Exploring the Role of Social Media in Transnational Advocacy

Floribert Patrick C. Endong
University of Calabar, Nigeria

A volume in the Advances in
Social Networking and Online
Communities (ASNOC) Book Series

Published in the United States of America by
IGI Global
Information Science Reference (an imprint of IGI Global)
701 E. Chocolate Avenue
Hershey PA, USA 17033
Tel: 717-533-8845
Fax: 717-533-8661
E-mail: cust@igi-global.com
Web site: http://www.igi-global.com

Library of Congress Cataloging-in-Publication Data

Names: Endong, Floribert Patrick C., 1983- editor.
Title: Exploring the role of social media in transnational advocacy / Floribert Patrick C. Endong, editor.
Description: Hershey : Information Science Reference, [2017]
Identifiers: LCCN 2017012028| ISBN 9781522528548 (hardcover) | ISBN 9781522528555 (ebook)
Subjects: LCSH: Social movements. | Social media.
Classification: LCC HM881 .E97 2017 | DDC 303.48/4--dc23 LC record available at https://lccn.loc.gov/2017012028

This book is published in the IGI Global book series Advances in Social Networking and Online Communities (ASNOC) (ISSN: 2328-1405; eISSN: 2328-1413)

British Cataloguing in Publication Data
A Cataloguing in Publication record for this book is available from the British Library.

For electronic access to this publication, please contact: eresources@igi-global.com.

Advances in Social Networking and Online Communities (ASNOC) Book Series

ISSN:2328-1405
EISSN:2328-1413

Editor-in-Chief: Hakikur Rahman, BRAC University, Bangladesh

MISSION

The advancements of internet technologies and the creation of various social networks provide a new channel of knowledge development processes that's dependent on social networking and online communities. This emerging concept of social innovation is comprised of ideas and strategies designed to improve society.

The **Advances in Social Networking and Online Communities** book series serves as a forum for scholars and practitioners to present comprehensive research on the social, cultural, organizational, and human issues related to the use of virtual communities and social networking. This series will provide an analytical approach to the holistic and newly emerging concepts of online knowledge communities and social networks.

COVERAGE

- Whole-Network Properties and Knowledge Communication
- Methods, Measures and Instruments of Knowledge Management
- Flourishing Knowledge Creation Environments
- Meta-data Representation and Management (e.g., Semantic-Based Coordination Mechanisms, Use of Ontologies, etc.)
- Communication and Agent Technology
- Knowledge as a Symbol/Model of Development
- Knowledge Acquisition Systems and Networks
- Leveraging Knowledge Communication in Social Networks
- Strategic Management and Business Process Analysis
- Leveraging Knowledge Communication Networks – Approaches to Interpretations and Interventions

IGI Global is currently accepting manuscripts for publication within this series. To submit a proposal for a volume in this series, please contact our Acquisition Editors at Acquisitions@igi-global.com or visit: http://www.igi-global.com/publish/.

The Advances in Social Networking and Online Communities (ASNOC) Book Series (ISSN 2328-1405) is published by IGI Global, 701 E. Chocolate Avenue, Hershey, PA 17033-1240, USA, www.igi-global.com. This series is composed of titles available for purchase individually; each title is edited to be contextually exclusive from any other title within the series. For pricing and ordering information please visit http://www.igi-global.com/book-series/advances-social-networking-online-communities/37168. Postmaster: Send all address changes to above address.

Titles in this Series

For a list of additional titles in this series, please visit:
https://www.igi-global.com/book-series/advances-social-networking-online-communities/37168

Online Communities as Agents of Change and Socia Movements
Steven Gordon (Babson College, USA)
Information Science Reference • ©2017 • 338pp • H/C (ISBN: 9781522524953) • US $195.00

Social Media Performance Evaluation and Success Measurements
Michael A. Brown Sr. (Florida International Univerity, USA)
Information Science Reference • ©2017 • 294pp • H/C (ISBN: 9781522519638) • US $185.00

Political Scandal, Corruption, and Legitimacy in the Age of Social Media
Kamil Demirhan (Bülent Ecevit University, Turkey) and Derya Çakır-Demirhan (Bülent Ecevit University, Turkey)
Information Science Reference • ©2017 • 295pp • H/C (ISBN: 9781522520191) • US $190.00

Power, Surveillance, and Culture in YouTube™'s Digital Sphere
Matthew Crick (William Paterson University, USA)
Information Science Reference • ©2016 • 317pp • H/C (ISBN: 9781466698550) • US $185.00

Social Media and the Transformation of Interaction in Society
John P. Sahlin (The George Washington University, USA)
Information Science Reference • ©2015 • 300pp • H/C (ISBN: 9781466685567) • US $200.00

New Opportunities for Artistic Practice in Virtual Worlds
Denise Doyle (University of Wolverhampton, UK)
Information Science Reference • ©2015 • 322pp • H/C (ISBN: 9781466683846) • US $185.00

Cases on Strategic Social Media Utilization in the Nonprofit Sector
Hugo Asencio (California State University – Dominguez Hills, USA) and Rui Sun (California State University – Dominguez Hills, USA)
Information Science Reference • ©2015 • 375pp • H/C (ISBN: 9781466681880) • US $195.00

For an entire list of titles in this series, please visit:
https://www.igi-global.com/book-series/advances-social-networking-online-communities/37168

IGI Global
DISSEMINATOR OF KNOWLEDGE

701 East Chocolate Avenue, Hershey, PA 17033, USA
Tel: 717-533-8845 x100 • Fax: 717-533-8661
E-Mail: cust@igi-global.com • www.igi-global.com

Table of Contents

Preface......xii

Chapter 1
Social Media Activism From an Information Warfare and Security Perspective......1
Brett van Niekerk, University of KwaZulu-Natal, South Africa

Chapter 2
Social Media as Alternative Public Sphere for Citizen Participation and Protest in National Politics in Zimbabwe: The Case of #thisflag......17
Collen Sabao, Midlands State University, Zimbabwe & University of Namibia, Namibia
Tendai Owen Chikara, Bindura University of Science Education, Zimbabwe & Solusi University, Zimbabwe

Chapter 3
Hashtag Activism and the Transnationalization of Nigerian-Born Movements Against Terrorism: A Critical Appraisal of the #BringBackOurGirls Campaign......36
Floribert Patrick C. Endong, University of Calabar, Nigeria

Chapter 4
Barriers to Social Media Advocacy: Lessons Learnt From the Project "Tell Them We Are From Here"......55
Aifheli Makhwanya, National Film and Video Foundation, South Africa

Chapter 5
From Jenin to Johannesburg: The Digital Intifada and Transnational Advocacy for Palestine......73
Suraya Dadoo, Media Review Network, South Africa

Chapter 6
Trans-National Advocacy and the Hashtag Black Lives Matter: Globalisation and Reception in the UK and France 101
Danella May Campbell, Manchester Metropolitan University, UK
Marie Chollier, Manchester Metropolitan University, UK

Chapter 7
Enhancing E-Transparency in Public Governance Through Social Media 136
Edison Wazoel Lubua, Institute of Accountancy Arusha, Tanzania

Chapter 8
Social Media Strategies of Political Power: An Analysis of the Ruling Party in Turkey 153
Hakan Yüksel, Independent Researcher, Turkey

Chapter 9
Euphoria and Delusion of Digital Activism: Case Study of #ZumaMustFall 179
Ufuoma Akpojivi, University of the Witwatersrand, South Africa

Chapter 10
Using Social Media to Advocate LGBT Rights in Black Africa: A Study of Nigerian and Cameroonian Gay Bloggers and "Facebookers" 203
Floribert Patrick C. Endong, University of Calabar, Nigeria

Related References 228

Compilation of References 267

About the Contributors 302

Index 305

Detailed Table of Contents

Preface.. xii

Chapter 1
Social Media Activism From an Information Warfare and Security Perspective 1
Brett van Niekerk, University of KwaZulu-Natal, South Africa

The use of social media in advocacy, and particularly transnational advocacy, raises concerns of privacy and security for those conducting the advocacy and their contacts on social media. This chapter presents high-level summaries of cases of social media in advocacy and activism from the perspectives of information warfare and information security. From an analysis of these, the impact and relationships of social media in transnational advocacy and information security is discussed. Whilst online advocacy can be considered to be a form of information warfare aligned to a Cyber Macht theory, it can be argued that social media advocacy negatively impacts information security as it encourages various actors to actively attempt to breach security.

Chapter 2
Social Media as Alternative Public Sphere for Citizen Participation and Protest in National Politics in Zimbabwe: The Case of #thisflag 17
Collen Sabao, Midlands State University, Zimbabwe & University of Namibia, Namibia
Tendai Owen Chikara, Bindura University of Science Education, Zimbabwe & Solusi University, Zimbabwe

The chapter examines and discusses the role and communicative potential of social media based platforms in citizen political participation and protests in Zimbabwe specifically focusing on the #thisflag movement on Facebook, Twitter and Whatsapp. #thisflag is a social media-based platform that rose to challenge the Zimbabwean government over the political and economic decay as well as rampant corruption characterising the country contemporarily. While a new phenomenon to Zimbabwe and Zimbabwean politics, the impact and communicative potential of social media as an alternative public sphere was recently tested in nationwide protest stayaway organised through the Facebook and Twitter movement under the #thisflag handle/brand. This chapter discusses the manners in which such social media platforms impact national politics in Zimbabwe as well as globally, specifically looking at the #thisflag movement as a case study.

Chapter 3
Hashtag Activism and the Transnationalization of Nigerian-Born Movements Against Terrorism: A Critical Appraisal of the #BringBackOurGirls Campaign 36
Floribert Patrick C. Endong, University of Calabar, Nigeria

This chapter describes how the Nigeria-based civil society initiatives have, of late, deployed digital activism in a bid to mobilize both endogenous and exogenous institutions against the terrorist group, Boko Haram. One of these anti-terrorism movements is the #BringBackOurGirls campaign which was launched in May 2014, following the abduction by Boko Haram of 276 schoolgirls, in the Northeastern village of Chibok (Nigeria). The #BringBackOurGirls" movement quickly attracted support from millions of voices (including Heads of States, their wives and celebrities) all over the world. In spite of its internationalization, the campaign has variously been critiqued. Many critics have arguably equated it with mere "clickitivism". Using empirical understandings, this chapter appraises the #BringBackOurGirls campaign vis-à-vis the fight against terrorism in Nigeria. The chapter starts by examining the genesis of the movement and its progressive trans-nationalization. It proceeds to exploring the extent to which the movement could be seen as "clicktivism"; and ends with a review of some of its successes.

Chapter 4
Barriers to Social Media Advocacy: Lessons Learnt From the Project "Tell Them We Are From Here"...55
Aifheli Makhwanya, National Film and Video Foundation, South Africa

This chapter describes how the latest statistics on social media usage shows Facebook as the biggest social networking site with over a billion users. With all the possibilities of the potential to grow transnational advocacy networks presented by the use of social media, its adoption and usage is not without limitations. A social media led campaign requires resources to ensure its effectiveness and should be used to complement a traditional advocacy campaign. Project Tell Them We are From Here, an anti-xenophobia campaign is used to explore some theories and demonstrate some of the resource challenges and how very few examples of true transnational advocacy can be found. This project is a collaboration of established non-governmental organisations with strong transnational links with a production company seeking to drive a social movement for unity and raising awareness of the daily plight of immigrants. Despite the campaign team's limited finances and capacity and shortcomings in the implementation of its social media campaign, the project demonstrates the affordances of social media for resource and capacity restrained activists.

Chapter 5
From Jenin to Johannesburg: The Digital Intifada and Transnational Advocacy for Palestine..73
Suraya Dadoo, Media Review Network, South Africa

Social media has given Palestinians around the world a voice with which to confront flawed media coverage of the Israeli occupation. This chapter will explore the use and rise of internet-based information and communication technologies (ICTs) and social media to expose Israel's colonial project in the Occupied Palestinian Territories (OPT) and advance pro-Palestine advocacy. The success and limitations of social media-based activism are examined, as well as the Israeli government's repressive response to these advocacy efforts. While social media has successfully challenged some deeply-entrenched media stereotypes about the Israeli occupation, it is a crucial tool for advancing Palestine activism globally. The chapter concludes that social media campaigns must be integrated with traditional advocacy, lobbying and grass-roots activism to end the Israeli occupation of Palestine and achieve a just peace for Palestinians and Israelis.

Chapter 6
Trans-National Advocacy and the Hashtag Black Lives Matter: Globalisation and Reception in the UK and France 101
Danella May Campbell, Manchester Metropolitan University, UK
Marie Chollier, Manchester Metropolitan University, UK

This chapter offers an insight into racial debates and equality advocacy in the 21st century and explores the emergence, the becoming and long-lasting effect of #BlackLivesMatter. The hashtag story is a traditional viral web content. Nevertheless, technologies allowed these initially local concerns, to become a world-wide plea. The first section summarises the past and current struggle for civil rights and equality in the USA. The second one focuses on the European reception of the hashtag in two structurally different countries. The last section discusses both outcomes and consequences in terms of social policies and international advocacy. A journalistic and critical analysis of the movement is here provided, with long term effects and reception case studies.

Chapter 7
Enhancing E-Transparency in Public Governance Through Social Media........136
Edison Wazoel Lubua, Institute of Accountancy Arusha, Tanzania

This chapter is a discussion on e-transparency. It is motivated by the trend where e-governance fails to significantly distinguish itself from the traditional governance, through embracing its secretive and prolonged nature of decision making. Both service delivery, and process and event models provided a basic background on enhancing transparency in governance activities. The emphasis is to make citizens the centre of governance processes. Moreover, key areas where citizen participation is desired, are discussed. The discussion integrates the role of ICTs is maximising participation. The later section of this chapter focuses on addressing contemporary challenges of e-transparency, in governance activities. Collectively, the modern society must embrace e-transparency, in ensuring that citizens decide their fate.

Chapter 8
Social Media Strategies of Political Power: An Analysis of the Ruling Party in Turkey 153
Hakan Yüksel, Independent Researcher, Turkey

This chapter analyzes the social media strategies of political power focusing on Turkey. By using inner-circle and outer-circle conceptualizations, it shows that the ruling party in Turkey simultaneously prevents and embraces social media in order to consolidate its power. The inner-circle strategies consist of practices facilitating an efficient use of social media whereas the outer-circle strategies are composed of judicial and technical measures to obstruct the democratic use of social media. By stressing that political power can also use social media efficiently, the chapter contributes to the literature in which social media is generally associated with emancipatory initiatives and the strategies of power are mostly explored in terms of restrictive measures. The chapter also describes the strategic role of social media in the increasingly violent power struggle in Turkey and the difficulties of using it in advocacy campaigns.

Chapter 9
Euphoria and Delusion of Digital Activism: Case Study of #ZumaMustFall...179
Ufuoma Akpojivi, University of the Witwatersrand, South Africa

This chapter seeks to question and problematize the concept of cyber-utopianism that has characterized the phenomenal increase of digital activism in the African continent in the last decade. Using tweets collected between November 1, 2015 and May 1, 2016 on the #ZumaMustFall digital activism as a case study, the chapter argues that the ability of new media technologies in digital activism to create awareness has created a sense of euphoria that digital activism can bring about political, economic and socio-cultural changes. The study revealed that #ZumaMustFall digital activism has had limited impact as Zuma has not fallen and this can be attributed to the elite nature of the movement that has excluded vast majority of ordinary South Africans from the activities of the movement. In addition, the racial coloration of the movement (i.e. identity) hindered the movement from reaching out to the public who could have actively participated in translating the movement from the online space to the offline space and achieve their goals and objectives.

Chapter 10
Using Social Media to Advocate LGBT Rights in Black Africa: A Study of Nigerian and Cameroonian Gay Bloggers and "Facebookers" 203
Floribert Patrick C. Endong, University of Calabar, Nigeria

The prevalence of draconian homophobic laws in Cameroon and Nigeria has systematically stultified sympathy for the LGBT communities and made pro-gay street activism a risky venture in these two countries. In view of this, a good number of gay rights activists have resorted to the social media as a suitable platform for a less risky advocacy. Using the social media has afforded them the opportunity to explore interactive, post-modern, and personified approaches to sensitizing and mobilizing their readership in favour of gay proselytism in Cameroon, Nigeria, and some other parts of Africa. Based on a content analysis of 200 blog posts and web/ facebook pages generated by Cameroonian and Nigerian gay activists, this chapter measures the extent to which gay activists adopt a national/local perspective versus the level to which they adopt an international perspective in their online advocacy. The chapter equally examines the degree to which these citizen journalist/activists construct their advocacy discourse from the prism of a cultural war between the West and Africa.

Related References 228

Compilation of References 267

About the Contributors 302

Index 305

Preface

The Internet and the social media have, in recent times, proved to be central to virtually all human activities. Their advent has remarkably revolutionized practices and doctrines in all domains of human endeavor, from administration/governance to education and from commerce to diplomacy. New and postmodern paradigms such as digital diplomacy, e-administration, e-government, e-participation, e-transparency, e-petitions, e-education and e-commerce among others have become popular emergent concepts which, to a great extent, (re)define human life in the twenty-first century. This increasingly strong influence of the social media and other digital technologies on human industries has warranted a plurality of scholarly efforts aimed principally at theorizing, schematizing and speculating on their use, function and future. There therefore exists a monumental and ever-growing body of literature devoted to the use of these digital technologies in almost all areas of research. In spite of the existence of this vast body of literature, additional research initiatives to further understand the use and potential of these digital technologies in various human industries remain laudable endeavors.

One of the human activities which have profoundly been reinvented by the Internet and the social media is socio-political activism. In effect, one easily observes that socio-political protests across the world are now increasingly driven by digital technologies. Such socio-political movements manifest in ways which range from classical typologies of social media campaigns (notably hashtag activism and e-petitions) to postmodern ones (notably "leaktivism" and "hacktivism"). Social media such as Facebook, Twitter, YouTube, and Internet blogging have thus been appropriated by various social influencers and political institutions (civil society initiatives and human right activists), even in poor countries, to grow political movements, shape public opinion and international perceptions of specific political issues; and mobilize pockets of supporters to various causes, all these in view of changing public policy in countries across the globe. The remarkable success of digitally driven campaigns such as the 2012 – 2016 "Black Lives Matter" movement and the 2011 Arab Spring uprisings are palpable evidences pointing to the fact that, for some decades now, national and international (political) activism on social media has "grown some teeth" and that, an intelligent use of this forms of activism may be very strategic in the global fight against colossal dilemmas ranging from environmental concerns to terrorism.

The necessity to enrich our understandings of contemporary forms of digital activism and their socio-political potential in today and tomorrow's technologically driven world has made most research efforts to focus on at least, four principal axes:

- Comparing the traditional or classical forms of activism (notably street protests) with social media assisted ones;
- Examining the neo and postmodern facets of digital activism and theorizing/ speculating on their future;
- X-raying the contribution of digital activism to the trans-nationalization or globalization of major economic and socio-political movements; and
- Exploring the potential of digital activism to effectively engender social and political change in the world.

As shown by the themes addressed by all contributors to the present volume, these research foci remain more than topical and interesting.

TRADITIONAL VS. NEW FORMS OF ACTIVISM

The Internet has affected the activism game at least in two ways: firstly, it has made conventional or classical activism to become more affordable and accessible; secondly, it has given birth to new and revolutionary approaches to advocacy, approaches which remarkably depart from the classical ones. These new approaches to advocacy have been categorized in many quarters as new social movements; this, in perfect contrast to old movements such as the labor, abortionist or suffragette movements of the nineteenth century. As kinds of paradigmatic shifts in the domain of activism, these new social movements are virtually non-hierarchical and non-vertical in their organizational structure. They have no clear delineating lines between leaders and followers as well as between members and non-members. As observed by many critics, the new forms of social movements are virtually leaderless, decentralized and not bound by an organizational structure. They are initiated or driven more and more by youths who have websites instead of offices as well as followers instead of remunerated staffs; and who craftily use open-source platforms instead of relying on robust budgets (Morozow, 2011). Additionally, the new forms of social movements are less predictable in their modus operandis, compared to old social movements which are mostly cause-based and which entail serious strategizing and planning.

Another striking aspect of the dichotomy between the old and the new social movements lies in the fact that, while the former are driven by well-defined causes (notably the abolition of slavery, the struggle for the right to vote, to unionize or to strike), the latter are most often centered on causes which are identity or lifestyle oriented. Such causes include issues like LGBT rights, civil rights and the protection of the environment among others.

In spite of the fact that the two types of activism differ considerably, it remains axiomatic that contemporary activists should bridge the gap between the two approaches to advocacy in their efforts towards socio-political change. This necessity is partially rationalized by the fact that effective change is most often the consequence of collective efforts manifested through various other platforms which are non-virtual. This evidently entails the cooperation of a multitude of both subtle and unsubtle players. These players may be civil society organizations, grass-root organizations, politicians, mainstream media, parliaments and presidential offices among others. How to meaningfully integrate and mobilize all these players for same causes has remained an interesting topic for research and debate. No doubt, chapters 5 and 9 of this book are focused on this issue.

CYBER ACTIVISM AS A POSTMODERN CULTURE

The ubiquity of Smartphones and the internet has engendered new and postmodern typologies of activism. Though the major internet assisted movements in the last two decades have mainly been "tweetered" (Twitter-driven), many other more or less muscled forms of activism such as "leakivism" and "hacktivism" among others, have emerged and attracted the attention of researchers. These new forms of activism bypass the existing world of politics, social movements and campaigns. They thus bypass the hierarchies and rigidities connected to traditional forms of activism. In the name of "hacktivism", online activists such as Anonymous, LulzSec and Guardians of Peace have been deploying Internet assisted tactics to attack the computer networks of rich and politically powerful quarters as well as terrorist organizations such as the Islamic State. In 2011, Anonymous launched its "Operation Tunisia" which among other things deployed DDoS (Distributed Denial of Service) attacks to deface over eight government websites; this in support of the Arab Spring (Howard & Hussein 2013; Machado, 2015). Other movements driven or supported by this group of hackers include "Operation Egypt" and "Operation Syria" which led to the harking and closure of government websites in Egypt and Syria during the Arab Springs.

With same degree of political commitment, adepts of "leaktivism" ("leaktivists") have been deploying the Internet to orchestrate leaks and disseminate sensitive documents with political ramifications. Issues like the Panama Paper and Wikileaks' political whistle blowing activities have had serious political repercussions in many western countries. The Panama Paper in particular has been at the root of political agitations aimed at overthrowing the head of State in Iceland and in UK. Similarly, the political whistleblower site Wikileaks has, in countless occasions, been used as a platform to declassify and leak confidential information between the U.S. State Department and many of its representatives in foreign climes (Jordan & Taylor, 2004; Kiel 2011).

Hacktivism and leaktivism have thus been a veritable transposition of political protests, political intervention, civil disobedience and low-level information warfare into the virtual space. Their adepts (hacktivists and leaktivists) are arguably profiled as postmodern political protesters. The obvious implication of this scenario is that the definition of digital activism remains dynamic and to an extent, elusive. Digital activism is not limited to classical models of digitally driven movements such as hashtag or Facebook assisted activism. It extends to paradigms – kinds of "guerilla activism" – which, at first sight, may seem disruptive, transgressive and liable to be problematized.

In spite of the fact that they tend to be motivated by the desire to draw public attention to specific causes, postmodern forms of political activism are subject to profound controversy and thus, represent excellent topics for further research in the domain of digital activism. The controversial nature of postmodern forms of digital activism is evidenced in the fact that social movements such as leaktivism and hacktivism have raised a number of issues bordering on the morality and legitimacy of deploying muscled digital tools – such as hacking and leaking confidential documents among others – for political ends. As remarked by Jordan and Taylor (2004), hacktivists and leaktivists have, on the basis of their advocacy methodologies, been branded in a number of pessimistic quarters as "rebels with a cause". In other words, hacktivism could paradoxically or technically be associated with rebellion and "vice". In tandem with this, the U.S. government has in several instances condemned Wikileaks' *modus operandis.* One of such condemnations was done in 2012, after the site served as platform for the dissemination of a series of classified and confidential information between the U.S. State Department and its representatives abroad.

THE SOCIAL NETWORKS AS VECTORS OF TRANSNATIONAL SOCIAL MOVEMENTS

It is an accepted premise that the social media have always constituted one of the key forces behind the redefinition of social and cultural geography. This is not unconnected to the fact that they (the social media) among other media of mass communication, systematically facilitate a high degree of interconnectedness across vast distances and "a temporal flexibility in social interaction" (Cammaerts, 2015;

Hjarvard, 2016). In other words, the social media have immensely contributed to the transformation of modern society into what is popularly termed a "network society" (Castells 1996). A network society is, one which, besides being part of a broad social structure, is subtly organized around a set of globalized and decentralized networks of capital, resources, production and information. The social media have thus facilitated transnationally distributed networks of information and communication; what a number of international communication theorists will term "transnational discursive spaces". The social media have facilitated these transnational or global discursive arenas by offering a unifying public forum where individuals, activists and civil society organizations across national borders can gather to discuss issues of global or international concern.

Such a development has been a welcomed opportunity for most contemporary activists and civil society organizations which, from many indexes, tend to increasingly be animated by the desire – or rather the craze – to globalize their movements. In effect, contemporary activists tend to increasingly be driven by the idea that their actions are susceptible to engender more globally integrative and participatory democracy. Even activists and civil society organizations which seek policy reforms and political change at national level increasingly tend to solicit the support of the international community (foreign governments and allies), thereby thinking global in their modus operandis or by internationalizing their protests – most often through a crafty mobilization of global communications. As noted by Keck and Sikkink (1998), contemporary civil society organizations have since embraced the culture of bypassing their states and directly searching out international allies to try to provoke exogenous political pressure on their states. Social media platforms (transnational discursive spaces) have constituted excellent tools to garner such an international support.

If the place of social media in the creation and growth of transnational advocacy networks (TANs) has since been documented, the systematic or subtle ways in which they (these networks) operate and impact both the national and the international socio-political ecology remain serious topics for debate and scientific investigation. Many contributions to this volume (notably Chapters 2, 3, 5, 6, and 10), critically address these topics through interesting case studies.

DIGITAL ACTIVISM OR SLACKTIVISM?

According to a number of studies, digital activism is based on a click-and-share formula which, in theory, is less fruitful than traditional activism paradigms (Barbera et al., 2015). A study conducted by Lewis, Gray and Meierhenrich (2015) revealed that large causes on social media – notably Save Darfur – have often been marred by the fact that, the donations (to support these causes) are hardy, nay never proportional to the evasive number of likes or online followers. The Save Dafur campaign for instance attracted over a million likes on social networks but amassed only $100,000 in guise of donations. Over 98% of the campaign's online supporters did not donate at all. Such findings coupled with similar other indexes tend to give credence to the myth stipulating that "return rates for charities on Facebook are a tenth of those whose charities take traditional routes" (Lewis, Gray & Meierhenrich 2015, p. 4). Such findings equally tend to rationalize the thesis which construes digital activism as a kind of armchair activism or "clicktivism"/"slacktivism", paradigm which is unsusceptible to bring about real policy change or political transformation in countries across the world.

However, it must be underscored that the myth which automatically equates digital activism with slacktivism is subject to controversy; and the bulk of contributors to this volume (particularly Chapters 3, 4, 5, and 9) contribute in various ways, to this virulent debate.

STRUCTURE OF THE BOOK

This book is organized in 10 chapters:

Chapter 1, titled "Social Media Activism From an Information Warfare and Security Purpose," critically explores some of the security and privacy risks associated with digitally driven transnational advocacy. It argues that in spite of its enormous potential, social media assisted advocacy may negatively impact information security as various actors (notably policy makers and hackers among others) may strongly embark on aggressive tactics that breach security.

"Social Media as Alternative Public Sphere for Citizen Participation and Protest in National Politics in Zimbabwe: The Case of #thisflag" (Chapter 2) by Collen Sabao and Owen Tandai Chikara examines the political impact the #thisflag campaign on Zimbabwean politics as well as their international implications. The chapter illustrates how the rise of this social media assisted movement successfully mobilized Zimbabweans in and out of their country, to challenge various government policies in view of "positive" political change.

The third chapter is "Hashtag Activism and the Trans-Nationalization of Nigerian-Born Movements Against Terrorism: A Critical Appraisal of #BringBackOurGirl Campaign" by Floribert Patrick Endong. The chapter assesses the #BringBackOurGirl twitter campaign vis-à-vis the fight against terrorism – particularly the Boko Haram group – in Nigeria. After exploring the genesis, structure and internationalization of the movement, the chapter questions and debunks tree myths stipulating that the campaign was a form of slacktivism or clicktivism.

Aifheli Cate Makhwanya's "Barriers to Social Media Advocacy: Lessons Learnt From the Project 'Tell Them We Are From Here'" (Chapter 4) x-rays the successes of the "Tell Them We Are From Here" campaign in the fight against xenophobia in South Africa. It suggests that despite the accessibility of social media, some resources and capacity must be dedicated to a campaign, to ensure that, the contents posted on Twitter and Facebook or whichever social networking sites that will serve the campaign, must be backed by a solid advocacy plan of action.

In Chapter 5, titled "From Jenin to Johannesburg: The Digital Intifada and Transnational Advocacy for Palestine," Suraya Dadoo demonstrates how social media assisted activism has been serving as a solid tool for the deconstruction and denunciation of the old and persistent media stereotypes and anti-Palestinian myths bordering on the Israel's colonial project, manifested by the Occupied Palestinian Territories (OPT). Highlighting some of the limitations of social media activism, she makes a case for the combine use of digital activism and traditional forms of protests to end what she perceives as Israeli occupation of Palestine, thereby enabling an era of peace between Israel and Palestine.

In Chapter 6, "Trans-National Advocacy and the Hashtag Black Lives Matter: Globalisation and Reception in the UK and France," Danella May Campbell and Marie Chollier explore an evocative case study (#BlackLivesMatter), which to many schools of thought, represents one of the greatest global successes of digital activism in recent times. The two scholars specifically review the genesis and trans-nationalization of the hashtag movement as well as its reception in two culturally different societies (Britian and France). The contribution also examines the campaign's socio-political implications for social policy designing and for international advocacy.

"E-Transparency in Public Governance" (Chapter 7) by Edison Lubua shows how the new information and communication technologies have phenomenally revolutionized the practice of governance, enhancing transparency in governance activities and putting the citizen at the centre of governance processes. The chapter identifies a number of key areas in which citizen participation is vital – ranging from electoral exercises to payment of utility bills – and succinctly demonstrates how the new ICTs could help foster such citizen participation. It also presents a non-exhaustive list of issues impending e-transparency in governance activities.

The eighth chapter of the book, "Social Media Strategies of Political Power: An Analysis of the Ruling Party in Turkey," by Hakan Yüksel, schematizes the Turkish government's more or less equivocative and hypocritical attitude towards the use of digital platforms for advocacy. The chapter argues that this government deploys "inner-circle paradigms to enable an efficient used by its members of digital activism (for public relations purposes) while also embarking on "outer-circle" strategies to obstruct democratic use of the social media by the opposition (the masses). These outer-circle approaches include restrictive laws and other technical measures.

The ninth chapter of the book, "Euphoria and Delusion of Digital Activism: Case Study of #ZumaMustFall" by Ufuoma Akpojivi, problematizes myths which support the infallibility of digital movements when it comes to shaping public opinion and engineering socio-political and cultural change in a setting. Hinging on interesting statistical data (primary data) generated on the #ZumaMustFall hashtag movement, the chapter illustrates the fact that, digitally driven movements may sometimes be as vertical and hierarchical as traditional forms of social movements, thereby having very limited social and political impact in a given context. The #ZumaMustrFall campaign for instance, visibly mobilized large pockets of followers but failed to cause the political fall of President Jacob Zuma; this, for reasons which range from its elite nature to its racist coloration.

The last chapter is "Using Social Media to Advocate LGBT Rights in Black Africa: A Study of Nigerian and Cameroonian Gay Bloggers and Facebookers" (Chapter 10). The work addresses the issue of Africans' use of Facebook and Internet blogging for international advocacy in favor of LGBT rights. It critically examines international versus national perspectives in the online contents generated by Nigerian and Cameroonian LGBT right activists.

REFERENCES

Barberá, P., Wang, N., Bonneau, R., Jost, J. T., Nagler, J., Tucker, J., & González-Bailón, S. (2015). The critical periphery in the growth of social protests. *PLoS One*, *10*(11), 1–15. doi:10.1371/journal.pone.0143611 PMID:26618352

Cammaerts, B. (2015). Social media and activism. In R. Hwa (Ed.), *The international encyclopedia of digital communication and society* (pp. 1027–1034). Oxford, UK: Willey-Blackwell.

Castells, M. (1996). *The rise of the network society*. Blackwell.

Edwards, F., Howard, P., & Joyce, M. (2013). *Digital activism and non-violent conflicts. Digital Activism Project*. Seattle, WA: University of Washington.

Gerbaudo, P. (2017). From cyber-autonomism to cyber-populism: An ideological history of digital activism. *Journal for a Global Sustainable Information Society*, *15*(2), 15–34.

Hjarvard, S. (2001). New media and the globalization of the public sphere. In S. Hjarvard (Ed.), *News in a globalized society* (pp. 1–16). Goteborg: Nordicom.

Howard, N. P., & Hussain, M. M. (2013). *Democracy's fourth wave?* Oxford, UK: Oxford University Press. doi:10.1093/acprof:oso/9780199936953.001.0001

Jordan, T., & Taylor, P. A. (2004). *Hacktivism and cyberwars. Rebels with a cause?* London: Routledge.

Keck, M., & Sikkink, K. (1998). *Activists beyond borders*. Ithaca, NY: Cornell University Press.

Kiel, C. (2011). How transnational advocacy networks mobilize: Applying the literature on interest groups to international action. *Josef Korbel Journal of Advanced International Studies*, *3*, 77–101.

Lewis, K., Gray, K., & Meierhenrich, J. (2014). The structure of online activism. *Sociological Science*, *1*, 1–9. doi:10.15195/v1.a1

Machado, M. B. (2015). Between control and hacker activism: The political actions of Anonymous Brazil. *Historica, Ciencias Saude*, *22*, 1–18.

Mora, F. A. (2014). Emergent digital activism: The generational/technological connection. *Journal of Community Informatics*, *10*(1), 1–24.

Morozow, E. (2011). *The net delusion: The dark side of Internet freedom*. New York: Perseus Book Group.

Reitan, R. (2007). *Global activism*. New York: Routledge.

Sivitanides, M. & Shah, V. (2011). The era of digital activism. *Conference for Information Systems Applied Research (CONISAR) Proceedings*, *4*(1842), 1-8.

Chapter 1
Social Media Activism From an Information Warfare and Security Perspective

Brett van Niekerk
University of KwaZulu-Natal, South Africa

ABSTRACT

The use of social media in advocacy, and particularly transnational advocacy, raises concerns of privacy and security for those conducting the advocacy and their contacts on social media. This chapter presents high-level summaries of cases of social media in advocacy and activism from the perspectives of information warfare and information security. From an analysis of these, the impact and relationships of social media in transnational advocacy and information security is discussed. Whilst online advocacy can be considered to be a form of information warfare aligned to a Cyber Macht theory, it can be argued that social media advocacy negatively impacts information security as it encourages various actors to actively attempt to breach security.

INTRODUCTION

Social media's primary purpose is that of information sharing, be it amongst friends, family, or colleagues. However, the prevalence that social media has gained in contemporary society raises a number of concerns related to privacy and information security at personal, organizational and national levels. A number of cases exist which show that social media is actively being aligned to military operations as a 'force multiplier', indicating its use in information operations and information

DOI: 10.4018/978-1-5225-2854-8.ch001

warfare. When considering advocacy and transnational advocacy, the use of social media immediately begins to raise the concern over information security for both the advocates, the targets, and others who get swept up in the online dialogue, and often the physical consequences that follow.

This chapter is an opinion piece based on previous research by the author and news reports of more recent cases; the fact that the incidents occurred is the relevant aspect to this chapter. The incidents are analysed based on the information security and information warfare models, from which key relationships between social media advocacy and information security can be inferred. The next section provides an overview of information security and information warfare with particular reference to the models against which the incidents are analysed. A number of cases involving social media advocacy and information security are then outlined, followed by a discussion on the impact transnational social media advocacy has had on information security.

INFORMATION SECURITY AND INFORMATION WARFARE: AN OVERVIEW

Information security is the preservation of the confidentiality, integrity and availability of information and the relevant systems. Essentially this means that information can only be accessed by those who have authorization to do so, there needs to be accuracy and assurance only authorized persons can modify it, and it needs to be available when the authorized persons require it. Another important concept is that of non-repudiation, which is a form of attribution in that someone cannot deny their involvement or action, akin to a signature on a piece of paper.

Information operations and information warfare are military activities to provide information superiority over an adversary, including deception, psychological operations, intelligence and counter-intelligence. Of these activities, cyber-warfare has become predominant in the media due to the threat of online attacks. Cyber-security and information security are often used synonymously, although they are not identical. Information security is concerned with information in all its forms; a relevant concept of information warfare is that it operates in the physical, virtual and cognitive domains. Cyber-security, however, is concerned primarily with activities occurring on networks, and according to the ISO/IEC 27032 Cybersecurity standard, it is a subset of information security.

When discussing cyber-warfare and cyber-security, Duggan (2016) contrasts the US approach which is based on structure Jominian and Clausewitzian military theory versus the Chinese approach based on Sun Tzu's *Art of War*. Duggan (2016) attributes the apparent challenges experienced by the US due to the structured nature of their philosophy, and the apparent Chinese success due to the deceptive and unpredictable basis of their theory. The Chinese therefore have a stronger emphasis on social and psychological aspects of cyber-warfare, versus the US tactical approach (Duggan, 2016). The Chinese approach is therefore ideal for the inclusion of social media, which can better leverage disinformation, deception, and social constructs. In this instance, the integrity of human mind is influenced, which is an important concept in advocacy.

The concept of Cyber Macht or Cyber Power (Armistead & Starsman, 2014) is the use of modern communication channels (including online or cyber-space) to project power in the form of global influence, or mass perception management through "information shaping" (Armistead & Starsman, 2015:14). The premise is that due to the open access to modern online communications this power also resides with smaller groups who can effectively transmit their messages using this medium (Armistead & Starsman, 2014). This is almost a combination and Sun Tzu's psychological approach and Clausewitz's (1832) concept of "war is merely the continuation of policy by other means". This theory is particularly pertinent when considering transnational advocacy via social media.

INCIDENTS

This section briefly describes a number of cases where social media advocacy had significant implications for information security. Some of these cases have been analysed in-depth elsewhere, therefore a summary of the key aspects related to information security and information warfare will be provided.

Wikileaks and Snowden

The release of US documents from the conflicts in Iraq and Afghanistan, and US diplomatic cables (Miller, 2010) has been commented on extensively. The initial leak originated from a US military intelligence analyst, Manning, who had access to the information (Poulsen & Zetter, 2010). This aligns to the information security concept of an insider threat: someone who has legitimate access to information or systems and commits some form of malicious act, usually motivated by revenge (disgruntled employee) or ideology. In this instance, the confidentiality of the information was breached. This was conducted due to an attempt at providing transparency, however it has had longer reaching implications on information security in that the hacktivist collective Anonymous in part grew out of this ideal. After the diplomatic cable leaks, some organizations stopped dealing with Wikileaks, and were then targeted by pro-Wikileaks activists, sparking a series of revenge attacks between Wikileaks supporters and opponents (van Niekerk & Maharaj, 2011).

A second leak committed by Edward Snowden in 2013 (Dencik & Cable, 2017) again illustrates these points. These leaks illustrated the surveillance capabilities and programs of the US and UK, which collected targeted intelligence against persons of interest, possible corporate and political espionage, and mass collection and analysis of meta-data from everyday citizen communications. Isin and Ruppert (2017) discuss the political and moral dimensions of Snowden's actions, however what is clear is that in order to bring attention to breaches of privacy and confidentiality, Snowden himself breached confidentiality. Due to user-generated content, the line between journalism and non-journalist reporting becomes blurred (Russel & Waisbard, 2017), similarly, there is a decreasing distinction amongst reporting, voicing opinions, and true advocacy. This affects the integrity of the information and how it is viewed. True advocates may have their message diluted as what can be considered ill-informed opinion. However, the leaks by Snowden do illustrate that government intelligence services are able to monitor personal communications through programmes such as XKEYSCORE (Agnihotri, 2015). These monitoring activities would be worrying for activists, as it gives the government's security apparatus the ability to identify and monitor activists.

In 2016 Wikileaks was again active in releasing information about US presidential candidate Hillary Clinton and the Democratic National Committee, which was reportedly hacked. This may have impacted the election to some degree (Entous, Nakashima & Miller, 2016). Another release of information in 2017 indicated government ability to compromise mobile phones and smart TVs in order to spy (Gross, 2017).

These incidents seem to encourage data breaches under the guise of advocacy for transparency or better security of personal information, however at the same time have exposed governments doing breaching privacy.

Arab Spring

The Arab Spring uprising were a series of anti-government protests, gaining international attention in 2011 after starting in Tunisia and moving to Egypt and Libya. These events are analysed in more detail in van Niekerk, Pillay and Maharaj (2011). From transnational advocacy and Cyber Macht perspectives, these protests are applicable due to the spreading of the protests, including a number of smaller protests were experienced in North Africa and the Middle East (Black & Chulov, 2011; Sky News, 2011) and the fact that national leaders participated in calling for the Egyptian president, Mubarak, to step down (Lee, 2011; Lekic, 2011; Robinson, 2011). This illustrates that a global audience was influenced to support the protests.

The Tunisian government responded to the use of social media in the unrest by recording the login details of users, possibly allowing them to 'hack' into the accounts (Madrigal, 2011). There are also reports of potential surveillance of users and their accounts (Comninos, 2011). From an information security perspective, this is a direct targeting of the privacy or confidentiality of the person's information. If access to the accounts were gained, they could be used to spread disinformation (affecting integrity), or to delete the accounts (affecting availability). In Egypt, Syria, and Libya a number of Internet and communication platforms (such as mobile telephony) were shut off (Associated Press, 2011; Flock, 2011; Kravets, 2011). From an information security perspective, this is an attack on information availability. In the broader sense, the use of the social media platforms in the protests can be seen to have 'resulted' in the governments targeting the social media user's accounts or their access to the Internet. This can be said to have resulted in a situation which inhibited information security.

Anonymous and the #Occupy Movement

The international hacker collective, Anonymous, often styling themselves as activists and advocating civil rights make use of social media extensively for publicity of their operations. They also strongly supported Wikileaks, and often targeted those hostile towards Wikileaks (Chabrow, 2012). From the core of Anonymous, more aggressive splinter groups began to form, such as LulzSec, who targeted Sony, HBGary, and the US Senate (Chabrow, 2012).

For instance, Anonymous Africa tweets what their target will be, prior to attacking them with distributed denial of service attacks. Their motivation for the attacks is to oppose perceived government corruption in Southern Africa (van Zyl, 2016a). They targeted a number of Zimbabwean websites in 2013, and stated that there was also activity in the real world, however they had to stop due to the Zimbabwean intelligence services getting close to identifying them. In 2016 they began targeting South African websites such as the South African Broadcasting Commission (Vermeulen, 2016). Unlike Anonymous Africa, the #OpAfrica campaign preferred to embarrass their targets by breaching data on the websites and releasing it (van Zyl, 2016b). It is interesting to note that both campaigns, whilst not officially affiliated with each other, were active at the same time. These campaigns strongly associated social media activism with hacktivism, intentionally breaching information security (either affecting availability or confidentiality) for a cause.

Anonymous supported physical protests, inspired by the Egyptian uprising in Arab Spring, which became the #Occupy movement (Kamzi, 2011). The first, Occupy Wall Street, saw the use of social media to identify police offers accused of using excessive force, and continuously call for peaceful protests. This example illustrates how social media activism, physical protest, and hacktivism can be coordinated (Kamzi, 2011). This movement can again be seen as a success for Cyber Macht, where a relatively small group effectively used online perception management to grow their ranks in the physical protest, and initiate a global movement.

The EuroMaidan Protests and the Russian Incursion Into Crimea

The events in Ukraine are analysed in more depth by Armistead and Starsman (2015) and van Niekerk (2015). The protests started in November 2013 after the pro-Russia government backed out of an agreement with the EU. The social media efforts used multiple platforms and three languages: Ukrainian, Russian and English, clearly meant to target a large audience. The images and videos of reportedly heavy-handed police tactics increased the public support for the protests, which began to escalate and a number if government buildings were occupied by the protestors. There was also a noticeable amount of memes on English humour websites taking a more satirical view of the events (van Niekerk, 2015). As the pro-Russian government went into exile, a number of documents were found and made available in a Wikileaks-style release, which was used to present the view of corruption by the pro-Russian government (Lokot, 2014). Due to a previous revolution in Ukraine, these protests and the ousting of the government provided an unparalleled opportunity to clearly assess the roles and effectiveness of social media in anti-government protests (Satell, 2014). The success of the protests was short-lived, as little was done to reassure the pro-Russian population, and the power of the social media was lost, and ultimately turned against the interim pro-EU government during the Russian incursion into Crimea (van Niekerk, 2015).

During the annexation of Crimea and the conflict in Eastern Ukraine, the pro-Russian movement and the Russian government employed well-orchestrated narratives using broadcast and online (including social) media, and the efforts clearly illustrate the Cyber Macht concept (Armistead & Starsman, 2015). These influence and perception management activities were also coordinated with military and cyber-activities; throughout the unrest and subsequent conflict a number of distributed denial of service attacks occurred, both as a protest activity, but also to hinder perception management activity (van Niekerk, 2015). Social media was used to post pictures and videos of Russian helicopters during the initial incursion, and photos attempting to prove Russian involvement in areas (which was denied by the Russian authorities) and staged Russian propaganda were circulated (van Niekerk, 2015). Social media was used in attempt to attribute the downing of flight MH17 to pro-Russian separatists, and an attempt to edit the Wikipedia entry about the incident was attributed to Russian supporters (Lowensohn, 2014; Rushe & Walker, 2014).

The use in perception management again illustrates the potential to affect information integrity, and the use to post document, and photos of military movements illustrates its use to affect confidentiality. In the case of the Russian soldiers, it was in some cases the soldiers themselves using social media on deployment which highlighted their involvement (Li, 2014); this again is an accidental breach of confidentiality which undermines operational security, benefiting those advocating against Russian involvement.

South African State Security Agency Leaks

The South African intelligence service, the State Security Agency, suffered a breach similar to the Manning and Snowden incidents, with a number of cables being leaked in 2015. The leak brought to light the concerns that the African intelligence agencies had regarding social media, however that they also recognised opportunities (de Wet, 2015). Also revealed were requests to spy of activists from foreign governments, and that some activists and rights advocates were spied on (Gumede, 2015). These two revelations may be telling: that activists and advocates are targets for national espionage, and that their social media activity will be one of the methods used to monitor them.

Student Protests

The student protests described in this section are analysed in depth by Ramluckan, Ally, and van Niekerk (2017). In 2011 students in Chile protested against the government's education fee policies and with the effective use of social media it became one of the most widespread the country has seen (García, Chauveau, Ledezma, & Pinto, 2013). The success is further illustrated by the fact that one of the protest leaders was voted into the Chilean Parliament (Franklin, 2013). In 2014 the Occupy Central, also known as the Umbrella Movement, encouraged student protests in Hong Kong. These protests had a strong social media presence after the students occupied square outside the government headquarters (Lee, 2014). As with some cases in the Arab Spring, the Chinese government attempted to censor social media posts about the protest (BBC, 2015).

In 2015 a series of isolated, campus-based protests in South Africa rapidly escalated over the period of a week under the #Feesmustfall banner, and besieged the Parliament in Cape Town, then a coordinated protest outside of the Executive buildings in Pretoria a few days later. These protests were largely successful in that the university fee increases were prevented (Ramluckan, Ally, and van Niekerk, 2017). All three protests achieved international recognition and support, with international students joining in both online and sympathy marches for the #Feesmustfall movement (BBC, 2015; Lee, 2014; Manning, 2014; Ramluckan, Ally, and van Niekerk, 2017). These protests again demonstrated the Cyber Macht theory, where small groups effectively used social media to gain influence and increase their support, which had noticeable long-term political implications in their various countries.

2016 US Election-Related Activity

The US presidential elections in 2016 exhibited a number of controversies, a number of which revolved around the candidates or advocates use of social media. This includes Wikileaks releases targeting the Democratic Party, as described previously. The use of shaming tactics, targeted amongst candidates, at other public figures, and at particular demographics (Segar, 2016) conducted both on social media and through other channels elicited reactions and dialogue across all channels, with a number of activist and advocacy groups taking to social media in response.

The term 'fake news' has become prevalent in the news reports at the time of writing. The first major use of the word was in relation to the 2016 US presidential elections, where rumours and conspiracy theories on social media were prevalent (Gentzkow & Allcott, 2017). However, other countries, such as India, are also affected by this phenomenon (Sawant, 2017). In this case, the use of the WhatsApp instant messaging application is considered to be part of the problem, as there is difficulty in tracing the source and users are often not aware that the news is fake (Sawant, 2017). The CEO of Uber withdrew as one of Donald Trump's economic advisory council members due to an online boycott of the application. This is due to what the CEO indicated as a misunderstanding that his involvement implied his endorsement of certain policies (Wong, 2017). This is a good illustration of a possible incorrect perception being used to affect a high-profile individual's behaviour, and is an indication of the strength of online misdirection.

DISCUSSION: THE INTER-RELATIONSHIPS BETWEEN TRANSNATIONAL SOCIAL MEDIA ADVOCACY AND INFORMATION WARFARE AND SECURITY

From the incidents discussed above, a number of commonalities emerge which illustrate the inter-relationships between Transnational Social Media Advocacy and Information Warfare and Security. The most predominant is that social media advocacy is a form of information warfare: the use of these online platforms by various groups, whether small or national governments, to exert mass influence to sway opinion of achieve their objectives is in its very essence an operalisation of Cyber Macht. There is an impact on the integrity of information through the way in which it is perceived. What is sometimes more difficult to determine is the integrity of the information as it is possible there is deception embedded in the communication if the form of selective or half-truths, and outright lies. The challenge becomes determining the truth from the deception. As with the Russian propaganda campaign around Ukraine, social media itself aided in identifying falsehoods in the official Russian stance.

The obvious effectiveness of social media as an advocacy and activist tool will encourage online propaganda or online reputation attacks. If posts go viral, there is the very real possibility of an outright lie becoming a de-facto truth through the sheer number of people who have fallen for the lie. This creates additional work in that the misperceptions need to be corrected while the truth is presented; this implies that the speed of communication (i.e. getting the correct message out first) can be crucial.

Social media advocacy appears to encourage attempts to breach confidentiality and privacy, as in the case of the various hacker groups supporting Wikileaks. From a hacktivist perspective, this is to either purely embarrass an organisation or country, or to bring to light some perceive misconduct. Ironically, those advocating for stronger privacy and systems security decrease the privacy by making compromised details publicly available. In the long-term there is a negative impact on information security, as hacktivists are encourage to breach the confidentiality of systems. What is of particular concern for corporations and intelligence services is that these high-profile breaches often are as a result of a trusted person with legitimate access. This implies not only have the information security structure strong from external hacks but also having to monitor employee activity, this again could raise privacy concerns if the organisation takes the monitoring too far.

Despite much of the online activism being around online privacy, the advocacy and activism itself encourages the opposite as it provides unique opportunities for national intelligence agencies to monitor the social media activity of the advocates. A respondent to a study on social media in crises situation openly stated that social media was useful for spying (Ramluckan, 2016). Often more totalitarian regimes will use concerns of safety and security to openly monitor and target advocacy group accounts. Even though there is no incriminating posts or activity on social media, it can be seen as a starting point to form a digital trace of a target, and form links to individuals or groups; supposedly anonymous social media posts may at some point give a trail back to the individual.

The scale of the concern for privacy and security of activists, social advocates and journalists can be evidenced by the number of mobile applications dedicated towards private and security communications. Applications such as Signal and Seecrypt provide encrypted instant messaging and voice communications (Communication Security Group, 2017; Open Whisper Systems, 2016). Application to hide information in images (known as steganography) also exist, along with anonymous remailers and email addresses. Virtual private networks encrypt traffic and disguise the location of the user. The Onion Ring Router (ToR) also provides anonymity, however it is also associate with illicit underground activity on the Dark Web (Wheatley, 2013). However, the use of such tools may immediately raise suspicion and attract the attention of intelligence and security services. The challenge also becomes in knowing if these supposedly secure systems are as private as they claim to be: vulnerabilities in web encryption and claims of government backdoors can make a privacy-conscious activist rather paranoid. The leaks that the CIA could leverage smart TVs to spy on people fuels such concerns.

To summarise, social media advocacy and information security are related as follows:

- The use to affect information integrity by altering how people view the information (perception management) or by spreading rumours and misinformation;
- Hacktivists are encouraged to actively breach information security to prove a point;
- Governments are encouraged to actively breach privacy on social media to monitor possible activist activity;
- Governments are encouraged to actively affect availability of services due to possible security concerns;
- Hacktivists are encouraged to actively affect availability of services to silence opposing views or for revenge.

CONCLUSION

Through a number of high-profile incidents, a linkage between the use of social media for online advocacy and information security has emerged. Of particular related to social media usage and its ability to rapidly disseminate information; this information may be illegally obtained through hacking, thus encouraging information security breaches. The information dissemination may be an attempt to exercise Cyber Macht, through mass influence using legitimate or misleading information. Activists and governments may actively try to block the information dissemination. Alternatively, governments might attempt to affect the privacy of advocates and activists by monitoring social media. The cases covered in this chapter are highly visible, and therefore it is possible that there are many more occurrences of social media advocacy affecting information security; some may not yet be discovered until the activists realise they are being monitored (if at all). It is therefore prudent to make use of privacy protecting applications and tools, and for organisations to ensure their information security is strong, including against possible insider threats.

REFERENCES

Agnihotri, M. (2015, July 2). XKEYSCORE: NSA's Google for the World's Private Communications. *LinkedIn*. Retrieved from https://www.linkedin.com/pulse/xkeyscore-nsas-google-worlds-private-communications-mayur-agnihotri?published=t

Armistead, A. L., & Starman, S. (2014). Global Influence and Cyber Macht. *Journal of Information Warfare*, *13*(1), 47–57.

Armistead, A. L., & Starman, S. (2015). Perception Shaping and Cyber Macht: Russia and Ukraine. In J. Zaaiman and L. Leenen (Eds.), *Proceedings of the 10th International Conference on Cyber Warfare and Security*, Reading, UK (pp. 14-19). Academic Conferences.

Associated Press. (2011, March 4). Libya Shuts Down Internet Service Ahead of Planned Anti-Government Protests. Retrieved from http://www.foxnews.com/world/2011/03/04/libya-shuts-internet-service-ahead-planned-anti-government-protests.html

BBC. (2015, September 19). China censors Hong Kong protest posts on social media. Retrieved from http://www.bbc.com/news/world-asia-china-29411270

Black, I., & Chulov, M. (2011, February 18). Bahrain, Libya and Yemen try to crush protests with violence. Retrieved from http://www.guardian.co.uk/world/2011/feb/18/bahrain-libya-yemen-protestsviolence

Chabrow, E. (2012, March 6). LulzSec Leader Strikes Deal with Feds, Government Information Security. Retrieved from http://www.govinfosecurity.com/articles.php?art_id=4558&opg=1

von Clausewitz, C. (1832). *On War* (M. Howard & P. Paret, Trans.). Oxford, UK: Oxford University Press.

Communication Security Group. (2017). Seecrypt. Retrieved from http://www.seecrypt.com/

Comninos, A. (2011, June). Twitter revolutions and cyber crackdowns, Association for Progressive Communications. Retrieved from http://www.apc.org/en/system/files/AlexComninos_MobileInternet.pdf

de Wet, P. (2015, February 27). What the 'spy cables' taught us, Mail and Guardian. Retrieved from http://mg.co.za/article/2015-02-27-what-the-spy-cables-taught-us

Dencik, L., & Cable, J. (2017). The Advent of Surveillance Realism: Public Opinion and Activist Responses to the Snowden Leaks. *International Journal of Communication*, *11*, 763–781.

Duggan, P. (2016, January 8). Why Special Operations Forces in US Cyber-Warfare? *The Cyber Defense Review*. Retrieved from http://www.cyberdefensereview.org/2016/01/08/why-special-operations-forces-in-us-cyber-warfare/

Entous, A., Nakashima, E., & Miller, G. (2016, December 9). Secret CIA assessment says Russia was trying to help Trump win White House. *The Washington Post*. Retrieved from https://www.washingtonpost.com/world/national-security/obama-orders-review-of-russian-hacking-during-presidential-campaign/2016/12/09/31d6b300-be2a-11e6-94ac-3d324840106c_story.html

Flock, E. (2011, June 3). Syria internet services shut down as protesters fill streets. *The Washington Post*. Retrieved from https://www.washingtonpost.com/blogs/blogpost/post/syria-internet-services-shut-down-as-protesters-fill-streets/2011/06/03/AGtLwxHH_blog.html?utm_term=.ee1d83e83848

Franklin, J. (2013, November 17). Camila Vallejo, student leader, gets ready for a seat in Chilean congress. *The Guardian*. Retrieved from https://www.theguardian.com/world/2013/nov/17/chilean-student-activists-congress

García, C., Chauveau, P., Ledezma, J., & Pinto, M. (2013, August 11-13). What can social media teach us about protests? In *Proceedings of the 4th International Conference on Collaborative Innovation Networks (COINs13),* Santiago de Chile.

Gentzkow, M., & Allcott, H. (2017, January). Social Media and Fake News in the 2016 Election. *Sanford University*. Retrieved from https://people.stanford.edu/gentzkow/papers

Gross, G. (2017, March 7). WikiLeaks' CIA document dump shows agency can compromise Android, TVs. *Computer World*. Retrieved from http://www.computerworld.com/article/3177797/security/wikileaks-cia-document-dump-shows-agency-can-compromise-android-tvs.html

Gumede, W. (2015, March 1). Spy leaks have revealed the rot, Independent Online. Retrieved from http://www.iol.co.za/sundayindependent/spy-leaks-have-revealed-the-rot-1.1825190

Isin, E., & Ruppert, E. (2017). Citizen Snowden. *International Journal of Communication, 11*, 843–857.

Kamzi, A. (2011, September 27). How anonymous emerged to occupy Wall Street, The Guardian. Retrieved from http://www.guardian.co.uk/commentisfree/cifamerica/2011/sep/27/occupy-wall-street-anonymous

Kravets, D. (2011, January 27). Internet down, tens of thousands protest in Friday of wrath. *Wired*. Retrieved from http://www.wired.com/threatlevel/2011/01/egypt-internet-down/#

Lee, M. (2011, February 1). Obama urges Mubarak to step down. *Columbia Missourian*. Retrieved from http://www.columbiamissourian.com/stories/2011/02/01/obama-urges-mubarak-step-down-now

Lee, D. (2014, October 30). The role of social media in Occupy protests, on the ground and around the world, The South China Morning Post. Retrieved from http://www.scmp.com/news/hong-kong/article/1628305/role-social-media-occupy-protests-ground-and-around-world

Lekic, S. (2011, February 11). Denmark prime minister Lars Loekke Rasmussen calls on Egypt's Mubarak to resign. *Huffingtonpost.com*. Retrieved from http://www.huffingtonpost.com/2011/02/11/denmark-lars-loekkerasmussen-mubarak-egypt_n_821804.html

Li, D. K. (2014, July 31). Soldier's selfies might prove Russia's direct role in Ukraine. *The New York Post*. Retrieved from http://nypost.com/2014/07/31/soldiers-selfies-might-prove-russias-role-in-ukraine/

Lokot, T. (2014, March 2). Ukrainian journalists take regime's corruption public with YanukovychLeaks. *Global Voices Online*. Retrieved from http://globalvoicesonline.org/2014/03/02/ukrainian-journalists-take-regimes-corruption-public-with-yanukovychleaks

Lowensohn, J. (2014, July 18). Russia Spotted editing Wikipedia page about downed Malaysia Airlines jet. *The Verge*. Retrieved from http://www.theverge.com/2014/7/18/5917099/russia-spotted-editing-wikipedia-page-of-downed-malaysia-air-jet

Madrigal, A. (2011, January 24). The inside story of how Facebook responded to Tunisian hacks. *The Atlantic*. Retrieved from http://www.theatlantic.com/technology/archive/2011/01/the-inside-story-of-how-facebookresponded-to-tunisian-hacks/70044/#

Manning, K. (2014, November 28). In Chile, Protesting Students Tweak Tweets to Win Global Support. *Wired*. Retrieved from http://www.wired.com/2011/11/chile-students/

Miller, G. (2010, December 21). CIA launches task force to assess impact of U.S. cables' exposure by WikiLeaks. *Washington Post*. Retrieved from http://www.washingtonpost.com/wp-dyn/content/article/2010/12/21/AR2010122104599.html

Open Whisper Systems. (2016). Privacy that fits in your pocket. Retrieved from https://whispersystems.org/

Poulsen, K., & Zetter, K. (2010, June 6). U.S. Intelligence Analyst Arrested in Wikileaks Video Probe. *Wired*. Retrieved from http://www.wired.com/threatlevel/2010/06/leak/

Ramluckan, T., Sayeed Ally, S. E., & van Niekerk, B. (2017). Twitter Use in Student Protests: The Case of South Africa's #FeesMustFall Campaign. In M. E. Korstanje (Ed.), *Threat Mitigation and Detection of Cyber Warfare and Terrorism Activities* (pp. 221–254). Hershey, PA: IGI. doi:10.4018/978-1-5225-1938-6.ch010

Ramluckan, T. (2016). Social Media as a Crisis Communications and Disaster Management Tool: A South African Governance Perspective [DAdmin Dissertation]. University of KwaZulu-Natal, Durban, South Africa.

Robinson, J. J. (2011, February 2). Maldavian president joins calls for Mubarak to step down. Retrieved from http://minivannews.com/politics/maldivian-president-joins-calls-for-mubarak-to-step-down-15715

Rushe, D., & Walker, S. (2014, July 20). MH17 crash: Kerry lays out evidence of pro-Russia separatists' responsibility. *The Guardian*. Retrieved from http://www.theguardian.com/world/2014/jul/20/mh17-crash-kerry-evidence-pro-russia-separatists-responsibility

Russel, A., & Waisbard, S. (2017). The Snowden Revelations and the Networked Fourth Estate. *International Journal of Communication*, *11*, 858–878.

Satell, G. (2014, January 18). If you doubt that social media has changed the World, take a look at Ukraine. *Forbes*. Retrieved from http://www.forbes.com/sites/gregsatell/2014/01/18/if-you-doubt-that-social-media-has-changed-the-world-take-a-look-at-ukraine/

Sawant, N. (2017, February 17). The Fake News problem in India can get out of hand if not controlled in due time; experts tell us why. *FirstPost*. Retrieved from http://tech.firstpost.com/news-analysis/the-fake-news-problem-in-india-can-get-out-of-hand-if-not-controlled-in-due-time-experts-tell-us-why-362791.html

Segar, M. (2016, November 30). Shame as a political weapon: Donald Trump and the US presidential election. *The Conversation Africa*. Retrieved from http://theconversation.com/shame-as-a-political-weapon-donald-trump-and-the-us-presidential-election-69029

Sky News. (2011). Middle East: See facts about all the countries in the region. Retrieved from http://news.sky.com/skynews/Interactive-Graphics/middleeast

van Niekerk, B., & Maharaj, M. S. (2011) The Information Warfare Life Cycle Model, SA Journal of Information Management 13(1). Retrieved from http://www.sajim.co.za/index.php/SAJIM/article/view/476

van Niekerk, B., Pillay, K., & Maharaj, M. (2011). Analysing the Role of ICTs in the Tunisian and Egyptian Unrest from an Information Warfare Perspective. *International Journal of Communication*, *5*, 1406–1416.

van Niekerk, B. (2015). Information Warfare in the 2013-2014 Ukraine Crisis. In J. Richet (Ed.), *Cybersecurity Policies and Strategies for Cyberwarfare Prevention* (pp. 307–339). Hershey, PA: IGI. doi:10.4018/978-1-4666-8456-0.ch012

van Zyl, G. (2016a, June 15). Hack attack threat for Gupta sites, Oakbay and Sahara down. *Fin24*. Retrieved from http://www.fin24.com/Tech/Cyber-Security/anonymous-threatens-hack-attacks-on-gupta-websites-20160615

van Zyl, G. (2016b, July 12). Anonymous 'hacks' Armscor website. *Fin24*. Retrieved from http://www.fin24.com/Tech/News/anonymous-hacks-armscor-website-20160712

Vermeulen, J. (2016, June 13). This is how I took down the SABC: Anonymous hacker. *MyBroadband*. Retrieved from http://mybroadband.co.za/news/security/168303-this-is-how-i-took-down-the-sabc-anonymous-hacker.html

Wheatley, M. (2013, September 12). Botnets and Porn: It's What Tor's All About. *SiliconAngle*. Retrieved from http://siliconangle.com/blog/2013/09/12/botnets-and-porn-its-what-tors-all-about/

Wong, C. W. (2017, February 3). Uber CEO steps down from Trump advisory council after users boycott. *The Guardian*. Retrieved from https://www.theguardian.com/technology/2017/feb/02/travis-kalanick-delete-uber-leaves-trump-council

KEY TERMS AND DEFINITIONS

Availability: A concept of information security whereby information or systems can be accessed by authorised individuals when the access is required.

Confidentiality: A concept of information security whereby only authorised individuals may access the information.

Cyber-Security: Protecting information, systems and networks from networked or online threats.

Denial of Service: An attack of information or systems to prevent legitimate access. An attack may come from multiple sources, known as a distributed denial of service.

Hacktivist: 'Hacker Activist' someone who hacks computer systems to raise publicity for an cause or ideology.

Information Warfare: A concept that revolves around gaining information superiority over an opponent, and comprises of various functions, including cyber security and psychological operations.

Integrity: A concept of information security whereby only authorised individuals may modify or create information, or that the source can be verified. All modifications should be logged.

Chapter 2
Social Media as Alternative Public Sphere for Citizen Participation and Protest in National Politics in Zimbabwe:
The Case of #thisflag

Collen Sabao
Midlands State University, Zimbabwe & University of Namibia, Namibia

Tendai Owen Chikara
Bindura University of Science Education, Zimbabwe & Solusi University, Zimbabwe

ABSTRACT

The chapter examines and discusses the role and communicative potential of social media based platforms in citizen political participation and protests in Zimbabwe specifically focusing on the #thisflag movement on Facebook, Twitter and Whatsapp. #thisflag is a social media-based platform that rose to challenge the Zimbabwean government over the political and economic decay as well as rampant corruption characterising the country contemporarily. While a new phenomenon to Zimbabwe and Zimbabwean politics, the impact and communicative potential of social media as an alternative public sphere was recently tested in nationwide protest stayaway organised through the Facebook and Twitter movement under the #thisflag handle/brand. This chapter discusses the manners in which such social media platforms impact national politics in Zimbabwe as well as globally, specifically looking at the #thisflag movement as a case study.

DOI: 10.4018/978-1-5225-2854-8.ch002

SOCIAL MEDIA BASED PROTESTS IN ZIMBABWE: A BRIEF BACKGROUND TO ITS RISE AND POPULARITY

The role of social media in citizen political participation and protests in Zimbabwe is a new phenomenon. Its impact and communicative potential was recently tested in nationwide protest stayaway organised through the Facebook and Twitter movement under the #thisflag handle/brand. Following this, the chapter discusses the manners in which social media platforms such as Facebook and Whatsapp impact national politics in Zimbabwe and on a global scale, specifically looking at the #thisflag movement as a case study. In the period between March and June 2016, there 'exploded' in Zimbabwe social media based protests against the Zimbabwean Zimbabwe National Union Patriotic Front (ZANU-PF) led government over the state of the economy. Since the controversial elections of 2013, Zimbabwe has been on an accelerated economic decline, characterised by the closure of the larger part of industry and a general degeneration of the fiscus.

The economic challenges faced by Zimbabwe had adverse effects on other economies as well, especially those of her border neighbours who had to 'accept' hordes of Zimbabwean economic migrants. The situation has become so bad that the government has been struggling, albeit failing to meet its civil service monthly wage bill commitment among other pertinent responsibilities. In this political climate characterised by political squabbling, rampant corruption, a general economic decay and severing of regional and international relations arose a social media movement named #thisflag, led by a Pastor Evan Mawarire. The movement arguably, while not political party driven, has managed to rattle the ZANU PF government into realising the potential of social media mass protests to the point that it eventually flighted threats to the citizenry over the use and 'abuse' of social media. In fact, the Zimbabwean government has since enacted into law a Cyber Security Law, an act seen as responding to fears of social media. The promulgation of the Cybercrime and Cybersecurity Act in Zimbabwe and the subsequent appointment on Patrick Chinamasa as first minister of the newly created Ministry of Cyber Security speaks to the fears of social media by the ZANU PF government. Sadly, because social media utilises the World Wide Web (WWW) which is internet based, it makes it a transnational phenomenon and more difficult a space to monitor and regulate. This was in light of the observation that the #thisflag movement successfully mobilised the nation to a day national boycott of work on the 6th of July through their submovement tagged #shutdownzimbabwe.

The participation of Zimbabweans living outside the country in countries such as South Africa, Botswana, Namibia, The United States of America and Europe in general as economic migrants, further solidifies the transnational impact that the movement had in the determination of the direction the country would take politically and economically. The success of this mass stayaway evinces the power of social media in citizen advocacy in Zimbabwe and thus warrants further study and examination.

As Sabao (2016) observes, since the attainment of independence from the British settler rule in 1980 up to the late 1990s, Zimbabwe *had* predominantly been a one-party state. The Zimbabwe African National Union Patriotic Front (ZANU PF) led by the incumbent president, Robert Gabriel Mugabe, was at the helm of the national political ladder, with little, if any, meaningful oppositional political resistance. The emergence of the Movement for Democratic Change (MDC) in 1999 saw the ZANU PF led government face the greatest opposition ever since independence. This is largely evidenced by the political inroads made by the newly formed MDC in the 2000 plebiscite, in which it won a resounding historic 57 of the possible 120 seats in parliament – a real political threat and shock to the ZANU PF political hegemony. This feat, to date, is still unparalleled in Zimbabwean politics. Since the emergence of the MDC the political scene in Zimbabwe has largely been pluralistic - tempting and inviting to other political actors. As such, the period saw the birth of several new political parties as well as breakaway faction from the mainstream political parties. Developments in the last decade in Zimbabwe, however, have witnessed a political rollercoaster. The nation and national affairs were defined by unstable political and socio-economic environments, characterized by economic meltdown, and incessant droughts. Several events, major among them the ZANU-PF led propagandistic motivated Fast Track Land Reform Programme of the late 1990s, the alienation of the country by the larger part of the world (especially Europe and the United States of America) through economic sanctions, gross economic mismanagement of the national fiscus and resources, incessant drought and political intolerance and violence have seen the country plunge into an economic and political quagmire of unprecedented proportions.

THE COMMUNICATIVE POTENTIAL OF SOCIAL MEDIA PLATFORMS

Over the last decade, social networking websites such as Facebook, Twitter, MySpace, Belbo and other social forums have exploded in popularity in the whole world, Zimbabwe included. These social networking sites have also become quite central as alternative public spheres, breaking stories before the mainstream official media does. The impact that such social networks have on contemporary society as platforms for group social interactions and news outlets should not be undermined. Social networking sites have become widespread and grown in popularity because they allow people to interact freely and to (re)construct and reveal their desired realities in the face of the gag of stringent media laws and regulatory frameworks. For example, Subrahmanyam et al (2008) estimate that sites such as MySpace and Facebook have over 100 million users between them, many of them adolescents and emerging adults. The chapter here examines the rise in popularity of social media platforms as representing the constructions of alternative public spheres where political debates, protests and messages are constructed, negotiated and consolidated. In doing this, the chapter uses the case study of the protest movement #thisflag and its success in leading political protests in Zimbabwe. The advent of web based networking sites however has meant that the questions of citizen advocacy and participation practices have to be (re)confronted and (re)interrogated. Of particular interest in proposed chapter is how this alternative digital public sphere has offered Zimbabweans 'an avenue to discuss a taboo subject in Zimbabwe without fear or being reprimanded by the secretive and authoritarian state. The 'taboo' in this context refers to issues that the state does not want discussed in public like the president's health, corruption, factionalism or succession debate and state sponsored corruption just to mention but a few. Most precisely, the chapter explores how the internet has challenged the elitist dominated domestic public sphere into a sphere where ordinary citizens interact among themselves and those in power' (Mpofu, nd). Moyo (2006) commenting on this condition and how it helped birth the rise of reliance on digital alternative media in Zimbabwe opines that:

Restricted democratic space has spawned a multiplicity of alternative public spheres that enable groups and individuals to continue to participate and engage in the wider debate on the mutating crisis gripping the country since the turn of the century... the diaspora are creatively exploiting new media to resist state propaganda churned out through the mainstream media. (p81)

Such are the issues the #thisflag largely discussed and challenged. Using the #thisflag movement as a case study, the chapter seeks to interrogate/demonstrate the power of social media in political and economic advocacy in Zimbabwe.

Observing the communicative potential of social networking sites to influence both change and development in society, we observe that these sites have the power to unite people with shared opinions and at times even diverse one to come together and discuss issues pertaining to their lives. We also recognise that social networking sites have by and large transformed themselves as a replacement of traditional communication channels. We thus explore the manners in which the internet has become an alternative platform for Facebook users (and Zimbabweans to be precise) to exercise their right to freedom of expression given the historically recorded repressive media regulatory conditions in the country. Theoretically the chapter utilizes the Digital Alternative Media Theory as well as Habermas' ambit of the public sphere. In an environment that does not promote media plurality and the proliferation of free speech and critical thinking such as the Zimbabwean environment of recent years, Mpofu (nd) envisions the internet and by extension citizen journalism as some extension of Habermas' public sphere. Habermas (1989) defines such a public sphere as,

[A] realm of our social life in which something approaching public opinion can be formed. Access is guaranteed to all citizens... with the guarantee of freedom of assembly and association and the freedom to express and publish their opinions—about matters of general interest. (p73-4)

The chapter explores, using the #thisflag movement, how the internet (and Facebook, Twitter and Whatsapp to be precise) has grown as a form of alternative media, reporting on and challenging the tabooed topics and issues in Zimbabwe. The proposed chapter seeks to demonstrate that the proliferation of citizen advocacy aided by the internet has made it possible for counter-hegemonic voices (Mitra, 2001) 'to upset the elite and politically dominated public spheres. The internet is credited for simultaneously enabling the user to exercise the right to freedom of expression through receiving and disseminating information, ideas and opinions visually or phonetically to large audiences at the lowest possible cost. Also, this evolution of technology has caused global dramatic changes in the field of citizenship participation.'

THE SOCIAL MEDIA PHENOMENON: COMMUNICATIVE POTENTIAL AND INFLUENCE IN 'NATIONAL' POLITICS

The power of social media to influence change and encourage citizen participation in the national affairs of their nations can never be overstated. Because if its capacity to conceal people's identities, social media encourages free participation of the citizenry in oftentimes sensitive matters they would not normally be free to participate in for fear or reprisals and victimisation by state security agents. Because of their potential to reach out to multitudes of people instantaneously, web based social media platforms have been able to rally masses of people behind a cause in the shortest amount of time. Because of the supersonic speed of information transmission offered by the internet, social media applications and platforms have been able to 'recruit' large numbers of followers with similar opinions to deliberate and debate on issues of national and oftentimes international interests which directly affect them. Through such kind of participation, citizens of several nationalities have been able to (re)shape, (re)invent and (re)negotiate their political fates and futures – sadly, not always with the best processes and outcomes. Several precedents of the power of social media to unite masses in protests and participation in life-changing social and political processes before the #thisflag movement are numerous. Examples can be drawn from the manner in which Facebook and Twitter played pivotal roles in the political transformations in Egypt, Libya, and Tunisia. More recent examples can be drawn from the student protests in neighbouring South Africa under the #feesmustfall and #rhodesmustfall movements.

In the political revolutions in Egypt, Tunisia and Syria (what has become known as the Arab Spring) for example, Facebook has been credited as having played a pivotal role in the coordination of protests. Social media helped in the shaping of political debates, the dissemination of information the world over about the ongoing in these countries' political revolutions and in the process assisted in a moderately peaceful manner to dislodge at least two regimes in Tunisia and Egypt. In Egypt, immediately after the Tunisian revolutions, coordination through the Facebook page "We Are All Khaled Said", the youth managed to mobilise, empower and coordinate online citizen protests into offline real protests. Howard, Duffy, Freelon et al (2011, p2) would opine in this regard that, '[s]ocial media played a central role in shaping political debates in the Arab Spring. A spike in online revolutionary conversations often preceded major events on the ground. Social media helped spread democratic ideas across international borders.' In essence, the communicative potential of social media based platforms manifests itself in the ability to disseminate information in real time, empower citizens, mobilise and fortify protesters. The downside to such web based protests is however that it usually serves the 'elitist' members of society. For example, in Tunisia and Egypt, 'evidence shows that social media was used heavily to conduct political conversations by a key demographic group in the revolution – young, urban, relatively well-educated individuals, many of whom were women. Both before and during the revolutions, these are individuals used Facebook, Twitter, and YouTube to put pressure on their governments' (Howard, Duffy, Freelon et al, 2011, p2). It would require a certain level of sophistication for citizens to become effective users of such platforms as Twitter and Facebook. In the Zimbabwean scenario however, the larger part of such protest communication was facilitated by a lesser complex platform, the smartphone based Whatsapp application – which we can safely but cautiously conclude is available to at least eighty percent (80%) of Zimbabwe's mobile phone users.

In South Africa, two national student protests evince the power of social media as an alternative 'democratised' space for facilitating national debate and participation in protests against and challenging ruling hegemonies. South African university students under the social media based banner and handle #feesmustfall coordinated nationwide protests against the government's proposal to increase university tuition fees by eleven percent (11%) in 2016. Beginning at the University of the Witwatersrand on 14 October 2015, the student lockdown of university soon spread to the universities in Cape Town and soon assumed a national outlook. Students were able to coordinate marches, protests and demonstration through the cyber network – managing to communicate in real time by sending messages, videos and images to each other. They also managed to attract the attention and oftentimes sympathy of the international community who sent messages of solidarity through the #feesmustfall pages on both Facebook and Twitter. So profound were the student protests that on October 23, President Jacob Zima was forced to announce that there would be no fees increases in 2016 marking a huge milestone in the communicative potential of social media in national politics. The #feesmustfall protests were soon to be rekindled in August 2016 in anticipation of the announcement by the Minister of Higher Education of the 2017 fees structures.

At the time of writing (October 2016), students in most Universities in and around Johannesburg (among them University of the Witwatersrand, University of Pretoria and Tswane University of Technology) are currently shut down as students are protesting against fees hikes proposed for 2017. Another online protest movement organised by successfully by South African university students was tagged the #rhodesmustfall campaign which began at the University of Cape Town in protest against the continued presence of relics of apartheid and colonialism. Students at the university demanded the removal from campus of all statues of colonisers and specifically the statue of Cecil John Rhodes. The protest, began and executed via social media immediately assumed a national face and students in universities around the country in solidarity with University of Cape Town and staged similar demonstrations of their own, with students at Rhodes University even demanding and immediate renaming of the institution.

The major motivation for the #rhodesmustfall campaign can be argued to be purely political in nature. The Jacob Zuma African National Congress (ANC) led South African government was also quick to point at the political nature of the student protests. Students argued that they found it absurd that a new black African government would continue embracing the heritage of colonialism especially considering the heinous racism that the legacy of Cecil John Rhodes represented in the national historical metanarrative of South Africa. The argument was that the removal of such colonial and by extension apartheid heritage would go a long way in expunging such a historically painful colonial past, which the continued erection of the statues seemed to ironically celebrate. True to the power and communicative potential of social medias based protests in national affairs, the South African government was forced to relent and the statues were taken down on 9 April 2015. Students across South African and the rest of the world, especially those who celebrate Pan Africanist agendas celebrated this as an inter/national victory against the colonial heritage and history.

ZIMBABWE IN THE LAST DECADES: POLITICAL LANDSCAPE AND PROCESSES AND THE RISE OF SOCIAL MEDIA

Zimbabwe's political and economic history in the last three decades has largely been characteristically turbulent. The ZANU-PF led government has been since 1980 used to be a one-party state. Following the entrance of the biggest opposition challenge to such a one-party hegemony by the Movement for Democratic Change (MDC) in 1999, the ZANU-PF government realised the need to hold on to power by all means necessary. Part of such measures was a stringent gag on the free flow of information, especially through the traditional media of broadcast and print news sources (which ironically the state then had a huge controlling state – being the sole television and radio broadcaster and owning one of the largest circulating national daily newspapers). The flow of information thus became highly regulated, often bordering on government propaganda. In order to avert counterbalancing news circulation, the government put in place measures that made it extremely impossible to register news reporting mediums such as newspapers and radio stations. Such restrictive media laws included the Access to Information and Protection of Privacy Act (AIPPA) and the Public Order and Security Act (POSA) we promulgated and were used together with previously existing laws such as the Official Secrets Act (OSA) and the Broadcasting Services Act (BSA).

The popularity of use of social media as a form of citizen journalism in Zimbabwe, as is the case with many other nations, can largely be attributed to the need to counterbalance 'regulated' information flow controlled by a dominating non-democratic hegemony. In other words, such popularity arises from the need to challenge 'the elitist dominated domestic public sphere into a sphere where ordinary citizens interact among themselves and those in power.' (Mpofu, n.d.). Up until around 2013, when the government seemed to ease up, the media regulatory framework in Zimbabwe has been regarded as one of the most draconian in the world, comparatively. Zimbabwean political evolutions from the year 2000, in which the then ruling political party, the Zimbabwe African National Patriotic Front (ZANU-PF), led by incumbent president Robert Gabriel Mugabe faced the strongest possible opposition ever to its traditionally 'one party state' hegemony from the Morgan Tsvangirai led Movement for Democratic Change (MDC) culminated in a serious gag on the media. Regarded as the fourth pillar of states, the power of the media in influencing public opinion, and by extension, political and social change must never be undermined. The high proliferation of a diversity of free speech and opinions is anathema to the sustenance of despotic political hegemonies. In the face of serious opposition, ZANU-PF realised that the control of the media was key to its continued survival. Stringent media regulating statutes such as the Access to Information and

Protection of Privacy Act (AIPPA) and the Public Order and Security Act (POSA) we promulgated.

Such laws, together with previously existing laws such as the Official Secrets Act (OSA) and the Broadcasting Services Act (BSA) made it nearly impossible for the freedom of expression to thrive. Many Zimbabwean began looking up to these for more diverse reportage of news from and in Zimbabwe. The embracing of these digital web based alternative forms of news can be credited as having played a critical part in Zimbabweans' embrace of the 'new' trend of citizen or participatory journalism. Mujere and Mwatwara (2015, p216) opine in this regard that, '...Zimbabweans have reacted to the narrowing of the democratic space by resorting to subterranean methods. Thus...a narrow media in Zimbabwe incubated the rise of citizen journalism'.

It became more clear that the majority if Zimbabwean began to use the internet not only as consumers but rather as 'prosumers' of information. 'Their status as 'prosumers' gives them freedom, power and a voice to speak up to authority and generate content. The internet offers an alternative digital public sphere where ordinary citizens meet and discuss issues they would not ordinarily discuss in government controlled public spheres because regimes of control have made discussions of these taboo topics impossible. In addition, the fact that public media stifle vibrant debate that speaks against state programmes, means people will forever be in the dark. To circumvent this, the internet, as a forum for power, voice and self-expression, has made it possible for debate and tensions between the elite and ordinary people to be experienced in a typical Habermasian public sphere fashion online' (Mpofu, nd, p7). So restricted was the free flow of information in Zimbabwe that several subjects, such as the President's health, ZANU-PF party politics and political processes such as corruption as well as the presidential succession and national political process such as elections were taboo to report on freely and 'objectively'. Instead, they could only be 'properly' reported on by the state controlled media (both broadcast and print). Because of the need for counter narratives from those of the 'despotic' ZANU PF government, there was need to (re)formulate new ways of dispersing information to the general public. 'A broad range of activities by the populace under the banner citizen journalism has also been deployed to counter the state metanarrative and of course in some cases to affirm it. Thus, citizen journalism has played an important role in shaping political attitudes, altering the boundaries of political interaction and bringing into existence new methods and channels for resistance since the build up to the 2008 elections and 2013 elections' (Mujere & Mwatwara, 2015, p216).

THE DIGITAL AGE: SOCIAL MEDIA AS ALTERNATIVE PUBLIC SPHERE

Social media as alternative public sphere has for some time been a very difficult phenomenon to characterise and ascribe parameters to. This has largely been because of the various dimensions that it has assumed in the dissemination of news and messages. It cuts across all web-based applications available on computers, iPads, tablets and smartphones such as Twitter, Facebook, Whatsapp, MySpace, etc. Whereas social media platforms once represented public spheres where individuals could (re) negotiate and (re)define their personas and identities without restraint, they have lately reinvented themselves by becoming a form of citizen journalism. They have metamorphosed into alternative digital public spheres where all aspects of human life are debated and negotiated, avenues through which politically citizens can without restraint speak to power. Through active participation in web based citizen journalism, tone citizenry has been empowered to 'freely' speak to each other and to power without fear of reprimands and harassment from the secret state security agents as well as the police and military. Bowman & Willis (2003, p9) believe citizen journalism to be 'the act of a citizen, or group of citizens, playing an active role in the process of collecting, reporting, analysing and disseminating news and information. Citizen journalism refers to the concept of an active audience in a new dispensation in which journalism has evolved significantly to cater to an audience equipped with the ability to not only consume but also produce media content. Citizen journalism appears thus, to be about 'a set of practices that are embedded with the everyday lives of citizens' (Atton 2002, p267). As a form of alternative digital public sphere, social media in Zimbabwe has gained momentum largely due to the very restrictive media regulatory frameworks that make is criminal to circulate any news messages viewed as directly attacking the incumbent ZANU-PF led government. The population thus seeks alternative channels to communicate such subversive materials through. This explains thus the potential exhibited by Facebook and Whatsapp to mobilize Zimbabweans to mass protest.

Citizen journalism seems to capture something of a countervailing ethos of ordinary person`s capacity to bear witness especially during a social or a political crisis (Allan 2009, p18). Citizen journalism is redefining the whole essence of journalism. Technological innovation has indeed enhanced the work of citizen journalists the world over though contrary to popular belief the concept is not entirely new (Mutsvairo, 2012). Citizen journalism can largely be viewed as an outgrowth of the internet and new media, which have given the readers opportunities to contribute to news production, not as just readers but also producers. For example, users are able to instantly share messages, images and videos and thus coordinate events and actions in real time.

Social media platforms thus empower the audience in such a way that they are no longer mere receivers but participants as they are platforms to debate issues released by the citizen journalist. Moyo (2011, p10) notes that in Zimbabwe citizens are no longer helplessly bombarded with messages by mass media but instead are also actively producing news and initiating news flows among themselves. The approach of professional journalism adopted on the coverage ensures the representation is clinical in its narration of the facts while simultaneously conveying both manifest and latent meanings that largely falls within the mainstream global framing (Chuma, 2005). Before the emergence of new media technologies so called deviants or dissidents had their grievances aired by foreign media organisations such as BBC; CNN; VOA (Chuma, 2005, p3). 'The intent of this participation is to provide independent, reliable, accurate, wide-ranging and relevant information that a democracy requires'. Largely viewed as an outgrowth of the internet and new media, such a form of citizenship participation in national politics through social network based citizen journalism is argued to have provided the citizenry with the prospects of contributing to unedited news production, not as just readers but also producers.' The concept itself has been defined in many ways and within different parameters. Goode (2009) opines that 'Citizen[ship] journalism' refers to a range of web-based practices whereby 'ordinary' users engage in journalistic practices. Citizen journalism includes practices such as current affairs-based blogging, photo and video sharing, and posting eyewitness commentary on current events.in doing this, the citizenry is empowered to share uncensored and unedited news in real time. This makes it easier to coordinate national protests and events. The notion of citizenship participation is often used quite broadly to include activities such as re-posting, linking, 'tagging' (labeling with keywords), rating, modifying or commenting upon news materials posted by other users or by professional news outlets, whereby citizens participate in the news process without necessarily acting as 'content creators'. Reflecting on the advent of citizenship participation through social media based citizen journalism, Papacharissi (2009, pi) opines that 'journalism is in the middle of sweeping changes in its relationships with the communities it serves, and the audiences for news and public affairs it seeks to address. Changes in technology have blurred the lines between professionals and citizens, partisan and objective bystanders, particularly in the emerging public zones of the blogosphere.'

#thisflag, #tajamuka, AND OTHERS: SOCIAL MEDIA AND NATIONWIDE PUBLIC PROTESTS IN ZIMBABWE

On 6 July 2016, Zimbabwe literally came to an economic standstill as the majority of working Zimbabweans, both in public and private employ, heeded a call to 'shut down Zimbabwe' in protest against the economic and political rot that has characterised the country for the last three decades. Organised under the leadership of Facebook and Twitter based protest movements, #thisflag and #tajamuka, the one day stay away represented possibly the biggest anti-government and anti-ZANU PF protests in the country since the 1998 stayaways and food riots. The rise of the two major social media based protests in Zimbabwe, #thisflag and #tajamuka took the nation by surprise. Especially surprised was the Robert Gabriel Mugabe led ZANU PF government. Formed under the leadership of a youthful clergyman, Evan Mawarire, #thisflag projected itself as a non-political movement whose main agenda as spelt out on both their Facebook and Twitter accounts as being 'the citizens of Zimbabwe [who] have decided to speak and be heard'. Posting a video online under the hashtag #thisflag, Mawarire, draped in the Zimbabwean national flag, proclaimed that he was not a politician but merely a citizen of Zimbabwe frustrated by the political and economic decay in Zimbabwe. He is quoted as having confessed that '[w]hen I look at this flag it is not a reminder of pride and inspiration, it feels as if I want to belong to another country'. The video, circulated nationally and internationally through the social media mediums of Facebook, Twitter and Whatsapp, managed to 'convert' other Zimbabweans both based in and outside the country who immediately began posting their own videos and pictures draped in the Zimbabwean national flag in solidarity with the protests and Mawarire. A period of a general hype of protests online through the three social media platforms of Twitter, Facebook and Whatsapp lasting approximately 25 days followed, culminating in the eventual call to shut down Zimbabwe. The protests to rise against the government were largely driven by 5 major demands:

1. Government should pay civil servants in time (This follows the government's failure to timelessly meet its monthly civil service wage bill commitment. The government had been struggling to meet its monthly civil service salary obligations, with salaries sometimes being paid half a month after they were due – half a month into the following month to be precise. Annual bonuses for 2015, for example, were only fully paid in August 2016).
2. Reduce roadblocks and stop police officers from harassing people for cash (This comes in the wake of the alleged rampant corruption characterising the Zimbabwe Republic Police. The generality of the Zimbabwean citizenry is agreed on the unnecessity of the high proliferation of roadblocks countrywide. It

would seem the police have abandoned their primary role of policing and have in fact become some 'fundraising' arm. Police are also accused of harassing motorists for bribes. It has become nearly impossible to pass a roadblock without event).

3. President Mugabe should fire corrupt officials (This comes amid allegations and suspicions of mass looting of national resources by those in Mugabe's close political circles as evidenced by the affluence of their lifestyles. A lot of national financial resources have for example just 'disappeared' unaccounted for).
4. Plans to introduce bond notes to ease cash shortages must be abandoned (Following the 'death' of the Zimbabwean economy in 2008, the Zimbabwean government introduced a multicurrency system, with the United States of America Dollar being the major currency. In the last year – 2015 – the government introduced bond notes, allegedly to curtail change shortages in the country. Currently it has proposed introducing bond notes to work side by side with other currencies including the United States dollar in order to allegedly alleviate shortages of cash blamed on the serious externalisation of the US currency by the Zimbabwean citizenry. The majority of Zimbabweans are opposed to this).
5. Remove a recent ban on imported goods (Through Statutory Instrument 61 of 2016, the Zimbabwean government imposed a general ban on the direct importation of goods by the general citizenry. Zimbabwean now need a special permit from the Zimbabwe Revenue Authority to import the restricted goods, which include among them basic foodstuffs, alcohol, building materials etc. Such a permit is only granted subject to the applicant successful making a case for why they did not opt for locally manufactured products. This was a big blow to the majority of Zimbabweans who, due to the economic hardships, had resorted to informal trading in imported goods, especially food and clothing items from neighbouring South Africa, Zambia, Botswana, Mozambique and Namibia. The government argues that this was in a bid to protect the local industries and local products, which sadly are always exorbitantly priced and also produced by companies owned by Mugabe's closest allies).

On the bedrock of these common complaints largely shared by the Zimbabwean citizenry, #thisflag managed to successfully organise a nationwide protest through social media. On 6 July, 2016, Zimbabweans across the political divide participated in one of probably the biggest anti-government protests in Zimbabwe's recent history. Several other minor protests were recorded in Zimbabwe's capital, Harare, immediately after the July 6 protest. It would seem that the success of the #thisflag led #shutdownzimbabwe campaign has fortified the resolve of Zimbabweans to seek change and redress in the political and economic systems of the country. Whilst the Mugabe led ZANU-PF government attempted to downplay the significance of the 'national' boycott through its state funded news outlets the national daily newspapers, *The Herald* and the national broadcasters (Zimbabwe Broadcasting Corporation run Zimbabwe Television as well as radio stations), the real effects of the nationwide boycott can only be explicated by the reactions of the government in the aftermath of the 6 July mass protest. On July 12, 2016 Mawarire handed himself over to the Zimbabwe Republic Police where he was formally charged with inciting violence and disturbing the peace, a charge later amended in court to 'attempting to overthrow a government'.

The new charge, treason, was only read to the accused Mawarire in court, prompting the judge presiding to dismiss the charges and release Mawarire. This was not the first time that the National Prosecuting Authority has failed to convict such 'high' profile figures. Politically motivated charges were once pressed on opposition party leader Morgan Tsvangirai, who was also acquitted of treason charges. These kinds of charges signify the desperation that the incumbent government has to silence any dissenting voices. Failing to prosecute Mawarire, the governments then resorted to its usual tactics of enacting draconian laws that inhibit any political processes perceived as opposition to ZANU-PF to commence. The Computer Crimes and Cyber Crimes Bill was thus quickly drafted in order to eliminate social media based protests such as #thisflag, #tajamuka etc. The use of the Zimbabwe national flag – a collective hieroglyph uniting #thisflag protestors – was also criminalised. The national flag, popularised by Mawarire, had become the nationally uniting symbol of protest against the ZANU-PF regime and criminalising its use meant curtailing any nationalistic coordinated protests against the ruling ZANU-PF elite.

AFTERWORD: THE POWER/POTENTIAL OF SOCIAL MEDIA IN NATIONAL PROTESTS AND TRANSFORMATION

The strength of social media as alternative digital public sphere in empowering, coordinating and popularising political processes and protests at both national and international platforms is borne testimony to by governments' reactions to such. In the aftermath of the Zimbabwean July 6 national protests, the ZANU-PF led government's reactions were largely threats of arrest and imprisonment, threats of tracing of individuals responsible through the national cellular phone registration database etc. The use of the national flag in protests was criminalised. What has been interesting is the manner in which Zimbabweans defied such a criminalisation of the use of the national flag in the recent mass protests that resulted in the resignation of Robert Gabriel Mugabe as president of the republic. In as much as the causes for the recent mass protests of November 18, 2017 were different from those of #thisflag, it is impossible to ignore how such a movement fortified Zimbabweans across the globe to rise against the regime. Again, Mawarire was quite instrumental in uniting Zimbabwean citizens all over the world to 'rebel'. Such a recognition and reaction to citizen protests coordinated over social media platforms are, however, not peculiar to Zimbabwe. In the Tunisian and Egyptian political revolutions, the governments of the two nations also acknowledged the immense power such an alternative source of 'unrestricted' and 'uncensored' information had and reacted the same. As Howard, Duffy, Freelon et al (2011) observe,

Governments themselves also recognized the power of opposition movements equipped with social media. In Tunisia, officials attempted to block Facebook and other social media sites and arrested bloggers and others who used social media to spread critical news about the government. What the found is that democracy advocates were tech-savvy and had the help of hackers and talented computer programmers who were able to shutter government services online and provide protestors with workarounds to censors. Likewise, Egypt attempted to choke off access to social media and found that the protestors in Cairo's Tahrir Square were nonetheless able to stay connected. The Muslim Brotherhood relied on bloggers whose servers were located in London and therefore couldn't be taken offline. (p3)

In the case of the South African government reaction to the student protests, true to reactions by many nationalistic governments, the first reaction was to try and militarise and securitise the universities in a bid to curtail not only information flow but also to clamp down of protesters. Sadly, the reactions of the government seem to actually inflame and fortify the students' resolve to demonstrate as such measure typically result in the student protesters becoming violent. 'The courts [in South Africa] attempted to ban students from using the #FeesMustFall, making it evident that the use of Twitter, Facebook, WhatsApp and other social media as alternative communication has been met with increased attempts by authorities to censor and control access to the new technologies as a way to stifle oppositional forces' (Mano and Mukhongo, 2016). Naicker (2016) commenting on the power of social media as a platform for speaking to power and challenging hegemonies opines that, 'The massive student protests that swept South Africa at the end of 2015, culminating in the 'fees must fall' movement resulted in a huge victory for university students, when President Jacob Zuma was forced to withdraw plans for a 11.5 per cent tuition fee hike for 2016, after students shut down universities all over the country. What began as a protest over proposed increases, soon led to a nation-wide call for free education, with thousands of students, workers, and parents on the streets in scenes reminiscent of the mass-based people's power movements of the 1970s and 1980s'.

In Zimbabwe, recognising 'social media and its power to put a human face on political oppression', the first reaction of the Zimbabwe government was to 'jam' the network signals of all cellphone service providers in Zimbabwe between 09:00 hrs and 11:00 hours on July 6 in order to frustrate and hamper the coordination of the nationwide boycott of work. Secondly, the government flighted advertisement/ notices (reproduced below as Fig 1) in almost all national media (both public and private) warning citizens against 'the abuse of social media for political reasons'. The ZANU-PF government, it seems, true to their historic banter, blamed and suspected the opposition political parties for conspiring against them and the national sovereign outlook.

Of interest to note is the threatening tone and language the government used in a bid to dissuade citizens from circulating messages it deems against national peace and national interest. The 'reminder' that all sim cards are registered and the government knows the owners is a clear indicator of the government realisation of the potential of the social media as a platform for protests and change in national politics and affairs. As an extra measure to curtail the role of social media in Zimbabwean politics, the ZANU-PF Robert Mugabe led government in early August 2016 further proposed the enactment of a law that can incriminate and incarcerate individuals for 'abusing' social media platforms for political purposes. While still at Bill level, if enacted into law, the Computer Crimes and Cyber Crimes Bill would empower the state security agents (military, police and the Central Intelligence Organisation) to intercept social media communications as well as to seize all electronic gadgets including laptops, computers and smartphones in order to squash social media based political communication. The same law would also make it possible for the Robert Gabriel Mugabe led government to extradite Zimbabwean citizens in the diaspora and other countries on the continent suspected of producing and disseminating through social media, messages suspected to be of a political nature and which undermine the ZANU-PF hegemony to face trial and be liable to a prison term of up to 5 years.

This however does not come as a surprise in a country that has a history of passing laws restricting the free flow of information in an attempt to curtail political communication by people or organisations regarded as critical of the government or opposition political parties. As Sabao and Chingwaramusee (2017) observe, it has become a norm for the ZANU-PF led government to enact draconian laws restricting the proliferation of free speech in order to curb opposition politics. For example, historically, 'in the face of serious opposition from the MDC, ZANU-PF realised that the control of the media was key to its continued survival. Stringent media regulating statutes such as the Access to Information and Protection of Privacy Act (AIPPA) and the Public Order and Security Act (POSA) we promulgated. Such laws, together with previously existing laws such as the Official Secrets Act (OSA) and the Broadcasting Services Act (BSA) made it nearly impossible for the freedom of

Figure 1. Zimbabwean government advertisement on the 'abuse' of social media following the 6 July 2016 national boycott of work
(Source: The Herald, 8 July 2016)

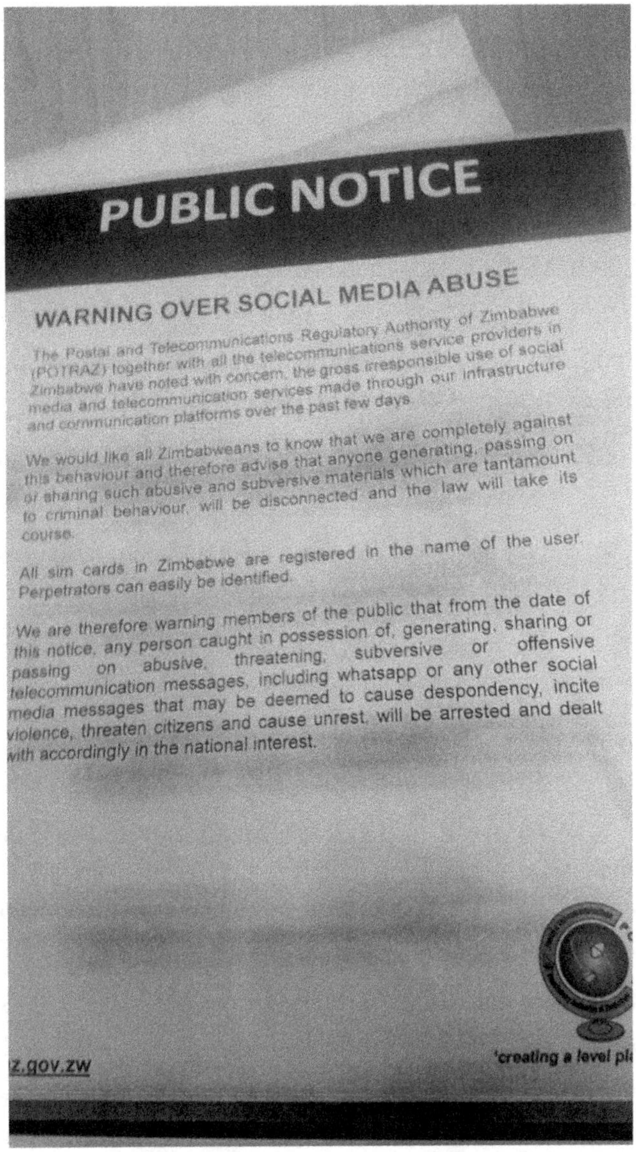

expression to thrive' (Sabao and Chingwaramusee, 2017). The 'abuse' of the national flag for purposes deemed political was also criminalised. This thus puts an end to the donning of the national flag as a protest tool, something that had become the protest face and mark of #thisflag campaign. In this regard, the government criminalised the reproduction, circulation and resale of replica Zimbabwean national flag as well as their use as a protest tool. Those found guilty of such an 'abuse' of the national flag would face prison terms of up to one year. Such forms of desperation by the Zimbabwean government simply evince their recognition of the power that social media as an alternative public sphere represents as well as its magnanimous potential to coordinate and effectively organise people to challenge elitist hegemonies.

REFERENCES

Dahlgren, P. (2000). Media citizens and civic culture. In M. Gurevitch & J. Curran (Eds.), *Mass Media and society* (3rd ed.). London: Edward Arnold.

Dahlgren, P. (2000). The Internet and the democratisation of civic culture. *Political Communication, 17*(4), 335–340. doi:10.1080/10584600050178933

Dahlgren, P. (2005). *Internet, public spheres and political communication*. London: Routledge.

Goode, L. (2009). Social news, citizen journalism and democracy. *New Media & Society, 11*(11), 1287–1305. doi:10.1177/1461444809341393

Habermas, J. (1989). *The structural transformation of the public sphere: an inquiry into a category of bourgeois society*. Cambridge, MA: MIT Press.

Mano W. & Mukhongo, L. L. (2016). Towards alternative media as critical media in Africa. *Journal of Alternative and Community,* (1).

Mhiripiri, N. A., & Mutsvairo, B. (2013). Social Media, New ICTs and the Challenges Facing the Zimbabwe Democratic Process. In A.A. Olorunnisola & A. Douai, (Eds.), New Media Influence on Social and Political Change in Africa (pp. 402 -421). Hershey, PA: IGI Global.

Mitra, A. (2001). Marginal Voices in Cyberspace. *New Media & Society, 3*(1), 29–48. doi:10.1177/1461444801003001003

Moyo, D. (2010). The new media as monitors of democracy. Mobile phones and Zimbabwe's 2008 election. *Paper presented at the conference on election processes, liberation movements and democratic change in Africa*, Maputo, April 8-11.

Moyo, D. (2010). 'The new media as monitors of democracy. Mobile phones and Zimbabwe's 2008 election'. Paper presented at the conference on election processes, liberation movements and democratic change in Africa, Maputo, April 8-11.

Mpofu, S. (n.d.). The power of citizen journalism in Zimbabwe. Unpublished manuscript.

Mujere, J., & Mwatwara, W. (2015). Citizen Journalism and National Politics in Zimbabwe: The Case of the 2008 and 2013 Elections. In B. Mutsvairo (Ed.), Participatory Politics and Citizen Journalism in a Networked Africa: A Connected Continent (pp. 215 – 228). London: Palgrave, MacMillan.

Mutsvairo, B. (2015). Recapturing Citizen Journalism: Processes and Patterns Citizen Journalism and National Politics in Zimbabwe: The Case of the 2008 and 2013 Elections. In B. Mutsvairo (Ed.), Participatory Politics and Citizen Journalism in a Networked Africa: A Connected Continent. London: Palgrave, Macmillan.

Naicker, C. (2016). From Marikana to #feesmustfall: The praxis of popular politics in South Africa. *Urbanisation, 1*(1), 53–61. doi:10.1177/2455747116640434

Papacharissi, Z. (2009). Introduction. In Z. Papacharissi (Ed.), Journalism and Citizenship: New Agendas in Communication. London: Routledge.

Sabao, C. (2016). Shades of the GNU in Zimbabwe (2009 – 13). Linguistic discourse analysis of representations of transitional politics in Zimbabwean newspapers. In D. O. Orwenjo, O. Oketch, & A. H. Tunde (Eds.), *Political Discourse in Emergent, Fragile, and Failed Democracies* (pp. 306–327). Hershey, PA: IGI Global. doi:10.4018/978-1-5225-0081-0.ch017

Sabao, C., & Chingwaramusee, V. R. (2017). Citizen journalism on Facebook and the challenges of media regulation in Zimbabwe. In N. A. Mhiripiri & T. Chari (Eds.), *Media Law, Ethics, and Policy in the Digital Age* (pp. 193–206). Hershey, PA: IGI Global. doi:10.4018/978-1-5225-2095-5.ch011

Chapter 3
Hashtag Activism and the Transnationalization of Nigerian-Born Movements Against Terrorism:
A Critical Appraisal of the #BringBackOurGirls Campaign

Floribert Patrick C. Endong
University of Calabar, Nigeria

ABSTRACT

This chapter describes how the Nigeria-based civil society initiatives have, of late, deployed digital activism in a bid to mobilize both endogenous and exogenous institutions against the terrorist group, Boko Haram. One of these anti-terrorism movements is the #BringBackOurGirls campaign which was launched in May 2014, following the abduction by Boko Haram of 276 schoolgirls, in the Northeastern village of Chibok (Nigeria). The #BringBackOurGirls" movement quickly attracted support from millions of voices (including Heads of States, their wives and celebrities) all over the world. In spite of its internationalization, the campaign has variously been critiqued. Many critics have arguably equated it with mere "clickitivism". Using empirical understandings, this chapter appraises the #BringBackOurGirls campaign vis-à-vis the fight against terrorism in Nigeria. The chapter starts by examining the genesis of the movement and its progressive trans-nationalization. It proceeds to exploring the extent to which the movement could be seen as "clicktivism"; and ends with a review of some of its successes.

DOI: 10.4018/978-1-5225-2854-8.ch003

INTRODUCTION

In recent times, social media such as Facebook, Twitter, YouTube, Instagram and Internet blogging among others, have constituted strategic instruments for political protests, democratic consolidation and many other forms of socio-political change in countries across the world. These media have revolutionized the conduct of political activism as they have made it possible for any computer-literate citizen to (i) organize large groups of people [without an organization], (ii) share ideas, messages, and viewpoints and (iii) support specific causes without passing through the established media of communication. In fact, with the aid of a social media click, one is today capable of taking direct and possibly militant actions in view of attaining well defined social or political aims. In tandem with this, it is more and more axiomatic that the social media offer for easier and quicker ways to support an organization or a cause (Gerbaudo 2017; Jordan & Taylor 2004; Morozow, 2011; Sivitanides & Shah 2011). They also represent strategic weapons for combating all forms of political problems (ranging from dictatorship to terrorism), and bringing about socio-political change in any setting. This aphorism is rationalized by the fact that, in recent years, many national and international political movements have known impressive success thanks to the social media. Egregious examples of these movements include the famous 2011 Arab Spring uprisings, the 2012 #OccupyWallStreet campaign, the UK Uncut movement, the #JeSuisCharlie campaign and the 2012 – 2016 Black Lives Matter movement among others.

In view of all the immense potential of the social media, a number of critics are of the persuasion that online activism may also be strategic in the fight against global terrorism in this present digital era as well as in the future. As reviewed by Morse (2014), hashtag activism has the potential to provoke the widespread condemnation of terrorist groups as well as the atrocities they commit. It may contribute to tarnishing their image and spurring governments and international opinion leaders to amplify their efforts against such groups. All these factors have the potential to affect terrorist groups' activities to a considerable extent. Morse thus opines that:

Groups like Al Qaeda and Al Shabab use social media extensively: it's not beyond the realms of possibility to imagine them employing a social media editor in the future. If hashtag activism really spits in their custard, such an employee may tell his boss 'this [online movement is] going to make our lives hell and it's just not worth it.' For all that is wrong with hashtag activism, it is only going to get more powerful in the future. It's not to be sniffed at. (p. 54)

Conscious of the great potential of the digital technologies, Nigeria-based civil society organizations and human rights activists have, in recent times, embarked on deploying online activism in a bid to mobilize both endogenous and exogenous institutions and supporters against the activities of the terrorist group called Boko Haram – a group which has been bent on wiping out vestiges of western education and culture through untold violent acts. One of these anti-terrorism movements conducted with the aid of social media has been the "#BringBackOurGirls" twitter campaign. This campaign was launched in early May 2014, following the abduction of over 276 school girls, by the terrorist group in the Northeastern community of Chibok (Nigeria). The "Bring Back Our Girls" movement quickly attracted the support of Heads of States and their wives as well as that of global opinion leaders and celebrities from across the globe. In spite of its phenomenal internationalization/globalization, the campaign has been subject to various critiques, some of which are negative. A number of critics are of the perception that the campaign was just of a kind of "clicktivism" and "slacktivism" which failed to mobilize sufficient or concrete support from the international community. Many have thus, likened the movement to a number of the ill informed digitally driven movements, one of which is the #Kony2012 viral Campaign, aimed at hunting down Ugandan Lord's Resistance Army leader Joseph Kony who recruited children as soldiers.

Using critical observations and secondary sources, this chapter seeks to appraise the "Bring Back Our Girls" campaign vis-à-vis the fight against terrorism in Nigeria. In its first part, the chapter provides a theoretical framework composed of the agenda-setting theory and the Transnational Discursive Space theory. The second part examines digital activism in Nigeria as a new – but more and more popular – form of political protest. In its third part, the chapter deals with the genesis of the #BringBackOurGirls movement and examines how the campaign became a transnational phenomenon. In its fourth part, the chapter examines the tenability of some of the myths which "relegate" the movement to mere "clicktivism"/"slacktivism while in the last part, it reviews some of its successes with respect to the fight against terrorism in the Sahel sub-region.

THEORETICAL FRAMEWORK

This discourse is anchored on two theories, namely: McComb and Shaw's Agenda Setting theory and the Transnational Discursive Spaces theory. The Agenda Setting Theory focuses on how the media – particularly the news media – influence the salience of topics on public agenda. In other words it seeks to demonstrate that the media have an immense ability to push audiences to prioritize certain issues over others and to ultimately shape public opinion. The theory has two main assumptions. The first stipulates that the media do not merely reflect reality but rather filter and shape it. The second stipulates that media concentration on specific issues and subjects pushes the public to view these issues and subjects as the most important. A very important tenet of this theory – as revised/upgraded over the years – is that different media have different agenda-setting potential.

In the present digital era, the social media have proven to be very powerful. They are, in many respects, more powerful than the traditional media. Citizen journalists, bloggers, Twitter and Facebook users (among which can be counted online activists), have platforms which by far are greater than local media at least in terms of reach. In line with this, it is often enthused that the social media have a very great agenda-setting potential (Commaerts, 2015; Kiel, 2011; Lewis, Gray & Meierhenrich, 2014; Machado, 2015). Given the fact that, in a social media context, anyone (citizen) can be part of the media production chain, it is often argued that even the common people can have great agenda-setting power by using online platforms. It could therefore be inferred that digital activism has great agenda-setting powers. Grzywinska & Batorski (2016) show five ways in which the agenda-setting powers of online activists are revealed in today's digital era when they note that:

1. Social Networking Sites (SNS) users decide what news is important by choosing what to share within their networks (basics agenda-setting effects);
2. Attributes regarding events are issued by SNS users under particular limitations (attribute agenda-setting);
3. In conditions of high uncertainty and relevance, SNS users can directly impact public opinion (psychological effects of agenda-setting theory);
4. SNS are becoming the source of traditional media agendas (sources of media agendas);
5. SNS users are reaffirming their opinions as a result of SNS homophily (consequences of agenda-setting effects); and users influence public figures within SNS (reverse agenda-setting effects) (p. 19).

The second theory driving analysis in this study is the Transnational Discursive Space Theory. This theory has some visible connection with the concept of "global public space" which among other things, supports the myth of the emergence of discursive arenas which transcend both the nation and the state. In other words, the Transnational Discursive Space Theory supports the two interrelated myths of the geographical expansion of the public space and the trans-nationalization of public opinion caused among other factors by the media of mass communication in general and the social media in particular. It is a clear extension of Habermas' (1989) conception of public space as, a "realm of our social life in which something approaching public opinion can be formed" and where access is guaranteed to all citizens. In such a space, citizens fully enjoy freedom of assembly and association as well as freedom to express and publish their opinions about matters of general interest (pp. 73-74).

In technical terms, the global public space is a virtual or imaginary place where people come together to discuss issues of common concern. It is a complex process which leads to the gestation or formulation of public opinion. The public space should therefore be construed here as an arena which is greater than the village, the small town, the country or any other situation where citizens can conceivably gather, talk and deliberate on issues of general or global concern.

To some of the proponents of the Transnational Discursive Arenas theory, the international communications (notably social media assisted communications) are not only key institutions but enablers of this public sphere (Castells, 1996; Edwards, Howard & Joyce, 2013; McQuail, 2009; Mora, 2014; Reitan, 2015; Schunemann, Stier & Steiger 2015). In fact, because of global communication, the public and its opinion have ceased to be substantial elements of the political system of a society. They have rather, gradually morphed into "a more or less autonomous global public sphere which cannot only be considered as a space between the 'public' and the state but between the state and an extra-societal, global community" (Volkmer, 1999, p.119). Sharing corollaries, Hjarvard (2016) contends that the radical change of the social geography of public and political communication is a 21st century reality. The formation of public opinion is now done across territorial/national boundaries and more importantly, "the 'opinion of the international community no longer refers unambiguously to the opinions of assemblies of state leaders or the cosmopolitan elite, but increasingly to a less tangible, phantomlike, and much more volatile phenomenon emerging from extensive media coverage of world events" (p.103). In other words, the international media and new ICTs offer a unifying public forum where individuals across countries may gather and discuss issues of international or global concern.

DIGITAL ACTIVISM AS POPULAR CULTURE IN NIGERIA

Like in other countries, most social institutions in Nigeria have recognized the versatility of the social media. They increasingly understand that these technologies can facilitate almost all forms of human activities, from commerce to territorial administration and from education to human rights promotion. Thus, the social media represent strategic instruments not only for official crusades launched by government against cybercrimes in the country but also for the organization of various forms of political and militant actions aimed at social change in the country.

From many indexes, digital activism in the country has emerged not really as a result of the globalization – or the 'craze' to globalize – cultural phenomena, ideas and political paradigms; but as a result of the ubiquity of the social media and the growing influence of citizen journalism in the country. Internet penetration in the country has been growing over the years, along with mobile connectivity/tele-density. According to the Nigerian Communication Commission [NCC] (cited in Adepetum, 2017), Nigeria has gone from about 72 million active mobile telephone subscribers (in 2009) to 184,148,420 active telephony users (in July 2017). Similarly, statistics reveal that 48.4 million people in the country have access to the Internet. Of this number, 58 percent access the Internet through their mobile phones. Active use of the Internet and mobile telephony particularly by the youths has been one of the vectors of guerilla journalism in the country. The ubiquity of the social media has facilitated the popularization of digital activism in the country. As remarked by many critics, Nigerians are increasingly appropriating digital platforms to call for more accountability from the political class.

In a country where "real democracy" still has a long way to go and where part of the traditional media has consciously or inadvertently adhered to unprofessional journalism, citizen journalists have quickly assumed the roles of political and social activists. The libertarian nature of the new ICTs has given them the power to report and denounce cases of human right crises in the country; this, has obviously been in a bid to attract the attention of the general endogenous public and the international community. A good example is Nigerian LGBT communities' constant use of digital activism – through blogging, tweeting and "Facebooking" – to promote their rights (Endong &Vareba, 2015). Popular LGBT people such as Olajide Macaulay, Yemisi and Bisi Alimi have for some years now based their pro-LGBT right campaigns on the use of social media. The growing urge among young Nigerians to deploy digital technologies such as the Internet and smart phones to challenge the political status quo or to advocate specific causes is further seen in the fact that, most student protests in Nigerian universities are now partly driven by social media campaigns, including hashtag activism (Ogundimu, 2013; Oladepo, 2016). A case in point is the social media driven campaigns organized by students at the University of Lagos in early 2016, to reverse a number of political actions taken by the Nigerian government. Actually, the student movement succeeded to "correct" the change of the name of their university from "university of Lagos" to "Mushood Abiola University".

The abovementioned advocacy efforts complement the actions of classical human right activists (civil society organizations) which have systematically harnessed the new media such as Twitter, Youtube, Facebook and Instagram among others to launch regional, nationwide as well as international campaigns. One of such nationwide campaigns – which, at a point, attracted the attention of the international media and community – is the #OccupyNigeria campaign launched in January 2012 by "Save Nigeria" and "Enough is Enough" groups. Inspired by the U.S. #OccupyWallStreet Campaign, the Nigerian movement was aimed at protesting against government's removal of subsidy for petroleum products, a policy which immediately caused a 100% increase in the price of petrol. It (the movement) succeeded in bringing large pockets of protesters to the streets, this in a country where mass public demonstrations are relatively rare. Human rights activist Osai (2014) reviews the immense success of the #OccupyNigeria thus:

The reaction to the #OccupyNigeria campaign was spontaneous and unexpected. Large numbers of people gathered in major cities (Abuja, Kano, and Lagos) to protest the fuel hike. For the first time in a long time, the crowds were made of ordinary citizens rather than members of CSOs or trade unions. They were angry about the increase in the cost of living caused by the fuel hike, so they assembled to demand a more socially responsive policy from the government. [...] The #OccupyNigeria campaign attributed its success to its hashtag activism. This in turn spurred many social activists to open social media accounts and study social media advocacy techniques. #OccupyNigeria represented a clear indication of the future of social advocacy and global movements. (para 6-7)

The campaign made the Nigerian government to review its policy on subsidy for petroleum products, leading to a reduction of the inflation in the price of fuel. Another good example of digital activism with international implications is the #BringBackOurGirls campaign of 2014. This campaign will be analyzed in greater details in the subsequent sections of this discourse.

GENESIS AND INTERNATIONALIZATION OF THE #BRINGBACKOURGIRLS TWITTER CAMPAIGN

The #BringBackOurGirls campaign started in early May 2014, shortly after nearly 300 teenager schoolgirls were kidnapped by the Islamist group Boko Haram, in the village of Chibok, a locality situated in the Northeastern part of Nigeria. The movement erupted as Nigerian civil society's response to the frequent killings and adductions of young girls and women by the terrorist group in the region, coupled with government's visibly poor management of the critical situation. The #BringBackOurGirls campaign therefore sprang as a citizen-driven movement aimed particularly at putting pressure on the Nigerian government to react promptly. It was equally a movement against the Boko Haram group whose activities against defenseless and innocent population (particularly children and women) in Northern Nigeria have been unprecedented and ravaging. It should be noted that since 2009, the group has perpetrated violent acts that have savagely claimed the lives of thousands of people, and caused wanton material destructions, displacement of people and massive abductions of people particularly in Northern Nigeria. The group's actions have mainly targeted schools and churches, institutions which it (the Islamic group) views as symbols and vectors of western culture and influence in Nigeria.

The identities of the principal brains behind the #BringBackOurGirls campaign have been subjects of profound controversy (Louw-Vaudran 2014; NBC News 2014; Sadighi 2017). However, Nigerian corporate lawyer Abdulahi Ibrahim is credited for being the first to have used the hashtag after which the campaign is christened. Abdulahi in turn, claims to have drawn his inspiration from former Vice President of the World Bank for Africa Obiageli Ezekwesili who employed the four words of the hashtag in a TV appearance. In effect, on April 23, 2014, Obiageli gave a speech in Nigeria where she strongly called on the Nigerian government to do everything within its powers to secure the release of the schoolgirls. In her speech she used the phrase "bring back our girls". This four-word phrase was soon borrowed by Twitter users in Nigeria and abroad to relay Obiageli's call for greater actions by the Nigerian government and the international community in view of securing the release of the abducted schoolgirls. Obiageli's campaign group stage managed the initial march in Nigeria's Federal capital, Abuja which triggered the online movement and series of vigils in Nigeria and abroad.

The #BringBackOurGirls campaign, however, started in a virtually unstructured manner. In effect, it is the regular tweets of a number of individuals seeking to raise national and international awareness about the plight of the abducted schoolgirls that actually gave birth to the online movement. As noted by Abdulahi Ibrahim, most Nigerians who tweeted from the outset, used phrases or hashtags that linguistically differed from the one that was finally adopted as the name of the movement; but which captured the essence and logic of the movement. He notes that:

I started tweeting about the abduction, trying to create more awareness because so many people did not know about what had happened. I was tweeting with so many hash tags then. At a time, it was #AbductedBornoGirls. I was tweeting with #ChibokGirls – several hashtags and maybe for a day or two and then I will start another one. I remember so many other people were tweeting with the hash tags I created or formed their own which I also used, trying to create more awareness on the abduction. (cited in Ibeh, 2016, p.12)

Early tweets were geared towards pushing the government to generate more information on the human rights crisis and provide some updates on the actions taken by government to rescue the captives. The ultimate aim of these tweets was to draw the attention of the international community to the plight of these schoolgirls and the insufficiency or lack of political will to promptly redress the situation.

In just a few days, the #BringBackOurGirls Twitter campaign became a global sensation as it phenomenally spread to over 69 countries with much of its external online support coming from Canada, the United States of America and Britain (as shown in the chart below). In such a brief period of time, millions of people all over the world declared their support for the movement. Prominent Heads of States (together with their wives), cinema celebrities, high profile women's rights activists and even international NGOs thus backed the movement to highlight the plight of the abducted schoolgirls. Some of these prominent figures include Barack Obama, his wife Michelle Obama, Hilary Clinton, former British Prime Minister David Cameron, Chris Brown and Malala Yousafzai (a Pakistani education activist). Michelle Obama, for instance, shared a photo of herself on social media, holding a sign bearing the inscriptions "#BringBackOurGirls". This happened on May 8th, 2014 on Twitter. The picture was re-tweeted more than 49,000 times. In the same line of thought, International NGOs such as Amnesty International and the UNICEF have adopted the "#BringBackOurGirls" in their various campaigns to raise international attention to the human rights crisis (the kidnapping of the school girls in Nigeria). The two international NGOs have constituted major influencers of the Bring Back Our Girls movement.

Initiatives such as Rama Mosley's #BringBackOurGirls Facebook page further helped globalize the Nigeria-based movement. The Facebook based initiative led

Figure 1.
Source: Sysomos Map (cited in Khalid, 2015)

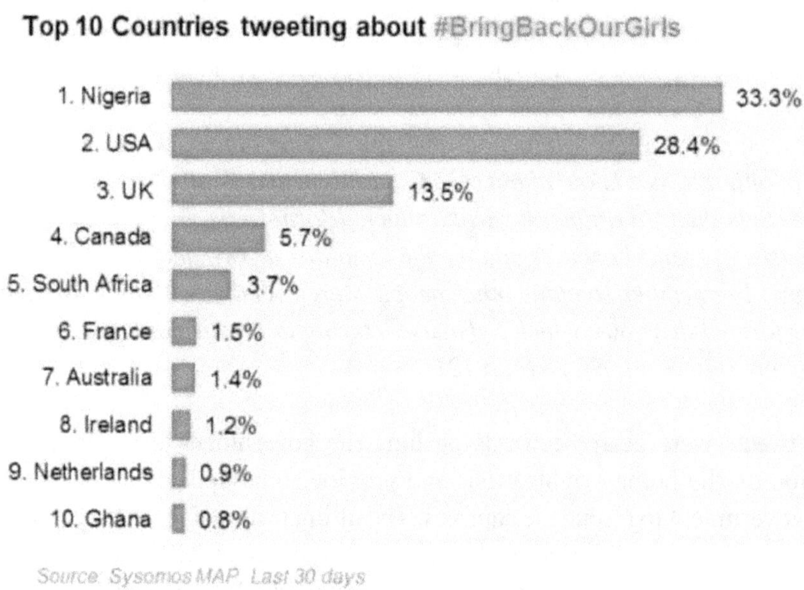

by Mosley had, as of May 2014, mobilized more than 98,000 members. The female activist reveals her desire to contribute to spreading the Nigeria #BringBackOurGirls" movement in the West when she states that: "I never claimed to have originated hashtag #BringBackOurGirls. [...] I heard the voices of Obiageli Ezekwesili, and Ibrahim Abdullahi, and I knew that in Nigeria, the story was being told but it wasn't being told in the United States and Europe" (cited in NBC News, 2015). Mosley's efforts have been so vocal that, at a point, it was (mistakenly) believed that she was the brain behind the BringBackOurGirls hashtags.

ROLE OF THE BRING BACK OUR GIRLS CAMPAIGN IN THE FIGHT AGAINST BOKO HARAM

The #BringBackOurGirls campaign contributed in no small measure to the fight against terrorism in Northern Nigeria. It tremendously increased international awareness of the destructive and inhuman activities of the Boko Haram group in Northern Nigeria. Exogenous publics who had never heard about the Islamic group as well as the nature and magnitude of its activities in the West African sub-region were increasingly informed; as national and international media coverage of Boko Haram's attacks, phenomenally increased from the debut of the online movement. This heavy media and worldwide attention has for some years now, put the Boko Haram group on the radar. This implies that the least crime committed or attack carried out by the group is susceptible to attract international media coverage as well as waves of condemnation from the international community which may be veritable foil for the movement. As put by Gibson (2014),

It's true that a hashtag alone can't even begin to combat the multiple systemic problems that have worked in conjunction to allow 276 girls to be taken from their very school, but it has shed some light on those problems. And even though it's true that not every person who has tweeted #BringBackOurGirls will give much thought to the Nigerian schoolgirls, the attention generated by the hashtag means that important people around the world are now doing just that. (p.24)

The #BringBackOurGirls campaign equally motivated many western countries to offer valuable military and technical assistance to the Nigerian government, aimed at locating and ultimately liberating the schoolgirls. For instance U.S. surveillance aircraft were deployed in Northern Nigeria weeks after the abduction in an attempt to track down the missing girls. Additionally, the campaign prompted a number of international summits and synergies to combat Boko Haram. A good example includes the May 2014 Paris Summit during which the then Nigerian President

Goodluck Jonathan met with some western leaders and some of his counterparts from neighboring countries to design synergistic actions to contain the terror of Boko Haram.

Furthermore, the #BringBackOurGirls campaign triggered endogenous and exogenous political protests which ended up pressurizing the Nigerian government to review and intensify its military campaigns against the Boko Haram group. The political pressure engendered by the campaign equally pushed the Nigerian government to show/develop greater enthusiasm to work towards the prompt liberation of the abducted schoolchildren. It goes without saying that the campaign could be counted among the factors that pushed the Nigerian government to abandon the lukewarm attitude it adopted at the initial stage of the human rights crisis, and to, at least make political promises to secure the liberation of the abducted girls. Weeks after the campaign was launched, Goodluck Jonathan (former Nigerian President) implicitly negated the former position of his government stating that the girls were rescued by the Nigerian Army, through his promise to do everything to locate and liberate the girls, wheresoever they were. Similarly, on coming to power, his successor (Mohamadu Buhari) repeated the promise thus:

We do not know if the Chibok girls can be rescued. Their whereabouts remain unknown. As much as I wish to, I cannot promise that we can find them. But I say to every parent, family member and friend of the children that my Government will do everything in its power to bring them home. (cited in Shearlaw 2015)

The online campaign, among other things, pushed the Nigerian government to initiate a number of negotiations with the terrorist group. These negotiations have so far led to the release of over 103 of the girls in two waves. The first release – which involved the liberation of 45 girls – happened in October 2016; while the second (involving the liberation of 82) took place in May 2017. Negotiations for the release of these schoolgirls involved the Swiss Government and the Red Cross in both cases. The number of schoolgirls released so far coupled with number of girls who succeeded to escape their captors has reduced the number of kidnapped Chibok girls to 113. It must be acknowledged that it is difficult to determine with mathematical precision the extent to which the efforts of hashtag activists led to this positive development (the rescue of the 103). However, it remains clear that the #BringBackOurGirls campaign seriously pressurized the Nigerian government and pushed it to give a greater thought to the issue of the Chibok girls and to take strategic (military and diplomatic) actions that led to the rescue of some of them.

It could therefore be surmised that the Bring Back Our Girls online campaign facilitated direct and effective communication between Nigerian citizens and their government on the one hand and the rest of the world on the other hand. It made

Nigerians see the extent to which the power of the social media could be harnessed to pressure or compel government to ensure accountability and give greater attention to issues of general interest. Thanks in part to the hashtag campaign, government rethought its military strategies against Boko Haram, accepting at a point, the technical help of some western countries and working with some of its African counterparts in coalitions against the Islamic group.

DEBUNKING THE MYTHS WHICH STIPULATE THAT THE #BRINGBACKOURGIRLS CAMPAIGN WAS CLICKTIVISM OR SLACTIVISM

As earlier mentioned, the #BringBackOurGirls campaign has variously been appraised by Nigerian and international observers. In some quarters, the movement has, on multiple grounds, been equated with slactivism or clicktivism. Having lauded the campaign in the preceding sections of this discourse, it will be expedient here to deal with myths which, in one way or the other, negate our position by associating the campaign with slacktivism. Before delving into an examination of these myths, it will be helpful to provide a conceptual definition of "clicktivism" and "slacktivism".

Clicktivism and slacktivism are portmanteau terms mostly used in a derogatory sense to refer to less effective or ineffective forms of advocacy. The former is derived from a combination of "click" and "activism" while the latter is comprised of "slack" and "activism". The two terms are often used in a pejorative sense to refer to actions taken for the sake of bringing about political or social change, but requiring only minimal commitment, effort, or risk. They equally refer to the casual "liking" or "retweeting" of online content in lieu of mobilisation or again the act of participating in a social or political cause just to feel good about contributing (Bulter, 1996; Smith, 2015). Shearlaw (2015) construes the two concepts as the lure of supporting a movement which is perceived to be in vogue before swiftly moving to the next. From the various definitions given to the concepts, it can be inferred that "clictivism" and "slactivism" are contrasted with "real activism" which integrates actions beyond campaign on social media spaces.

Skeptical observers who associate the #BringBackOurGirls campaign with slacktivism anchor their argumentations on various factors. This section addresses three of these factors. It precisely attempts to debunk the three following myths:

- The campaign did not garner sufficient support from the international community
- It was militarily and psychologically innocuous to the Boko Haram group
- It was short-lived or rather quickly aborted

The Myth Stipulating That the #BringBackOurGirls Campaign Failed to Garner Sufficient International Support

One of the arguments advanced by Skeptical critics is that, although it contributed enormously to putting the Boko Haram terrorist group on the radar and to creating greater awareness about the plight of the Chibok girls, the #BringBackOurGirls campaign did not triggered decisive actions on the ground, that could lead to the prompt liberation of the abducted girls (Gibson, 2015; Shearlaw, 2015; Tran, 2016). Such skeptical critics are of the persuasion that the initiators of the movement did not attract sufficient support from western powers; and so very little was actually done by the international community to rescue the abducted schoolgirls. According to Morse (2014), instead of taking such consequential actions, most western supporters (Heads of States and Celebrities) gave the impression that they were capitalizing on the online movement to update their status. She writes:

[Hashtag activism] can be a brilliant way to bring a campaign to people's attention, but presumably those using the hashtag #BringBackOurGirls want to do more than just spread awareness-they want those girls brought home. Getting people like Michelle Obama and David Cameron to hold up a slogan and pull a concerned face is not mission accomplished. We, the people, use a hashtag because we don't have the power that these leaders have. I want influential people to act, not update their status. (p.53)

In the same line of thought, Pakistani human rights activist Malala Yousafzai denounced the slacktivism of some western powers when she succinctly wrote on her blog that:

Nigerian leaders and the international community can and must do much more to resolve this crisis and change their weak response to date. If these girls were the children of politically or financially powerful parents, much more would be done to free them. But they come from an impoverished area of north-east Nigeria and sadly little has changed since they were kidnapped. (cited in Tran, 2015, para 3)

Although it remains clear that most well meaning quarters would have expected greater commitment from the international community, it will be inappropriate to neglect or overlook the contribution of foreign supporters of the movement. As earlier underscored, the movement spurred many foreign nations (such as the U.S., Canada and Britain) into providing militarily support to the Nigerian army, in view of containing the Boko Haram group and liberating the Chibok girls. Though such cooperation was for the most part discontinued because of Nigerian army's abysmal human rights records and The Nigerian government's questionable policy not to over rely on western allies for intelligence, it remains on record that, the campaign provoked a positive reaction from some western powers. The later manifested a clear desire to help the Nigerian government. A month after the girls were abducted, the U.S. dispatched some 80 military personnel to neighboring Chad in view of assisting the Nigerian army locate the abducted girls and support their safe return to their homes. It is even purported that, on locating some of the missing girls, the U.S. and British surveillance experts revealed their findings to the Nigerian army. Unfortunately, the latter did not follow-up.

Additionally, one should not lose sight of the fact that the movement pushed a number of foreign countries and international NGOs to be at the forefront of negotiations with the terrorists to liberate the girls. The Swiss Government and the Red Cross for instance, immensely helped the movement by taking part in a number of fruitful negotiations that led to the release of 103 out of the 276 kidnapped schoolgirls. Such exogenous support given the movement is really invaluable.

The Myth Stipulating That #BringBackOurGirls Campaign Did Not Really Affect Boko Haram

Another argument advanced by skeptical critics is that the #BringBackOurGirls campaign has, in many respects, been politically, psychologically and militarily innocuous to Boko Haram. This position is principally anchored on the fact that, the Islamist group continued to perpetrate similar abductions in the region, visibly in total disregard of the international outcry provoked by its 14 April 2014 crime. In November of the same year (that is seven months after its abduction of the Chibok schoolgirls), Boko Haram repeated its crime, by kidnapping over 300 schoolgirls in Damasak, another locality situated in Northeastern Nigeria. A report released by Amnesty International in 2015 revealed that the group had continued its acts of kidnapping in the region, increasing the total of its captives to over 2000 (Amnesty International 2015). Such indexes have, in a way pushed observers such as the American conservatives to perceive the #BringBackOurGirls campaigns as mere "exercises of self-esteem" that have been – and would be – of no concern to the Boko Haram group.

The abovementioned arguments are relatively pertinent but not irrefutable. In effect, it must be underlined that the #BringBackOurGirls campaign has pushed the Nigerian government to manage the crisis with a high amount of urgency and to embark on intensive military solutions to the problem. As earlier mentioned, the campaign pushed the Nigerian army to rethink its military tactics and to do more to mitigate or tame the activities of Boko Haram in Northern Nigeria. Dealing with the Boko Haram menace became a top issue in government's agenda. This is evidenced by the promises made by both the out-going and new President (Goodluck Jonathan and Mohammadu Buhari), promises in which it was implied that the government was determined to use all weapons at its disposal (including coercion) to ensure the location and liberation of the Chibok girls.

Furthermore, the campaign has been one of the principal factors which engendered an international military coalition against Boko Haram involving neighboring countries such as Cameroon, Chad and Niger. This laudable synergy has, of recent, enabled many military breakthroughs to the credit of the three countries, leading to the recovery of many territories previously under Boko Haram's control. All these are palpable indexes pointing to the fact that, far from being militarily or psychologically innocuous to the Islamic militia, the #BringBackOurGirls campaign has, in conjunction with some other variables, "spat in Boko Haram's custard" making the group to be perceived as the common enemy of multiple armies.

The Myth Stipulating That the #BringBackOurGils Was Short-Lived

A number of critics have described the #BringBackOurGirls campaign as a movement whose premature end was predictable. This category of critics equally claim that the Twitter campaign did not live long to bear optimum fruits. In some sense, the movement "dominated the spring and was gone by summer, replaced by new viral causes". They also argue that the search for and liberation of the schoolgirls dragged into months and eventually years. The fate of the abducted girls quickly became symbolic of the ineffectiveness of most of the actions taken by both the Nigerian government and their Western backers. A related argument is that, although some of the schoolgirls continue, till date, to be in captivity, the #BringBackOurGirls campaign is mostly spoken of in the past.

It is indisputable that at one point or the other, the #BringBackOurGirls campaign witnessed moments of reduced intensity. However, supporters of the movement have, from May 2014 to ending 2016, struggled to keep the spirit of the campaign alive through various strategic actions. Indeed, *s*everal global initiatives have sought to revive the spirit of the #BringBackOurGirls movement, even when it seemed to be dormant. One of these initiatives has been the Global School Girl March organized in 2016 by volunteers around the world, in a bid to ensure that the girls are not forgotten. A similar program has been the worldwide week of actions staged in Nigeria in October 2015 by Nigerian human rights activists in favor of the still missing Chibok girls. The two above mentioned events and many others really caught the attention of both local and international media. The fact that activities in line with the movement were stage managed for more than 2 years clearly establishes the fact that the #BringBakOurGirl campaign has never been short-lived. Also, so long as there continue to be vocal voices that are clamoring for the liberation of the remaining Chibok girls and other people abducted by Boko Haram, the movement remains relevant, memorable and why not eternal? As noted by Obiegeli, "as long as one person is still holding out a candle for the kidnapped, we haven't failed. That one voice can grow into millions eventually" (cited in Shearlaw, 2015).

CONCLUSION

Hashtag activism has for some time now, been a popular culture in Nigeria. Nigerian citizen journalists and civil society organizations have systematically embraced it as a strategic weapon to change the political status quo in the country and advocate for various causes. Through hashtag activism, the Nigerian civil society has in many cases enabled the internationalization of some indigenous movements against bad governance, corruption and other socio-political issues of national and even international concern. The #BringBakOurGirls Twitter campaign is an egregious example of how the Nigerian civil society has deployed social media-assisted activism to enable the trans-nationalization of locally initiated movements against terrorism and the Boko Haram insurgency. Backed in many international quarters, the #BringBackOurGirls succeeded in mounting tremendous pressure on both the Nigerian government and Western leaders to give a modicum of attention to the fight against terror in Northern Nigeria.

The hashtag campaign brought awareness to the international community of the carnage the Boko Haram group has been perpetrating in the northern part of Nigeria for years. The campaign equally pushed the Nigerian government to accept military help from its western and African counterparts, help which somehow enabled a number of decisive military actions against the Boko Haram group. Indeed, thanks partially to the campaign, military coalitions against the Islamic militia were formed, leading to impressive results on the battle ground: the recovery of many territories previously under the control of Boko Haram and the negotiated release of hundreds of people abducted by the militia.

Furthermore, the campaign exposed the initial lukewarm attitude of the Nigerian government and army towards this human rights crisis, contributing partially to the political fall of the party in power. In effect, it is popularly believed that the campaign has been at the root of the antigovernment tone of many national and international media outlets. This contributed enormously to antigovernment public opinion and Goodluck Jonathan's losing the 2015 Presidential elections. In view of all these indexes it could be surmised that the #BringBackOurGirls campaign has considerably been fruitful. The successes of the campaign clearly mitigate, if not neutralize most of the myths which rather "relegate" the movement to a mere form of clicktivism carried out by uninspired entities who fail to profoundly understand the complexity of the Nigerian politics, and who seem to overlook the axiom stipulating that real political change requires more than mere discourse or publicity.

REFERENCES

Amnesty International. (2015). *"Our job is shoot, slaughter and kill". Boko Haram's reign of terror in North-East Nigeria.* London: Amnesty International Ltd.

Barberá, P., Wang, N., Bonneau, R., Jost, J. T., Nagler, J., Tucker, J., & González-Bailón, S. (2015). The critical periphery in the growth of social protests. *PLoS One, 10*(11), 1–15. doi:10.1371/journal.pone.0143611 PMID:26618352

Bogart, N. (2014, May 9). Can social media really help #BringBackOurGirls and end terrorism in Nigeria? *Global News*, 32-36.

Butler, M. (1996). Clicktivism, slacktivism or real activism. Cultural codes of American activism in the internet era. A M.A. Thesis submitted to the faculty of graduate School, University of Colorado.

Cammaerts, B. (2015). Social media and activism. In R. Hwa (Ed.), *The international encyclopedia of digital communication and society* (pp. 1027–1034). Oxford: Willey-Blackwell.

Castells, M. (1996). *The rise of the network society. Malden MA: Blackwell.*

Edwards, F., Howard, P., & Joyce, M. (2013). *Digital activism and non-violent conflicts. Digital Activism Project.* Seattle: University of Washington.

Endong, F. P. C., & Vareba, A. L. (2015). Resisting anti-gay laws through media advocacy and online communities of meaning: A study of Nigerian homosexuals. *Journal for Studies in Management and Planning, 10*(2), 94–106.

Gerbaudo, P. (2017). From cyber-autonomism to cyber-populism: An ideological history of digital activism. *Journal for a Global Sustainable Information Society, 15*(2), 15–34.

Gibson, M. (2014, May 7). Can a social media campaign really #BringBackOurGirls? *TIME Magazine*.

Grzywinska, I., & Batorsski, D. (2016). How the influence of social networking sites challenges agenda-setting theory. *Nonteksty Spoleczne, 4*(1), 19–32.

Habermas, J. (1989). *The structural transformation of the public sphere: an inquiry into a category of bourgeois society.* Cambridge, MA: MIT Press.

Hjarvard, S. (2001). New media and the globalization of the public sphere. In S. Hjarvard (Ed.), *News in a globalized society*. Goteborg: Nordicom.

Howard, N. P., & Hussain, M. M. (2013). *Democracy's fourth wave?* Oxford: Oxford University Press. doi:10.1093/acprof:oso/9780199936953.001.0001

Ibeh, N. (2014, June 14). Interview: Meet the man who generated #BringBackOurGirls hashtag. *Premium Times*, 32-36.

Jordan, T., & Taylor, P. A. (2004). *Hacktivism and cyberwars. Rebels with a cause?* London: Routledge.

Karatzogiani, A. (2017). Beyond hashtag: How a new wave of digital activists is changing society. *The Conversation*. Retrieved November 3, 2017, from https://theconversation.com/beyond-hashtags-how-a-new-wave-of-digital-activists-is-changing-society-57502

Keck, M., & Sikkink, K. (1998). *Activists beyond borders*. Ithaca: Cornell University Press.

Khalid, I. (2015, September 1). From Chibok to global reckoning: The impact of social media on the #BringBackOurGirls campaign. *Native Edge*. Retrieved November 2, 2017, from http://nativedge.com/blog/from-chibok-to-global-reckoning-the-impact-of-social-media-on-the-bringbackourgirls-campaign/

Kiel, C. (2011). How transnational advocacy networks mobilize: Applying the literature on interest groups to international action. *Josef Korbel Journal of Advanced International Studies*, *3*, 77–101.

Lewis, K., Gray, K., & Meierhenrich, J. (2014). The structure of online activism. *Sociological Science*, *1*, 1–9. doi:10.15195/v1.a1

Machado, M. B. (2015). Between control and hacker activism: The political actions of Anonymous Brazil. *Historica, Ciencias. Saude*, *22*, 1–18.

McQuail, D. (2009). *Mass communication theory* (5th ed.). London: Routledge.

Mora, F. A. (2014). Emergent digital activism: The generational/technological connection. *Journal of Community Informatics*, *10*(1).

Morozow, E. (2011). *The net delusion: The dark side of Internet freedom*. New York: Perseus Book Group.

Morse, F. (2014, May 13). The bring back our girl campaign is working: Boko Haram should be scared of a hashtag. *The Independent,* 51-56.

Moyer, J. (2017). Political activism on social media has grown some teeth. *Pacific Standards*. Retrieved November 3, 2017, from https://psmag.com/social-justice/social-media-activism

News, N. B. C. (2015). Hashtag wars: Who is behind the Nigeria #BringBackOurGirls movement? *NBC News*. Retrieved from https://www.nbcnews.com/tech/social-media/hashtag-wars-whos-behind-nigeria-bringbackourgirls-movement-n100771

Ogundimu, N.K. (2013). Facebook and digital activism: Conversation about peace building in Nigeria between a President and his "friends" on Facebook. *International Journal of social Sciences and Humanities Reviews*, *4*(1), 218-206.

Oladepo, T. (2016). Digital activism and Nigeria's emerging public sphere. *Journal of Law. Social Justice and Global Development*, *13*(4).

Osai, O. (2014). Hashtag activism makes the invisible visible. *The Mantle*. Retrieved November 3, 2017, from http://www.mantlethought.org/other/hashtag-activism-makes-invisible-visible

Reitan, R. (2007). *Global activism*. New York: Routledge.

Sadighi, D. (2017). How hashtag activism helped raise awareness about Boko Haram. *Teen Vogue*. Retrieved November 3, 2017 from https://www.teenvogue.com/story/hashtag-activism-raise-awareness-boko-haram/

Schroeder, R. (2017). Towards a theory of digital media. *Information Communication and Society*, *33*(1), 1–18.

Schunemann, W. J., Stier, S., & Steiger, S. (2015). Is there a transnationalisation of public sphere? A comparism of two global political issues. Presented at ECPR General conference, Montreal, August 26-29.

Shearlaw, M. (2015, April 14). Did the #BringBackOurGirl campaign make a difference in Nigeria? *The Guardian*.

Sivitanides, M. & Shah, V. (2011). The era of digital activism. *Conference for Information Systems Applied Research (CONISAR) Proceedings*, *4*(1842).

Smith, C. (2015). The technology of hope: Twitter and the #BringBackOurGirls campaign [M.A. Thesis]. Royal Roads University.

Tran, M. (2015). Malala Yousafzai criticizes weak effort to free girls kidnapped by Boko Haram. *The Guardian*. Retrieved November 15, 2017, from https://www.theguardian.com/world/2015/feb/08/malala-yousafzai-criticises-efforts-free-nigerian-girls-boko-haram

Chapter 4
Barriers to Social Media Advocacy:
Lessons Learnt From the Project "Tell Them We Are From Here"

Aifheli Makhwanya
National Film and Video Foundation, South Africa

ABSTRACT

This chapter describes how the latest statistics on social media usage shows Facebook as the biggest social networking site with over a billion users. With all the possibilities of the potential to grow transnational advocacy networks presented by the use of social media, its adoption and usage is not without limitations. A social media led campaign requires resources to ensure its effectiveness and should be used to complement a traditional advocacy campaign. Project Tell Them We are From Here, an anti-xenophobia campaign is used to explore some theories and demonstrate some of the resource challenges and how very few examples of true transnational advocacy can be found. This project is a collaboration of established non-governmental organisations with strong transnational links with a production company seeking to drive a social movement for unity and raising awareness of the daily plight of immigrants. Despite the campaign team's limited finances and capacity and shortcomings in the implementation of its social media campaign, the project demonstrates the affordances of social media for resource and capacity restrained activists.

INTRODUCTION

The purpose of this article is to make a case for social media as a tool for civic activism and advocacy. In the context of parliamentarian politics, Uldam and Vestergaards (2015) distinguish between formal participation such as voting and civic engagement

DOI: 10.4018/978-1-5225-2854-8.ch004

(activism, volunteerism, participation in community driven initiatives. Civic engagement refers to "engagement with political and social issues, an engagement expressed in a variety of ways that do not always adhere to traditional perceptions of parliamentarian politics" (Uldam & Vestergaards, 2015, p. 2). The authors make a case for alternative modes of participation in parliamentarian politics that are emerging and how social media facilitates or contains such participatory modes. Camay and Jordan (1998) define advocacy as a process where civil society organisations work with like-minded groups or individuals through sustained effort for systematic and peaceful change to policy or conditions that affect people's lives. *Tell Them We Are From Here*, a campaign against xenophobia – the hatred of people from other countries. There are many references for people from other countries. These range from legal terminology such as citizens, non- nationals, refugees to commonly used words such as foreign nationals, immigrants and sometimes derogatory terms which hints on levels on intolerance for immigrants. A context of the problem of xenophobia and its manifestations in South Africa is later in the chapter.

This chapter is comprised of the following sections. The introductory section gives an overview of how social media is used in South Africa for advocacy and civic engagement to galvanize support for calls for free education, a stop to women abuse, political campaigning and xenophobia. A context of social networking sites uptake in South Africa is provided to give an indication of how accessible and the potential reach for the targeted audience for the campaign. The campaign critique takes the form of an analysis of the social media campaign for *Tell Them We Are From Here*, specifically its use *of* social media as tool for advocacy and civic engagement. Akin Omotoso, the founder of the campaign is a film producer and a writer. His call to action to firstly produce the film *Man on Ground,* which is used as a tool to facilitate dialogue and understanding of the plight of immigrants adds another dynamic to the campaign. Constraints of the social media campaign are discussed and how these were navigated by partnering with international actors active in South Africa to give the campaign its transnational legs. With that said, narratives that were emerging of tensions between Germans and Syrian immigrants provided a transnational advocacy opportunity that was missed by the actors. Considering the involvement of the Goethe Institut in the campaign in South Africa, lessons learnt from South Africa would have provided insights on the subject. Social media in this context would have been a tool to enable transnational advocacy and engagement. The conclusion highlights emerging trends and ways to enable and empower individuals and civil society with limited resources and capacity to utilise social media to make their causes visible to the global community.

THE RISE OF SOCIAL MEDIA USAGE IN ADVOCACY

There are many uses of social media that have emerged in the 21st century enabled by digital technologies. Piccinini, Gregory, Kolbe define digital technologies as "the combinations of information, computing, communications and connectivity technologies such as social media, mobile devices, analytics and cloud computing" (2015 p. 1634). Whether it be for personal or business objectives, the uptake and growth in numbers of social networking sites globally is a continuing phenomenon. According to the latest report on the social media landscape in South Africa, social media is an indispensable tool for South African marketers, politicians, artists, activists, reporters and media reporters (World Wide Worx & Ornico South Africa, 2017).Three recent examples of social media campaigns indicate hashtags used for online campaigns against social ills in South Africa indicate the growing trend of advocacy campaigns that are using social media space to call for action and change. The Rhema Bible Church in South Africa recently launched #Notinmyname, a campaign against the abuse and killing of women while #16DaysofActivitism and #ThatsNotOK are examples of 2017 national campaigns that are currently running on social media in South Africa. The 16 Days of Activism of No Violence against Women and Children is a worldwide campaign that runs annually from 25 November to 10 December every year. On the political front, the African National Congress (ANC), the ruling party in South Africa is also active on social media particular social media campaigns that are part of campaigning for leadership positions leading up to the party's elective conference in December 2017. One of the candidates for the party, current deputy president of South Africa's campaign used a #CR17 while Dr Nkosazana Zuma, former African Union chair and member of the South African parliament's election campaign is #NDZ17. Both hashtags for their campaigns are made up of abbreviations of their respective names and the year of the conference (2017).

Notably, Cammaerts (2015) makes a case for social media as instrumental and a constitutive role for activists the world over in their efforts to disseminate social movement discourses, mobilisation and coordination of direct actions online and offline and self-meditate acts of resistance potentially leading to movement spill overs. The author explains the affordances of social media; the one-to-many, one-to-one; and many –to-many forms of communications. Cammaerts quotes Gibson's (1977, p. 75) definition of affordances which mean the 'unique combination of qualities that specifies what the object affords us' which represent an object's opportunities or potentialities for a set of actions whether perceived or not. Monaghan (2003) uses an example of football fan activism to demonstrate how social media as a low cost online communication enables a resource poor and powerless resistance to organise against a resource rich and powerful opposition.

Enablers of Social Media Use in South Africa

South Africa is a country of contrast; it has one of the most liberal constitutions in the world while at the same time dealing with the triple challenges of poverty, inequality and unemployment typical of developing economies. The Constitution's preamble recognises that South Africa belongs to all who live in it – and the provisions for naturalisation and citizenship by birth are provided for in the Immigration Act No. 13 of 2002. South Africa ranks 95 out of 171 countries in terms the International Telecommunications Union (ITU) information and communications technologies (ICTs) Development Index (IDI) (International Telecommunications Union, 2017). The IDI gives an indication of a country's readiness towards the information society by combining access to ICTs, use and skills into a single comparative measure. The ICT use measure is important for this chapter; it measures individuals' use of Internet, fixed broadband subscriptions and mobile broadband subscriptions). South Africa ranks third after Mauritius and Seychelles in the African continent in terms of use values that that also exceed those of developing economies. In this context, the ITU recognises that ICTs are used for both economic and personal development objectives. The focus is on personal use objectives – the use of social media for civic engagement and advocacy.

The importance of access to ICTs in the digital era and the information economy is a well-established principle globally; a fundamental tool for democratic participation, communication and interconnectedness. However, for countries in the Global South, it is the recognition that ICTs have the potential to help reduce inequalities by enabling access to information and knowledge to disadvantaged segments of society especially women, girls and people living with disabilities according to the ITU's 2017 report.

World Wide Worx & Ornico South Africa's 2017 report on social media has found that public debate has moved from the periphery to the heart of activism citing the popular #FeesMustFall campaign. The report indicates that 14 million South Africans are on Facebook, Twitter at 7.7 million, LinkedIn at 5.5 million, Instagram at 3.5 million and lastly 8.74 YouTube users. Facebook and Twitter will be discussed further in section 3 as tools for the campaign's social media presence. From a marketing perspective, there is an acknowledgement that a significant portion of participation by members of an online community is a prerequisite for any online community to thrive (Tuten & Solomon, 2015). Facebook is an example that is given for an online community that provides members with many options to participate that include status updates, video uploads, making comments, uploading photos etc. (Cammaerts, 2015). The rise of online communities and removal of geographical boundaries enable connections all over the world that are important for transnational advocacy and the ability to bring geographically dispersed people together in the same communicative space (Sergeant & Tagg, 2014).

Social Media Opportunities and Challenges for Transnational Advocacy

Many business models and traditional ways of doing business have been disrupted by the introduction of social media as a form of communication and marketing. The disruption brings with it many opportunities and challenges for corporates, governments and organisations to embrace social media in order to communicate with customers, citizens, funders/sponsors and policy makers whichever the case may be. Social media is a space for connecting with and conversing with people, a space for presentation of the self; they have become personal or public spaces despite ownership by private players (Motion, Heath & Leitch, 2016).There are many definitions on the Internet that seek to explain what social media is; and it is immediately apparent that the definition of social media is multi -faceted and keeps evolving. The International Telecommunication Union (ITU), an agency of the United Nations responsible for the driving the use of information communication technologies (ICTs) globally, uses a definition that makes the connection between social media and transnational advocacy apparent. As a starting point, the ITU makes reference to well established types of social media which are social network or networking sites (SNS), blogs, wikis, podcasts, forums, content communities and microblogging. Focus will be on SNS for the purpose of this chapter. SNS refers to web based services that allow an individual to construct a public or semi-public profile with a bounded system (International Communications Union, 2015). Some of the benefits highlighted by the ITU definition focus on coordination and mobilisation of social action. Social media are a huge contrast to the traditional types of advocacy; this is in terms of scale and reach. Traditional types of advocacy is used in this context to distinguish it from the emerging use of social media.

In the context of non-governmental originations (NGOs), Guo and Saxton (2002) acknowledge that social media sites provide a way to expand advocacy networks of community of actors and by mobilizing those networks to take action. On the other hand, Scott and Maryman (2016) caution that social media alone are not sufficient for promoting social change, but should be used to enhance traditional organizing tools. Traditional organising tools are discussed in greater details as direct and indirect advocacy strategies. Action is an international NGO championing advocacy to control tuberculosis internationally. The organisation's 2007 Best Practices Guide for Advocacy provides useful information on strategies, tools and tactics for advocacy. Generally, a direct or indirect advocacy strategy is used in relation to a targeted audience to mobilise support according; the use of direct means to engage and inform public policy decision making by initially attempting to shape social agendas and mobilise larger groups of influence as opposed to the use of direct means to personally engage and educate decision makers. A detailed table which differentiates various types of advocacy by their immediate audience developed provides good summary of examples, tactics, champions and the immediate audience. Bureaucratic, protest, legal and policy advocacy make up the direct forms of advocacy targeted at policy enablers, political obstructers, courts and decision makers respectively. Indirect advocacy through research, coalition and mass advocacy targets opinion leaders, multipliers and sustainers. The latter is applicable in so far as it related to the formation of a coalition amongst some of the actors discussed in section 3.2 below.

Literature seems to suggest a complementary relationship between the use of traditional advocacy strategies and tactics as well as social media (Scott & Maryman, 2016). They argue that social media can be used to augment organisers' existing strategies for communicating about public issues, building relationships and collaborations with supporters and encouraging greater involvement among supports. Social media as a communication tool enhances traditional advocacy strategies as it is considered cost effective (Monaghan, 2003) and brings increased speed of collaborative communication (Scott & Maryland, 2016).

The main challenge that the campaign team continues to grapple with in the implementation of their social media campaign is inadequate resources; both financial and human resources. None of the members of the campaign had any experience in advocacy work in the formal sense. As a result, there was no formalised structure or entity under which the campaign was designed and managed. All the work was conceived and planned under the auspices of the production company (T.O.M Pictures initially, whose two shareholders later formed Rififi Pictures with a new third shareholder) whose primary business is film production. Scott & Maryman (2016) highlight planning as a prerequisite of a quality social media campaign that successfully engages supporters which further requires the allocation of sufficient resources.

Despite the lack of advocacy experience, the team was quite clear from the onset what the strategy was all about. They would combine film, a powerful medium to tell stories through moving images and dialogue around the various themes that have emerged as part of the xenophobia discourse in South African politics and society. These were the themes of fear, suspicion, competition for resources and criminality to mention a few that were incorporated as part of the script.

CONTEXTUALISING THE CAMPAIGN PROBLEM: XENOPHOBIA

In 2008, xenophobia attacks broke and led to the killings and displacement of many foreign nationals living in South Africa making international headlines. A number of scholarly works and reports by international and local non-governmental organisations have highlighted some of the following broad factors as fueling anti-immigrant sentiments that are in the main directed at African immigrants. Firstly, the many years of isolation from the rest of the world has contributed to major challenges that have made relationships with other countries in the continent a difficult one. Reintegration into the global community has also required post-apartheid South Africa not only to integrate within the regional, continental and global structures. For instance, Klaaren and Naamji (2001) paint a rather gloomy picture of minimal coordination among migration policy enforcing agencies such as Home Affairs, South African Police Service, and South African National Defence Force. Unfortunately, as at 2010 almost a decade later, there has been very minimal improved coordination as indicated by the South African Human Rights Commission (SAHRC).

Secondly, South Africa is regarded as the gateway to doing business in the continent and has been the continent's economic super power for many years. The SAHRC in its 2008 report on xenophobia highlighted the response of government between May and October when the first public violence against immigrants took place (South African Human rights Commission, 2010). Although the report extensively analysed the role and government response at national, provincial and local level and respective departments that are involved in this area, focus will be on the response at national level for the purpose of this chapter. The report found that weaknesses in intergovernmental coordination and institutional processes hindered the response to the crisis (South African Human Rights Commissions, 2010 p. 12). Crush and Ramachandran (2009, p7) found that "the policies and practices of state institutions reinforce extreme xenophobia by undermining rights and aggravating insecurity" supports findings by the SAHRC.

The International Organisation for Migration's latest (2015) global migration figures are more telling in two trends that are relevant in this chapter. Firstly, number of international migrants, which refers to people residing in a country other than their country of birth was the highest ever recorded at 244 million. Secondly, South to South migration flows between developing countries continues to grow compared to South to North movements. Statistics of documented immigrants in South Africa released by Statistics South Africa every year based on data received from the Department of Home Affairs are not very useful in comparable terms to the report produced by the IoM. The main reason for the limitation of this is that data analysed focuses on all permits that are applied for which include visitors, study, work, family, business, waiver residents permits that are received and processed by Home Affairs

(Statistics South Africa, 2015). It is however useful for the Africa region that the majority of immigrants are from Zimbabwe, Nigeria, Democratic Republic of Congo, Lesotho, Angola, Malawi, Ghana and Cameroon. Statistics on the number of immigrants whether documented or undocumented remain a contentious issue. According to the latest census, there are more approximately 2.2 million immigrants living in South Africa (Statistics South Africa, 2015).In the National Development Plan which outlines Vision 2030 for South Africa, it is recognised that there is a need for South Africa to focus on its position in the geopolitics of the continent and a focus on how to take advantage of a skilled migrant labour force to contribute to the country's economy and society (National Planning Commission,2009). This approach is a mutually beneficial for both migrants as well as South Africa.

The Actors in the Anti-Xenophobia Campaign

There are a number of civil and non-governmental organisations both local and international who have a number of programmes to assist refugees and immigrants in South Africa. I will focus on profiling those that participated in *Project Tell Them We are From Here* campaign.

The Open Society Initiative of Southern Africa (OSISA), according to its website (http://osisa.org/) is "a growing African institution committed to deepening democracy, protecting human rights and enhancing good governance in the region. OSISA's vision is to promote and sustain the ideals, values, institutions and practices of open society, with the aim of establishing vibrant and tolerant Southern African democracies in which people, free from material and other deprivation, understand their rights and responsibilities and participate actively in all spheres of life. Its vision is implemented through a number of support programmes that engender open society ideals in the Southern African region. OSISA's approach its partners' advocacy work in relevant countries or joining partners in advocacy work on shared objectives and goals. OSISA directly initiates and leads in advocacy interventions, along the key thematic programmes that guide its work. OSISA also intervenes through the facilitation of new and innovative initiatives and partnerships, through capacity-building initiatives as well as through grant making. It was established 19 years ago in 1997 with a presence in 10 Southern African countries including South Africa. Its offices are in Johannesburg.

The International Organisation for Migration (IoM) has been in the forefront of the plight of immigrants and refugees globally. Part of the United Nations, its role is to provide leadership in migration management and to uphold human dignity and wellbeing of migrants. It offers a wide range of specialist services that range from basic migration services for immigrants to specialised services on research and programmes aimed at a coordinated and informed global approach to manage various factors of migration according to its website. Its offices in South Africa are located in Pretoria. The IOM has been involved in a number of interventions as a response to this specific crisis. The obvious emergency relief response related to the displacement of many immigrants who had to flee for their lives with nothing losing their homes and in some cases business which were looted and destroyed during the attacks on foreign national that took started in the township of Alexander on 11 May 2008. The South African History Online website (www.sahistory.org.za) gives a detailed timeline dating from the 1980s to the incidents of 14 April 2015 where attacks took place in Durban.)

The Goethe Institut, in Johannesburg, South Africa is the cultural institute for the Federal Government of Germany with a presence in other parts of the world according to its website. Its main activity is to encourage international cultural exchange including a German language service offering.

Rififi Pictures is a South African film and television production company based in Johannesburg. Two of its shareholders, Akin Omotoso and Robbie Thorpe developed and produced the film *Man on Ground* under a company that they used to co-own. Omotoso is the founder of the campaign while Mothobi managed the social media campaign that the company developed.

The players introduced in this section are different in terms of status as well as areas of interest in the migration discourse. The collaboration of two NGOs, a production company and a cultural institute over a common objective to raise awareness on the daily plight of migrants is not a usual one. The writer concedes that it does not fit the definition of transnational advocacy in all its facets. However, it is submitted that "coalition" between these different entities for a common shared objective to raise awareness on xenophobia is a unique one. Lessons and observations made on this case study offer a dynamic on social movements and the need for collaboration outside established frameworks of transnational networks. Later in the chapter, a link will be attempted outside scholarly approaches that make a case for a transnational nature of this campaign.

A Civil Call to Action?

"The process started with the picture of Ernesto Nhamuave. I saw the picture and was immediately struck by the horror of it. I phoned Hakeem Kae-Kazim and Fabian Adeoye Iojede and said we had to do something cinematic, but we didn't have a story. We commissioned the research. The lady we hired came back three months later with tons of files, videos, testimonies, books, pictures-everything. We then poured through the research and from that we started teasing out the story. Last year after the World Cup (where there were rumours of attacks) the story came to us and we started writing" (Mail and Guardian, 13 October 2011).

The film,*Man on Ground* (IMBD, 2011) is a product of the reflections captured in the 2011 Mail & Guardian when Omotoso spoke about the inspiration for the film. The film tells the story of a Nigerian-British banker Ade based in the United Kingdom who visits South Africa to see his estranged half-brother Femi. Upon his arrival in South Africa, he discovers that Femi has been missing for a week. With the help of his brother's fiancée, he investigates his brother's disappearance. It soon emerges that his brother's disappearance coincides with a recent period of xenophobic violence.

CAMPAIGN OBJECTIVES, CHALLENGES, AND OPPORTUNITIES

During the 2008 and later the 2011 attacks, there were large scale mobilisation by churches, organisations and civil society to come to the assistance of the many displaced immigrants that received a lot of media coverage. The 2011 outbreaks led to long periods of displacement in temporary shelters provided by the South African government even though the humanitarian and emergency services were being provided by the likes of the IOM.

Objectives of the Campaign

Project Tell Them We are From Here is a civil society led anti- xenophobia campaign that seeks to raise awareness about the challenges that many immigrants face and social inclusion. The short description on the Facebook page captures the campaign objective as follows: "The goal of the campaign is to support the ongoing fight against xenophobia. Its main message is one of inclusion, reminding mankind that people are people regardless of where we come from".It is through the film, that many South Africans and immigrants have been encouraged to have a dialogue on xenophobia, anti-immigrants sentiments and also giving both sides of the community an opportunity to share their views and experiences regarding migration and xenophobia. These dialogues take place in the context of the South African and foreign national experiences. As discussed in greater detail in section 4, the major shortcoming of the campaign may have been its oversimplification of an otherwise complex discourse of politics, globalisation and migration.

In summary, the awareness campaign was targeted at inception stage as explained by Omotoso as follows:

South African Citizens

The ordinary South African citizen in any part of South African society whether in an urban or rural part of the country, black and white, male and female and from all sectors of society whether religious, language, ethnic and cultural. However, a special emphasis was given to black South African township and informal settlements dwellers where friction amongst South Africans and non-South Africans were experience. For examples, Musina in Limpopo is a border town with neighbouring Zimbabwe where there is a large population of Malawian, Zimbabwean and Mozambican nationals who live in neighbouring communities.

Governments

The issues of migration and xenophobia manifesting in South Africa are not a unique to South Africa but rather a global phenomenon which requires international cooperation. However, the response of the South African government to both outbreaks in 2008 and later in 2011 is important for setting the tone amongst others for regional interventions that include neighbouring countries in the Southern African Development Community (SADEC) and countries such as Somalia whose township informal owned businesses have been specifically targeted in townships. This of course does not presuppose the lack of political unwillingness between South Africa and these countries but recognises that foreign nationals are refugees who cannot return to their countries of birth. Messaging in this context was focused on highlighting the plight of immigrants and by promoting unity amongst South Africans and non-South African nationals. To bring back into light the role of the IoM, their role of expertise to give advice and best practise methodologies on how governments can use statistics and trends to manage migration and take advantage of a migrants skilled labour force in a mutually beneficial and sustainable approach based on the needs of member states is important. Their involvement in the migration issues globally gives the NGOs a perspective from an informed position as an NGO that provides humanitarian services for immigrants and refugees as well as specialised services for government players.

The campaign team also expressed their willingness to partner with the South African government as part of their partnership strategy. The Department of Arts and Culture (DAC) is a key national government department that would have been an ideal partner. The Department as part of its strategy, is responsible for driving social cohesion in South Africa. The DAC defines social cohesion "as the degree of social integration and inclusion in communities and society at large, and the extent to which mutual solidarity finds expression among individuals and communities"

(DAC, 2016). The definition is further unpacked to indicate that cohesion only takes place in a society or a community wherein inequalities, exclusions and disparities based on ethnicity, gender, class, nationality, age, disability or any other distinctions which engender divisions distrust and conflict are reduced and/or eliminated in a planned and sustained manner. The definition further refers to active participation by community members and citizens working together for the attainment of shared goals, designed and agreed upon to improve the living conditions for all. Unfortunately, the campaign team was not able to secure a partnership with the DAC who would have been a natural fit in terms of the scope of the portfolio and the social cohesion programme that they are responsible to implement. There is merit to arguing that such a partnership would have gone a long way to engender social cohesion by also further incorporating the soft power of arts and culture as a vehicle for community engagement (Department of Arts and Culture)

Established Network of Already Existing Local, Regional, and International NGOs Involved in Transnational Advocacy Work

Partnerships with already established international advocacy groups as already discussed based on shared objectives with the IoM, OSISA and the Goethe Institut. The partnership involved some funding for the art of exhibition and film screenings across South Africa in communities to raise awareness about xenophobia and its terrible effects on the safety, dignity and security of thousands of African immigrants. Along with funding from OSISA, a partnership with the Maboneng Township Arts Experience, which is a national public arts exhibition that turns homes in townships into galleries and the outdoor spaces into performance districts boosted the campaign's reach to South Africans living in the townships. The IOM also facilitated the production of the film through production funding from the Swedish International Development Cooperation Agency and the Norwegian Foreign Ministry on the basis that the film portrayed the day-to-day challenges faced by migrants highlighting the plight of migrants in their search for a better life (see note Ventura, 2011). The Goethe Institut in South Africa, Johannesburg funded the photographic exhibition as well as marketing and promotional support for the community outreach programmes. The writer has not been able to establish with the Goethe Institut at this stage if there is any intention to use the film to raise awareness about the plight of immigrants. This is an interesting development as Germany has been reported to have received over 1 million refugees from Syria; with reports of growing xenophobic sentiments and attacks fueled by similar sentiments of fear and mistrust which bear a striking resemblance to the South Africa circumstances.

Implementation of the Campaign on Social Media

The team used Facebook and Twitter to activate their social media campaign. A Facebook Community Page called *Man on ground: We are From Here Campaign* and a *@ManonGroundWeareFromherecampaign* Twitter handle was also set up. The timeline photographs on the Facebook page is a combination of powerful portraits and views shared by some of the community members who participated in the community outreach programmes. The last post on the page was on 26 January 2015 which is quite dated with a total number of 336 likes. This has been largely attributed to the lack of resources and time to ensure regular posts. Upon further scrutiny, it is obvious that there has also not been a lot of conversations or debates either in response to posts or comments sent by the administrator. The Facebook page however, was well utilised from a messaging point of view as well as promoting the film screenings and exhibitions which were posted and shared on the page. There were also shares of pages and other information relating to topics of xenophobia and immigration.

An interview with the campaign's social media manager Ms Rethabile Mothobi, one of the shareholders in Rififi Pictures is more telling. Mothobi confirms that Twitter and Facebook were used for the campaign. These social media platforms were used as indicated earlier, to initially promote the film and events around it. However, the major turning point took place around May 2015 when the 5thanniversary of the xenophobic attacks was imminent. It was around this period that the team started dialogue to engage both foreign nationals and South Africans in grassroots communities around the events that had taken place with a view to raise awareness and to ask difficult questions. The major sources of content for messaging came from images (photographs) as well as quotes from community members who had participated in the various screenings and exhibitions.

The team strategy was to also disseminate information that they had collected in the different parts of the country where exhibitions were shown. This was supplemented by various feeds of topical news articles and powerful images on a regular basis. This has since fallen away due to their lack of capacity. The team is involved in the production of other projects which is their core business. Despite this, Omotoso admits that more could be done if they had a dedicated social media campaign media to keep the social media presence current and alive. On further questioning, he reveals that although the campaign is "dormant", the team will be in a position to activate the campaign should the need arise. It is an awkward admission during the interview that there is a possibility that xenophobic attacks may manifest at some stage. As a result, the campaign founder as part of a long-term vision he has had, is to find resources and an appropriate mechanism to focus on the campaign's long-term objective.

Mothobi admits that interaction from members of the community was disappointing. Despite the sometimes candid and social (informal) nature associated with social media, it was in fact quite startling that engagement either in the form of Facebook posts or comments in response to messaging was either limited or a rehash the same old rhetoric that formed part of the negative narrative about foreign nationals. In that sense, no robust engagement or debate was noted during such interactions. It was in fact face to face interactions with community members who came to attend exhibition that turned out to be more meaningful around the debate.

The role of the IOM was instrumental in ensuring that the campaign team was able to get into the community in the first place. Mothobi describes the IOM's role as exceptional. One of the biggest challenges was getting together foreign nationals and locals in the same venue in the various townships that were visited. The team experienced first-hand the fear and anger experienced in varying degrees between community members considered foreign and those who are South Africans. It was at this stage that the complexities of working on a limited budget, logistics and ensuring people's safety proved to be a burden the team could not handle. It was the IOM intervention through the provision of local "peace keepers" who helped bridge the gaps between the "the outsiders" and the local community when inviting them to come to the film screening.

In conclusion, both Omotoso and Mothobi indicate their intention of making the campaign more of a social movement. This will entail shifting focus from an exhibition only to more of a travelling road show as part of a long-term strategy to grow the advocacy campaign. For now, the focus seems to be in South for the travelling road show aspect while the film will continue to be relevant as a tool to raise awareness on immigration and its related challenges that include xenophobia and other forms of intolerances.

General Critique of the Campaign

I have summarised three main critiques of social media in the context of protest movements that are discussed in greater detail by Cammaerts (2015). These are digital divides which are referred to in the context of access and narrowcasting which I will unpack. The other two constraints relate to social media's "Me"-centric disposition (Cammaerts, 2015 p 99) as opposed to its social characteristics and lastly corporate ownership of social media spaces and government surveillance. Corporate ownership and government surveillance concerns are extremely valid; but will not be discussed further as they have not played out since the campaign was founded. To expand further on the digital divide constraint which applies to this scenario; there is merit to its contribution to the poor levels of participation and engagement by the targeted audiences for the campaign. For instance, the ITU's website describes its role of advocating for digital inclusion to ensure that access to ICT is used for the social and economic development of people with specific needs such as indigenous peoples, those living in rural areas; people living with disabilities; women and girls; and youth and children. In the Global South, including South Africa activists have to be mindful of the digital divide and where possible, resort to traditional advocacy that are a fit for their social movements or causes.

At a social media strategy level, there are some fundamentals that should have been adhered to. For instance, it should have been a given that all the actors who participated in the campaign should have committed a resource, whoever it was to post on both Facebook and Twitter every time there was an event (film screenings, exhibitions, community engagements) or any mentions of migration, xenophobia on these platforms. An agreed upon hashtag by all actors could have given the campaign more visibility. Additional hashtags such as #immigration, #xenophobia, and #globalisation would have made it easier for Twitter and Facebook users to find information about the campaign. A hashtag symbol is used as a form of metadata labelling for a topic of the post so that it can be found by others (Zappavigna, 2014). The *@ManonGroundWeareFromherecampaign* Twitter handle is too long and should ideally be separated so that the campaign can stand on its own. In that way, the film is not given too much prominence over the campaign.

There is no doubt that the team's ability to partner with already existing NGO networks in South Africa with both local, regional and global networks has been enriching in terms of appreciating the civil organisations as well as advocacy environment. The collaboration between a non-traditional advocacy vehicle (a production company in this case) and established NGOs such as IOM, OSISA and the Goethe Institut makes for an interesting case study on the efficiencies and challenges of such collaborations.

CONCLUSION

Tell Them We are From Here campaign offers interesting insights on collaboration and the reality that despite the accessibility of social media, some resources and capacity must be dedicated to a campaign to ensure that content that is posted on Twitter and Facebook or whichever social networking sites that will serve the campaign must be backed by a solid advocacy plan of action. Although the campaign in its nature was multifaceted through its use of film, photographic exhibition and community dialogue, the combination of its non-traditional approach to advocacy by its founders shows the capacity of social movements that can grow into meaningful and impactful interventions at community level where it matters the most. The campaign's very limited presence on social networking site (Facebook and Twitter) is an example of how social media does not necessarily solve all problems related to communication in general and their ability to connect to similar and like-minded NGOs, communities and networks.

There is no doubt based on this case study that social media requires expertise and resources to be effective and relevant. It is therefore much easier for well-established NGOs to use social media platforms to grow their network with targeted audiences at local, regional and international level. The reality of a social networking site that is outdated and not providing commentary or sharing of information on similar events that were unfolding in Germany for instance is a missed opportunity for all the actors in this campaign to share experiences from the South African campaign and continued advocacy for immigrants globally. It is argued that such an opportunity to expand this campaign will go a long way in ensuring that the campaign assumes a truly transnational character and find supporters and networks in other parts of the globe.

Although the issue of effectiveness of the campaign was not explored in this context, lessons learnt show the possibilities of partnership between well-established NGO networks who are willing to explore partnerships to utilise a different advocacy tool to further their own advocacy objectives. Guo and Saxton (2013, pp. 71-75) suggested two dimensional views of advocacy communication on social media where messages can meaningfully be examined in terms of basic communication and the direct relevance to the core advocacy is an important development that introduces an element of effectiveness in the use of social media in non-profit advocacy. Indicators for both messaging and direct relevant will have to put in place for measurement to take place.

ACKNOWLEDGMENT

I would like to thank Akin Omotoso and Rethabile Mothobi for making time to respond to telephonic, one on one interviews and e-mail correspondence. Akin, thank you for giving me unconditional access to material for this chapter.

REFERENCES

Action.org. (2007). Best practices for advocacy; A dozen tactics, tools and strategies. Retrieved November 2007, from http://www.action.org/documents/ACTION_Best_Practices_Guide_small.pdf

Camay, P., & Gordon, A.J. (1998). *Advocacy in Southern Africa: Lessons for the future*. Johannesburg: Cooperative for Research and Education (CORE).

Cammearts, B. (2015). 'Technologies of self – medication: Affordances and constraints of social media for protest movements. In J. Udam & A. Vestergaard (Eds.), *Civic Engagement and Social Media: Political Participation Beyond Protest* (pp. 87–110). New York: Palgrave Macmillan. doi:10.1057/9781137434166_5

Crush, J., & Ramachandran, S. (2014). *Xenophobic violence in South Africa: Denialism, minimalism & realism.* Cape Town: International Migration Research Centre.

Department of Arts and Culture, South Africa. (2016). *Social cohesion programme*. Retrieved from http://www.dac.gov.za/social-cohesion

Department of Justice and Constitutional Development, Republic of South Africa. (1996). Constitution of the Republic of South Africa.

Geneva International Organisation for Migration (2013). Advocacy role. Retrieved September 28, 2016 from, http://www.unhcr.org/advocacy.html

Guo, C., & Saxton, G. (2013, January). 8). Tweeting social change: How social media are changing non-profit advocacy. *Nonprofit and Voluntary Sector Quarterly*, 43–57.

International Communications Union. (2017). Measuring the Information Society Report (Vol. 1).

International Organisation for Migration. (2015). 'Global migration trends fact sheet, Retrieved September 26, 2016 from, https://www.iom.int/news/iom-releases-global-migration-trends-2015-factsheet

Khagram, S., Riker, J. V., & Sikkink, K. (2002). *Restructuring world politics: Transnational social movements, networks, and norms: Project MUSE*. Minneapolis: University of Minnesota Press.

Monaghan, F. (2003). Seeing red: Social media and football fan activism. *The Information Society*, *6*(20), 143–168.

Mothobi, L. (2016, September). (telephone interview) (e-mail communication).

Motion, J., Heath, R. L., & Leitch, S. (2016). *Social media and public relation: Fake friends and powerful publics*. New York: Taylor & Francis Group.

National Planning Commission, South Africa. (2009). *National development plan of South Africa 2030: Our future, make it work. The Department in the Presidency of South Africa*. Pretoria: Government Printers.

Omotoso A (2016, September). (Interview).

Piccinini, E., Gregory, R., & Kolbe, L. M. (2015). Changes in the producer-consumer relationship – Towards digital Transformation. In *Proceedings of the 12th international Conference on Wirtschaftsinformatik*, Osnabruck, Germany, March 4-6.

Scott, J. T. & Maryman, J. (2016). Using social media as a tool to complement advocacy efforts. *Global Journal of Community Psychology Practice*, 7(5).

Sergeant, P., & Taggs, C. (2014). *The language of social media: Identity and community on the Internet*. New York: Palgrave MacMillan. doi:10.1057/9781137029317

South African Human Rights Commission. (2010). *Report on the SAHRC investigation into issues of rule of law: Justice and impunity arising out of the 2008public violence against non-nationals*. Johannesburg: Human Rights Commission.

Statistics South Africa. (2015). Documented immigrants in South Africa. Statistics South Africa 10, Retrieved September 27, 2016, from http://www.statssa.gov.za/publications/P03514/P035142013.pdf

Tuten, L., & Solomon, M. (2015). *Social Media Marketing Strategy*. New York: Sage Publications.

Udam, J., & Vestergaard, A. (2015). *Civic engagement and social media political participation beyond protest*. New York: Palgrave MacMillan.

United Nations. (2016). *Security Council Report of the Secretary General S/2016/796*. Geneva: UNO.

United Nations ACICIT-ESCAP. (2014). Academy of ICT essentials for government leaders Version 2.0 Module 11: Social Media for Development. Republic of Korea. Retrieved June 11, 2014 from, http://www.unapcict.org/academy

World Wide Web & Omico South Africa. (2017). South African social media landscape. Retrieved September 11, 2017 from http://www.worldwideworx.com/wp-content/uploads/2016/09/Social-Media-2017-Executive-Summary.pdf

Zappavigna, M. (2014). CoffeTweets: Bonding Around the Bean on Twitter. In P. Sergeant & C. Taggs (Eds.), *The language of social media: Identity and community on the Internet* (pp. 139–160). New York: Palgrave MacMillan. doi:10.1057/9781137029317_7

Chapter 5
From Jenin to Johannesburg: The Digital Intifada and Transnational Advocacy for Palestine

Suraya Dadoo
Media Review Network, South Africa

ABSTRACT

Social media has given Palestinians around the world a voice with which to confront flawed media coverage of the Israeli occupation. This chapter will explore the use and rise of internet-based information and communication technologies (ICTs) and social media to expose Israel's colonial project in the Occupied Palestinian Territories (OPT) and advance pro-Palestine advocacy. The success and limitations of social media-based activism are examined, as well as the Israeli government's repressive response to these advocacy efforts. While social media has successfully challenged some deeply-entrenched media stereotypes about the Israeli occupation, it is a crucial tool for advancing Palestine activism globally. The chapter concludes that social media campaigns must be integrated with traditional advocacy, lobbying and grass-roots activism to end the Israeli occupation of Palestine and achieve a just peace for Palestinians and Israelis.

INTRODUCTION

While social media is currently playing a significant role, and becoming an important space for transnational and global activism for Palestine, Palestinians have been able to successfully mobilise citizen-enabled protests and mass actions, decades before the advent of internet-based information and communication technologies (ICTs).

The most sustained and effective non-violent protest movement and mobilisation that occurred in the Occupied Palestinian Territories (OPT) of the West Bank, Gaza

DOI: 10.4018/978-1-5225-2854-8.ch005

Strip and East Jerusalem was the pre-internet-era First *Intifada*.[1] Grassroots Palestinian organisations primarily used leaflets and mosques to direct and co-ordinate a six-year mass civil disobedience campaign of boycotts, strikes, stone-throwing and demonstrations against the Israeli military occupation of Palestine.

Pioneering forms of internet activism by Palestinians within the OPT and in the diaspora in the late 1990s and during the Second *Intifada* in 2000 focused on countering stereotypes in mainstream media about Palestinian resistance to the occupation. This was achieved by providing first-hand accounts of the humanitarian and political realities of life under occupation in the OPT. Jenin, a city in the occupied West Bank, was an important site of resistance during the Second *Intifada*, and is referred to in the title of this chapter.

A political and legal background to the Israeli occupation of Palestine is provided. A brief examination of mainstream media coverage of the Israeli occupation and the portrayal of Palestinians as 'terrorists' then follows. The author then explains how early ICT-enabled activism challenged this flawed narrative. Focus is then placed on how the internet and social media transcends Israeli checkpoints and barriers to free movement to create an online, global, borderless community, thus allowing Palestinians trapped in the OPT to connect with activists around the world.

Significant transnational social media campaigns exposing the brutality of the Israeli occupation, and advocating for a free Palestine, are examined in this chapter, together with the way they have reached and challenged traditional media outlets, and the public at large. There is an emphasis on South African actions, as the author is the social media coordinator for the National Coalition for Palestine (NC4P), an umbrella body representing over 40 South African civil society structures, dedicated to ending the Israeli occupation of Palestine and achieving a just peace for Palestinians and Israelis.

POLITICAL AND LEGAL CONTEXT

On November 29, 1947 the United Nations (UN) - without the consent of the indigenous population - voted in favour of dividing Palestine into two states: a Palestinian state and a Jewish state (with Jerusalem to be administered by the UN). Although the leadership of the indigenous Palestinian population rejected the UN Partition Plan, the leaders of the Zionist Movement in Palestine unilaterally declared the independence of the state of Israel on May 14, 1948. The borders of this state were never specified.

On that same day, fighting broke out with several Arab states. To Israelis, this was a War of Independence, and to Palestinians this was the *Nakba* (catastrophe). The Arab-Israeli War followed, and lasted until 1949. There were over 860 000 indigenous Palestinians living in the territory that was to become the state of Israel. The creation of Israel resulted in the forced displacement of over 750 000 Palestinians and the depopulation of 400 Palestinian villages (Pappé, 2006). The large-scale expulsion of Palestinians began long before the armies of neighbouring Arab states became involved. Between 250 000 and 350 000 Palestinians had already been expelled from their homes by Zionist para-militaries between the passage of the UN Partition Plan in November 1947 and Israel's declaration of independence on May 14, 1948 (Khalidi, 2006, p.131).

The majority of displaced Palestinians ended up in refugee camps in the area west of the Jordan River (the West Bank), the Gaza Strip, and neighbouring Arab states. By 1949, the new state of Israel comprised 78% of historic Palestine. Israeli forces ended up seizing a significantly larger state, compared to the UN Partition Plan that apportioned 52% of historic Palestine to the Jewish state.

In June 1967, Israel militarily conquered the West Bank, East Jerusalem, the Gaza Strip, the Sinai Peninsula in Egypt, and the Golan Heights in Syria. UN Security Council Resolution 242, passed on 22 November 1967, ordered Israel to immediately withdraw from these occupied territories.

Not only did the Israeli government refuse to comply with Resolution 242, but it began the construction of residential areas (settlements) for Israeli citizens in the West Bank in late 1967. Settlement construction also began in occupied East Jerusalem, the Gaza Strip and the Golan Heights. The construction of these settlements are illegal under international law, and a violation of the Fourth Geneva Convention that forbids states from transferring their citizens to occupied land. The UN calls the settlements a "flagrant violation" of international law with "no legal validity" (UN Security Council Resolution 2334, 2016). The UN has called on Israel to stop the construction of illegal settlements and fulfil its obligations as an occupying power under the Fourth Geneva Convention. The Israeli government, however, has not halted the construction of settlements, and there are now over 400 000 Israelis living in settlements in the West Bank, and over 200 000 Israelis living in occupied East Jerusalem (Peace Now, 2017).

In 1979, Israel returned the Sinai Peninsula to Egypt after the signing of a peace treaty between the two countries. Israel continues to occupy the Golan Heights in Syria, where 20 000 Israeli settlers live in 30 illegal settlements. In 2005, Israel withdrew its settlers and soldiers from within the Gaza Strip, but retained absolute control over the movement of people and goods via Gaza's airspace, territorial waters, and land borders. Since 2007, following Hamas's victory in internationally-monitored elections for the Palestinian Authority parliament the previous year, Israel blockaded Gaza's border crossings, permitting only limited passage of goods and people.

Since Israel has de facto control over virtually all entry and exit points into Gaza, it retains unconsented-to 'effective control' - the legal definition for qualifying as an occupying power (Ferraro, 2012). Israel's military blockade also subjects Gaza's population to collective punishment, in contravention of The Hague Conventions on the laws of war, and Article 33 of the Fourth Geneva Convention (Legal Centre for Freedom of Movement, 2008).

Israel's status as an occupying power in Gaza has been affirmed by the UN, international human rights organisations such as Amnesty International and Human Rights Watch, and the United States Department of State (Amnesty International, 2017; Human Rights Watch, 2006; UN General Assembly Human Rights Council, 2010; U.S Department of State, 2011).

Israel enforces its occupation of the West Bank and East Jerusalem through a brutal regime that controls almost every aspect of Palestinian life in those areas. Palestinian freedom of movement is restricted through a permit system and military checkpoints. Palestinians are subject to home demolitions, arbitrary arrest, torture, and detention without trial (Amnesty International, 2017). Human Rights Watch (2010) concluded that Palestinians face systematic discrimination based on their race, ethnicity, and national origin, and are deprived of electricity, water, schools, and access to roads.

Although the Israeli government disputes that the West Bank is occupied territory, Israel's status as an occupying power was confirmed by the International Court of Justice (ICJ) when it ruled that the Fourth Geneva Convention was applicable in the Palestinian territories (ICJ, 2004). This ruling is important since the ICJ is the principal judicial organ of the UN. Elements of the Israeli occupation of Palestine were also found to constitute forms of colonialism and apartheid (Dugard, 2007; Falk, 2010; Tilley, 2009). The Israeli government was found to have potentially committed war crimes and crimes against humanity during its military invasion of the Gaza Strip, codenamed Operation Cast Lead in 2008/9 (UN General Assembly Human Rights Council, 2009).

References to Israel as an occupier, and to its practices as colonialism and apartheid are not a subjective assessment of the author, but based on the above-mentioned reports that are grounded in international law.

MAINSTREAM MEDIA: OCCUPIED TERRITORY

Western mainstream media portrays the Israeli occupation of Palestine as a conflict revolving around security and terrorism, with Israel the victim. Consequently, the issue is understood as a conflict of land and borders between two peoples who have equal claims - not as an occupation with Israel being the military occupier, and Palestinians the occupied. A lack of analysis and context in the reporting of events in the Occupied Palestinian Territories (OPT) by British and American media is so deeply entrenched that people have no idea that there is an Israeli military occupation of Palestine (Ackerman, 2001; Oborne & Jones, 2009; Philo & Berry, 2004).

Inaccurate terminology relating to illegal Israeli settlements, 'terrorism' and 'extremism' further blurred the reality of the occupation (Fisk, 2001). The context of Palestinian resistance against a violent Israeli occupation was often missing from the reporting of corporate network reporting. There are wide discrepancies between the way that Israeli deaths are discussed and how Palestinian fatalities are reported. Israeli citizens – whether illegal settlers or soldiers – are presented in a humane way, Palestinians are not (Friel & Falk, 2007; Jhally & Ratzkoff, 2003).

Israel's continuous disregard of the provisions of the Oslo peace process throughout the 1990s, combined with its restrictions on freedom of movement, illegal settlement construction, and Israeli Prime Minister, Ariel Sharon's, provocative visit to the Al Aqsa Mosque led to the eruption of the Second *Intifada* in September 2000. Yet, mainstream media overwhelmingly reported that the cause of the Second *Intifada* was Palestinian leader, Yasser Arafat's, rejection of peace accords at Camp David in July 2000. A picture was created of a peaceful Israel prepared to make 'historic' offers while Arafat turned his back on negotiations and incited the Palestinian people to violently revolt (Aouragh, 2012).

Major news outlets have hidden the extent of Israel's occupation and violation of basic human rights from media consumers worldwide, and severely diminished their understanding of the occupation of Palestine. However, internet-based ICTs and social media has provided Palestinians a means of challenging this skewed media coverage. The next section will explore the use and rise of the internet and social media to expose Israel's colonial project in the OPT.

THE BEGINNINGS OF THE DIGITAL INTIFADA

In 1996, Palestinian internet service providers, PalTel and Palestine Online, began to offer internet connections, and the first internet cafes emerged in the OPT that year. By 1999, only 3% of Palestinians had access to the internet (Aouragh, 2012).

Palestinians soon realised that the internet provided a platform for them to tell their own story - a story that was being ignored and shut out of mainstream media. In September 1999, Palestinian American, Ramzy Baroud, established the *Palestine Chronicle* website. The site featured a commentary and analysis section, book reviews, photos, and an art section. The 'Daily News' section documented personal accounts of life under occupation. Through *Palestine Chronicle*, Baroud, who himself was born and raised in a refugee camp in the Gaza Strip, hoped to provide a platform for many talented writers inside the OPT to tell their story.

Shortly after the Second *Intifada* began in September 2000, Ali Abunimah, Arjan El-Fassed, Laurie King-Irani, and Nigel Parry formed *Electronic Intifada*, an English website that aimed to counter the strongly pro-Israel slant in Western mainstream media. In April 2002, Israel launched Operation Defensive Shield, the most extensive military operation since Israel occupied the West Bank, Gaza Strip and East Jerusalem in 1967. All of the West Bank, the Gaza Strip and East Jerusalem was sealed off, and Palestinians completely isolated from the outside world following an Israeli ban on all journalists in the OPT. In response, *Electronic Intifada* launched 'Diaries: Live from Palestine', daily accounts from local residents detailing life under a punishing curfew and military occupation. With the media blackout, *Palestine Chronicle* and *Electronic Intifada* were the only voices heard from the OPT during Operation Defensive Shield (Zayyan & Carter, 2009).

Baroud and the *Electronic Intifada* co-founders were engaging in, what is now termed, 'citizen journalism.' Allan (2009, p.18) argues that while there are various ambiguities and definitions related to the term, 'citizen journalism' refers to "the ordinary person's capacity to bear witness." Iazzolino (2010) tracked the emergence of Palestinian citizen journalism, and found that a growing number of Palestinians had followed the examples of *Palestine Chronicle* and *Electronic Intifada* in using ICTs to expose the brutality of the Israeli occupation. Allan and Thorsen (2009) documents the rise of citizen journalism and the meaningful impact it has had in the fight for democracy and human rights inside different countries, including Brazil, India, Iran, China, Kenya, Australia and Vietnam.

A State for the Stateless

Most advocacy efforts assume and involve the existence of a nation state. This is not the case for Palestinians, who are scattered throughout the OPT, within Israel, in refugee camps in the Middle East, and throughout the world. Websites like *Palestine Chronicle* and *Electronic Intifada* provided Palestinians in the OPT to communicate-for the first time - with those inside Israel, in refugee camps in the Middle East, in the diaspora and with pro-Palestine allies throughout the world. Abunimah (2009) corroborates this point:

The Internet provided me, as a Palestinian who grew up in the diaspora, with a real sense of community, connection and empowerment. It became in one sense a virtual country where Palestinians could meet, debate and even coordinate joint action in defence of their rights.

By 2001, six percent of Palestinians could access the internet. This jumped to 20% by 2004. As ICT access increased, more Palestinians began using social media to enter the virtual state of Palestine.

SOCIAL MEDIA CAMPAIGNS

Here the chapter will focus on the increased use of social media by Palestinians, and the use of transnational social media campaigns by pro-Palestine advocacy groups.

#GazaUnderAttack

Israel has launched four major invasions of the Gaza Strip, under the guise of security. In 2006, Israel invaded the Gaza Strip and southern Lebanon in Operation Summer Rains. In December 2008, Operation Cast Lead was launched, killing 1400 people. In 2012, Operation Pillar of Defence killed over 167 Palestinians. In July 2014, over 2100 Palestinians were killed during Operation Protective Edge.

According to Cook (2008) only the representatives of major (mostly American) media outlets were permitted to cover Israel's 2006 invasion of Gaza and Lebanon. Through bureaucratic censorship and intimidation, Israel effectively purged Gaza of any alternative journalists who could challenge the narrative of Israeli self-defence. With less than 3% of Palestinians in Gaza having internet access, social media had not yet been used to expose Israel's atrocities in Operation Summer Rains (Aouragh, 2012).

Operation Cast Lead was a culminating moment for both online and offline Palestine resistance and activism. By 2007, eighteen percent of Palestinians had an internet connection at home and 30% of Palestinians had internet access through internet cafes. With a literacy rate of 92%, it was not surprising that Palestine was the Middle East's fastest social media adopters (Aouragh, 2012; UNESCO Institute of Statistics, 2013).

Israel enforced a ban on reporters entering the Gaza Strip during Operation Cast Lead in 2008/9. Only reporters embedded with the Israeli forces were allowed to cover the military assault as it happened. Other reporters were given access to Gaza after the attacks were over (Chehata, 2010). Cast Lead was being portrayed as a conflict between two equal forces. There was no mention of the disproportionate use of force being employed by the Israeli military, or its use of internationally-prohibited white phosphorous and cluster bombs. The message being transmitted was of Israel merely responding to Hamas rockets.

Palestinians, however, were covering the attacks from inside the Gaza Strip, and used the internet and social media to disseminate news and pictures of Israel's attacks on schools, hospitals and mosques to an international audience. Al-Jazeera English allowed people to upload videos from their cell-phones directly on to the channel's YouTube account. All of the video material was then made available to anyone, including rival broadcasters. Gazans uploaded images on Flickr, and eyewitness accounts were uploaded on to blogs, while others tweeted details of attacks. Some mainstream media did utilise the information being put out by residents. Social media accounts from Gaza challenged Israel's sophisticated media operations and the sanitized accounts provided by journalists embedded with the Israeli military.

By 2012, thirty two percent of Palestinians could access the internet, 55% owned a computer in the West Bank and 44% in the Gaza Strip. This resulted in Palestinians employing greater use of social media during Operation Pillar of Defence in 2012. Activists used blogs, online forums, Facebook, YouTube, Twitter, and other social media platforms as media tools.

The Israeli government again enforced a media blackout on Gaza, but 'citizen journalists' like Rana Bakr and Harry Fear allowed Twitter users to hear real-time explosions, sirens, screams, and cries while reading live updates from Gaza. When the electricity and Internet connections were destroyed in Gaza, friends and colleagues in the West Bank offered to tweet on their behalf if they sent them the updates through the cellular network.

The BBC, Al-Jazeera English, CNN, *Sunday Times*, and *Guardian* either followed Bakr on Twitter, or contacted her directly for updates. Media outlets embedded Bakr's links into their live blogs and articles so that users without Twitter or Facebook accounts were still able to access and listen to these recordings. The recordings were also aired on radio stations around the world (Bakr, 2012). Ola Anan, co-founder of Diwan Ghazza, an online group consisting of bloggers and social media activists in Gaza, also used Twitter and Facebook to report Israeli bombings and share updates during the war, helping to spread news of mounting casualties and mobilise international support.

At the end of the first day of attacks, *Washington Post* reported that variations of the hashtag #GazaUnderAttack, used by Palestinians in Gaza was tweeted 120 000 times, compared with only 808 for the pro-Israel #PillarOfDefense. Six days later, a subsequent count by the Russia Today television channel found #GazaUnderAttack and #PrayForGaza were outpacing pro-Israel hashtags #IsraelUnderFire and #PrayForIsrael by factors of 10:1 and 20:1, respectively (Catron, 2012). Diwan Ghazza member, Maram Humaid, focused on reaching Francophone followers and tweeted in French. Another member contacted a friend at the Japanese Communist Party, who helped translate tweets from English into Japanese. Social media also helped drive activists to protest around the globe, spawning hundreds of offline actions.

While the scale and brutality of Israel's 2014 Operation Protective Edge was unprecedented, so too was internet connectivity and the use of social media as a tool of Palestinian resistance, campaigning and organising. In 2014, thirty seven percent of Palestinians in the Gaza Strip and 59.4% of those in the West Bank used a smartphone; 55.6% of Gaza Strip residents and 66.9% of residents in the West Bank had access to a computer; 51.4% of houses in the West Bank and 42.2% of homes in the Gaza Strip were connected to the internet (UNESCO, 2014).

More than 1.7 million Palestinians in the OPT were using Facebook and the WhatsApp messaging app, with 300 000 using Twitter and Instagram (Qawasmi & Othman, 2016). Having witnessed the effectiveness of social media-based 'citizen journalism' in countering Israeli propaganda during Operation Pillar of Defence in 2012, increasingly connected Palestinians in the West Bank and Gaza Strip armed with smartphones and computers took to social media to share information, images, video, and sound files of the bombing of Gaza.

The Israeli government's sponsored social media 'war rooms' churned out infographics depicting Israel's rationale for the war in Gaza as 'self-defence'. However, up against real-time reports and graphic pictures of dead women and children, these explanations were unconvincing. Millions of ordinary Twitter users showed their solidarity with Gaza, using the hashtag #GazaUnderAttack. In July 2014, #GazaUnderAttack was used more than 4 million times, while the hashtag #IsraelUnderFire was used less than 200 000 times (Dadoo, 2014).

In South Africa for instance, #GazaUnderAttack accounted for 76% of all Twitter traffic between July 20, 2014 and August 17, 2014, trending above #Ebola and #ISIS which were also making headlines in the same period (T. Khoury, personal communication, August 19, 2014). Crucially, the massive online campaign around #GazaUnderAttack translated into diverse, offline, awareness campaigns and protests in almost every province in South Africa. Approximately 200 000 South Africans protested in Cape Town on August 9, 2014, making this the largest march in post-apartheid South African history.

On the same day, the National Coalition for Palestine (NC4P) presented a memorandum to the South African parliament, demanding the expulsion of the Israeli ambassador to South Africa. Local Twitter users, coordinated by the Media Review Network (MRN) took to Twitter in large numbers with a message to the South African government and Israel's ambassador to South Africa, Arthur Lenk. #ExpelIsraeliAmbassadorToSA was the number one trending topic in South Africa on July 14 and 15, 2014 - surpassing Germany's victory in the soccer World Cup and news of the death of South African literary icon, Nadine Gordimer. #Israel, #Palestine, and #Gaza consistently featured in the top 10 trending topics throughout July, with contributions from South African celebrities bolstering exposure.

Through these online campaigns, attention was drawn to the sale of Israeli products in South African stores. NC4P launched the #BoycottWoolworths campaign and the consumer boycott of Israeli products gained traction in South Africa. South Africans posted pictures of creative protests of Israeli products in shops, and major South African retailers were forced to field queries about their decision to stock Israeli goods. Digital activism was being translated into real actions.

#HungryForFreedom

The hunger strike of the prisoner, Khader Adnan, translated into one of the most successful pro-Palestine transnational social media campaigns. Adnan, a 34-year old Palestinian man from the West Bank village of Arraba, was arrested for the eighth time on December 17, 2011. He began a hunger strike on the first day of his arrest, and continued for 66 days until a deal was reached for his release. On January 8, 2012, Adnan was sentenced to administrative detention[2] for four months, based on secret evidence.

Adnan continued with his hunger strike, and maintained that he would continue the hunger strike until he was either charged or released. 'Hungry for Freedom' became the main slogan of the worldwide campaign. Online activists and bloggers picked up Adnan's story after he passed the fortieth day of his hunger strike. Until then, no single Palestinian political prisoner had continued on such a prolonged hunger strike.

Apart from a few Arab and Palestinian websites and blogs, Adnan's story was publicised entirely through Twitter. Palestinian Twitter users and their supporters around the world, including South Africa, coordinated a number of hashtags that trended globally on Twitter more than five times. It was through these repeatedly-trending hashtags that some mainstream media picked up the story. The trending hashtags included #KhaderIsAlive, #Khader61Days, #Respect4Khader, and #HungerStrike63Days (Nabulsi, 2014).

Activists were also quick to use new features on social media and apply it to their political campaigning. For instance, a few months before the Khader Adnan campaign, Twitter introduced its 'Discover' feature which allowed Twitter users to read about the top 10 most popular stories from around the globe. Each time, Adnan's name trended, a story about him would remain in the 'Discover's top 10 section for over six hours, allowing Twitter users to learn more about Adnan and Israel's administrative detention policy against Palestinians.

The Twitter activity forced human rights groups like Amnesty International, Human Rights Watch, and Physicians for Human Rights-Israel to also launch campaigns around administrative detention. Nabulsi (2014) argues that for international organisations to follow the lead of social media activists who first launched the campaign is a notable phenomenon. This indicates that social media activists have been able to influence important organisations.

The social media campaign was also supported by NGO's campaigning against administrative detention. The Palestinian Prisoner Support and Human Rights Association (Addameer) published an activist toolkit on its website containing templates of letters people could send to their governments and to Israeli embassies in their country. In this way, the campaign was not simply a form of 'keyboard activism' but integrated traditional lobbying methods in its approach. Samidoun, a Canadian-based Palestinian prisoner solidarity network, posted flyers, templates, social media avatars, information and fact-sheets for activists to use in their social media campaigns. A blog set up by Palestinian youth activists managed to gather 500 letters of support, written by people around the world, in support of Khader Adnan and other Palestinian political prisoners. Transnational video messages of support were also posted on YouTube.

A digital poster of Adnan, with a lock on his mouth signifying his refusal to eat and speak, went viral on social media. The image soon found its way into the real world and was spray-painted on walls throughout the OPT and even within Israel. Protesters also printed the image and displayed it during protests and sit-ins around the world. Khader Adnan had moved from Twitter timelines to the real world. By the end of the second month, *New York Times*, *Los Angeles Times,* CNN, and other major media outlets covered the story.

In April 2012, as Palestinians marked Prisoners Day and Khader Adnan awaited his release, over 1200 Palestinian political prisoners began a hunger strike in Israeli jails protesting the policy of administrative detention. The strikes came to be known as the al-Karama strikes.

Palestinian civil society organisations also called for action to be taken against G4S, the British-Danish security corporation contracted to provide security equipment to Israeli prisons at which Palestinian political prisoners are held. #BoycottG4S then became an integral part of the social media campaign for Palestinian political prisoners. This was an attempt to make corporations, which both enable and directly profit from Israel's continued violations, accountable.

Using the hashtag #PalHunger, Twitter users publically called for solidarity actions throughout the world. Significantly, the hashtag was also used by local and international organisations, including UN agencies, when issuing official statements via Twitter. During the al-Karama strikes a picture of a faceless, blindfolded prisoner dressed in brown clothes with the word *Shabas*, the Hebrew abbreviation for the Israeli prison services, circulated widely on social media. The image was inspired by Facebook's well-known default profile picture. News reports estimate that up to 27 million people used the image as their profile picture (Nabulsi, 2014). Facebook and Twitter users posted screenshots of their contacts list almost entirely covered in brown from the image. Khader Adnan was released on April 18, 2012 after being on hunger strike for 66 days. On July 8, 2014 he was rearrested under the administrative detention policy, and re-released in July 2015.

A similar campaign was launched to free Mohammad Alan, who was administratively detained for six months in November 2014, with his detention then being renewed for an additional six months. On June 17, 2015 Alan launched a hunger strike in protest of his administrative detention. Alan's hunger strike was accompanied by a social media campaign, under the hashtag #Mohammad_Alan. Palestinian Twitter activists accompanied Alan's mother to Ashkelon hospital, where Alan was held. These activists then became the central information source for media on Alan's situation.

The social media campaign was supported by the Palestine Solidarity Campaign (PSC) in South Africa whose members held protests at the Israeli Trade Office in Johannesburg. Members of the PSC, who themselves were South African political prisoners and detainees, posted a video message on YouTube in solidarity with the hunger strikers in Palestine. In November 2015, Alan was released from prison.

#ShootingBack Through YouTube

Sharing snippets of daily life in the Occupied Palestinian Territories (OPT) on social media platforms challenges the dominant narrative of the Israeli occupation as a conflict between two equal sides, with Palestinians as the aggressors. In 2007, the Israeli Information Centre for Human Rights in the Occupied Territories (B'tselem) launched Shooting Back, a project aimed at empowering Palestinian communities by distributing video cameras to film human rights violations perpetrated by settlers and the Israeli army.

Eighty cameras were distributed in the West Bank. Since then, B'tselem has collected 1500 hours of footage that have been shared on YouTube and broadcast worldwide. Crucially, they have highlighted the issue of illegal Israeli settlements in the OPT as one of the main obstacles to peace. The videos were also used as evidence in 84 complaints filed by B'tselem and have led to the opening of 15 investigations against settler crimes.

In March 2016, footage of Israeli soldier, Elor Azaria, shooting dead a disarmed Palestinian man in Hebron went viral after it was published by the Palestinian Human Rights Defenders group and shared by B'tselem on Facebook. Within hours it had been picked up by news outlets around the world, sparking international condemnation, and a rare statement from the Israeli authorities criticising the soldier's actions. Azaria was subsequently found guilty of manslaughter and is currently serving a 14-month prison sentence.

In July 2015, following campaigning from Palestinian activists, SnapChat called on its users to publish photos under the hashtag #WestBankLife. Palestinians answered this call by publishing videos of daily life in several cities in the occupied West Bank. Most of the videos related to the reality of the occupation, checkpoints, and home demolitions (Qawasmi & Othman, 2016). Cameras and smartphones are now potent tools of resistance, and videos act as a humanizer for Palestinians.

Corporate Accountability: #BDS Targets

In 2005, inspired by the success of the South African anti-Apartheid movement, Palestinian civil society called on people of conscience all over the world to impose broad boycotts and implement divestment initiatives against Israel, similar to those applied to apartheid South Africa. The boycott, divestment and sanctions movement (BDS) as it is known, would be enforced against Israel until it recognises Palestinian rights in full compliance with international law (Barghouti, 2011).

BDS activists target products and companies that profit from the Israeli occupation and the violation of Palestinian rights, as well as Israeli sporting, cultural and academic institutions. Campaigners call on consumers not to buy Israeli goods or support those companies complicit in Israeli Apartheid and occupation. BDS social media campaigns have successfully targeted companies profiting from the Israeli occupation.

Ahava Cosmetics

In 2009, the CODEPINK group initiated the Stolen Beauty campaign against cosmetics company Ahava, whose factory was located in Mitzpe Shalem, an illegal Israeli settlement in the occupied West Bank. Through social media, the group aggressively targeted retailers of Ahava products. In December 2009, Rula Borelli wrote a letter to the Costco retailer asking them to remove Ahava products from their shelves. Borelli then started a Facebook group called 'Ask Costco to remove AHAVA from their shelves' with the intention of mobilising more people to contact Costco via the social networking site.

The group soon grew to over 200 members, and bombarded Costco with messages about Ahava. Borelli also encouraged the group's members to join Costco's fan page on Facebook, where they posted messages about Ahava's operations in an illegal settlement. These messages were read by Costco fans. Borelli and others received non-committal formal replies from Costco representatives. Within a month, the company stopped stocking Ahava products (End the Occupation, 2010).

In May 2011, CODEPINK activists disrupted a Twitter marketing promotion between Ahava and online cosmetics retailer, Birchbox. Members of the public were invited to submit beauty-care questions using #AhavaReborn (the slogan for Ahava's rebranding campaign) with the lure of a prize of $300 worth of Ahava products for the best query. CODEPINK then alerted other BDS activists about the marketing campaign, and suggested using the opportunity to subvert Ahava's rebranding effort. Campaigners from the U.S, U.K, Netherlands, Belgium, South Africa, Singapore, and the OPT then flooded the Twitter stream of #AhavaReborn with hundreds of witty, creative messages advocating the boycott of Ahava products (Mondoweiss, 2011).

As people who hoped for the prize tweeted #AhavaReborn with their beauty questions about cracked heels, blemishes and dry skin, BDS campaigners used ready-made tweets that CODEPINK had sent out. Some examples of these tweets include:

@Arabian_Babbler: My trigger finger is dry from shooting too many Palestinians around my settlement. What moisturizer do you recommend? #AhavaReborn

@bethlehemballet: I was helping to demolish Palestinian houses today and I chipped a nail! Do you have a product that will strengthen them? #AhavaReborn

BDS campaigners also posted tweets with links to the Stolen Beauty website for background information on Ahava for those who wanted to know more. BDS campaigners had turned Ahava's social media rebranding attempt into a platform for BDS and pro-Palestine messaging.

In March 2013, South African activists were alerted to a competition being advertised by online retailer, Spa Shop South Africa, that promised customers 10% off all Ahava products and a free hand cream during the month of March. BDS activists wrote to the owners of the Spa Shop about the illegality of Ahava products, but these attempts at engagements were ignored by the owners.

At 7 PM (South African time) on March 28, 2013 the hashtag #AhavaCrimes was posted and South Africans in Johannesburg, Cape Town, Durban, and hundreds of smaller towns were joined by Twitter users from across Africa, U.S, U.K, Australia, Italy, and Brazil. People used expressions and words particular to South African political struggles to express their outrage. Twitter users also shared factual information about Ahava, offering links to news articles about the boycott campaign and human rights reports about the company's occupation profiteering.

With thousands of people joining in worldwide, #AhavaCrimes trended at the number one spot on South African Twitter for 3 hours while #Ahava stayed in the top ten trends list. The continued interest in the topic left #AhavaCrimes staying in the list of top 10 trending topics until 11:30AM the following morning (Dadoo, 2013). In March 2016, the Stolen Beauty campaign was declared successful when Ahava announced plans to move their factory out of the occupied West Bank.

What is significant about the Ahava campaign is that it did not rely on social media campaigning alone. In London, protesters picketed outside the Ahava store for two years on an almost daily basis, until the store was forced to close down. In South Africa, pro-Palestine solidarity groups, Open Shuhada Street and BDS South Africa, lobbied the South African Department of Trade and Industry to introduce new labelling legislation that would correctly identify goods originating from illegal settlements. The Stolen Beauty campaign against Ahava combined transnational social media activism with traditional offline protests and lobbying to successfully target a company, and change its corporate behaviour.

Woolworths (South Africa)

In August 2014, the National Coalition for Palestine (NC4P) launched the #BoycottWoolworths campaign, which called for the complete boycott of the South African retailer, Woolworths, due to its Israeli trade relations. This was the first comprehensive consumer boycott of a South African retailer since 1994.

As a retailer that claimed to stock ethically-sourced products, Woolworths was bombarded with questions on all its social media platforms about its continued stocking of Israeli goods. Users also posted pictures of the then recently-ended Operation Protective Edge, reminding the retailer that the sale of its Israeli goods contributed, in some way, to funding the devastation in Gaza. Four days after the campaign was launched, #BoycottWoolworths remained in the top 10 trends on South African Twitter. The campaign sparked a media frenzy, and every media outlet in South Africa covered the boycott. The campaign also attracted international media attention, and was featured in *New York Times*, *Rolling Stone* magazine and on the Al-Jazeera TV network.

This strong social media campaign was followed up with monthly, in-store protests led by BDS South Africa and supported by other groups within the NC4P. These actions included die-ins, flash-mobs, till jams, and the placing of 'Boycott Israeli Apartheid' stickers on Woolworths Israeli goods (BDS South Africa, 2014; Gumede, 2015). These actions were widely encouraged via social media platforms, and were tweeted as they happened, streamed lived, and videos posted to YouTube immediately. An aggressive social media campaign had made its way to the shop-floor of Woolworths.

Palestine solidarity activists then dominated the company's Annual General Meeting (AGM) with questions around the ethics of stocking goods from a military occupier. This action, too, was covered live by the social media accounts of NC4P affiliates, and picked up by South African media. In November 2014, Woolworths instituted legal action against BDS South Africa. In legal papers served against BDS South Africa that the author has seen, Woolworths stated that an "aggressive social media [campaign] started to translate into action." The intensive, sustained social media presence of the hashtag #BoycottWoolworths was inflicting brand and reputational damage to the company (Voice of the Cape, 2014).

While the company was able to legally suppress physical protests within its stores, it conceded in its legal papers that it could not police social media and prevent users from using #BoycottWoolworths. The campaign reached over 4 million people through social media networks. Between 2015 and 2016, consumers were then encouraged to write letters to Woolworths store managers, questioning the continued stocking of Israeli goods. Images of the letters were shared widely on social media, thus encouraging others to do the same.

The campaign had enormous successes over the last two years. The #BoycottWoolworths had brought the BDS boycott of Israel into people's homes and lives. Driven by social media the campaign had taken, what had been an abstract concept for many up until then, and made it a real-life campaign. At its 2015 AGM, Woolworths affirmed that the retailer will not purchase Israeli goods originating from illegal settlements in the OPT.

THE ISRAELI GOVERNMENT RESPONSE TO TRANSNATIONAL SOCIAL MEDIA ADVOCACY

Here the chapter will focus on the Israeli government's use of censorship, intimidation and propaganda to counter pro-Palestine transnational social media campaigns.

Policing Social Media

Over the past two years, the Israeli government has tried to blame an upsurge in confrontations between Palestinians in the OPT and Israeli soldiers and settlers on 'incitement' in social media. Under this pretext, the Israeli government intends introducing legislation that would force social media networks to censor its users. The bill passed a preliminary reading in the Knesset (Israeli parliament) on July 20, 2016, and proposes a fine of $78 000 for users that do not remove 'offensive' posts on social networks (Gur and Winer, 2016).

While the Israeli government claims the legislation is simply aimed at curbing 'incitement to terrorism' on social networks, the Israeli state is engaging in what Kuntsman and Stein (2015) term "digital militarism"- the interplay between social media and Israel's militarist politics. The Israeli government is, in effect, trying to occupy Palestinian spaces on social media.

Between October 2015 and January 2016, Israeli police arrested 150 Palestinians based on 'Incitement through Social Media'. Some Palestinians received prison sentences of up to a year, based on the content of social media posts, and the number of 'likes' and 'shares' that these posts received (Qawasmi & Othman, 2016). The Israeli government is stretching the definition of 'incitement' with the goal of suppressing Palestinian voices on social media.

Foreign BDS activists using social media are being monitored by Israel, while the Shin Bet (Israel's internal security service) monitors local Israeli and Palestinian BDS groups and activists. The transnational pro-Palestine movement, and its successful social media campaigns, are viewed as a strategic threat by the Israeli government (Hitchcock, 2016).

A website called Canary Mission provides a 'blacklist' of American students involved in pro-Palestine and pro-BDS activism, and publicises details of their personal Twitter and Facebook accounts, in an attempt to tarnish their reputations, paint them as anti-Semites, and prevent them from obtaining future employment (Blumenthal and Carmel, 2015). The policing of social media by the Israeli government serves to restrict Palestine and BDS-related social media campaigns, as activists may fear for their future employment prospects.

Pressure on Facebook

There are more than a million Facebook users in the Occupied Palestinian Territories (OPT), and the OPT is ranked 62nd in the world in terms of Facebook users with 37% of the population using the social networking site (UNESCO, 2014:104). While the site has become a vital tool for Palestine and BDS-related campaigning, Facebook management has also come under intense pressure and ceded to Israeli government demands to censor Palestinians and pro-Palestine activism.

In early March 2011, a Facebook page called 'The Third Palestinian Intifada' was created. The page was a rallying call for thousands of Palestinian refugees to march to the Syrian, Lebanese, Jordanian, and Gaza-Israel borders on May 15, the day that Palestinians traditionally commemorate as the *Nakba* – the displacement of hundreds of thousands of indigenous Palestinians from their homes in 1948 to make way for the state of Israel. The page attracted 230 000 'likes' within two weeks of its creation. On March 29, Facebook removed the page, after the company had received a complaint from the Israeli government that the page was an 'incitement' to violence. The management of Facebook maintained that the page was found to 'promote violence.' The page, however, was promoting a march - a form of non-violent protest, and did not encourage violence in any way (Morrow & al-Omrani, 2011).

By August 2016, Israel had submitted 158 requests to Facebook to remove 'inciting' content, and Facebook has accepted those requests in 95% of the cases (*Guardian*, 2016). In September 2016, the Israeli government and Facebook agreed to work together to silence Palestinians after the Israeli government attempted to legislatively force Facebook to censor content - deemed by Israeli officials - to be improper (Greenwald, 2016). A Mossad-linked group, Shurat HaDin, filed a $1 billion lawsuit against Facebook claiming the company serves as a platform for what Israel calls 'terrorist groups' (Silver, 2016).

On September 23, 2016 Facebook disabled the Facebook accounts of the editors of *Quds* newspaper which has more than five million 'likes', and Shehab News Agency, which has more than six million 'likes' (Abunimah, 2016). The editors of both media outlets believe that the suspensions were directly related to the collaboration between Facebook and the Israeli government to monitor what Israel claims is 'incitement' by Palestinians. Following a social media outcry, Facebook restored the editors' accounts within 24 hours, and apologised. At the time of writing, Palestinian journalists had launched a campaign to protest censorship on Facebook under the hashtag #FBCensorsPalestine.

While Facebook not only supported - but enabled - youth movements in Egypt and Tunisia during the Arab Spring, the company is working against young Palestinians seeking to end the Israeli occupation. Facebook is selective in its commitment to fight incitement on its site. During Israel's invasion and bombing campaign of Gaza in 2014, hundreds of Israelis posted messages inciting genocide against Palestinians (Sheen, 2014). Yet, Facebook did not remove, or censor, those posts.

Facebook is interpreting slippery concepts such as 'hate speech' to please the Israeli government. By caving in to intimidation from the Israeli government, the company is setting a dangerous precedent that will have far-reaching implications, not just for Palestinians, but for all social media-based advocacy efforts.

Propaganda War-Rooms

Since the outbreak of Operation Cast Lead in 2008, Israel invested almost $2 million in 'new media warriors' to control messaging during its attack on Gaza (Kestler-D'Armours, 2011). Israel's Foreign Ministry established a special undercover team of paid workers who were to surf the internet 24 hours a day, spreading positive news about Israel. Branded as 'propaganda trolls' by pro-Palestine online activists, these internet-savvy Israeli youngsters were recruited to pose as ordinary internet surfers while providing the Israeli government's messaging. Their key messages included the claims that Hamas broke a ceasefire agreement with Israel; that Israel's aim was to defend its citizens; and that Hamas is a terrorist organisation. These war rooms were activated again during 2012 and 2014 when Israel invaded Gaza during Operations Pillar of Defence and Protective Edge, respectively.

CHALLENGES OF SOCIAL MEDIA-BASED ADVOCACY

Here the chapter will explore the challenges facing pro-Palestine transnational social media advocacy campaigns.

Israeli Control of Palestinian ICTs

A key component of the Israeli occupation is its stranglehold on Palestinian telecommunications. Palestinian cellphone operators, Jawwal and Wataniya, are forced to license their wireless spectrum from the Israeli government and route their traffic through Israel. Israel also licenses far less spectrum to Jawwal and Wataniya, than to Israeli firms. (Quartz, 2015). Low amounts of spectrum results in slower connection speeds, severely hampering digital activism in the OPT.

In 2015, Israel's government granted fourth generation (4G) licenses to six Israeli mobile operators in Israel, yet refuses to grant the Palestinian Authority a licence to launch third generation (3G) mobile services that are required for wireless internet access, in the OPT (Al-Jazeera, 2016). A lack of 3G access is also the reason why Twitter usage lags behind Facebook in the OPT. Twitter is centred around breaking news, and Twitter users must have an internet connection to live-tweet a demonstration or an arrest in real-time, otherwise, the whole point of tweeting is lost (UNESCO, 2014).

Effect on Israeli Government Policy

Social media advocacy efforts have raised global awareness about the Israeli state's unprecedented brutality against Palestinians in the besieged Gaza Strip; government-enabled Israeli settler violence against Palestinians in the OPT; home demolitions; and the ongoing colonisation of Palestinian land. These campaigns have also had a significant impact on the corporate behaviour of settlement businesses like Ahava, and forced some to relocate outside of the OPT. However, social media advocacy has not had any impact on the policies of the Israeli government.

Administrative detention continues, despite long-running campaigns around Israel's 'detention without trial' policies. The siege, blockade and violence on Gaza persists, despite the intensive social campaigns around #GazaUnderAttack. Despite B'tselem's successful #ShootingBack campaign, settler violence continues with impunity, reaching unprecedented brutality. The scale and degree of Israeli racism has never been higher, with Israelis hunting Palestinians in the street, chanting 'Death to Arabs' (Sheen, 2014). Israeli government ministers have openly called for the genocide of Palestinians, and the denial of a Palestinian state (IMEU, 2015). Israel's occupation and apartheid practices have never been more entrenched.

International governments, too, have not only ignored the BDS call to boycott Israel until it upholds international law, but actually enable the occupation by providing financial and diplomatic support to the Israeli government. In September 2016, then U.S president, Barack Obama, announced a $38 billion military assistance package to Israel over the next decade, the largest such aid package in American history. It remains up to global civil society to pressure governments to hold Israel accountable for breaches of international law.

RECOMMENDATIONS

This section will explore how to improve the effectiveness of transnational social media campaigns advocating for the end of the Israeli occupation of Palestine.

Development of Palestinian ICTs

The international community must take measures to ensure that Palestinians can access the ICTs they require. In October 2010, the International Telecommunication Union acknowledged that the Palestinian telecommunication network had been "significantly damaged in recent years" and that the international community had "an important role in assisting Palestine to develop a modern and reliable telecommunication network" (UNESCO, 2014). This is essential if Palestinians are to have a platform to expose the illegality of the Israeli occupation.

Integration of Online and Offline Advocacy

All social media campaigns and resources must be integrated with traditional methods of lobbying. The case of Ahava showed how a consistent, sustained social media presence was supplemented by activists engaging in regular in-store protests, and leafleting to educate people about the theft of Palestinian land, and the pillaging of Palestinian resources. South African groups lobbied their government to change labelling laws relating to the sale of settlement goods. An advocacy effort based entirely on social media interactions simply amounts to 'keyboard activism' and will not be effective without offline actions. No amount of tweeting, Facebook posts, YouTube videos, Instagramming, 'shares' or 'likes' is as effective as traditional mobilising based on personal interactions and government lobbying.

Taking Social Media Resources Offline

YouTube videos posted by Palestinians allow users to experience the everyday reality of life under occupation. Al-Jazeera publishes short, concise, factual videos about various aspects of the occupation through its social media-based AJ Plus offering. The Visualising Palestine website effectively explains the occupation and Israeli apartheid in easy-to-understand graphic form. These resources can only be utilised by those with internet access. In countries where high data costs limit internet access for the majority of the population, it is essential to download resources and use them as teaching aids in educational workshops. In this way, these resources reach those who are unable to access social media.

CONCLUSION

For the last 50 years, the image of Palestinians as 'terrorists', and Israelis as 'peace-seekers', has dominated mainstream media portrayals of the Israeli occupation of Palestine. This flawed narrative, coupled with Israeli government censorship of foreign journalists, has meant that the true horrors of the Israeli occupation have largely remain hidden from the world. Social media, however, has given Palestinians a voice with which to challenge flawed media coverage and Israeli government propaganda.

The rise of 'citizen journalism' in the OPT, particularly since Operation Cast Lead in 2008, has brought the brutality of the Israeli occupation to the world. Through Facebook, Twitter, YouTube and other social media, Palestinians have been able to circumvent Israeli checkpoints and other restrictions on movement. They have been able to take the world to the Occupied Palestinian Territories (OPT) to experience occupation, siege, colonialism and apartheid.

There are, however, limitations to the effectiveness of social media campaigns. Campaigns around Palestinian political prisoners highlighted Israel's administrative detention policies. Other campaigns have forced settlement businesses to relocate, fundamentally changing corporate behaviour. However, these campaigns have not ended administrative detention or the construction of illegal settlements, and have had a negligible impact on Israeli government policies. It is only when social media campaigns are combined with traditional advocacy and activism efforts that it will become an important weapon to bring about a just peace for Palestinians and Israelis.

REFERENCES

Abunimah, A. (2009). An ideal medium for a stateless people. *Electronic Intifada*. Retrieved September 1, 2016 from https://electronicintifada.net/content/ideal-medium-stateless- people/9745

Abunimah, A. (2016). Facebook disables accounts of Palestinian editors. *Electronic Intifada*. Retrieved September 29, 2016 from https://electronicintifada.net/blogs/ali-abunimah/facebook- disables-accounts-palestinian-editors

Ackerman, S. (2001, January). Uprising without explanation. *EXTRA!* Retrieved September 5, 2016 from http://fair.org/extra/uprising-without-explanation/

Al-Jazeera. (2016, April 26). Waiting for 3G: Palestinians call for connections. *Al-Jazeera*. Retrieved November 20, 2017 from http://www.aljazeera.com/news/2016/04/waiting-3g-palestinians- call-connections-160426133858205.html

Allan, S. (2009). Histories of citizen journalism. In S. Allan & E. Thorsen (Eds.), *Citizen journalism: global perspectives* (pp. 17–32). New York: Peter Lang Publishing.

Allan, S., & Thorsen, E. (Eds.). (2009). *Citizen journalism: global perspectives*. New York: Peter Lang Publishing.

Alsaafin, L. (2013). Israel restricts entry of foreigners into Palestinian territories. *Al-Monitor*. Retrieved September 30, 2016 from http://www.al-monitor.com/pulse/originals/2013/03/israel- restricts-foreign-nationals-entry.html

Amnesty International. (2017). Israel and the Occupied Palestinian Territories. Retrieved November 19, 2017 from https://www.amnesty.org/en/countries/middle-east-and-north-africa/israel- and-occupied-palestinian-territories/report-israel-and-occupied-palestinian-territories/

Aouragh, M. (2012). *Palestine online: Transnationalism, the internet and the construction of identity*. London: I.B Tauris.

Bakr, R. (2012). How we made the world hear Gaza, as citizen journalists. *Electronic Intifada*. Retrieved August 29, 2016 from http://electronicintifada.net/blogs/rana-baker/how-we-made-world- hear-gaza-citizen-journalists

Barghouti, O. (2011). *Boycott, divestment, sanctions: The global struggle for Palestinian human rights*. Chicago: Haymarket.

Blumenthal, M., & Carmel, J. (2015). Exposed: Pro-Israel modern day McCarthyites going to extremes to slime human rights activists. *AlterNet*. Retrieved September 30, 2016 from http://www.alternet.org/tea-party-and-right/modern-day-mccarthyists-are-going-extremes-slime- activists-fighting-israels

Catron, J. (2012). Gaza thwarts Israeli propaganda with Twitter. *Electronic Intifada*. Retrieved August 26, 2016 from http://electronicintifada.net/content/gaza-thwarts-israeli-propaganda- twitter/11964

Chehata, H. (2010). Israeli censorship. *Middle East Monitor*. Retrieved September 8, 2016 from http://www.middleeastmonitor.com/reports/by-dr-hanan-chehata/1449-israeli-censorship

Cook, J. (2008). *Disappearing Palestine: Israel's experiments in human despair*. London: Zed Books.

Cook, J. (2009). Internet users paid to spread Israeli propaganda. *Electronic Intifada*. Retrieved September 19, 2016 from http://electronicintifada.net/content/internet-users-paid-spread-israeli- propaganda/8355

Dadoo, S. (2013). Using Twitter to spread the word about #AhavaCrimes. *Mondoweiss*. Retrieved September 27, 2016, from http://mondoweiss.net/2013/04/twitter-spread-ahavacrimes/#sthash.Vqh2gyZ9.dpuf

Dadoo, S. (2014, August 4). Israel is losing the war in Gaza one tweet at a time. *The Star*. Retrieved September 27, 2016 from http://mediareviewnet.com/2014/08/israel-is-losing-the-war-in- gaza-one-tweet-at-a-time/

Dugard, J. (2007). Report of the Special Rapporteur on the situation of human rights in the Palestinian territories occupied since 1967. Retrieved November 19, 2017 from http://www.diakonia.se/Documents/public/IHL/Publications/Dugard_January2008.pdf

End the Occupation. (2010). 'Stolen Beauty' victory: Costco feels the love. *End The Occupation*. Retrieved September 29, 2016 from http://blog.endtheoccupation.org/2010/01/stolen- beauty-victory-costco-feels-love.html

Falk, R. (2010). Report of the Special Rapporteur on the situation of human rights in the Palestinian territories occupied since 1967. Retrieved November 19, 2017 from http://www.un.org/ga/search/view_doc.asp?symbol=A/65/331

Ferraro, T. (2012). Determining the beginning and end of an occupation under international humanitarian law. *International Review of the Red Cross, 94*(885), 133–163. Retrieved November 19, 2017 from https://www.icrc.org/eng/assets/files/review/2012/irrc-885-ferraro.pdf doi:10.1017/S181638311200063X

Fisk, R. (2001, September 3). CNN caves in to Israel over its references to illegal settlements. *The Independent*. Retrieved September 3, 2016 from http://www.commondreams.org/headlines.shtml?/headlines01/0903-01.htm

Friel, H., & Falk, R. (2007). *Israel-Palestine on record: How the New York Times misreports conflict in the Middle East*. London and New York: Verso.

Greenwald, G. (2016, September 12). Facebook is collaborating with the Israeli government to determine what should be censored. *The Intercept*. Retrieved September 30, 2016 from https://theintercept.com/2016/09/12/facebook-is-collaborating-with-the-israeli-government-to- determine-what-should-be-censored/

Guardian. (2016, September 12). Facebook and Israel to work to monitor posts that incite violence. *Guardian*. Retrieved September 30, 2016 from https://www.theguardian.com/technology/2016/sep/12/facebook-israel-monitor-posts-incite-violence- social-media?CMP=twt_gu

Gumede, P. (2015, September 3). Till jam protest at Woolworths. *South Coast Fever*. Retrieved September 30, 2016 from http://www.news24.com/SouthAfrica/Local/South-Coast-Fever/Till-jam- protest-at-Woolworths-20150902

Gur, H., & Winer, S. (2016, July 20). Bill cracking down on social media incitement passes initial reading. *Times of Israel*. Retrieved September 29, 2016 from http://www.timesofisrael.com/bill-cracking-down-on-social-media-incitement-passes-initial- reading/

Hitchcock, J. (2016, January-March). Social media rhetoric of the transnational Palestinian-led boycott, divestment, and sanctions movement. *Social Media + Society*, *2*(1). doi:10.1177/2056305116634367

Human Rights Watch. (2006). Written statement: Human Rights Council special session on the Occupied Palestinian Territories. Retrieved November 19, 2017 from https://www.hrw.org/news/2006/07/05/human-rights-council-special-session-occupied-palestinian- territories-july-6-2006

Human Rights Watch. (2010). Separate and unequal: Israel's discriminatory treatment of Palestinians in the Occupied Palestinian Territories. Retrieved November 19, 2017 from http://www.hrw.org/en/reports/2010/12/19/separate-and-unequal

Iazzolino, G. (2010). Digital shahid: From broadcast media to citizen journalism in Palestine. *Arab Media and Society*. Retrieved September 25, 2016 from http://www.arabmediasociety.com/?article=763

Institute of Middle East Understanding (IMEU). (2015). In their own words: Senior Israeli officials on the Palestinian question. Retrieved September 30, 2016 from http://imeu.org/article/in- their-own-words-senior-israeli-officials-on-the-palestinian-question

International Court of Justice. (2004). Legal consequences of the construction of a wall in the Occupied Palestinian Territory (Request for advisory opinion). Retrieved November 19, 2017 from http://www.unrod.org/docs/ICJ-Advisory2004.pdf

Jhally, S., & Ratzkoff, B. (2003). Peace, propaganda and the promised land. *Media Education Foundation*. Retrieved August 5, 2016 from https://www.youtube.com/watch?v=GSXFNSvInIE

Kestler-D'Amours, J. (2011). Israel investing $1.6 million in 'new media warriors'. *Electronic Intifada*. Retrieved September 8, 2016 from http://electronicintifada.net/content/israel-investing-16- million-new-media-warriors/9245

Khalidi, R. (2006). *The iron cage: The story of the Palestinian struggle for statehood*. Boston: Beacon Press.

Kuntsman, A., & Stein, R. (2015). *Digital militarism: Israel's occupation in the social media age*. Stanford: Stanford University Press.

Legal Centre for Freedom of Movement (Gisha). (2008). Gaza closure defined: Collective punishment position paper on the international law definition of Israeli restrictions on movement in and out of the Gaza Strip. Retrieved November 19, 2017 from http://www.gisha.org/userfiles/file/publications/GazaClosureDefinedEng.pdf

Mondoweiss. (2011). Stolen Beauty boycott culture jam turns Ahava's online marketing contest into a social media #FAIL. *Mondoweiss*. Retrieved September 29, 2016 from http://mondoweiss.net/2011/05/stolen-beauty-boycott-culture-jam-turns-ahava%E2%80%99s-online- marketing-contest-into-a-social-media-fail/#sthash.DeAZ27TO.dpuf

Morrow, M., & al-Omrani, K. (2011). Activists preparing for 'third intifada.' *Electronic Intifada*. Retrieved November 22, 2017 from https://electronicintifada.net/content/activists-preparing- third-intifada/9937

Nabulsi, M. (2014). “Hungry for freedom”: Palestine youth activism in the era of social media. In L. Herrera (Ed.), *Wired citizenship: Youth learning and activism in the Middle East* (pp. 105–119). New York: Routledge.

Oborne, P., & Jones, J. (2009). The pro-Israel lobby in Britain. *Open Democracy*. Retrieved September 18, 2016 from http://www.opendemocracy.net/ourkingdom/peter-oborne-james-jones/pro- israel-lobby-in-britain-full-text

Palestinian Central Bureau of Statistics (PCBS). (2015). Statistics on internet usage in the OPT. Retrieved September 6, 2016 from http://pcbs.gov.ps/portals/_pcbs/PressRelease/Press_En_IntDyInfoSoc2015E.pdf

Pappé, I. (2006). *The ethnic cleansing of Palestine*. London: Oneworld.

Peace Now. (2017). Settlements data – population. Retrieved November 18, 2017 from http://peacenow.org.il/en/settlements-watch/settlements-data/jerusalem

Philo, G., & Berry, M. (2004). *Bad news from Israel*. London: Pluto Press.

Qawasmi, H., & Othman, D. (2016). *Hashtag Palestine: Palestinian social media activity during 2015*. Haifa: Arab Centre for Social Media Advancement (7amleh). Retrieved September 4, 2016 from http://www.7amleh.org/en/article/62

Quartz. (2015, November 19). Israel is finally allowing Palestine to have 3G. Retrieved September 28, 2016 from http://qz.com/554746/israel-is-finally-allowing-palestine-to-have- 3g/

Rashid, S. (2003). An overview of the role of the international media regarding the Palestinian-Israeli conflict. *Paper presented at the Alternative Information Centre seminar*, Boston. Retrieved September 27, 2016 from https://electronicintifada.net/content/role-international-media-palestinian- israeli-conflict/4853

Robbins, A. (2016). BDS victory: Ahava moving factory out of occupied West Bank. *Mondoweiss*. Retrieved September 29, 2016 from http://mondoweiss.net/2016/03/bds-victory-ahava- moving-factory-out-of-occupied-west-bank/

Sheen, D. (2014). Incitement to hate: Testimony to the Russell Tribunal on Palestine. Retrieved September 30, 2016 from https://www.youtube.com/watch?v=SDNFdjwolaI&list=PLBDtcbghfMdsKkGO9MFG5MPxC3s8gy GES&index=5

Silver, C. (2016). Mossad-linked group sues Facebook for $1 billion. *Electronic Intifada*. Retrieved September 30, 2016 from https://electronicintifada.net/blogs/charlotte-silver/mossad- linked-group-sues-facebook-1-billion

South Africa, B. D. S. (2014). Successful #BoycottWoolworths "Seng Khatele" flashmob. *YouTube*. Retrieved September 30, 2016 from https://www.youtube.com/watch?v=_6Y- oHEw61U&list=PL_FuAw3qkivow_Li9JWKSI-OhlmU21A68&index=4

Tilley, V. (2009). Occupation, colonialism, apartheid? A re-assessment of Israel's practices in the Occupied Palestinian Territories under international law. Human Sciences Research Council, Pretoria. Retrieved November 19, 2017 from http://www.hsrc.ac.za/en/research- outputs/view/4634

UNESCO Institute for Statistics (UIS). (2013). *Adult and youth literacy: National, regional and global trends, 1985 – 2015*. Retrieved September 30, 2016 from http://www.uis.unesco.org/Education/Documents/literacy-statistics-trends-1985-2015.pdf

United Nations Educational, Scientific and Cultural Organization (UNESCO). (2014). *Assessment of media development in Palestine*. Retrieved September 21, 2016 from http://unesdoc.unesco.org/images/0022/002277/227784e.pdf

United Nations General Assembly Human Rights Council. (2009). Report of the United Nations fact-finding mission on the Gaza Conflict. Retrieved November 19, 2017 from http://www2.ohchr.org/english/bodies/hrcouncil/docs/12session/A-HRC-12-48.pdf

United Nations General Assembly Human Rights Council. (2010). Report of the international fact-finding mission to investigate violations of international law, including international humanitarian and human rights law, resulting from the Israeli attacks on the flotilla of ships carrying humanitarian assistance. Retrieved November 19, 2017 from http://www2.ohchr.org/english/bodies/hrcouncil/docs/15session/A.HRC.15.21_en.pdf

United Nations Security Council Resolution 2334. (2016). Retrieved November 19, 2017 from http://www.un.org/webcast/pdfs/SRES2334-2016.pdf

United States Department of State. (2011). 2010 country reports on human rights practices: Israel and the Occupied Territories. Retrieved November 19, 2017 from https://www.state.gov/j/drl/rls/hrrpt/2010/nea/154463.htm

Voice of the Cape FM. (2014, November 14). Taking BDS to court 'risky': analyst. Retrieved September 29, 2016 from http://www.vocfm.co.za/taking-bds-to-court-risky-analyst/

Zayyan, H., & Carter, C. (2009). Human rights and wrongs: Blogging news of everyday life in Palestine. In S. Allan & E. Thorsen (Eds.), *Citizen journalism: global perspectives* (pp. 85–96). New York: Peter Lang Publishing.

KEY TERMS AND DEFINITIONS

BDS Movement: The Palestinian-led boycott, divestment and sanctions (BDS) movement calling for Israel to be politically, diplomatically and economically isolated until that state complies with international law in respect of its occupation of Palestinian territories.

Blog: An abbreviation for weblog. This is a regularly updated website typically run by an individual, consisting of entries, with the most recent entry appearing first.

Censorship: The suppression of information by governments, authorities, media or social media outlets on the grounds that it is dangerous, politically incorrect or harmful.

Citizen Journalism: The dissemination of information (text, pictures, audio and video) by the public through the internet and social media.

Hashtag: A hashtag is a keyword, phrase, talking point or topic that is preceded with a pound (#) sign, e.g. #GazaUnderAttack. Often used on Twitter and Instagram, it allows people to search for posts based on particular subjects.

Infographics: Graphic, visual representations of data that present complex information quickly and clearly.

National Coalition for Palestine (NC4P): An umbrella body representing over 40 South African civil society structures dedicated to achieving a just peace in Palestine-Israel.

Propaganda: Biased and misleading information, ideas, spread widely to promote a political cause or point of view or to harm a group, movement, or nation.

Trending: On Twitter this refers to a hashtag-driven topic that is immediately popular at a specific time.

Twitterstorm: A sudden spike in activity, often started by a single person or a few accounts using an original hashtag, around a specific topic on Twitter. The tweet, and its related hashtag, quickly spreads as people re-use the hashtag with subsequent tweets and retweets.

ENDNOTES

1 The word *intifada* means 'to shake off.' It is often translated into English as 'uprising.'

2 Administrative detention is a procedure that allows the Israeli military to hold - mainly Palestinians from the Occupied Palestinian Territories - indefinitely on secret evidence without charging them or allowing them to stand trial.

Chapter 6
Trans-National Advocacy and the Hashtag Black Lives Matter:
Globalisation and Reception in the UK and France

Danella May Campbell
Manchester Metropolitan University, UK

Marie Chollier
Manchester Metropolitan University, UK

ABSTRACT

This chapter offers an insight into racial debates and equality advocacy in the 21st century and explores the emergence, the becoming and long-lasting effect of #BlackLivesMatter. The hashtag story is a traditional viral web content. Nevertheless, technologies allowed these initially local concerns, to become a world-wide plea. The first section summarises the past and current struggle for civil rights and equality in the USA. The second one focuses on the European reception of the hashtag in two structurally different countries. The last section discusses both outcomes and consequences in terms of social policies and international advocacy. A journalistic and critical analysis of the movement is here provided, with long term effects and reception case studies.

INTRODUCTION

For the majority of African-Americans, the reality is unemployment, barriers to education and health services and insufficient housing in poor urban areas highly militarized by the police. American statistics show that Black men are 31% more

DOI: 10.4018/978-1-5225-2854-8.ch006

likely to be pulled over by the police than white men and 15 to 34-year-old black men are nine times more likely to be killed than any other person. American police killed around 1,100 black people in 2015 compared to three killed by police in the UK; it has one of the highest murder rates in the developed world and three million privately owned firearms (Murdoch, 2016). The ongoing war against police brutality in the United States persists for African-Americans.

From Malcolm X's marking of the 'movement' in the sixties as a nightmare… to King's dream attributed as a dream deferred, the killing of Michael Brown undoubtedly triggered the re-affirmation of the struggle for Blacks in America. The story of #blacklivesmatter is a lens through which both American and international racial inequalities can be analysed. This chapter offers an insight into racial debate and equality advocacy in the 21st century, based on journalistic and academic works.

The first section briefly summarises the past and current struggle for civil rights and equality in the USA documenting the birth and journey of BLM within the current social and political settings of America and identifying the political triggers contributing to a black uprising. It acts as a documentation of the timeline and adaptation of BLM, from hashtag, to movement, transcending to its recognition as a global network and describes how new technologies and social media offer new channels for advocacy, leading to potential new agencies.

The second one focuses on the European reception of the hashtag in two structurally different countries, the UK and France, exploring the transferability of an online movement born in the USA to other national contexts. The last section discusses both outcomes and consequences in terms of social policy, international advocacy and potential impact on people's lives interrogating the internationalisation of BLM as a global movement and its proficiency to advocate for the poorest of Black people in an ever-increasing globalised world.

BIRTH AND RISE OF THE #BLACKLIVESMATTER (#BLM): AMERICAN HISTORY

From Slavery to Civil Rights: A Brief History of Black Rights Movements

American history is complex. The structure of society and the legality are organised according to several levels leading to diverse impact and consequences. Several dates and historical periods are important to recall regarding the topic of this chapter.

Reconstruction Amendments

The first date is the abolition of slavery in 1865. The reformation following the civil war, led to Reconstruction Amendments and a will from President Lincoln to guarantee rights and equality to all citizens. The 13th amendment of the constitution - examined on January 31 and ratified on December 6 – declares "…neither slavery nor involuntary servitude, except as a punishment for crime whereof the party shall have been duly convicted, shall exist within the United States, or any place subject to their jurisdiction…" (Constitution of the United States of America, 1865/2016). The reformation following the civil war, led to Reconstruction Amendments and a will from President Lincoln to guarantee rights and equality to all citizens. Nevertheless, slavery even though abolished, found new social expressions (Daniel, 1979). One of the forms of slavery perpetuated in Southern states was through peonage (even if legally abolished) and sharecropping (Daniel. 1973; Nieman, 1994). Indeed, labour organisation and southern agriculture maintained a form of lifetime exploitation and implicit transmissibility to descendants.

From "Separate but Equal" to Structural Equality

In 1896, the law case Plessy v Ferguson confirmed the up to then latent doctrine of "separate but equal" (Groves, 1951). In 1890, Louisiana State passed the Separate Car Act (Rountree, 2004) that required separate railway cars and accommodations for Black and White people. Homer Plessy, an octoroon free man (reportedly of seven-eighths European descent and one-eighth African descent), bought a first-class train ticket but was refused the 'white' wagon. Homer Plessy appealed to the law for equal treatment. However, the Supreme Court followed the jurisprudence stating that separation was not anti-constitutional. Further to Plessy v Ferguson, national Black civil rights movements encompassed local communities and aimed at forming a national alliance. The national movement became organised and structured after World War 1 (for comprehensive details, see Maslow and Robinson, 1953), through the creation of different organisations, such as the Universal Negro Improvement Association[1]. From 1896, the doctrine (Roche, 1951) seemed officially promoted, considering the separation of public space between White and Black people (defined by one ancestor) as not entailing the 13th Amendment. The legal turn came in 1954 when the Supreme Court stated that separate public schools were unconstitutional (Brown v. Board of Education of Topeka).

Subsequently, a de-segregation process operated. However, mentalities and interpersonal relationships cannot be guided by legal decisions. The next decade saw the rise of two seminal works on prejudice (Allport, 1954) and stigma (Goffmann, 1963). Indeed, these works studied empirically, racial and religious prejudice and stigma in post 1954 America. These seminal works investigated, firstly, the social perpetuation of diverse types of prejudice against visible minorities, namely Black (up to then discriminated against) and Jewish people, secondly, how some members of these communities were ostracised. Further to this, racial and social preference studies started in the USA after the end of racial segregation in schools (Brand et al, 1974). Many of them focused on children's groups re-creating segregation (i.e. not playing together) and trying to formalise interventions or a good-enough environment to promote equality. Current studies focus on the conceptual acquisition of the notion of race/ethnicity (Cockerham, 2011) and racial favouritism (Rutland et al, 2015; Aboud, 2003). Almost Decades later, both the persistence of this field of study and the events leading to the rise of the #BLM indicate the structural shift from an unequal to a theoretically equal system is not enough to implement and achieve social change and equality.

Technologies and Advocacy: From Black Activism to Black Digital Activism

The history of Black Rights and Black Rights campaigning in the USA is not unequivocal and should be historically and geographically contextualised, as it determines both means and aims. The organisation and the modes of campaigning used to rely on in-person, sometimes hidden meetings, spreading by word of mouth and relying on printed materials when not prohibited (Cashmore and McLaughlin, 1991; Painter, 2006). Therefrom, the main impact of new technologies relates to the dematerialisation of both organisational aspects and campaigning materials and therefore to the rapidity of diffusion and potential snowball effect (Franklin, 2014).

New technologies and social media represent a new possible means for social interactions, personal and collective expression (Moore & Selchow, 2012). Virtual or online communities are dematerialised communities that can gather around specific common features; in the context of this chapter, around a common cause and purpose. This is named digital or online activism (Breindl, 2010); hashtag activism (Stache, 2015), sometimes spelled hashtactivism (Ibahrine, 2017), as one of its subtypes. The codes and rules of writing and using the hashtag have been studied from a linguistic perspective, underlining the condensing mechanism aiming to produce a strong effect (Caleffi, 2015). More than a new linguistic practice condensing words, the hashtag and related social practices (e.g. posting, sharing) are a new way to aggregate both language and people when aiming at visibility and awareness. If the hashtag has a linguistic structure, each hashtag has an intrinsic sociolinguistic and socio-political meaning attached to it, as it most of the time relates to the combination of an event and a cause. Hence, #BLM is one of many cases of hashtag activism and other famous ones have related to similar events such as, the Arab Spring (Jansen, 2010) or more generally children and human rights (#BringBackourGirls, for a critical analysis see Loken, 2014 or the recent #metoo, adding to the many calls and actions against sexual violence).

In the specific context of Black activism, the structuration of online communities appears both generic and specific: generic as human rights and equality-based (De Choudury et al., 2016), specific when concerned with an event (Bonilla & Rosa, 2015) or an identified movement (e.g. Black feminism, see Williams, 2015). It is maintained in this chapter that the #BlackLivesMatter movement is both generic and specific, both the product and the cause of new narratives and social agencies (Campbell, 2005; Yang, 2016). Therefore, the next sections will explore the preceding social structures to the hashtag and the movement, its exportability and transferability to other national contexts, and its consequences in terms of potential new agency.

The Story of #BlackLivesMatter

George Zimmerman's Acquittal, Michael Brown's Murder and a Chronology of Publicised Cases

The hashtag #blacklivesmatter was created by Alicia Garza, Patrisse Cullors, and Opal Tometi in response to the trial and acquittal of George Zimmerman, responsible for the shooting and killing of 17-year-old Trayvon Martin in 2012.

The rise of the hashtag as a communicative method and of political identification has proliferated the cries of "Black Lives Matter!", "hands up, don't shoot", "I can't breathe" and "WhatHappenedToSandraBland" across the globe.

In research published by Pew Research Center (Anderson & Hitlin, 2015) from its first use mid-2013 to March 2016 #BLM has been used almost 11.8 million times on Twitter, spiking at key events in 2015, including the deaths of Eric Garner on December 1, Freddie Gray on April 27 and Sandra Bland on July 20. Its biggest spikes on Twitter since its formation have exploded at other key political events; the rejection of indictment for police officers in the case of Eric Garner, 2014 (189, 210 times: the most it has been used in a single day); the Presidential campaign debate where by Senator Bernie Sanders defended the movement, 2015 (more than 127, 000); and finally, the one-year anniversary of Michael Browns death, August 9, 2015 (120, 067 and 98, 518 the preceding day).

In 2014 #BLM was the American Dialect Society's 2014 Word of the Year (Steinmetz, 2014). Chair of the New Words Committee told TIME "it's a time to recognize that hashtags are an innovative linguistic form that deserve our attention."

It was also voted into the top 12 world changing hashtags of 2014, but 'in the age of the Internet, conflict comes with corresponding online movements (Weedston, 2014). Undoubtedly this is the case for the BLM movement in relation to the emergence of #AllLivesMatter (#ALM), a corresponding social media campaign rooted in opposition to the political statement, made specific to the state of black lives.

In June 2015, the massacre of nine Black worshippers by White supremacist, Dyllan Roof, in an African-American church sparked further outrage and protests in Charleston. The Black Liberation Movement declared what happened here was an act of terrorism, the media refuses to label this as terrorism, they want us to wait until all of the details come out, but had it been one of us, to go into a white church and gun down nine people, it would have been terrorism (Murdoch, 2016).

Social media has presented an array of online video footage to the public that has documented the murder and mistreatment of Blacks, most importantly from all different backgrounds, demographics and walks of life. Whether it be the Dallas pool party (2015), where teenagers were thrown to the ground and held at gunpoint or Sandra Bland (2015) whose death, ruled a suicide, provoked questions and interrogation into what happens behind the prison cell walls, or the shooting of Richard Ramirez (2014).

The killing of Walter Scott (2015) was a key moment in the run up to the official establishment of Black Lives Matter. Not only did the video portray a man being shot in the back but it captured police officer, Michael Slager, stating "he grabbed my taser" [conducted electrical weapon, part of the equipment of the police forces in the USA, UK and France] and whilst continuing to walk over to his body and plant the taser next to him.

The BLM movement's message has echoed, sparking solidarity protests in the UK, Ireland, Germany, The Netherlands, Amsterdam, Canada and South Africa against anti-black racism and violence worldwide, triggered by the deaths of Alton Sterling (2016) in Baton Rouge, Louisiana, and Philando Castile (2016), Minnesota.

The movement gained the backing of black elites sparking the US National Anthem protests, predominantly within the National Basketball Association (NBA) and National Football League (NFL), most notably sparked by Colin Kaepernick who sat during a national anthem whilst playing for the San Francisco 49ers in August 2016. This sparked a national campaign with other elite players joining and taking a knee before games and was backed by the former President Barack Obama as exercising his political right (Jones & LoBianco, 2016).

With over 40 chapters, worldwide, BLM was awarded with the 2017 Sydney Peace Prize, in particular for its Australian chapters and its fight for the aborigine struggle; becoming in addition, a recognised global network (Wahlquist, 2017).

America's 'Post-Racial' Proposition

The success of a minority of black elites such as the election of Barack Obama, corporate executives, government officials as well as celebrities means America, became the epitome of a "post-racial" society (Balkaran, 2015) largely attributed to the success of its first Black President. At the time, this was considered representative of a change in attitudes towards race with the success of a relative few African-Americans upheld as a vindication of the United States' color-blind ethos and a testament to the transcendence of its racist past (Taylor, 2016).

Overall statistics show, concerning education, voter turnout, number of congressional representatives and life expectancy, these have all increased in the US (Plumer, 2013). Although mass incarceration for black men has fallen over the last decade, Plumer (2013) highlights that, between 1960 and 2000, there had been a huge continual increase of the number of incarcerated blacks. Statistics published by Pew Research Centre document the incarceration rate of Black men as six times higher than White men, increasing since 1960, where it measured at five times more likely. Additionally, the poverty gap between Blacks and Whites has remained stagnant for the last fifty years (PEW, 2013). Lack of economic opportunities; particularly within the jobs market was researched: black people were half as likely to get a job offer or call back when submitting an identical resume of a White counterpart; and a Black person with no criminal convictions was not more successful than White applicants who had recently been released from Prison (Denver, 2003; Vaidyanathan, 2016).

As Murdoch points out, the Klu Klux Klan (KKK) are still very much the poster boys of White supremacy and he highlights research undertaken by The Southern Party Law Centre which claim that the number of active Klan groups increased in 2015 to 190 klans in America from 72 the year before.With KKK members declaring for a long time, that their members lie in the midst of ranks within various organisations and professions including, police officers, politicians and congressional representatives (Murdoch 2016). The #BLM has been about political action against the institutional racism reinforced within a capitalist system that stems from elite positions of power and infiltrates society throughout the remaining classes.

Footage of protests show both Black and White protestors at public marches. One benefit of social media is the opportunity to promote unity of black groups within local communities. Being unified under the hashtag allows them to relate to and present a uniformed identification for the cause and a unified message. The #BLM is not only the leading affiliate for all black movements but also the direct message to the world, which encapsulates the overall aim and the epitome of the black struggle on a global scale.

However, despite the level of global support for the BLM movement, there is still tension amongst White and Black supporters. One member of a local community group (Murdoch 2016) who faced problems with a White Trump supporter who had infiltrated the group and asked all whites to leave, explained,

...we created an African only space for a second just to re-group and think about security and who's who, and some of our European alliances who are very consistent, that we love, they felt a little upset and so we had to explain to them why there's that tension and the only example we could give them is Dylann Roof who sat in church and prayed with our elders for an hour and they welcomed him with open hands and he shot each one of them execution style in the back.

Many ask why social media is focused around the police. The BLM's focus on 'white supremacy as a system of oppression stretching through policing, politics and education gives the movement relevance in a globalised context. After all, globalisation refers mostly to the sharing of Western ideals but with white supremacist systems in practise within this, it's hard to see how Blacks will fare well.' Alternatively, without living in a globalised world driven by the developments in technology, social media campaigns such as BLM would not exist. Arguably, on both sides the #BLM may or may not survive in invoking social and political change for Blacks and only time will tell whether this campaign will accomplish the same successes as the Civil Rights Movement did but it most definitely impacts the Black demographic of political campaigning.

Trump's America: The Current Political Climate

January 20, 2017 saw Donald Trump become the 45th President of the United States and with it a tumultuous white America. Predominantly secured by a white vote, America had elected a man who openly targeted people's freedoms; endorsing a white transphobic, misogynist power who openly targeted the vulnerable within his own political audiences and the American people. A resurgence of whiteness, white power and the re-empowerment of the white American voter resurfaced in America; one rooted in anger and resentment from discontented Republican voters, a diverse class of people who felt cheated of 'their legacy: a bright, white future' (Hughes, 2017).

This was a post-Civil Rights political epoch, where we did not just see institutional controls overtly at work, but we saw white power divulged at the lower levels of society reverting to scaremongering tactics of the segregation era with localized groups mobilizing to threaten and target black minority ethnic voters. It was also one where by the New Right and neoliberal groups had previously appropriated Civil Rights political discourses, evoking empowerment and equality and accused by some of rolling back Civil Rights legislation and policies to aid colour-blind policy and a post-racial ideology; one deemed by some scholars as post-racial or colour-blind racism (Makovsky, 2017) in that it attributes racial inequality to non-racial dynamics such as cultural and biological limitations as opposed to historical enslavement and discrimination (Mullings, 2005).

Makovsky's (2017) coining of white nationalist post-racialism demonstrates this political shift well. Defined as paradoxical politics of the twenty first century; they define this term as a white resentment whose exponents aim to re-claim America for white Americans, whilst paradoxically denying ideological investment in white supremacy. Subsequently, Trump's America embodies an implosion in national identity politics, where racial identity specifically has been pushed to the forefront and the political sphere has become a black/white binary mirroring America's dominant and enforcing racial spectrum; this is backed by an establishment that counteracts BLM as a global movement; spear-headed by the anti-globalist and anti-immigrant leader convivial to white nationalist rhetoric.

An Epoch of Hate

The FBI Uniform Crime Reporting (UCR) program's 2016 hate crime statistics show a five per cent increase from the year 2015-16 with a total of 6,121 reported criminal incidents (FBI, 2017); 57.5% motivated by race, ethnicity or ancestry, 21.0% religious, 17.7% sexual orientation, with remaining incidents motivated by gender identity, disability and gender.

Trump's stance on perpetrators of terrorism as people of colour; attributed to anti-Islam and anti-Muslim sentiments in comparison to white terrorists and government policies against the black right to protest, organisations and activists have been consistently identified; most notably in the failure of the President to denounce and condemn Virginia white supremacists in the case of Charlottesville where a car ploughed into counter protestors at an organised white nationalist rally in opposition to the removal of the statue of Confederate general, Robert E Lee, killing one person dead (Jacobs and Murray, 2017).

This is in addition to an increase in mass shootings committed by white perpetrators; the most recent that of the First Baptist Church, Sutherland springs, where 26 people were gunned down by Devin Patrick Kelley and the Harvard Music Festival; 58 people were killed by Stephen Paddock who fired from the 32nd window of the Mandalay Bay Resort and Casino in Las Vegas. Reinforcement of these attacks of white terrorism of cases attributed to mental health issues as opposed to America's growing gun crisis and gun legislation (Shapiro, 2017) is in stark contrast to that of BLM; added to the FBI's terror watch list and the dedicated surveillance of black organised activism and activists declaring 'black identity extremists a violent threat and motivated to the targeting of law enforcement officers (FBI, 2017).'

Internationalisation

One media sensation that has taken both the US and Europe by storm since the Iraq war has been the concept of terrorism which has been a contributing factor to the evoking of racial hate against ethnic minorities, has driven stereotypes and swayed public opinion to be anti-immigrant and anti-refugees.

Social media has become a method of information, consumption and mobilization resulting in a demonstrable shift in power-play and the development of a collective consciousness for Blacks that adopts the movement's strategy as a cultural process. (Black Liberation Movement, Murdoch, 2016). Primary video material pertaining black injustice becomes a localised safeguarding measure and method to enforce accountability.Throughout the emergence and disappearance of periodic hashtags, #BLM has remained and from this has developed into a trans-national, socio-political movement for Black people and this is mostly attributed to the fact that it puts the issue of systemic racism at the forefront (Weedston 2014).

Taylor (2016) writes the advent of social media has almost erased the lag between when an incident happens and when the public becomes aware of it, time and geographical barriers are removed. The case of #BLM demonstrates not only a significant shift in the sharing and consumption of news but arguably as a multimedia platform operating with more freedom for social engagement, determined by the sharing of news being preliminarily in the control of the user. To some extent, it could be argued that for social movements in favour of oppressed minorities, social media is a necessity to the survival of a social movement as opposed to facing definitive barriers determined from an elite agenda (Noam Chomsky's Filters of Bias) which mainstream media operates within.

Co-founder of Black Lives Matter Toronto, Janaya Khan (2015) states that:

...the reach of anti-black racism is not confined to the borders of North America. Black Lives Matter has become a transformative outlet for all black people from different historical, cultural, socioeconomic and political identities. It is a source of solidarity for the survivors of colonization, exploitation, capitalism and police brutality.

The hashtag's international relevance and momentum has developed from its use in other international social media campaigns and as political identification with other oppressed groups such as #Palestine2Ferguson, connecting the murders of Palestinians in Gaza to the suffering of blacks in the US (Khan, 2015). The resonance of BLM was further reinforced in Ethiopia when the Israeli police attacked a member of the Israeli army highlighting 'anti-black racist discrimination' against Ethiopians living in Israel. This protest became affiliated to the #BLM movement, with Ethiopian Jews demanding an end to discrimination and police brutality in Israel.

White supremacist society has not only been challenged within a social and political context, but an environmental one too; solidarity for the cause was also demonstrated at The annual United Nations climate summit in Lima, Peru, with the 'climate-justice movement to symbolically join the increasingly global #BLM uprising staging a "die-in" outside the convention center much like the ones that have brought shopping malls and busy intersections to a standstill, from the US to the UK' (Klein, 2014).

To some, the reasons as to why this is the case, in places such as the UK does not seem so apparent, statistics show that police in the UK have reportedly shot four people fatally in 2016 compared to 957 in the US (Mortimer, 2017).The BLM movement is at the conjunction of acute events and historical construction of racial oppression or colonial history, as American, British and French examples show (Tharoor, 2016). The following section explores the internationalisation and re-contextualisation of the movement in two European countries.

THE RECEPTION OF BLACK LIVES MATTER IN EUROPE

To illustrate the diversity of #BLM reception, it appeared relevant to assess the responsivity to #BLM in two other structurally different but historically related Western countries. The colonial history (Cooper, 1996) and current structural differences between the French assimilative model and UK multiculturalist are well documented (Favell, 2001; Bertaux, 2016). Both models provide different social structures leading to different social treatments of migration (Freeman, 2015), integration of cultures and faith (Brahm-Levey & Modood, 2009; Durham, 2015). Each case study focuses on ethnic and discrimination statistics to contextualise the relevance of #BLM, then analyse its public reception and media coverage.

United Kingdom

Ethnic Statistics

To provide a clearer picture of ethnic statistics within the UK, we can refer to the ethnic demographic data from the 2011 census (Office for National Statistics, 2012a). According to the official report, the population was 56.1 million people. The statistical breakdown was as follows, White: 86.0%, Mixed/Multiple Ethnic Groups: 2.2%, Asian/ Asian British: 7.5%, Black, African/ Caribbean/ Black British: 3.3% and Other Ethnic Groups: 1.0%

In relation to specific regions of the UK and to provide an overview of ethnic demographics of the UK, the key relevant findings (2012a) were as follows:

- The most ethnically diverse region within the UK was London (2012a: 2) and contained the highest proportion of ethnic minority groups at 3.4 percent and White at 59.8 percent (2012a:7). London had above average quantities for minority groups which included African (7.0%), Indian (6.6%), Caribbean (4.2%) and other whites (12.6%), (2012a:7). This was followed by the West Midlands; the second most diverse region, which also had a higher than average of minority ethnic groups including Pakistani (4.1%), Indian (3.9%) Caribbean (1.5%) and a lower average regarding White ethnic groups (82.7%) including White British (79.2%) (2012a:7).
- In addition, relating to international migrants, the top ten local authority areas with the highest proportion of residents born outside of the UK (2012b: 15) were in London.
- The White majority ethnic group accounted for 86.0 percent (48.2 million), of this White British was the largest group at 80.5 percent (45.1 million), (2012a:2)
- Wales was found to be the least diverse area in the UK (2012a:2) followed by the South West and North East (2012a:7). The report highlights that 95% of the population in these areas identified as White.

The population of people belonging to Black groups according to statistics provided in the 2011 census would accumulate to just over 1.8 million people (mixed/multiple ethnic groups not included).

Minorities and Police Discrimination in UK

Since 1990, there has been 171 Black, Asian and Minority Ethnic (BAME) deaths in police custody or following contact with police, including 16 shootings, 155 deaths in custody and 493 deaths in prison within England and Wales (INQUEST, 2017). These include ten unlawful killing verdicts returned by juries at inquests however to date, from the point of monitoring; there have been no successful murder or manslaughter prosecutions of government agents involved in a death in police custody (this includes deaths resulting from police contact or deaths occurring whilst in prison). Restraint, use of force and mental health related issues are dominating features of deaths in custody and two times more likely to be a contributing factor in BAME cases. The research documents levels of racial disparity in relation to white counterparts and raises the issue of institutional racism as a contributing factor.

Although critics argue that the UK remains dissimilar to the USA regarding criminal justice, independent research (Prison Reform Trust, 2017) concluded that BAME groups are considerably over-represented within the prison system: prisoners are 10% Black and 6% Asian, which is significantly different from the general population of 2.8%. Overall, authors suggest Black prisoners account for the largest number of minority ethnic prisoners at 49% and add that at the end of June in 2014, 28% of minority ethnic prisoners were foreign nationals. The official statement comments that according to the Equality and Human Rights Commission, there is now greater disproportionality in the number of Black people in prisons in the UK than in the United States.

This can be explained by a racial bias in police stop and searches. The Institute of Race Relations (IRR, 2011) found that people from BAME groups are more likely than whites to be stopped and searched by police in the UK:

...police were 28 times more likely to use 'Section 60' stop-and-search powers (where officers do not require suspicion of the person having been involved in a crime) against Black people than White people. In the year 2013-2014, 59% of people stopped under Section 60 by London's Metropolitan Police Service were either Black British or Asian British.

BAME groups are still two times more likely to be stopped and searched by police; for Black people, specifically, this rises to 4.2 times the rate of white people (Stopwatch, 2016). In 2014, blacks were four times more likely to be arrested than whites were. A retrospective study of over a million court records suggested prison sentences were more likely for a black offender than a white one (44%more likely for driving offences, 38% for public order offences or possession of a weapon, 27% for possession of drugs (IRR, n.d.)

As Athwal and Burnett (2014) investigated, biases are also found in lack of legal enforcement. There have been 93 known or suspected racially motivated deaths since the death of Steven Lawrence in 1999 (preceded by the Macpherson report). They argue 'the racially motivated aspect of cases is being filtered out by the police, the CPS and the judiciary' often leaving families of victims to challenge police decisions and mobilising the media to exert pressure into recognition of the racial element (IRR, 2014).

Additionally, in a report on racial violence (IRR, 2013) in the UK, Burnett (2013) identifies that in 2011/12 there were more than 37,000 racial or religious recorded aggravated crimes, no longer predominantly found in 'urban centres' which bare a historic association. The impact of pauperisation in areas with little to no history of diversity is pointed out (IRR press release, 2013).

Disempowerment arises also from the inability to access the criminal justice system and trigger legal proceedings. The Report of the Independent Review of Deaths and Serious Incidents in Police Custody (Lindon & Roe, 2017) commissioned by Prime Minister, Theresa May highlighted a number of inequalities within the current system. These included i) imbalances within the coronial process due to family of the deceased having no automatic right to funding for legal representation despite different branches of the state having access to senior legal representation throughout the process (2017, p. 13), as well as ii) the vulnerability of individuals suffering mental health issues and the proficiency and use of NHS services in these cases as opposed to police custody (2017, p. 16).

Post EU referendum has seen an increase in racially motivated hate crimes with reports to police increasing by 42%, more than 3,000 allegations of hate crime were made across the UK in the week before and the week after the vote (Dodd, 2016). Although it is important to note that these racial experiences were encountered by a variety of people of mixed ethnicities including that of Eastern-Europeans; distinct attributions to the image of that of a refugee or immigrant were reinforced by the mainstream press that were attributed to 'blackness'. As far back as 2013, Nagarajan explored mainstream media's 'anti-immigrant rhetoric as common public opinion. Trans-national histories become lost in a country where by Black-British history is disregarded.

Organisations such as the English Defence League and right wing political parties such as the British National Party (BNP), United Kingdom Independence Party (UKIP) and some members of the Conservative Party, have powered this 'anti-British' concept. These public backers of the 'Leave Campaign', figure-headed by Nigel-Farage and Boris Johnson led a racist, anti-immigration campaign endorsing political tactics that used refugees as political targets.

Post-Brexit poses a risk to the British judicial process with regards to BAME rights and protections with the process currently enshrined and protected by Article 2 of the *European Convention on Human Rights*, which imposes a procedural obligation on the UK 'to conduct an active, impartial, independent and prompt investigation into deaths for which the State might be responsible. This Article also forms one of the Convention rights incorporated in the Human Rights Act 1998' (2017, p. 12). The UKs intention to scrap the human rights Act 1998 and Britain's sanctioning of Article 50 to withdraw as a member of the European Union means that the ramifications on legal proceedings and people's rights remain unknown and in a stagnant state of legal and societal vulnerability.

Seminal UK Case: Mark Duggan and the London Riots

On 4thAugust 2011, the shooting of Mark Duggan, an unarmed black man in Tottenham, London, initiated social unrest and racial tension across the country. This act triggered what is now known as 'The London Riots' which saw the spreading of rioting across the London boroughs and the continuation across the main major cities within the UK.

Starting on August 4, 2011, the riots saw thousands of people take to the streets up and down the country. The protest, which began peacefully involving 300 members of the community at Tottenham police station quickly turned into violence resulting from a confrontation between a teenager and the police (BBC, 2011). The first night saw 49 primary fires, looting, violence and clashes with police. Over the next week, two police stations were set on fire, major shopping centres were targeted and five deaths were being investigated. Across the country, 1436 arrests had been made by forces and as of August 12, 2011, 838 people had been charged (BBC, 2011). In London, Solihull and Manchester, courts stayed open throughout the night to fast track those in custody for disorder related offences (BBC, 2011).

BLM UK Today

On July 15th 2016, the official Twitter account was established for Black Lives Matter UK, the first post being "We are #BlackLivesMatterUK. In Solidarity with our black family all over the world fighting against racist violence. Join us. Follow us" (@ UKBLM, posted 2016, July 15). In addition to this introductory post, early tweets relate to US events and re-tweets from prominent US Black media organisations. Alternatively, media organisations and twitter users with articles or information on race-related issues in the UK have used this as a platform to tweet @BLMUK, with latest research and news pieces directly communicating with UKBLM's following.

In the Statement of Solidarity with the UK, the message from Black Lives Matter was "We send you solidarity, as we see Mzee Mohammed. We see Sarah Reed, we see Jermaine Baker, the 1,558 people killed by police in the UK and your struggle to gain justice for them…" (@BLMUK, 2016, July 16). The March *Justice for Mohammed*, 2016, July 17, held in protest to the death of the 18 year old who died in police custody in Liverpool after being restrained by Merseyside officers at a shopping centre.

The death of Mohammed sparked BLM protests in London and Liverpool (Bulman, 2016). Traynor (2016) for the Liverpool Echo reported, "The movement, currently sweeping America and the UK - with demonstrations throughout the country since the fatal shootings of Philando Castile and Alton Sterling by police officers in the

USA - came to Merseyside this afternoon. Cries of "Black Lives Matter, Mzee's Life Mattered" were shouted out as the march snaked through the city centre." The London march in the capital the next day coincided with the BLM rally in Melbourne Australia, highlighting the treatment of Aboriginal Australians.

BLMUK have circulated numerous Black cases of injustice ranging from Leon Patterson (1992), Errol McGowan (1999), Sean Rigg (2008) and Mark Duggan (2011) which continue to hold precedence for the fight for black rights evident in the more recent killings of Jermaine Baker (2015), professional footballer, Dalian Atkinson (2016) and Rashan Charles (2017).

Since the launch of UKBLM on Twitter, like the BLM in the USA, the group has mirrored an intersectional formation with the creation of localised UKBLM Facebook groups for each specific region, as are the American chapters.

In August 2016, UKBLM organised a nationwide #shutdown across the UK preceding the march *Tottenham Remembers* to mark the five-year anniversary of the killing of Mark Duggan. The shutdown included marches and rallies in Manchester (estimated at 3000 people by Pidd, 2016), Birmingham, Nottingham, Bristol and London, involving the shutdown of tramlines and road blockades throughout the city. A rally in London was led by the mother of Sean Riggs who died in police custody in 2008, after being restrained.

The organisation tweeted: #BlackLivesMatterUK @ukblm, Aug 5 "This morning we #Shutdown major transport hubs because the conventional avenues to justice have been shutdown to us". (@UKBLM, posted 2016, Aug 5)

As well as larger scale protests across major cities, local rallies for UKBLM have also taken place, most prominently on the issue of immigration and brought the attention to the treatment of migrants; with specific focus on the case of Luqman Onikosi where students did a sit in at Sussex University. Onikosi was an international student fighting deportation on the grounds no treatment for Hepatitis B was available in his country and would result in death. He eventually had his degree cancelled by the institution and was deported by the UK home office (Lentin, 2016).

One BLM protest in the UK that has created controversy has been the shutdown of London City Airport where nine environmental activists staged a protest under the BLM banner. The group faced public criticism for being a predominantly White group and were accused by anti-racist campaigners of being "white left-wing activists hijacking the Black Lives Matter banner" (Grierson, 2016). Whilst this was one perception of public opinion circulated by the mainstream, other organisations used the opportunity to inform the public on how climate change has a disproportionate effect on black people globally; re-affirmed as a 'racist crisis', by UKBLM activist, Kelbert (2016). Whilst these responses can be gauged as a reflection of mainstream media, there has not been enough research done into how people have engaged with

UKBLM other than levels of physical engagement in active protests and social media metrics i.e. number of likes and followers, given above.

Additionally, collaboration between BLM and other movements has become precedent, the United Families and Friends Campaign (UFFC) annual march was promoted by BLMUK and by use of #BLM in conjunction with its news sharing of prominent deaths in custody and police killings on all of its social media platforms.

France

The French system is marked by a form of idealism, in its conception of society and identity (Favell, 2001). Indeed, the egalitarian aspiration and memories of previous labelling led to decades of a national policy preventing any ethnic and religious statistics from the state (Spire & Merllié, 1999), and so was the legal decision to ban the word race from any official documents in 2015. However, as the end of separate but equal doctrine in the USA, structural and legal equality is theoretical and differs from a social reality sometimes in denial or unable to accept its history (Nidiaye, 2008). If race can be thought of as construction to impose power, the ideal of a colour-blind French system fails to address discrimination and stigma related to cultural and ethnic background or skin-colours (Begag, 2016).

Ethnic Statistics

So far, the French system is aware of its discrepancies. On the one hand, at the structural level, banning the word race from the constitution was a symbolic attempt to promote an egalitarian ideal. On the other hand, facing reality, civil society finds ways to fight against discrimination based on ethnicity, religion or any other label. Indeed, civil society institutionalised the equality promotion through non-governmental organisations (e.g. SOS Racisme) but also consultative community groups (e.g. Representative Council of Black Associations of France - CRAN) and state-funded agency (The National Consultative Commission of Human Rights - NCCHR).

French National Institute of Statistics and Economic Studies (INSEE, 2015) do not report ethnic or religious backgrounds of the French population. However, surveys and other research could provide an estimation through side approaches. Beauchemin et al (2010a, 2010b) estimate that 10% of the people living in France are migrants, 12% of people living in France are direct descendants of at least one migrant. Main countries or areas of origin are Northern Africa with more than a million people (Morocco, Algeria, Tunisia), European Union with more than a million people, Sahel and Central Africa with over 350 000 people, other areas include Turkey,

South Asia and other countries. If these statistics provide an overview of origins, no information can be deduced regarding either ethnic or religious background, even less, on how people identify.

In the same national survey (Beauchemin, Lagrange and Safi, 2011), one-third of interviewees agreed to the statement that "to be accepted in France you have to forget your origins". Authors interpret this as a reflection of the assimilationist idea and ideal therefore questioning the sense and possibility of transnational practices.

In 2006, the Representative Council of Black Associations commissioned the first poll including self-reported ethnic data to investigate experience of discrimination (CRAN, 2007); for the first time how people identify was investigated. Main categories and distribution were as follows: not belonging to any visible ethnic minority 90%, Black 3.2%, Arabo-Berber 3.2%, Mixed 1.4%, Asian 0.5%, Indian-Pakistani 0.2 and other 1%. It has been estimated that approximately 4% (including people identifying as mixed with one Black descent) over 1.8 million people, of the French population is black. 57% of the Black respondents do report experiencing discrimination. This discrimination occurs for 62% in public space or transportation and ranges from disrespectful attitude to actual violence. 61% of the Black people have reported a discriminatory event within the past twelve months. This alarming number is amplified by the very slow proportion of people engaging in legal recourse or in taking action. Other studies specified the different types of discrimination, notably regarding employment (SOS Racisme, 2016)

Minorities and Police Discrimination in France

The survey on racism (NCCHR, 2016) showed that anti-Muslim acts more than tripled and racist acts increased to 17.5% in 2015 compared to the previous year. Specific scopes also analysed anti-Semitic and anti-Romany acts. However, this refers to the analysis of justice statistics and seems far from the daily experiences of discrimination. Official statistics show an increase in the number of complaints against the police, but it is residual.

Nevertheless, the past decade saw the rise of media coverage and press releases related to police violence. One of the most prominent cases was the death of two young boys (one French-Black and one French-Arab) aged 15 and 17, who were chased by the police and hiding close to an electric substation were electrocuted and died. The teenagers were chased after information of a robbery and fled when seeing the police. This event was the trigger of French Riots in 2005 and led to the systematic focus on police officers. At the time and contingent to the riots, social reaction blamed the police. Families of the victims filed against the police but after a decade of legal procedures the sense of justice and the legal accountability of police officers remains uncertain.

This event is very similar to the UK and the USA ones, in the fact that it led to riots denouncing the ghettoization and the social inequalities suffered by the suburban population. Similarly to the UK, at the time, the lower classes and poorest people were at the heart of the French riots.

Seminal French Case: Adama Traore

From the very beginning, #BLM movement has been spread and supported in France. Discrimination of minorities and police violence has been recognised and has led to general emotional reaction and condemnation; however, it did not relegate the movement. Adama Traore died in police custody after being chased and arrested. The autopsy revealed he died of asphyxia.

This event and the secrecy around the autopsy, the absence of any criminal record gave the media grounds to question the relevance and the possibility of a French Black Lives Matter (Zappi, 2016). The first protest in the name of the BLM movement occurred on July 2, 2016, in Paris (Citiletti, 2016). Families of up to then forgotten cases joined the march. This march is the symbolic date of a French chapter of the BLM movement with the actual website http://blmfrance.com/. After this first protest, journalists started documenting more comprehensively and re-inspecting previous tragedies, such as the death of Babacar Gueye. In December 2015, the 27-year-old man, who was living undocumented in Rennes was shot with five bullets. Police invoked his aggressiveness to justify the shooting but it appeared the man was having a panic attack and dealing with mental health issues.

Indeed, the Adama Traore case highlights the French discrepancies and newspaper coverage reflects an international scope. Interestingly, French newspapers released foreign criticisms and reference to the BLM movement in the press seems to alert on police impunity (Gauthier-Faure, 2016).

During the spring and summer 2016, Facebook pages of BLM France (Facebook page and timeline can be tracked back to July 29) and BLM Paris started launching protest marches in different cities. The delocalisation of the protests to small cities, such as Bordeaux shows the concern and mobilisation out of the capital quite early on. If the number of followers on the BLM France Facebook page remains low (less than a thousand) mobilisation and media coverage shows a higher number of shares, re-tweets and global agreement.

Other events, such as the case of Theo L., a 22-year-old Black French young man who had an altercation that degenerated into a fight with four policemen. The four police officers were later charged, three of them for assault and last one for rape. The rape charge was abandoned and the four police officers were convicted for assault. This could have been the breeding ground for the rise of the BLM movement in France. Instead, it led to a social movement against police brutality and institutional investigations. The scarcity of studies on this topic raises concerns; however, French system tends to support initiatives from the civil society.

In October 2016, the first French Black Newspapers was launched, as an official response to this lack of visibility and representation in the public space and medias. Again, it seems that the social structure requires local adjusted means to reach an equality, awareness and visibility goal. The remaining question is can the #BLM movement translate into social action (McAuley, 2016) in the French context? If so, the next question is will it be a #BLM movement or a #ALM movement incorporating all discriminated minorities and fitting the colour-blind French system?

CRITICAL ANALYSIS: SHOCK WAVE, GLOBALISATION AND ADVOCACY

The power of social media is encapsulated in its ability to bypass professional journalism and sees activists able to use their own media production to mobilize the people. The circulation of visual footage has also challenged racial stereotypes and has 'erased the imaginary line between "respectability politics" - the concept that if black people are upstanding they won't experience racism and the lived experiences of black people; destroying the myth that black lives worth protecting are those of moral citizens' (Thrasher, 2015).

On a trans-national scale in relation to the BLM movement globalisation becomes about the globalised identification of being 'Black' and as well as identification with social and economic disparities, solidarity becomes also an acknowledgement of cultural hegemony across borders linked by historical references to colonization and enslavement. From a cultural perspective, trans-national relations between Blacks are further strengthened by the historic relevance to previous conquests, of which, are re-affirmed by the BLM movement, in this case through visual imagery. Take for example the Pan-African flag used in protest; this holds cultural resonance for all Africans but within a national context, for British-Blacks and French-Blacks, reflects the national significance for the movement for Blacks within the UK and France through historic association with the Pans-national congress.

Social Media Statistics and Impact

The increased usage of the smartphone worldwide has broadened possibilities of mobile social networks and this has been attributed to the development of location-based services (Statista, n.d.) Facebook is the leading social network worldwide with 1.71 billion monthly active users followed by Whatsapp and Facebook messenger, each with a billion monthly users. Twitter is 9th leading worldwide with 313 million active users (Statista, 2016). A recent report on the *number of social media network users worldwide 2010-2020* show that in 2016 there were an estimated 2.34 billion users globally; data analysis predicts these figures will increase to 2.67 billion in 2018 and 2.95 billion in 2020 (Statista, n.d.).

Collating statistics on the state of digital, mobile and social media usage on a global scale, there are 2.31 billion active social media users, 31% of the overall population of which 27% of these are mobile social users (We Are Social, 2016). Social media usage was measured around the globe, showing a stark contrast between different regions of the world. North America has the highest level of usage (59%), followed by South America (50%), Western Europe (48%) and Eastern Europe (45%). Regions with the lowest levels of usage included Central Asia (6%), South Asia (11%) and Africa (11%), (We Are Social, 2016).

To highlight the specific countries focused on within this chapter, the percentage of social media use by country were the following, USA (59%), UK (59%) and France (50%), (WAS, 2016).

Currently 59 percent of the United Kingdom have active accounts on social media (this data was specific to the top social networking site in the country, WAS, 2016). On Twitter, Black Lives Matter UK currently has 17.2K followers (Metrics: tweets: 275, following: 261, likes: 66, taken 2016, Sep 29, 18:53 GMT @UKBLM, Twitter).

Take the case of Africa, with a population of just over 1.2 billion, only 349 million are active internet users; 129 million are active social media users (WAS, 2016). One key point that must be paid attention is the BLM movement's principal focus concerning the social position of Blacks and racial injustice within a white supremacy system. Alternatively, to blacks living within these westernised systems, there are a Black population who may not relate to power structures based on a racial hierarchy, but have been exploited by it historically and are affected by it globally in relation to environmental challenges and social economic stability. Can therefore, this trans-national movement advocate a cause that will benefit the poorest of blacks?

Global Integration of Communication Technologies and Distribution of Media

Cole (2015) identifies the three main aspects of globalization as economic, cultural, social and political, which are powered by the following core areas: 'technological development, the global integration of communication technologies and the global distribution of media.'

Globalised advances in technology particularly in the 'smart-era' with the developments of the smart phone has seen a new generation of communicative methods and being connected particularly amongst young people. Technology advances have given us more power, control and access to social networking. All elements combined, ranging from video quality, to internet speed; the development of 4G and in particular the development of 'the app' has made information easier to access and faster to put out and circulate. The ranges of 'like', 'share' and 'tweet' features make accessibility and distribution an extremely fast process that spread quickly amongst online communities. Today often breaking news now comes over the internet first, followed then by TV and newspapers that cover it due to public interest.

This study however, highlighted core barriers in relation to specific varied properties of individual social media platforms (Giglietto, Rossi & Bennato, 2014). Facebook privacy settings can inhibit the circulation of news sharing and further inhibit data analysis of closed groups. On both Facebook and Twitter, originality was a major issue when identifying official BLM affiliated pages. Different variations of the hashtag i.e. #AllBlackLivesMatter led to a varied collation of circulated material; including related news. Variations on the hashtag such as this, although connected to the original hashtag, made search optimisation difficult and socio-behavioural patterns difficult to observe, further study should be done as to the effects on the overall follower demographic of the official organisation.

These advances in technology have benefited the globalised world when it comes to accountability of the state and the establishment and have developed as accessible resources to be used as protective methods. These developments in the modernised world have opened the door for resources to be made for specific groups including the minorities and the marginalised. See the example of the new ACLU Cell phone App, (Wiener, 2015) 'Mobile Justice CA app' which automatically preserves videos of police encounters and geographic information which are directly transmitted to the ACLU, so even if the phone is damaged or destroyed the footage is protected.

Patrice Cullors, the director of the Truth and Reinvestment Campaign at the Ella Baker Center, which is working with the ACLU of California explains:

People who historically have had very little power in the face of law enforcement now have this tool to reclaim their power and dignity, our vision is that this app will ultimately help community members connect and organize to respond to incidents of law enforcement violence, and then share their experiences and knowledge with others.

However, barriers to these developments are founded in state law in the US, to combat this the ACLU affiliates in other states have developed other versions for use in those states: 'residents of New York should use the "Stop and Frisk Watch" app; in New Jersey, it's the "Police Tape" app; in Oregon and Missouri it's the "Mobile Justice" app.' (Wiener, 2015) Arguably globalisation means that technology developments are equipped to be re-developed for each geographic demographic with economic interests vested in both the UK and the US. The constitutional set-up of the US makes this more difficult as unlike the UK which has one governing law, problems arise within different parts of America such as the one in Texas where 'a proposed law would make it a crime for ordinary people to videotape police actions—on the grounds that it was "interference" with police activity. In California, on the other hand, the state senate this month approved legislation providing clear legal protection to people who videotape police activity without interfering with investigations.'

This example displays the different aspects of globalisation on both a technological, economic and political scale and the implications it can present at a local level. But if we look at globalisation as a whole specifically with regards to internet users and social media, there is cause to question as to whether the #BLM can impact social and political change for the poorest people of colour.

Consequences of the Hashtag

Not all black people identify with the hashtag #blacklivesmatter (Freelon, 2016) including younger demographics of black communities. Further studies explore the breakdown of racial categories (Bonilla-Silva, 2004), and unsure Americans regarding the future distribution of power. The study presents the case for racial tension with the hashtag resulting from formal groupings aligned to on the basis of identity politics and in relation to racial categories which have formed on opposing hierarchical notions of race within what England, (2009:198) refers to as 'the logic of the colour continuum'. Although physical protests show a wide demographic of people in attendance, further exploration is needed into how individualised, categorised ethnic groups i.e. Asian, Hispanic, Latino engage with the movement. The movement has received criticism (Morrison, 2015) for its lack of coverage of other ethnic groups. Nevertheless, on a trans-national level the alliances built in the case of #Palestine2Ferguerson did progress interconnected issues of the mistreatment of people of colour across borders.

The strength of the hashtag results from its agility in use as a political statement and as a form of social identification where by Black political groups and organisations under a socially mobile political label, can capture the aims and direct message of a unified socio-political movement. Its durability arises from relevance to mirrored social justice situations and a broad resonance of socio-political issues that affect Black people (McLaughlin, 2016).

CONCLUSION: #BLM IN NON-AMERICAN CONTEXTS – RESPONSIVITY AND RETERRITORIALIZATION

Seen from a social construction approach (Hoberman, 1997; Boulle, 2002; Machery & Faucher, 2005; Steinberg, 1989); deconstructed and demystified by scientific studies (Smedley and Smedley, 2005; Sussman, 2014), race as an empirical concept is erroneous but persists as a social category. The #BLM movement is spreading widely and supported all over the world. However, its embodiment in other countries seems to depend on local contexts, local social constructions of race or ethnicity and social reality of minorities' integration.

Responsivity and the Need for a Similar Case

The French case study showed how police-related violence against minorities is not enough to embrace the cause. Indeed, if African-Americans are an important minority in the USA, historically, France has a different migration history. Moreover, terrorist attacks endured since 2015 has led to the social targeting of Arab descendants and Muslim people more than the Black community. This led to the social responsivity to what is perceived as a cold-blooded killing, as an unfair and evitable drama. Adama Traore is (rightly) becoming an archetype of the innocent, victim of a suspicious system, discriminatory state and authoritarian state.

Reterritorialization, Embodiment, and Reframing

A dominating ideal amongst Western countries has been the 'post-racial' one, whether through 'colour-blindness' as evidenced in the French system or the multiculturalist British or American ones. Currently, in these systems, nationalist ideals arise and with them a new form of White superiority. Nationalism counteracts with globalisation and reinforces the idea of an elite power structure (Sabanadze, 2010). BLM is a decentralized network with a grouping of local chapters including members from all different communities, which reflects the idea of the local first.

Regarding the French context, events are too recent to enable any interpretation. Nevertheless, the re-contextualisation of the movement in the UK shows an interesting becoming. The struggle and oppression is worse for the lower classes/ poorer people. Historically, within the UK, Black rights have been tied to working class movements. This explains why not only Black people protest against the establishment, but Whites too.

It is an example of how, counterintuitively, even ordinary white people have an interest in exposing the racist nature of US society, because doing so legitimizes the demand for an expansive and robust regime of social welfare intended to redistribute wealth and resources from the rich back to the working-class—Black, Brown and white. Conversely, it is also why the political and economic elites have such a vested interest in colorblindness and in the perpetuation of the myth that the United States is a meritocracy (Taylor, 2016).

Using the hashtag is to make a political statement. As a form of social identification under a political label Black groups and organisations can send the key and direct message of a holistic socio-political movement. From a trans-national perspective, the same capitalist system is mirrored within Europe, magnifying comparable social issues that in conjunction, oppress Blacks within that system and is embedded within key institutional elements such as politics, education and criminal justice.

One of the consequences of BLM in relation to global struggles is the perpetuated definition of racism as one confined in a black/white schema of racism; a reflection of America's racial history and structure. How then can BLM advocate for those affected by other racisms such as ethnic cleansing, religious and cultural persecution, committed by distinctive groups amongst people of colour that sit beyond the boundaries of a social reality constructed within black-white terms? Racism is a global phenomenon, with a diverse and ever-changing form (Castle, 2000). Subsequently, BLM becomes, in part, a paradox: pertaining to advocate for Black people in different national and demographical contexts whilst simultaneously reinforcing a restrictive narrative of oppression, which was created for the rights and citizens that lay within the boundaries of a Westernised context.

REFERENCES

Aboud, F. E. (2003). The formation of in-group favoritism and out-group prejudice in young children: Are they distinct attitudes? *Developmental Psychology*, *39*(1), 48–60. doi:10.1037/0012-1649.39.1.48 PMID:12518808

Allport, G. W. (1954). *The nature of prejudice*. Cambridge, MA: Addison-Wesley.

Anderson, M., & Hitlin, P. (2016). *Social Media Conversations About Race*. New York: Pew Research Center.

Athwal, H., & Burnett, J. (2014). Investigated or ignored? An analysis of race-related deaths since the Macpherson Report. *Race & Class*, *56*(1), 22–42. doi:10.1177/0306396814531694

Balkaran, S. (2015, May 27). Post Racial America in the Age of Obama. The Huffington Post. Retrieved September 27, 2016, from http://www.huffingtonpost.com

BBC. (2011). England riots: Maps and timeline. Retrieved from http://www.bbc.co.uk

Beauchemin, C., Borrel, C., & Régnard, C. (2010b). Migrations : Les immigrés et les autres. In P. Simon, C. Beauchemin, & C. Hamel, (Eds.), Trajectoires et Origines. Enquête sur la diversité des populations en France. Premiers résultats (Ch. 2). Paris: Institut national d'études démographiques, pp 19-24.

Beauchemin, C., Hamel, C., Simon, P., & Equipe Te, O. (2010a). *Trajectoires et origines : enquête sur la diversité des populations en France. Premiers résultats.* Paris: Institut National d'Études Démographiques.

Beauchemin, C., Lagrange, H., & Safi, M. (2011). *Transnationalism and immigrant assimilation in France: Between here and there?* Paris: HAL et INED.

Begag, A. (2016). La France en panne d'intégration. *Contemporary French Civilization*, *41*(2), 273–277. doi:10.3828/cfc.2016.14

Bertaux, S. (2016). Towards the unmaking of the French mainstream: The empirical turn in immigrant assimilation and the making of Frenchness. *Journal of Ethnic and Migration Studies*, *42*(9), 1496–1512. doi:10.1080/1369183X.2015.1119651

Bonilla, Y., & Rosa, J. (2015). # Ferguson: Digital protest, hashtag ethnography, and the racial politics of social media in the United States. *American Ethnologist*, *42*(1), 4–17. doi:10.1111/amet.12112

Bonilla-Silva, E. (2004). From bi-racial to tri-racial: Towards a new system of racial stratification in the USA. *Ethnic and Racial Studies*, *27*(6), 931–950. doi:10.1080/0141987042000268530

Boulle, P. H. (2002). La construction du concept de race dans la France d'Ancien Régime. *Outre-mers*, *89*(336/337), 155–175. doi:10.3406/outre.2002.3987

Brahm Levey, G., & Modood, T. (2009). *Secularism, Religion and Multicultural Citizenship.* Cambridge: Cambridge University Press.

Brand, E. S., Ruiz, R. A., & Padilla, A. M. (1974). Ethnic identification and preference: A review. *Psychological Bulletin*, *81*(11), 860–890. doi:10.1037/h0037266

Breindl, Y. (2010). Internet-based protest in European policymaking: The case of digital activism. *International Journal of E-Politics*, *1*(1), 57–72. doi:10.4018/jep.2010102204

Brown v. Board of Education of Topeka, 347 U.S. 483, 74 S. Ct. 686; 98 L. Ed. 873. (1954).

Bulman, M. (2016). Death of black teenager detained by police sparks Black Lives Matter protests in UK cities. *The Independent*. Retrieved from http://www.independent.co.uk

Burnett, J. (2013). *Racial Violence: Facing Reality*. London: Institute of Race Relations.

Caleffi, P. M. (2015). The 'hashtag': A new word or a new rule? *Skase Journal of Theoretical Linguistics, 13*(2).

Campbell, K. K. (2005). Agency: Promiscuous and prote-an. *Communication and Critical/Cultural Studies*, *2*(1). doi:10.1080/1479142042000332134

Cashmore, E., & McLaughlin, E. (Eds.). (1991). *Out of Order: Policing Black People*. Routledge.

Castelliti, C. (2016, July 24). Reportage au cœur de la première manifestation "Black Lives Matter France. *Les Inrocks.* Retrieved from http://www.lesinrocks.com/2016/07/24/actualite/reportage-coeur-de-manifestation-black-live-matter-france-11855472/

Castles, S. (2000). *Ethnicity and globalization: From migrant worker to transnational citizen*. London: Sage.

Cockerham, C. (2011). The defining moment: Children's conceptualization of race and experiences with racial discrimination. *Ethnic and Racial Studies*, *34*(4), 662–682. doi:10.1080/01419870.2011.535906 PMID:21532908

Cole, N. (2015).h What is Globalization, A Sociological Definition: About Education. Retrieved from: http://sociology.about.com/od/Ask-a-Sociologist/fl/Globalization.htm

Cooper, F. (1996). *Decolonization and African society: The labor question in French and British Africa*. Cambridge University Press. doi:10.1017/CBO9780511584091

CRAN. (2007). Les discriminations à l'encontre des populations noires de France (short report). Retrieved from le-cran.fr/document-cran-associations-noires-de-france/63-tns-sofres-premiere-enquete-statistique-sur-les-noirs-de-france.pdf

Daniel, P. (1973). *The Shadow of Slavery: Peonage in the South, 1901-1969*. London, Oxford: Oxford University Press.

Daniel, P. (1979). The Metamorphosis of Slavery, 1865-1900. *The Journal of American History*, *66*(1), 88–99. doi:10.2307/1894675

De Choudhury, M., Jhaver, S., Sugar, B., & Weber, I. (2016). Social Media Participation in an Activist Movement for Racial Equality. AAAI In (Ed.), *Proceedings of the Tenth International AAAI Conference on Web and Social Media* (pp. 92-101).

Dodd, V. (2016). Police blame worst rise in recorded hate crime on EU referendum: The Guardian. Retrieved September 20, 2016 from https://www.theguardian.com

Durham, C. W. (Ed.). (2015). *Religion and the Secular State*. Madrid: International Center for Law and Religion Studies, Universidad Complutense.

England, S. (2010). Mixed and multiracial in Trinidad and Honduras: Rethinking mixed-race identities in Latin America and the Caribbean. *Ethnic and Racial Studies*, *33*(2), 195–213. doi:10.1080/01419870903040169

Favell, A. (2001). Philosophies of Integration. Immigration and the Idea of Citizenship in France and Britain (2nd ed.), New York: Palgrave in association with Centre for Research in Ethnic Relations, University of Warwick. doi:10.1057/9780333992678

FBI. (2016). Hate Crime Statistics: Criminal Justice Information Services Division: Government website. Retrieved November 22, 2017 from https://www.fbi.gov/news/stories/2016-hate-crime-statistics

FBI. (2017, August 3) Black Identity Extremists Likely Motivated to Target Law Enforcement Officer. Counterterrorism Division, Government report: Retrieved November 22, 2017 fromhttps://assets.documentcloud.org/documents/4067711/BIE-Redacted.pdf

Franklin, S. M. (2014). *After the rebellion: Black youth, social movement activism, and the post-civil rights generation*. NYU Press. doi:10.18574/nyu/9780814789384.001.0001

Freelon, D., McIlwain, C. D., & Clarke, M. D. (2016). *Beyond The Hashtags: #Ferguson, #Blacklivesmatter and the online struggle for offline justice*. Washington, DC: Centre for Media & Social Impact. American University.

Freeman, G. P. (2015). *Immigrant labor and racial conflict in industrial societies: The French and British experience, 1945-1975*. Princeton University Press.

Gauthier-Faure, M. (2016, July 31). Mort d'Adama Traoré: le New York Times dénonce l'impunité de la police française. Retrieved from http://www.marianne.net/mort-adama-traore-new-york-times-denonce-impunite-police-francaise-100244747.html

Giglietto, F. A., Rossi, L., & Bennato, D. (2014). The Open Laboratory: Limits and Possibilities of Using Facebook, Twitter, and Youtube as a Research Data Source. In K. Bredl, J. Hunniger, & J. L. Jensen (Eds.), *Methods for Analyzing Social Media* (pp. 5–19). London, New York: Routledge.

Goffman, E. (1963). *Stigma: Notes on the management of spoiled identity*. London: Pelican Books.

Grierson, J. (2016). Black Lives Matter activists admit trespass after City airport protest. Retrieved from, https://www.theguardian.com

Groves, H. E. (1951). Separate but Equal--The Doctrine of Plessy v. Ferguson. *Phylon, 12*(1), 66–72. doi:10.2307/272323

Hoberman, J. M. (1997). *Darwin's Athletes: How Sport has Damaged Black America and Preserved the Myth of Race*. Boston: Houghton Mifflin Co.

Ibahrine, M. (2017). Women Hashtactivism: Civic Engagement in Saudi Arabia. *World Academy of Science, Engineering and Technology. International Journal of Information and Communication Engineering, 11*(3), 79.

INQUEST. (2017). BAME deaths in police custody. Retrieved from http://inquest.org.uk/statistics/bame-deaths-in-police-custody

IRR. (2013). Facing up to racial violence. Retrieved September from http://www.irr.org.uk/news/facing-up-to-racial-violence/

IRR. (2014). Investigated or ignored? Press Release. Retrieved from http://www.irr.org.uk/news/investigated-or-ignored/

IRR. (n.d.). Criminal justice system statistics. Retrieved from http://www.irr.org.uk/research/statistics/criminal-justice/

Jacobs, B., & Murray, W. (2017, August 13) Donald Trump under fire after failing to denounce Virginia white supremacists. *The Guardian*. Retrieved November 22, 2017 from www.theguardian.com

Jansen, F. (2010). Digital activism in the Middle East: Mapping issue networks in Egypt, Iran, Syria and Tunisia. *Knowledge Management for Development Journal, 6*(1), 37–52. doi:10.1080/19474199.2010.493854

Jausset, J. S. (2016, Aug 8). France: abattu par la police, Babacar Guèye a été accusé de tentative de meurtre par deux des policiers. Jeune Afrique http://www.jeuneafrique.com/346546/societe/abattu-par-police-babacar-gueye-accuse-de-tentative-de-meurtre/

Jones, A., & Lobianco, T. (2016, September 5). Obama: Colin Kaepernick 'exercising constitutional right'. *CNN*. Retrieved from http://edition.cnn.com

Kelbert, A. W. (2016). Climate change is a racist crisis: that's why Black Lives Matter closed an airport. *The Guardian*. Retrieved from https://www.theguardian.com

Khan, J. (2015). Black Lives Matter has become a global movement. The root. Retrieved from: https://www.theroot.com

Klein, N. (2014) Why #BlackLivesMatter Should Transform the Climate Debate. *The Nation*. Retrieved September 5, 2016 from: https://www.thenation.com

Lentin, A. (2016) Luqman Onikosi's deportation shows we are all being asked to become border guards. *The Guardian*. Retrieved from, https://www.theguardian.com

Lindon, G., & Roe, S. (2017). *Deaths in police custody: A review of the international evidence. Research Report 95*. London: Home Office, Crown Copyright.

Loken, M. (2014). #BringBackOurGirls and the Invisibility of Imperialism. *Feminist Media Studies, 14*(6), 1100–1101. doi:10.1080/14680777.2014.975442

Machery, E., & Faucher, L. (2005). Social construction and the concept of race. *Philosophy of Science*, *72*(5), 1208–1219. doi:10.1086/508966

Maskovsky, J. (2017). Toward the anthropology of white nationalist postracialism: Comments inspired by hall, goldstein, and Ingram's "The hands of donald trump". *HAU*, *7*(1), 433–440. doi:10.14318/hau7.1.030

Maslow, W., & Robison, J. B. (1953). Civil Rights Legislation and the Fight for Equality, 1862-1952. *The University of Chicago Law Review. University of Chicago. Law School*, *20*(3), 3. doi:10.2307/1597662

McAuley, J. (2016). Black Lives Matter movement comes to France. But will it translate? Washington Post.

McLaughlin, M. (2016). The Dynamic History of #BlackLivesMatter Explained, This is how a transformed into a movement. *The Huffington Post*. Retrieved June 30, 2016, from http://www.huffingtonpost.co.uk

Moore, H. L., & Selchow, S. (2012). 'Global Civil Society' and the Internet 2012: Time to Update Our Perspective. In M. Kaldor et al... (Eds.), *Global Civil Society 2012* (pp. 28–40). Palgrave Macmillan, UK. doi:10.1057/9780230369436_2

Morrison, K. (2015, July 30). Social Media Activism: Sandra Bland, Police Brutality and #BlackLivesMatter. *Adweek.com*. Retrieved from http://www.adweek.com

Mortimer, C. (2017, January 3). M62 Shooting: Charts show difference between police shootings in the US and the UK. *The Independent*. Retrieved November 19, 2017 from http://www.independent.co.uk

Mullings, L. (2005). Interrogating Racism: Toward an Antiracist Anthropology. *Annual Review of Anthropology*, *34*(1), 667–693. doi:10.1146/annurev.anthro.32.061002.093435

Murdoch, D. (2016). *Black power: America's armed resistance*. Documentary, UK: BBC; Retrieved from http://www.bbc.co.uk/programmes/p03t9g3j

Nagarajan, C. (2013). How politicians and the media made us hate immigrants (Blog post). *Open Democracy Online*. Retrieved from https://www.opendemocracy.net/transformation/chitra-nagarajan/how-politicians-and-media-made-us-hate-immigrants

NCCHR. (2016). *Report on the prevention of racism, anti-semitism and xenophobia*. Paris: CNCDH.

Ndiaye, P. (2008). *La condition noire. Essai sur une minoritéfrançaise*. Paris: Calmann-Lévy.

Nieman, D. G. (1994). *From Slavery to Sharecropping: White Land and Black Labor in the Rural South, 1865-1900*. London: Garland.

Office for National Statistics. (2012a). *Ethnicity and National Identity in England and Wales: 2011. National Identity*. London Crown Copyright.

Office for National Statistics. (2012b). *Ethnicity and National Identity in England and Wales: 2011. Migration*. London: Crown Copyright.

Pager, D. (2003). The Mark of a Criminal Record. *American Journal of Sociology*, *108*(5), 937–975. doi:10.1086/374403

Painter, N. I. (2006). *Creating black Americans: African-American history and its meanings, 1619 to the present*. USA: Oxford University Press.

Pew Research Center. (2013). King's Dream Remains an Elusive Goal; Many Americans See Racial Disparities. Retrieved from http://www.pewsocialtrends.org/2013/08/22/kings-dream-remains-an-elusive-goal-many-americans-see-racial-disparities/4/

Pidd, H. (2016). Thousands attend Black Lives Matter solidarity march in Manchester. The Guardian. Retrieved from https://www.theguardian.com/uk

Plessy v. Ferguson, 63 U.S. 537, 16 S. Ct. 1138; 41 L. Ed. 256. (1896).

Plumer, B. (2013, Aug 28). Ten charts show how the U.S. has changed for the better since MLK's speech. *The Washington Post*. Retrieved August 28, 2016 from www.washingtonpost.com

Prison Reform Trust. (2016.). Projects & Research. Retrieved from http://www.prisonreformtrust.org.uk/ProjectsResearch/Race

Racisme, S. O. S. (2016, July 12). Les discriminations dans l'accès à l'emploi public: un rapport bienvenu. Retrieved from http://sos-racisme.org/communique-de-presse/les-discriminations-dans-lacces-a-lemploi-public-un-rapport-de-bienvenue/

Roche, J. P. (1951). The Future of "Separate but Equal". *Phylon*, *12*(3), 219–226. doi:10.2307/271632

Rutland, A., Hitti, A., Mulvey, K. L., Abrams, D., & Killen, M. (2015). When does the ingroup like the out-group? Bias among children as a function of group norms. *Psychological Science*, *26*(6), 834–842. doi:10.1177/0956797615572758 PMID:25888686

Sabanadze, N. (2010). Globalization and Nationalism: The Relationship Revisited. In *Globalization and Nationalism: The Cases of Georgia and the Basque Country* (pp. 169–186). Central European University Press.

Scheper-Hughes, N. (2017). Another country? racial hatred in the time of trump: A time for historical reckoning. *HAU*, *7*(1), 449–460. doi:10.14318/hau7.1.032

Shapiro, R. (2017, November 6). Trump says deadly Texas shooting isn't a guns issue, it's a mental health problem. *The Huffington Post*. Retrieved November 22, 2017 fromhttp://www.huffingtonpost.co.uk

Smedley, A., & Smedley, B. D. (2005). Race as biology is fiction, racism as a social problem is real: Anthropological and historical perspectives on the social construction of race. *The American Psychologist*, *60*(1), 16–26. doi:10.1037/0003-066X.60.1.16 PMID:15641918

Spire, A., & Merllié, D. (1999). La question des origines dans les statistiques en France. Les enjeux d'une controverse. *Le Mouvement Social*, *188*(188), 119–130. doi:10.2307/3779961 PMID:22029101

Stache, L. C. (2015). Advocacy and political potential at the convergence of hashtag activism and commerce. *Feminist Media Studies*, *15*(1), 162–164. doi:10.1080/14680777.2015.987429

Statista. (2016). UK Social Media Statistics for 2016. Leading social networks worldwide as of September 2016, ranked by number of active users (in millions). Worldwide; We Are Social; WhatsApp; Tumblr; LinkedIn; Google. Retrieved from https://www.statista.com

Statista. (n.d.). Number of social media users worldwide 2010-2020. Retrieved from https://www.statista.com/statistics/278414/number-of-worldwide-social-network-users/

Steinberg, S. (1989). *The ethnic myth: Race, ethnicity, and class in America*. Boston: Beacon Press.

Steinmetz, K. (2014) #blacklivesmatter Is the American Dialect Society's 2014 Word of the Year: TIME online. Retrieved June 19, 2016 from http://time.com

Stopwatch. (2015). Stop and Search Statistics 2014/2015. Retrieved from http://www.stop-watch.org/news-comment/story/new-stop-and-search-statistics-2014-2015

Sussman, R. W. (2014). *The myth of race: The troubling persistence of an unscientific idea*. Cambridge: Harvard university press. doi:10.4159/harvard.9780674736160

Taylor, K.-Y. (2016). *From #Blacklivesmatter To Black Liberation*. Haymarket Books Chicago.

Tharoor, I. (2016). Black Lives Matter is a global cause. *The Washington Post*. Retrieved September 5, 2016 from https://www.washingtonpost.com

Thrasher, S. W. (2015). Black Lives Matter has showed us: the oppression of black people is borderless. *The Guardian*. Retrieved March 7, 2015 from https://www.theguardian.com/uk

Traynor, L. (2016, July 16). Pleas for "justice" for 18-year-old Mzee Mohammed at Black Lives Matter march in Liverpool. Liverpool Echo. Retrieved from http://www.liverpoolecho.co.uk

@UKBLM (n.d.). Official Twitter Page Black Lives Matter UK. Twitter. Retrieved from https://twitter.com/ukblm

Vaidyanathan, R. (2016). The compass: America in black and white: Criminal Justice. *BBC*. Retrieved September 17, 2016, from http://www.bbc.co.uk/programmes/p03db7zh

Vaidyanathan, R. (2016). The compass: America in black and white: Economic Opportunity. *BBC*. Retrieved September 17, 2016, from http://www.bbc.co.uk/programmes/p03drnpt

Wahlquist, C. (2017, May 22). Black Lives Matter awarded 2017 Sydney peace prize. *The Guardian*. Retrieved November 18, 2017 from https://www.theguardian.com/uk

We Are Social. (2016). Digital In 2016. Retrieved from http://wearesocial.com/uk/special-reports/digital-in-2016

Weedston, L. (2014). 12 Hashtags That changed the world in 2014. *YES Magazine*. Retrieved from http://www.yesmagazine.org

Williams, S. (2015). Digital defense: Black feminists resist violence with hashtag activism. *Feminist Media Studies*, *15*(2), 341–344. doi:10.1080/14680777.2015.1008744

Witte, G. (2015, June 11). Do Britain's gunless bobbies provide answers for America's police? *The Washington Post*. Retrieved September 5, 2016, from https://www.washingtonpost.com

Yang, G. (2016). Narrative agency in hashtag activism: The case of# BlackLivesMatter. *Media and Communication*, *4*(4), 13–17. doi:10.17645/mac.v4i4.692

Zappi, S. (2016). Rassemblement à Paris de "Black Lives Matter France" après la mort d'Adama Traoré. Le Monde. Retrieved from http://www.lemonde.fr/police-justice/article/2016/07/23/rassemblement-a-paris-de-black-lives-matter-france-apres-la-mort-d-adama-traore_4973930_1653578.html#7zT5dvQqPYTMwEgm.99

KEY TERMS AND DEFINITIONS

Activism: The policy or action of using vigorous campaigning to bring about political or social change.

Advocacy: Individual or collective public support for or recommendation of a particular cause or policy.

Assimilationism: Doctrine of cultural integration.

Colour-Blindness: Doctrine related the social integration of minorities thought to be not influenced by racial prejudice.

Hashtactivism: Activism using online media and subversion of social media into online campaigning

Multiculturalism: Doctrine of cultural cohabitation.

ENDNOTE

1 The Universal Negro Improvement Association was created in 1914 in Jamaica by Marcus Garvey and was settled in the USA in 1916.

Chapter 7
Enhancing E-Transparency in Public Governance Through Social Media

Edison Wazoel Lubua
Institute of Accountancy Arusha, Tanzania

ABSTRACT

This chapter is a discussion on e-transparency. It is motivated by the trend where e-governance fails to significantly distinguish itself from the traditional governance, through embracing its secretive and prolonged nature of decision making. Both service delivery, and process and event models provided a basic background on enhancing transparency in governance activities. The emphasis is to make citizens the centre of governance processes. Moreover, key areas where citizen participation is desired, are discussed. The discussion integrates the role of ICTs is maximising participation. The later section of this chapter focuses on addressing contemporary challenges of e-transparency, in governance activities. Collectively, the modern society must embrace e-transparency, in ensuring that citizens decide their fate.

BACKGROUND

Authors propose different factors defining governance in the public sector. The study by Weiss & Steiner (2006) considers the rule of law, accountability, and transparency as key to quality governance. Moreover, the International Federation for Accountants (2013) advocates a strong commitment to integrity, ethical values, the rule of law, openness, and stakeholders' engagement in the governance process. On the other hand, the Collaboration on International ICT Policy in East and Southern Africa

DOI: 10.4018/978-1-5225-2854-8.ch007

(2015) and Lubua (2014) cite accountability, citizen empowerment and transparency (in government operations) as important pillars of good governance. Collectively, transparency is acknowledged by many studies, as key in ensuring good governance, and the ultimate objective is to ensure the execution of government operation, in favour of citizens.

Generally, transparency provides the required level of openness to government operations. This is through allowing the scrutinisation of the basis used in decision making (Lubua & Maharaj, 2014). Internally, key strategic decisions and operations must receive a collective approval from its stakeholders (Berggren & Bernshteyn, 2007). Moreover, the operation system must acknowledge the role of external stakeholders in approving the quality of governance through allowing feedbacks, while operating under transparent environment (Weiss & Steiner, 2006; Acosta, 2013). As the result of this scrutinisation, decision makers act with an understanding that they are viewed by the public. Hence, transparency becomes an agent for enforcing the sense of accountability and the rule of law among actors (International Federation for Accountants, 2013; Boyoung & Jinwoo, 2001).

While many government institutions acknowledge the importance of transparency in operations, the status of its implementation remains to be a concern. For example, the study by Gideon & Alouis (2013) reports low transparency in revenue collections and expenditure in the African context. Based on the scale by the Transparency International of 2015, many African countries receive a very low approval from their citizens on the issue of transparency in decision making (Transparency International, 2015). Arguably the received approval relates to the perceived level of corruption in respective countries. This observation is supported by several other studies (e.g. Ukah, 2009; Berggren & Bernshteyn, 2007; International Federation for Accountants, 2013). Countries which allow public organisations to operate in closed doors provide the room for leaders to exercise their authority unethically, and enrich themselves with natural resources illegally (Acosta, 2013).

On the other hand, the use of social media and web 2.0 related tools, offer a platform for elevating the level of transparency in governance. Social media allow stakeholders to communicate information across different platforms in a more convenient manner(Lubua & Maharaj, 2014; Banday & Mattoo, 2013). The exchange of information is characterised by efficiency, because multiple users can access and communicate the same information at the same time, more reliably (Darwish & Lakhtaria, 2011). Advanced tools supported by social media technologies facilitate live interactions between communicating individuals through text messages, audio, images and even video files (Darwish & Lakhtaria, 2011; Bidabad, Amirostovar, & Sherafati, 2017). Moreover, social media in support of other web 2.0 related tools allow the deployment of online survey tools, which are used in soliciting opinions from stakeholders of governance.

Currently, evidence shows that different world communities show interests on engaging ICTs in governance activities (Darwish & Lakhtaria, 2011). The purpose is to take advantage of the benefits brought by ICTs and associated tools in governance. Their interest is demonstrated through the establishment of recognised bodies to ensure quality implementation of e-services. One of the politically supported consortium is the Open Government Partnership (OGP), which brings about 70 countries in a common platform. Specifically, the consortium provides an international platform for reformers to make their governments more accountable, open, and responsive to citizens. In Southern African Development Countries (SADC), there is a common plan directing the development of ICT infrastructures useful in governance activities and service provision to citizens (Southern African Development Community, 2012). In the East African Community (EAC), the framework for harmonising ICT policies across member states is adopted (East African Community, 2013). This framework is known as the Protocol on Regional Information and Communication Technology. The purpose is to ensure a common direction is adopting ICTs in governance activities. Arguably, the multinational agreements are to be replicated by individual countries, through establishing policies and organs supporting the adoption of ICTs and related tools in governance activities.

So, what is in the local ground? The adoption of ICTs comes with its prospects and challenges. It is promising to note that a large part of the African continent is linked to the world, through reliable internet backbones (Lubua E., 2014). Moreover, the number of internet users is increasing, and this is partly attributed by the increase of mobile phone users (Tanzania Communication Regulatory Authority, 2016). Furthermore, government institution shows a desire to use ICTs, policies governing the use of ICTs are enacted, while the infrastructure is further developed (Christoph, Enrico, & Alison, 2013). Nevertheless, studies point out a frequent inability of clients to enjoy the benefits associated with ICT enabled services in governance (Christoph, Enrico, & Alison, 2013; Lubua & Maharaj, 2014). Moreover, some local governments do not show a true commitment to standards by international bodies advocating transparency. Therefore, this chapter offers a scholarly and practical perspective, on factors linked to the implementation of ICT enables services, where social media are at the centre of transparency.

MODELS SUPPORTING SOCIAL MEDIA BASED TRANSPARENCY AND CITIZEN PARTICIPATION

Modern societies are in the digital era. Accordingly, their governance requires a proper integration of digital tools. A proper integration of digital tools in governance activities should result to openness and participation of citizens in governance activities

(Bidabad, Amirostovar, & Sherafati, 2017). In this chapter, openness in governance activities based on ICT tools (and social media in particular) is simply represented by the term "e-transparency". Currently, a number of theories are in place defining expectations of e-transparency stakeholders, on digital governance. The Interactive Service Model (Figure 1) is among contemporary models for e-transparency in service delivery in the public sector. The model opens a possibility for a direct participation of individuals in governance processes. This is through establishing digital platforms, which facilitates interactions between stakeholders and the governing body. Social media and other web 2.0 based platforms make a good case because of their ability to support users in content development and sharing (Bannister & Connolly, 2011). The participation is direct, and not through the use of representatives; therefore, it evokes a sense of empowerment to participants (Kim & Lee, 2011).

Basically, Figure 1 provides a summarised relationship between the variables of the Interactive Service Model. This model places citizens at the centre of all relationships in governance activities. A well-established interactive model demands a two-way flow of information between the relating variables (Berggren & Bernshteyn, 2007; Kim & Lee, 2011). In the context of this chapter, the emphasis is on the flow of information between government authorities and citizens.

Additionally, the Process and Event Model" present more arguments on enhancing e-transparency. The focus of the model is on elements formulating a complete procedure for attaining a given result in services offered by the public sector. In all procedures for attaining services in the public sector, transparency is mandatory to satisfy customers with the rate and quality of output (Berggren & Bernshteyn, 2007; Darwish & Lakhtaria, 2011). The model received detailed improvement to form a Data, Process and Decision model (Bannister & Connolly, 2011). Figure 1

Figure 1. Interactive service model
Source: (Digital Governance Initiative, 2016)

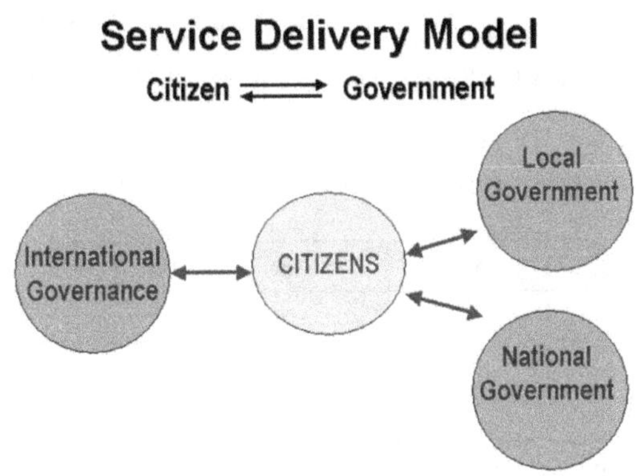

summarises the model, through questions which must be asked in each component of the model, for enhanced transparency.

Transparency in data makes the first key element of the Data, Process and Decision model. In Tanzania, transparency in data form the basic right of citizens, as articles 18(1 and 2)of its constitution acknowledges the right to access information for all citizens. They must be able to access public data without restrictions, unless such data justifiably endanger the security of the nation. The type of data may be government statistical information, government-business data, and to some extent the access to internal information such as salaries (Bannister & Connolly, 2011; Lubua E., 2014). Moreover, in incidents where such data are analysed to obtain the results, which may impact the direction of the nation, the transparency of methods used (to capture such data) is necessary to enhance the sense of validity and reliability within the society (Boyoung & Jinwoo, 2001; Bolarinwa, 2015). The level of transparency is summarised by the following questions, in the Data, Process and Decision model: What data to be accessed? Who is to access? And, where are they available? However, valid these questions are, more often than not, government officers (in the African continent) limit the accessibility of data through the enactment of secretive laws. A good case for this scenario (based in Tanzania) is explained in the next section of this chapter.

Moreover, government stakeholders desire transparency indifferent processes for acquiring public services. Business processes are formed through a series of steps to be taken to achieve a certain result (Lubua & Maharaj, 2014; Christoph, Enrico, & Alison, 2013). The complexity of processes differs depending on the result expected. Someone applying for admission in a university, is likely not to share a complete process with a VISA applicant. Although ICT tools are used in processes, there are many times where they require the input form attendants. Eventually, their delay, or error affects the pace of providing expected results. Transparency in processes enables the client to understand a complete status of the request submitted. Equally, attendants become active because they know that they are viewed (Bannister & Connolly, 2011). Transparency in processes is summarised through the following questions: Where is the process happening? When is it happening? And, how is it

Table 1. Questions to assess transparency

	What	Who	Where	When	How	Why
Data	√	√	√			
Process			√	√	√	
Decision					√	√

Source: (Bannister & Connolly, 2011)

happening? The applicant must be aware of these. Like other types of web pages, social media offer the opportunity for public organisations to link their backroom processes, to the public. For example, the Public Services Recruitment Secretariat of Tanzania, is actively sharing the information about stages of the recruitment process, to its stakeholders, through Facebook, Instagram and Twitter.

The last part of the Data, Process and Decision model calls for transparency in in decision making. Decisions are the output of the data captured and the process. Though data and process stages are transparent, the applicant must be able to understand how attendants arrive to a certain conclusion (Ojo, 2013; Kim & Lee, 2011). Failure to be open in decision making, is likely to dissatisfy the applicant of the service. Moreover, transparency is required in complex decisions by the government; examples of these decisions include the formulation of governance laws. The coordinating body has the responsibility of soliciting opinions from stakeholders for inclusive decisions. Social media have the ability to facilitate the decision-making process, through allowing live discussions and polls, in dedicated pages. This is key in winning the confidence of citizens in government business. In decision making, the applicant of service (citizen) must be able to answer the following: How is the decision arrived? And, why is it arrived in that fashion? Justification is required to all levels of citizen participation.

Together with the discussed models, scholars suggest different areas that need a close citizen collaboration (in government business), as a key aspect for enhanced transparency. One way to which the relationship between the government and citizens is desired, is in the policy making process or planning (Lubua & Maharaj, 2014; International Federation for Accountants, 2013). While the policy formulation process varies across countries, certain components (of the process) are shared. At one point, the problem to be addressed by the policy must be identified. After the problem is known, it is necessary to engage a debate to receive opinions from stakeholders (on different aspects of the policy or law). In the African context, debates are conducted through organs representing citizens. Nevertheless, the engagement of citizens through e-media increases the level of transparency in the process. Accordingly, the engagement increases the chance of the proposed law to receive the consent from citizens.

Arguably, social media provide an improved environment for the engagement of citizens in the policy formulation process (Darwish & Lakhtaria, 2011). This is because the government can share the content of the legislation to stakeholders, this ignites the debate. Social media allow participants to generate their content and share. Therefore, social media allow citizens to understand the debated subject, and use the opportunity to provide instant comments, where necessary (Gideon & Alouis, 2013). Unfortunately, in the East African Context, instead of providing live feeds on debates in progress, the social media pages communicate information on concluded topics(Collaboration on International ICT Policy in East and Southern Africa, 2015). This is without the room for direct contribution from citizens. In many cases, emails are used as the main tool for communication. However, emails are limited. With emails, it is difficult to have an open platform presenting a clear trend of opinions (submitted by citizens) in support or against a proposed legislation. This limits the ability of the legislative process to receive useful inputs from citizens on time.

Moreover, the government must adequately engage its stakeholders in resolving issues of national concern. This is before establishing a legal framework for governance. Such things are likely to endanger peace and tranquillity, if the nation fails to engage the community in the decision making process. The following are few examples of such matters in recent years: the voting of the UK government out of the European Union, the constitution process in Tanzania, and the unpopular extension of presidential terms by some states in Africa. Social media extend the platform for such national discussions in different ways. In the year 2011 after the Tanzanian government decided to review its constitution, Facebook was used in obtaining opinions from stakeholders (Collaboration on International ICT Policy in East and Southern Africa, 2015). In this exercise, 2,729 people submitted their opinions through Facebook. Moreover, tools for collecting opinion polls through survey were used. Online survey tools provide a more efficient way of making decisions on defined topic (Ojo, 2013). In addition, tools used in the Tanzanian case, video and audio clips are another type of tools. This is more relevant in contemporary environment since there are more online facilities to provide free hosting and access. The YouTube is an example of such facilities.

Regardless of the power of these social media (in engaging the community in national discussion), it is unfortunate that there are times where the political will, differs from that of the people. Therefore, those in power may decide to twist the technology, to portray the results in their favour. On the other hand, social media channels presenting opinions opposing those of government leaders may be obstructed. Such behaviour abuses the validity of social media in deciding national matters (Weiss & Steiner, 2006; Bidabad, Amirostovar, & Sherafati, 2017).

Likewise, social media tools are suitable in facilitating the submission of grievances from citizens. In a similar motive, in 2007, the President of the United Republic of Tanzania, directed the Ministry of Information Affair, to establish a central portal, used as a point to receive grievances from citizens. These grievances are associated with the quality of public services. It is the expectation of citizens that tools of this nature must address challenges associated with the traditional ways of handling grievances. Such challenges include process ineffectiveness, and low transparency (Lubua, 2014; Collaboration on International ICT Policy in East and Southern Africa, 2015). It is unfortunate that such systems are still characterised by ineffectiveness. There are times where citizens with grievances are obliged to make physical visitations, just to make sure that their requests get the required attention (Dombeu & Rannyai, 2013). On the issue of transparency, activities supported by traditional ICT tools are still lacking the required level of openness. Regardless of the setbacks, there are few public organisations which have shown the intent to improve their situations in enhancing transparency in service provision and decision making. They set criteria for decision making, and allow all involved stakeholders to view the progress and have a policy based reason for whatever decision made. Such systems provide a way for stakeholders to appeal, where they are not satisfied with available decisions. Transparency and efficiency must form basis for governance in the public sector, and social media has a role to play.

Moreover, automated services are important in enhancing the performance of public institutions (Ojo, 2013; Darwish & Lakhtaria, 2011). The use of ICT tools makes the best option in automated services. The availability of most of government services online would improve the availability of services to citizens without unnecessary struggles. Additionally, such services are characterised by the low access cost. In East Africa, this is one area which has received several improvements. Citizens are able to make payments for different services such as electricity, water, transport, insurance, and medical bills. Accordingly, some components of taxation are also automated. Taxpayers can make self-tax estimations, with the aid of established e-transparency tools hosted by government portals. Nonetheless, regardless of the value brought by automated services, their level of reliability is still low (Collaboration on International ICT Policy in East and Southern Africa, 2015). The services are characterised by a frequent breakdown, which leads to delayed services. In this aspect, social media could be used to provide chat rooms and live feeds, where users of automated services may be assisted. Moreover, social media can be linked with databases offering different customised solutions to the system under use.

Generally, ICT tools are important in electoral activities. They are useful in registration and voting activities. This is essential in avoiding duplicates, which may nurture electoral fraud. In countries with national identification cards, the same can be used in identifying citizens qualifying for the process. Nevertheless, even the countries whose citizens are not known (based on their registration numbers), other means of identifying them may be devised. However, in all cases the electoral machines are capable of identifying duplicates through fingerprints. The credibility of the election process depends on a number of factors, one being transparency in counting votes. The system must be open enough to allow people to be confident of the results. It is unfortunate that in the African context, the credibility of results is low, because key stakeholders are denied the opportunity to witness the tallying process, in an open manner. E-transparency can improve this situation, provided that actors are willing. Moreover, in this context, social media may act as an educative platform to citizens.

The above discussed part of this chapter introduced key areas of services, which would benefit the local African community if they were available through ICT channels, and social media in particular. However, it is valuable to note that it would be difficult to attain the required level of self-services availability, unless a proper legal framework is in place (Lubua & Maharaj, 2014; Ojo, 2013). In the era where most of government institutions have access to the internet, it is the right time to make it mandatory for certain services to be available online. Likewise, prohibitive clauses of the law need a review (Dombeu & Rannyai, 2013). These are clauses which restrict citizens to access some information, while the same could expose the misconducts due to unethical governance. Other things such as the maximum waiting time (before the requested service is received), the reliability of electricity in supporting the e-transparency systems, and the competency of service providers must be strengthened for a proper service provision. Some of these things require an authentic legislative framework for proper implementation.

ADDRESSING CONTEMPORAY CHALLENGES OF E-TRANSPARENCY

This part of the chapter discusses a number of issues, which need improvement to enhance e-transparency in governance. As explained earlier (in this chapter), this is the type of transparency in governance activities felicitated through electronic media, including social networks. First, transparency in Revenue Collection and Spending must be improved. Studies show that African governments are overwhelmed by corruption acts (Gideon & Alouis, 2013; International Federation for Accountants, 2013). The study by Transparency International (2015) exclusively concludes that Africa is in the dark part of corruption. On average, the corruption free score is 33%, across Sub-Saharan Africa. The challenge of corruption has a significant impact to the development of linked countries, because it paralyses lawful revenue collection (Fjeldstad & Moore, 2009). Governments fail to collect revenue to their full capacity because of corruption. On the other hand, sources of revenue, which would benefit the entire community, are unethically handled to investors. Investors end up abusing such economic means while being granted excessive privileges as the result of contracts which were discussed and signed in total darkness. This is possible in a state where the state law and/or those who are trusted to enforce it are weak and corrupt. E-transparency, through media such as social networks, would allow other stakeholders to share their opinions on the matter, hence, avoid the misuse of natural resources (Dombeu & Rannyai, 2013; Lubua, 2014). This is through providing an open platform for developing laws governing revenue collection, without the influence from investors. Moreover, the use of the e-transparency tools to trace the value of an object of sale (from the point of manufacturing or importation to the final selling point) is inevitable. Such tools include Electronic Fiscal Devices (EFDs) and scanners, which are integrated into the Enterprise Resources Planning System of the revenue authority.

Furthermore, it is valuable to acknowledge that corruption negatively affects the way government funds are used. Basically, the parliament is entrusted with the role to develop laws governing the use of public funds (Ukah, 2009; Weiss & Steiner, 2006). Nevertheless, before the law is debated and concluded, in most cases, its development emerges from government executives. Throughout the process, e-transparency tools can be used in accommodating discussions, which integrate different stakeholders. Government portals and social media make a good case for providing open discussions. The emphasis is to have an open dialogue, which leads to a common direction in establishing laws governing expenditures. It is unfortunate that such positive practices for law enactment are limited.

Moreover, in recent days, we are witnessing stakeholders of development who advocates for open contracts between the government and business companies. Secretive contracts are famous at benefiting government executives and business companies. In Tanzania, there has been an outcry for the government to negotiate with large investors, in an open manner; possibly through the parliament (Manley & Lassourd, 2014). This is because citizens are victimised through unchecked contracts in many ways. Operations in this environment are in a way that, where the government is to secure services through such contracts, the price is escalated, and excessive exemptions are offered (Uwazi, 2010). This is to accommodate the fact that such contracts were concluded in a corrupt environment. Besides, if a company wants to enter a new business venture through resources owned by the public, the price tag for accessing such business contracts may be too low, when compared to the actual value (Uwazi, 2010; Manley & Lassourd, 2014). All these are happening to cover for corruption. Where the government is willing, e-transparent tools are useful in addressing challenges associated with selling or acquiring services by the government. The challenge is that in most cases, government executives may prefer an open system of data collection, but hide the process from stakeholders, to avoid criticism (Berggren & Bernshteyn, 2007). Therefore, while there are e-transparency tools in place, they are likely not to be fully used.

Additionally, the government must establish and strengthen Open Portals for Public Requests and Information Sharing. This may be through traditional pages or the use of social media. Many government legislations agree that citizens have the right for information. For example, article 18-b of the constitution of Tanzania states that "every person has a right to be informed at all times of various important events of life and activities of the people and also of issues of importance to the society".

The Kenyan Constitution (Article 35-1) suggests that "every person has the right to access the information held by state". Moreover, Article 16-1 of the South African Constitution provides "the freedom to impart and receive the information" held by the state. The cited countries represent those whose constitution acknowledges the democratic process of governance. Such legislations would be more beneficial if the information was readily available to citizens. The socioeconomic information is more important because, it renders citizens the power to make decisions, where necessary, even the change of regime. Equally to this, the information on the governance of publicly owned projects is invaluable. It is unfortunate that government executives fail to provide such information to citizens who are key stakeholders (Government Expenditure on Human Capital Development, 2011). This is one key indicator for poor governance, since government executives use this privilege to hide unethical acts.

Moreover, there are several cases where laws governing access to information are contradicted by inhibiting laws. One side of the law may grant the privilege to information access, while the other grab it. In Tanzania while the constitution provides access to information, the Cybercrime Act (2015) threatens the right to access through allowing the police force to criminalise actions under freedom of expression and access to information. Laws of a similar nature are likely to be spotted in other sovereign. These affect the ability of citizens to share and access the information.

Moreover, the establishment of data repository for open access is necessary. The question is – why should data which are to be available to citizens, be accessed through bureaucratic procedures? There is a need to establish open portals and associated media to disseminate the information to citizens on different subjects (Southern African Development Community, 2012). Other types of information are desired on a real-time basis, and may be useful in engaging citizens in valuable discussions which leads to meaningful decision making (Kim & Lee, 2011). Besides, other information enables citizens to carry out their economic operations in a manner which brings them more profit. For example, a farmer would benefit from accessing the information providing technical directives on the modern way of farming. The challenge is that where portals are available, many lack the information addressing the needs of citizens. Such information would propel self-service within the community. Moreover, the information would be useful for researchers, and other stakeholders who are in need.

Moreover, government portals, which liaison citizens' grievances to executives are to be open. Not all the time that citizens are comfortable to relay their grievances through third parties. In traditional environments, citizens with such needs are blocked from meeting those who are entrusted with the most power, simply to maintain bureaucratic demands. As the results, they barely submit their request through the channel which make them uncomfortable – hence, they end up frustrated. It is important to acknowledge that citizens are equally entitled to the information on the status of different requests they make (Bolarinwa, 2015). The feedback must be time bound, and able to inform the applicant reasons for delay, where there is a delay. Another important feature is the information about basis used in decision making, where the final verdict is made. It is necessary to accommodate these qualities to the e-transparent system of the public sector.

Accordingly, it is valuable to consider the importance of data recovery plan, in a case where a fault occurs. Under e-transparency, citizens have a complete dependency to online media in accessing services. Therefore, it is recommended that e-transparency tools are to operate all the time to support the idea of convenience, effectiveness and efficiency. Nonetheless, there are many cases where stakeholders fail to access e-transparency platforms because of different reasons. One of the reason for such interruption, is an attack to data storages. Arguably, there are many forms of attacks, and they all need a well-established mechanism to avoid damage. While some of the attacks focus on denying users access to the system (for commercial of political gains), some of them focus on stealing the information. Attacks which deny users access to the system may damage the setup of the infrastructure to redirect or block the flow of information. In whatever form of the attack, they all affect users and the organisation. Therefore, appropriate frameworks must be in place, to ensure the protection from such attacks, and even recovery should the attack materialise.

This section gives weight to all discussed points, in enhancing the performance of e-transparent tools for proper governance in the public sector. However, the importance of competent and dynamic Information and Communication specialists cannot be over emphasised. Technical people have the general responsibility of installing and maintaining the system. However, technical people in government Institutions are equally affected by the pragmatic system of government operations. Most of them can hardly take initiatives to engage themselves in a new technology and responsibility. This is the reason why they are rigid at adopting new technologies, and if they should, they outsource services which could be handled internally. This tendency diminishes the value of their existence, creates more implementation cost, and exposes internal systems to outsiders – that is hired technicians. It is the right time for the public sector to demand more value from its officers, while promoting environments that allow innovation to enshrine. Until then, the public sector will lowly benefit from its technical staff; as the result, they will fail to realise the benefits of e-transparency.

E-TRANSPARENCY IN THE FUTURE

The chapter discussed the unquestionable importance of e-transparency in governance. E-transparency, is an improvement to e-governance. Unfortunately, the e-governance concept fails to make a significant difference from the traditional way of governing, except that it is online. For example, there are those who simply consider it as an act of doing governance activities over the internet. Such a system does not necessarily take into consideration, the inherent challenges of traditional governance. Therefore, in this case, e-governance is still a traditional way of governing, except that it is done through online media. While citizens see e-government from the public side (online), the most important part of it is paralysed. The paralysed part is the internal government operations. This impedes users from having full benefits of online governance.

In acknowledging the shortcomings of traditional e-governance; e-transparency comes with a clear advocacy, on attaining a required level of openness in governance activities. Eventually, openness stirs the sense of responsibility among actors. This chapter is of the opinion that governing bodies are obliged to redirect their perspective, from simply automating their systems, to making sure that they are open enough to win the confidence of their stakeholders. Otherwise, operations in darkness will diminish the sense of accountability, and cause civil unrest in the African societies. In this case, social media can be useful in linking with citizens, because they subscribe in a large number.

Besides, it is convincing to suggest that many governing bodies ignore the potential of making the required investment to its manpower, policies and processes. This study does not ignore the importance of effort invested in online tools, including social media. Nevertheless, these efforts yield minimum impact if the government do not have qualified people. Moreover, policies must not obstruct information sharing and access to services in the most transparent manner possible. Moreover, government processes must be open, and address the traditional bureaucracy for enhanced performance. These aspects call for restructuring of the online government systems, for enhanced performance through transparent processes.

Moreover, collaboration and cooperation among public institutions is inevitable. A proper body with the mandate to monitor the collaboration is necessary. While some countries may have such bodies in place, they lack statutory power to apply carrot and stick where necessary. A well-defined framework for supervising the implementation of e-transparency services, would ensure the implementation meeting national strategic objectives. Collectively, in all undertakings, users are at the centre of e-transparency.

CONCLUSION

Collectively, this chapter concludes that a proper governance is an important determinant of the prosperity of any society. This type of governance is centred to citizens. Its operations are determined by the level to which operations and decisions are carried out in an open manner. Operations under transparent environment enhances the confidence of citizens toward their government. Besides, it offers an alert to government actors that they are constantly monitored by their key stakeholders, and any misconduct will call them for accountability. Arguably, the introduction of electronic media (and social media in particular) sets new expectations on enhancing governance. This is through allowing the provision of quality services to citizens and other stakeholders of the government. Nevertheless, this is not the case in many African countries. While a good number of public organisations boost to have online platforms (for example in East African Countries), the level of transparency must be enhanced in operation levels. This is key in making sure that government systems are citizens-centred. Citizens must be able to understand where the process of service provision is halted, and what they must do to ignite the process. Moreover, they must understand conditions used in making decisions about their requests. This is the essence of e-transparency, which is an important pillar of governance in modern time. To maximise the level of transparency, the chapter recommend the use of electronic platforms, subscribed my many citizens, for information sharing. Social media are the favourable case. Generally, it is time for African government to address challenges hampering e-transparency; this includes operation procedures, technical matters, and guiding legislations.

REFERENCES

Acosta, A. M. (2013). The Impact and Effectiveness of Accountability and Transparency Initiatives: The Governance of Natural Resources. *Development Policy Review*, *31*(1), 89–105. doi:10.1111/dpr.12021

Banday, M. T., & Mattoo, M. M. (2013). Social Media in e-Governance: A Study with Special Reference to India. *Social Networking*, 2(2), 47–56. doi:10.4236n.2013.22006

Bannister, F., & Connolly, R. (2011). The Trouble with Transparency: A Critical View of Openness in e-governance. *Policy and Internet*, *3*(1), 1–30. doi:10.2202/1944-2866.1076

Berggren, E., & Bernshteyn, R. (2007). Organizational transparency drives company performance. *Journal of Management Development*, *26*(5), 411–417. doi:10.1108/02621710710748248

Bidabad, B., Amirostovar, A., & Sherafati, M. (2017). Financial transparency, corporate governance and information disclosure of the entrepreneur's corporation in Rastin banking. *International Journal of Law and Management*, *59*(5), 636–651. doi:10.1108/IJLMA-01-2016-0003

Bolarinwa, O. A. (2015). Principles and methods of validity and reliability testing of questionnaires used in social and health science researches. *The Nigerian Postgraduate Medical Journal*, *22*(4), 195–201. doi:10.4103/1117-1936.173959 PMID:26776330

Boyoung, I., & Jinwoo, J. (2001). *Using ICT for Strengthening Government Transparency*. Retrieved September 20, 2016, from http://www.oecd.org/dataoecd/53/55/2537402.pdf

Christoph, S., Enrico, C., & Alison, G. (2013). Internet going mobile: internet access and use in 11 African countries. *info*, *15*(5), 34-51.

Collaboration on International ICT Policy in East and Southern Africa. (2015). *ICT in Governance in Tanzania*. Kampala: CIPESA. Retrieved September 29, 2016, from http://www.cipesa.org/?wpfb_dl=205

Darwish, A., & Lakhtaria, K. I. (2011). The Impact of the New Web 2.0 Technologies in Communication, Development, and Revolutions of Societies. *Journal of Advanced Information Technologies*, *2*(4), 204–216.

Digital Governance Initiative. (2016). *Interactive Service Model*. Retrieved September 30, 2016, from http://www.digitalgovernance.org/index.php/models/interactive-service

Dombeu, J., & Rannyai, N. (2013). African E-government Research Land Scape. *African Journal of Information Systems*, *6*(3), 85–119.

East African Community. (2013). *Protocol on Regional Information and Communication Technology*. Retrieved September 5, 2016, from www.eac.int

Fjeldstad, O.-H., & Moore, M. (2009). Revenue Authorities and Public Authoriesin Africa. *The Journal of Modern African Studies*, *47*(1). doi:10.1017/S0022278X08003637

Gideon, Z., & Alouis, M. (2013). Systems, Processes and Challenges of Public Revenue Collection in Zimbabwe. *American International Journal of Contemporary Research, 3*(2), 49–59.

International Federation for Accountants. (2013). *Good Governance in the Public Sector*. New York: IFAC.

Oluwatobi, S.O., & Ogunrinola, O.I. (2011). Government Expenditure on Human Capital Development: Implications for Economic Growth in Nigeria. *Journal of Sustainable Development, 4*(3), 72–80.

Kim, S., & Lee, J. (2011). E-Participation, Transparency, and Trust in Local Government. In *Proceedings of the 1st Global Conference on Transparency Research*. Newark: Rutger University.

Lubua, E. (2014). E-Transparency and Information Sharing in the Public Sector. *International Journal of Computer Science and Business Informatics, 14*(1), 1694–2108.

Lubua, E. W., & Maharaj, M. (2014). State Information Protection Laws and e-Transparency. In *ST-Africa 2014 Conference Proceedings*. Younde: IIMC International Information.

Manley, D., & Lassourd, T. (2014). *Tanzania and Statoil: What Does the Leaked Agreement mean to Citizens*. Retrieved November 20, 2017, from https://resourcegovernance.org/sites/default/files/Tanzania_Statoil_20140808.pdf

Mbarawa, M. (2014). (Interview). Retrieved August 28, 2016, from http://www.the-report.net/tanzania/nov2014/1166-interview-professor-makame-mbarawa-minister-of-communications-science-and-technology

Ojo, J. (2013). E-governance: An imperative for sustainable grass root development in Nigeria. *Journal of Public Administration and Policy Research, 6*(4), 77–89. doi:10.5897/JPAPR2013.0264

Southern African Development Community. (2012). *ICT Sector Plan*. Retrieved August 30, 2016, from http://www.sadc.int/files/9413/5293/3532/Regional_Infrastructure_Development_Master_Plan_ICT_Sector_Plan.pdf

Tanzania Communication Regulatory Authority. (2016). *Quarterly Communication Statistics Report*. Retrieved September 28, 2016, from http://tcra.go.tz/images/documents/telecommunication/CommStatMarch16.pdf

Transparency International. (2015). *Corruption Perception Index 2016*. Retrieved August 29, 2016, from https://www.transparency.org/news/feature/corruption_perceptions_index_2016

Ukah, O. C. (2009). General Expenditure Management and Control Within the Framework of Ethiopia Economy. *African Research Review*, *3*(1), 206–213. doi:10.4314/afrrev.v3i1.43566

Uwazi. (2010). *Tanzania's Tax Exemptions: Are they too high and making us too dependent on foreign aid?* Retrieved November 23, 2017, from http://twaweza.org/uploads/files/Tax%20Exemptions.PDF

Weiss, F., & Steiner, S. (2006). Transparency as an Element of Good Governance. *Fordham International Law Journal*, *30*(5), 1545–1580.

KEY TERMS AND DEFINITIONS

E-Governance: Enhancing governance activities through ICT tools.

Electronic Fiscal Device: An electronic device used in business, which complies with certain defined laws.

Enterprise Resource Planning System: Is a process by which a company manages and integrates important parts of its business.

E-Transparency: Enhancing transparent environment through the use of ICT tools.

Governance: Governance refers to all process in government or corporate activities, which shows who has power to make decisions, and how other players make their voice heard and how the justification is provided.

Model: Is simply a framework defining or describing a situation.

Portal: An internet site providing access to other sites.

Social Media: These are websites and applications that enable users to create and share content.

Transparency: Honest and Openness in governance activities.

Chapter 8
Social Media Strategies of Political Power:
An Analysis of the Ruling Party in Turkey

Hakan Yüksel
Independent Researcher, Turkey

ABSTRACT

This chapter analyzes the social media strategies of political power focusing on Turkey. By using inner-circle and outer-circle conceptualizations, it shows that the ruling party in Turkey simultaneously prevents and embraces social media in order to consolidate its power. The inner-circle strategies consist of practices facilitating an efficient use of social media whereas the outer-circle strategies are composed of judicial and technical measures to obstruct the democratic use of social media. By stressing that political power can also use social media efficiently, the chapter contributes to the literature in which social media is generally associated with emancipatory initiatives and the strategies of power are mostly explored in terms of restrictive measures. The chapter also describes the strategic role of social media in the increasingly violent power struggle in Turkey and the difficulties of using it in advocacy campaigns.

INTRODUCTION

Social struggles are being transformed due to the development of communication technologies. The Arab Spring in the Middle East, the Occupy Wall Street Movement in the USA, anti-austerity movements in Europe, the Gezi Park Protest in Turkey are among the many examples of how social media has changed the organization

DOI: 10.4018/978-1-5225-2854-8.ch008

and action of social protests against the powers that be, thus, enriching the related literature in social sciences. With this transformation, it has become necessary to inquire into social advocacy in current circumstances. This is important for democracy at both global and local levels. The development of social media, however, is not linear. As with emancipatory movements, power organizations are also searching for strategies for using social media efficiently and in order to reach the democratic ideals, this issue must also be explored.

This chapter analyzes social media strategies of political power focusing on Turkey within the framework of inner-circle and outer-circle conceptualizations that contribute to the literature. It shows that social media strategies of power are not limited to bans, restrictions and surveillance but also include embracing social media. Accordingly, the outer-circle strategies consist of constraining practices that prevent the democratic use of social media and can be analyzed at the levels of the judicial and technical. Conversely, the inner-circles strategies embrace social media. They are composed of proactive practices that benefit from social media and can also be analyzed at two levels; that of the official and unofficial.

Turkey is a suitable focus for such an investigation. It is among the developed countries in terms of the Internet and mobile technologies, and the use of social media is very common. Furthermore, social media is one of the strategic domains in the ever-increasing power struggle in Turkey. Different actors utilize different strategies within social media and their attitudes are changing due to their interaction. The violent nature and multiple facets of the power struggle render Turkey a laboratory, in which the strategies that political powers can apply or be subject to can be analyzed. International organizations confirm this by defining Turkey as a "swing state" and emphasizing that the strategies shaped in this country would constitute a democratic or repressive model for others. This chapter focuses mostly on Twitter because it is the main battlefield in the political struggle on social media.

The chapter consists of four sections. The first concerns the literature on social media and the approaches adopted by political powers around the world. The second section describes the socio-political context, Internet infrastructure and social media diffusion in Turkey in order to better comprehend the political struggle and social media strategies of the ruling party. The third and fourth sections focus on the inner and outer circles strategies. The consequences of the strategies for the advocacy initiatives in Turkey are analyzed in the concluding section. This section also contains information gathered through the interviews done with Turkish activists in order to verify the results.

SOCIAL MEDIA IN THE LITERATURE

The distinctive aspect of social media literature is the contrast between techno-optimists and techno-pessimists (Gerbaudo, 2012, pp. 5-9; Fuchs, 2012a, pp. 777-779). While the optimists claim that social media strengthens democracy and facilitates emancipation, pessimists argue the opposite. With a unidimensional perspective, both approaches represent extreme positions regarding social media.

The optimistic literature can be categorized into two branches according to the focus of their research. The first branch explores the role of social media in institutional politics and emphasizes that it can be useful in broadening public discussion and participation in political processes. Given that social media platforms empowered by the interactive technology provide more opportunities for users to manage the Internet content and communication, it is underscored that people are able to affect political party strategies and policies by producing and disseminating their messages on the Internet, and candidates can have a direct contact with their electorate (McNair, 2011, p. xviii; Williams and Gulati, 2007; Vergeer, Hermans & Sams, 2011; Vergeer, 2012 p. 10; Demirhan, 2014, pp. 286-287). The success of 2008 Obama campaign in using social media during the presidential race of the USA is particularly emphasized in this literature.

The second branch of the optimistic literature deals with the role of social media in social change. Witnessing massive social protests that occurred in various countries in the late 2000s and early 2010s, such as the popular protests in Europe and the USA against the economic crisis and social injustice or the popular revolts in the Middle East causing the fall of dictators, optimists emphasize the transformative potential of social media. Andrew Sullivan (2009) and Clay Shirky (2011, pp. 30, 35) stress that social media, as a new technology destroying the institutional control over the media and information flow, offers new opportunities for the organization, coordination and mobilization of opposition forces. As people develop a shared awareness through social media, the usual tactics of censorship and propaganda of ruling elites become unworkable (Shirky, 2011, pp. 35-38). This optimistic but also technologically deterministic approach that associates the new technology of social media directly with more democracy and freedom (Fuchs, 2012a, p. 778) paves the way for the dominant discourse emphasizing the "Twitter Revolution" or the "Facebook Revolution", which was also adopted by the USA administration, especially after the Arab Spring at the beginning of 2011 (Morozov, 2009a, p. 10-11; Gladwell, 2010, p. 42-43; Fuchs, 2012a, p. 777; Gerbaudo, 2012, p. 6).

Manuel Castells (2015) presents a sophisticated version of the optimistic claims by stating that the "networked social movements of the digital age represent a new species of social movement" and can be qualified as "harbingers of social change in the 21st century" (Castells, 2015, pp. 15, 18). These movements are formed firstly on the Internet and social media platforms, which constitute a safe and autonomous space to organize and mobilize the anger of people against power, and then occupy streets and places (Castells, 2015, pp. 46, 108, 249-250). Through the use of more democratic organization and decision-making processes, these movements also bear the promise of a more democratic society (Castells, 2015, pp. 131-135, 181-187, 316). According to Castells' logic, the Internet and social media created these movements and the subsequent massive social protests around the world and there would be no such historical protests without these technologies (Fuchs, 2012a, p. 780).

These optimistic claims, which constitute the dominant discourse in policy circles and media, are severely criticized by pessimists. After stressing that the resistance against powerful actors and groups naturally contains high risks and requires strong ties and disciplined hierarchy between activists, Malcolm Gladwell (2010, pp. 45-49) argues that social media activism is qualified by weak group ties and leaderless organization and does not impact on power structures even if social media makes it easier for activists to express themselves. Moreover, Evgeny Morozov (2009b) considers social media activism as "slacktivism" and argues that it does not have a political or social impact though people in these virtual campaigns feel "an illusion of having a meaningful impact on the world without demanding anything more than joining a Facebook group". Morozov also asks whether slacktivism is destroying traditional and proven forms of activism.

Additionally, Morozov (2009a, p. 12) argues that Twitter use in Iran was so rare despite the Green Movement protest in 2009 shook the established power in the country to the extent that optimists labeled it as the "Twitter Revolution". Contrary to the optimistic claims stressing the leaderless and spontaneous nature of the new social protests, Morozov emphasizes the well-planned organization of these actions. Furthermore, he argues that repressive regimes are using social media for surveillance and to track dissidents (Morozov, 2009a, p. 12; Morozov, 2011).

It can be argued that social media can be used both for emancipatory and repressive purposes. The problem lies in ignoring the fact that social media and other communication technologies are a field of struggle shaped through clashes of competing interests, and presenting excessive optimist and pessimist claims which deny alternatives courses of technology.

In that struggle, it is also important to notice that companies operating social media platforms are also major players and their interests can be in conflict with the purpose of emancipation. Accordingly, not only States wishing to have control over their societies, but also private companies monitor social media users for gathering their data and selling the information, as emphasized by Christian Fuchs (2011a; 2011b; 2012b; 2014; 2015), and Daniel Trottier and David Lyon (2012). Surveillance studies related to social media are so abundant that they constitute the third specific field in the social media literature in addition to studies concerning political participation and those of social movements.

In the literature, it is not difficult to find empirical studies on censorship and surveillance in different countries. Thomas Poell (2015) explored the cases in Tunisia, Iran and China, where there are powerful authoritarian tendencies. While the powers in these countries use various censorship strategies in their attempts to suppress dissident movements that emerge and develop through networks, the activists have developed a range of strategies to tactically maneuver within the social media landscape, such as using symbolic language, pseudonyms and misspelling to cover identity, and changing proxy settings or using VPN to circumvent censorship (Poell, 2015, pp. 190, 199, 200).

Investigating internet control strategies in different countries since the mid-2000s, Ronald Deibert and Rafal Rohozinski (2010; 2012) present a comprehensive picture. According to their studies, repressive powers consolidate their control on the Internet and social media through a new generation of strategies. In addition to the first-generation control strategies mostly consisting of filtering and access bans, authoritarian countries also use the legal framework and other offensive strategies to intimidate, discredit and demoralize the opposition in the networks. Among the examples of the second and third generations strategies are; making informal removal requests to internet service providers (ISPs), organizing network attacks against dissident websites or social media accounts, starting State-sponsored information/disinformation campaigns and applying data mining measures against opponents.

Thus, according to the new generation of control strategies, it is necessary for repressive powers to be active in social media. This is why Chinese officials are very interested in the discussions held over the networks (Shirk, 2011, p. 26) and hundreds of thousands of people working for Chinese government are engaged in manipulative activities on the Internet and social media (Yang, 2009, pp. 51-52; King, Pan & Roberts, 2013). These people, commonly labeled as "50 cent party members", adopt anonymous identities to participate in online discussions aiming to prevent the development of critical ideas and to guide the direction of the debates in accordance with the principles of the power. In Russia, there are also online armies promoting the policies of the President Vladimir Putin on the Internet and social media (Walker, 2015).

Against the challenge of online opposition, the political power responds by adjusting and refining its institutions and methods of control. During the Arab Spring and subsequent social protests, the political powers were unprepared to deal with social media and for this reason, they resorted to violence against the masses who had been mobilized through social media, thus amplifying the scale of protests. This is why the user side has become the focal point in the literature. This is also valid for Turkey since after the experience of massive social protests, the political power in Turkey also decided to become organized and utilize social media instead of ignoring it. In order to better comprehend the issue in Turkey, it is useful to explore the context of the country, which shapes the strategies and actions of the government.

THE CONTEXT IN TURKEY AND SOCIAL MEDIA

Turkey has a relatively advanced telecommunication infrastructure, and social media usage in the country is very popular. There are more than 50 million broadband internet subscribers in Turkey, constituting more than 60 percent of the population, and nearly 74 million mobile subscribers, creating a 93.7 percent penetration rate (The Information and Communication Technologies Authority [BTK], pp. 31, 37). Of the Internet users in Turkey, 82.4 percent use social media for creating profile, sending messages and sharing visual materials, 74.5 percent watch videos, 69.5 percent read online news and articles, 65.9 percent undertake searches on health, 65.5 seek information on goods and services, and 63.7 percent listen to music (Turkish Statistical Institute [TUIK], 2016).

The report of We Are Social, titled *Digital in 2016*, provides data on the Internet use in Turkey (2016, pp. 450-459). There are 42 million active internet users in the country, constituting a 53 percent penetration rate. 36 million of these users connect through mobile devices and 77 percent go online every day. Of the total web traffic, 51 percent is generated through laptop and desktop computers, 46 percent through mobile devices, and 4 percent through tablets. The report underscores that people use the Internet and social media more than watching television. Users spend 4 hours 14 minutes on personal computers and tablets, and 2 hours 35 minutes on mobile devices. Internet users using these two ways of connection spend 2 hours 32 minutes on social media platforms in comparison to 2 hours 18 minutes on television. According to the report, Turkey is 19th in the world list ranking concerning the Internet use, and 12th in social media usage (2016, pp. 23, 34).

Thus, social media constitutes a significant opportunity for social advocacy initiatives in Turkey where there are deep divisions across society. In the mostly Muslim but constitutionally secular country, the conflict between secularism and Islam has persisted for decades, like the struggle of Kurds, who make up almost 20 percent of the population, for the recognition of their identity. The Kurdistan Workers' Party (PKK) has been waging an armed struggle since the 1980s, making terrorism a sensitive subject. Due to the hegemony of Sunni Islam, other religions and Islamic sects have been experiencing difficulties. In these circumstances, different social actors are using social media for their struggles.

The political power in Turkey is an effective user of social media. The Justice and Development Party (AKP) has been in power since 2002 and has struggled with crises threatening its rule and legitimacy in recent years. In face of the crises, it has not only been tightening its grasp on power, resulting in claims of authoritarianism, but also developing abilities related to social media. Two crises that erupted in 2013 and subsequent events are especially influential in this respect.

The Gezi Park Protest, which originally started in the last days of May 2013 against the construction of a shopping mall in the center of Istanbul, suddenly turned into a nationwide revolt after the brutal police intervention and millions of people staged street protests against AKP policies. Then, in the last days of 2013, police arrested the sons of three AKP ministers on "corruption" charges and wiretap recordings related to the case were shared on YouTube. AKP considered the scandal as a coup attempt to discredit and overthrow the government and accused its old allies, Gülen Movement supporters in the judiciary and police ("Turkey PM Erdogan," 2014) of being behind the scandal. During the ascension to power, AKP had collaborated with Gülenists in key State positions. The two Islamo-conservative forces neutralized the old strictly secular establishment but then began to conflict with each other.

These crises are determinant for the social media strategies of AKP. As a reaction to being ignored by the mainstream Turkish media, protesters at the Gezi Park used social media effectively not just to circumvent censorship but also to get organized and resist. Though AKP leader Recep Tayyip Erdoğan described Twitter as a curse that was spreading lies during the protest (Oremus, 2013), the government learned important lessons concerning the potentials of social media, which will be elaborated below.

The feud in the power bloc, erupted as the "corruption" scandal, further reinforced AKP's concerns. Social media accounts in line with the Gülen Movement have been harming the government and profiting from the anonymity of the Internet. The recordings of the "corruption" case, which were considered by AKP to have been fabricated, were posted from anonymous accounts. With the intensification of the feud, the government closed many media outlets of Gülenists but could not find a solution to the problem of the social media. Thus, this time, Erdoğan pledged to wipe out Twitter ("Twitter is blocked," 2014).

Twitter is the main battleground given that an anonymous account until its deactivation was persistently posting new and delicate information concerning AKP. The *Fuat Avni* account, which stopped posting five days after the failed coup of July 15 in 2016 amid the massive crackdown on the Gülenists and other government opponents, had more than 2.9 million followers. Until the deactivation, the account holder was able to access critical government information, such as secret meetings or future police operations. It even gave information on Erdoğan's daily routine, proving that its sources were within the close circle of the power. There was heavy pressure on the government given that despite serious efforts the account owner had not been identified for many years. Fuat Avni is also an example of manipulative use of social media. Though Gülenists were removed from the critical posts after the "corruption" scandal, the Fuat Avni Tweets released classified information, that the mainstream media would never print, and exposed the government's wrongdoings, attracting the attention of ordinary people. However, it also posted erroneous information to discredit the government.

The actions in social media, generally associated with the Gülen Movement, can hardly be described as democratic. Nevertheless, they cannot be ignored in assessing the role of social media in advocacy initiatives given that they showed the limits of governments in facing opposition in social media and the importance of anonymity in dealing with a powerful government.

INNER-CIRCLE STRATEGIES

The official level of the inner-circle can be defined from the social media accounts of the political power and digital propaganda. As is the case in many countries, the actors and institutions of power in Turkey use social media. For example, President Erdoğan and ministers have verified Twitter accounts. Institutions also have confirmed accounts, such as the Turkish Presidency, the Prime Minister's Office and various other ministries. However, a sense of dislike for social media and a lack of unified action are found in the highest echelons.

President Erdoğan's Twitter account has more than 9 million followers as of August 2016 and this provides him an enormous opportunity for political influence. The Turkish Presidency has also two Twitter accounts, one in Turkish and the other in English, which have 3.6 million and 684,000 followers, respectively. However, Prime Minister Binali Yıldırım does not have a Twitter account but his office does have an account, which was created in May 2016, the month in which the previous Prime Minister Ahmet Davutoğlu resigned. During his time in the office, Davutoğlu used his own account and his title was given as "Prime Minister of Turkey" and "President of the AKP". After his resignation, it became necessary to create a new account for the office of the Prime Minister given that Davutoğlu immediately deleted his titles and Yıldırım does not have a personal account which indicates his new position.

The President of Turkey does not like social media and his last declaration of his dislike was in June 2016, after the ISIS attack in Istanbul Atatürk Airport ("Erdoğan: Biliyorsunuz," 2016). Speaking about social media comments after the attack, he said, "As you know, I am against social media. Many people have attacked me for this reason. [...] I am not using social media but there are people using it in my name. This is different". Conversely, lower ranking officials of the AKP appear to like Twitter. Their use is categorically different from their superiors whose accounts are monitored by their aides and have been subject to control. Lower ranking officials monitor their own accounts and write whatever they wish, which sometimes sparked arguments between AKP and opposition.

The other aspect of the official level is digital propaganda. In the autumn of 2013, news organizations argued that Erdoğan had ordered AKP to be more active in social media (Sokollu & Demir, 2013; "AK Parti'den 6 bin kişilik," 2013; Kasapoğlu, 2014). Hence, AKP decided to deploy more than 6,000 people to engage in social media communication, especially to present digital propaganda prior to the local election of March 2014. The news in media stressed that these people would be recruited from AKP organizations in all 81 cities of Turkey and receive training in the party headquarter in Ankara in order to digitally present AKP policies, create content, and rapidly share visual and written material ("AK Parti'den 6 bin kişilik," 2013; Kasapoğlu, 2014).

Pro-government and opposition figures share common ground in the Gezi Park Protest being the beginning of the mobilization of AKP in social media. Taha Ün, who monitors one of the most important pro-government Twitter accounts, emphasized that of all political parties, AKP is the leader in understanding the importance of social media and the fastest to become organized after the protest (Kasapoğlu, 2014). Tayfun Kahraman, the spokesperson of the Taksim Solidarity Platform, which was the voice of protesters at the Gezi Park, also said, "With the Gezi Park, the power of social media is understood" (Sokollu & Demir, 2013). Yaşar Adanalı, a political scientist and sociologist, declared that "The only way for the government is to be active in these platforms" given that "the decentralized opposition using social media effectively shook its power" (Sokollu & Demir, 2013).

In 2013 and 2014, there was a huge imbalance in the social media resources of the political parties. Adanalı argued that the size of AKP's social media team consisting of 6,000 people was to ensure that effective propaganda would be delivered and indicated that this would require a massive budget and the collaboration of several firms to establish the network (Sokollu & Demir, 2013). According to Adanalı, the required human resource could be provided from the Youth Group of the party but it is also probable that many fake accounts could be operated given that it is possible to buy 10,000 Twitter followers with 20 Euros. The election campaign of Ekmeleddin İhsanoğlu, the rival of Erdoğan in the presidential election of August 2014, offers a striking comparison. İhsanoğlu was the common candidate of the two largest opposition parties of the time, the Republican People's Party (CHP) and the Nationalist Movement Party (MHP), but his social media team only consisted of 35 full-time workers and 60 volunteers (Kasapoğlu, 2014).

Speaking in July 2013 while there were still clashes between the police and protesters, Süleyman Soylu, an AKP leader, said their social media initiative had indeed started in April and it was a "total coincidence" that the initiative and the Gezi Park Protest happened simultaneously ("AK Parti'den sosyal medya," 2013). He also complained about the defamation, disinformation and manipulation that was staged with fake accounts during the protest and emphasized that their 9 million party members are important for social media campaigns. Thus, the AKP is flexible in its use of social media given that it took the decision to utilize these platforms just after the Gezi Park Protest and started to implement this communication few months later; therefore, it would be incorrect to only focus Erdoğan's comments denouncing social media.

AKP was successful in gaining support in the local and presidential elections in 2014. There was also a general election in July 2015 and AKP started a new initiative. The New Turkey Digital Office (NTDO), a unit of 180 people, was formed to present the official propaganda in social media (Altuntaş, 2015a). According to Gökhan Yücel, the director of NTDO, the employees were engaged under full-time contract and were responsible of four specific tasks; namely content creation, interaction, monitoring, and field communication (Altuntaş, 2015a). Contrary to the comments of the party officials emphasizing that the office would continue its activities, the NTDO disappeared after the election.

At that time, Yücel emphasized that the NTDO was an official organization working only with institutional accounts and strongly denied the presence of "Aktrolls"in the office (Altuntaş, 2015a). According to the director of the unit, the reason for founding the office was indeed to overcome the general perception that associates the concept of troll with AKP. He also stressed that they were not creating negative propaganda or acting unethically as the group of social media users who were often referred to as Aktrolls did. The then Deputy Chairman of the AKP, Beşir Atalay declared that the rumors on Aktrolls working secretly in favor of his party must be over with the formation of NTDO, which represents an institutional stance (Altuntaş, 2015a).

The unofficial level of the inner-circle is mainly occupied by Aktrolls and AKP has denied the existence of Aktrolls given that their usage of social media is problematical. Contrary to AKP, which started to ignore the thousands of party members that had been trained to present information in social media, opponents have begun to discuss the issue concerning the 6,000 Aktrolls and have been investigating their activities and their relationship with the political power. Since government sources do not offer information on this topic, the available data mainly comes from opposition sources and this is a reason why some degree of caution is required in considering the information given below.

Accusations against Aktrolls are long and severe described as insulting, defaming, lying, intimidating, social lynching, snitching and spreading hate speech. According to allegations in media, in their attacks against opposition, they mostly use fake accounts and profit from the anonymity of Twitter ("Aktroller ne kadar," 2015; "10 maddede Aktrolleri," 2015). In addition, they open fake accounts in the names of opponents to discredit as Sezgin Tanrıkulu, a CHP parliamentarian, reported ("Sezgin Tanrıkulu: Profiline," 2016). Aktrolls use opposition party symbols and logos in these fake accounts and make postings contrary to common sense.

Moreover, they mobilize in times of crisis, when social reaction is oriented against the government, as was the case of the funerals of fallen soldiers in the summer of 2015. After the end of the peace process with PKK, the funerals of the fallen soldiers became a sensitive issue for the government, especially when the grieving relatives publicly criticized AKP. Public sympathy for their grief increased and their comments were shared in social media. However, opposition newspapers referred to the lynching campaign of Aktrolls in social media at the same period by emphasizing the circulation of messages about treason and lack of patriotism ("Aktroller ne kadar," 2015; "10 maddede Aktrolleri," 2015).

In March 2016, 30 parliamentarians requested an official investigation into Aktrolls. They emphasized that people were becoming afraid of freely using social media and that hate speeches had reached an alarming level ("CHP, 'AKtroller' için," 2016). The messages of Ün, the owner of the *Sağlam İrade* Twitter account, can be displayed as examples of the concerns. He referred to a meat cleaver as the only method of communication with PKK members and said that he misses the 1990s, the period in which extra-judicial killings were common ("Kürtlere 'satır gösteren'," 2015). He implicitly described Alevis, people from the Shiite branch of Islam, as insects and praised the attacks of Sunni Saudis against Shiite Houthis in Yemen ("Kürtlere 'satır gösteren'," 2015). Commenting on the repression against opponents in social media, he declared that "AKP would never be the one that casts the first stone but it would also never turn the other cheek if it is hit" (Kasapoğlu, 2014).

According to the news published in the Gülenist newspaper *Taraf* but presented by other media organizations, Aktrolls were organized after the Gezi Park Protest (as cited in "Aktroller ne kadar," 2015; as cited in "10 maddede Aktrolleri," 2015; as cited in "'Sövme Timi'," 2015). The news articles comment on many aspects of Aktrolls such as their identity and administration. Aktrolls are generally between 20 and 25 years old and mainly recruited from the AKP Youth Group. For security reasons, they are from the close circle of the AKP leaders and are managed by a core team of 30 people who decide on the targets. The core members mobilize them by posting the first tweet against the target. It is also argued that aides in the Presidential Palace and in the AKP headquarter are involved in strategy making and have fake social media accounts.

The same news argues that Twitter's refusal to detect the identity of users after the Gezi Park Protest provides a cover for Aktrolls. Another cover is the indirect payments for Aktrolls. Private firms receiving contracts from AKP municipalities are intermediaries for the payments. The minimum monthly payment is 1,000 Turkish Liras but successful Aktrolls can obtain contracts with public banks and institutions or private firms close to AKP, making it possible to gain bigger payments.

This information must be viewed cautiously because of its Gülenist origin; however, news from other media organizations are in line with the allegations. For example, a map that displays the interaction of some well-known Aktroll accounts with other Twitter accounts was published and according to the map, Mustafa Varank's Twitter account is situated at center of the web of interaction ("'Ak Trol'lerin haritası," 2015). Varank is the Senior Advisor to President Erdoğan. There is also a controversial recording on YouTube in which Varank is allegedly discussing the mobilization of Aktrolls with Sümeyye Erdoğan, the President's daughter (https://www.youtube.com/watch?v=bEBV7icWaWM). Furthermore, Ahmet Sever, the Senior Advisor of ex-President Abdullah Gül, claimed that Aktrolls are ruled from the Presidential Palace and indicated that Varank was the main leader ("Gül'ün eski danışmanı," 2016). He also argued that President Erdoğan is well aware of Aktrolls, and claimed that the system is built to intimidate. In response, Varank sued Sever.

According to Sever, Aktrolls' mobilization against the founding members and former leaders of AKP, such as Abdullah Gül, Bülent Arınç, Hüseyin Çelik and Sadullah Ergin, is a proof of the lack of tolerance against any criticism ("Gül'ün eski danışmanı," 2016). For example, Arınç, who is also the ex-President of Turkish Parliament, condemned the Aktrolls attacks, which occurred after his harsh comments on the government and the President ("Arınç'tan Ak Trol," 2016).

There are also other indications of the relationship between Aktrolls and the political power. Within the framework of a judicial investigation possibly conducted by Gülenists, the owner of the *Esat Ç.* Aktroll account was identified. He was born in 1991 and was found to be a member of the AKP Youth Group ("'Ak Trol' Esat Ç.'nin," 2015). In another investigation opened upon the demand of Umut Oran, a CHP parliamentarian, following lies being spread about him from a Twitter account, it was detected that the account had been monitored from three different IP addresses; the Prime Minister Office, the Ankara office of a pro-government newspaper, and the Istanbul headquarter of another pro-government newspaper ("10 maddede Aktrolleri," 2015). Additionally, President Erdoğan was a witness to the marriage of Taha Ün, whose wife is the aide of Turkish First Lady ("Kürtlere 'satır gösteren'," 2015). Moreover, Tanrıkulu claims that successful Aktrolls are being appointed to government posts ("Trollere ne kadar," 2016).

As a result of a manipulative blog, which was created because of the power struggle within AKP, it is understood that each AKP faction wants its own troll team.

According to the long text shared in May 2016 in *Pelikan Dosyası* (The Pelican File) blog, the then Prime Minister Davutoğlu was deliberately acting against the President in order to weaken him (https://pelikandosyasi.wordpress.com). The text also claims that Davutoğlu wanted to found his own media organization with its own troll team by employing Ün. The blog has not shared another text since then but only one text was sufficient to cause Davutoğlu's resignation.

Bot accounts are another aspect of the unofficial level and have become obvious with the critical visit of the President to the USA in March 2016. At that time, the international popularity of Erdoğan was questionable and a Twitter campaign started with the hashtag of "weloveerdogan". Following 300,000 Twitter messages, the hashtag became a trending topic on Twitter but the company deleted it ("Turkish ministers accuse," 2016). It is possible that many messages could have been produced by automated bots. Turkish ministers reacted harshly and accused Twitter of censoring Erdoğan. However, bot accounts allegations even existed in 2014 with Ün strongly denying them in that period (Kasapoğlu, 2014). Also in 2015, the CHP social media team declared that they found Facebook more trustworthy than Twitter and indicated the abnormal interactivity of the AKP accounts (Altuntaş, 2015b). Furthermore, Phil Howard, who investigates bots at the Oxford Internet Institute, claims that Mexico and Turkey are two cases where bots have been particularly widely used (Baerthlein, 2016).

OUTER-CIRCLE STRATEGIES

For the judicial level of the outer-circle, it must be said that laws and regulations in Turkey are not settling disputes but amplifying them. The Transparency Report of Twitter for the second half of 2015 gives a clue on the issue (https://transparency.twitter.com/removal-requests/2015/jul-dec). Among 486 court orders for removal that Twitter received from all over the world, 450 were from Turkey. 1,761 of 4,131 removal requests undertaken by government agencies without a court decision were from Turkey and submitted by the Presidency of Telecommunication and Communication (TİB), an institution which was closed after the failed coup and handed over its remits to the Information and Communication Technologies Authority (BTK). Thus, Turkey was the world leader in content removal requests before Russia, with 2,211 of all 4,617 removal requests being from Turkey; thus, constituting 48 percent of the total. Additionally, 3,003 of 3,353 tweets that were withheld were related to Turkish demands. In response, Twitter declared that they made their objections in the Turkish courts and achieved a 6 percent success. The first half of 2015 was not bright either (https://transparency.twitter.com/removal-requests/2015/jan-jun) with 408 of 442 court orders for removal coming from Turkey in addition to 310 of 561 requests without court decision. As a result of these demands, Twitter withheld 125 accounts, constituting 79 percent of all 158 accounts withheld. Russia followed Turkey with 22 accounts. Among the 2,354 tweets withheld, 1,667 were from Turkey.

These restrictive activities are closely related with the developments in Turkey, which are summarized by Yaman Akdeniz (2015), a law professor working on Internet freedom. Turkey only sent one court order and six other requests in 2012 to Twitter but nothing was done. In 2013, though authorities decided to inspect 5 million of 13 million tweets posted during the Gezi Park Protest and detained 34 people for inciting revolts in social media, Turkey only sent five court orders and four requests without a court order in relation to 32 accounts and again Twitter took no action. According to Akdeniz, Turkey's rise in Twitter censorship started in the first half of 2014 after the "corruption" scandal and the release of the wiretap recordings.

With the amendments made by the initiative of the government in February 2014, it has become possible to ban access to the Internet without waiting for a court order by claiming "violation of private life" ("İşte 10 maddede," 2014; "9 Soruda yeni internet," 2014). Concerning these violations, TİB (now BTK) has the authority to ban the Internet access and to force the Union of Internet Service Providers to put the ban in force within four hours. Bans issued by TİB must be submitted to a judge within 24 hours and the judge has to decide within 48 hours. This means that it has become possible to impose a ban on access for three days without a court order. Furthermore, Akdeniz (2015) claims that judges confirm bans in cases related with corruption, state violence and criticism against politicians.

Furthermore, the government also has the authority to ban access without a court order (Karakaş, 2015; Akgül, 2015; "İnternet 'zincir'lendi," 2015). After the revealing on YouTube of a secret conversation on Syria between the Head of Intelligence and the Foreign Minister, AKP attempted to include the violation of national security in the jurisdiction of TİB. However, the Constitutional Court decided that TİB could not take decisions on national security. The law was changed again in March 2015 and the cabinet members were given the right to ban access in relation to "protection of people's life and property, national security, protection of public order, prevention of crime and protection of public health". The ministers' bans have to be put in force within four hours and to remain valid, the ban must be confirmed by a judge within 48 hours.

Though the procedure seems to be under judicial control, in practice, the government has total control given that most of the bans are confirmed, encouraging the requests for the removal of content from social media platforms. By submitting objections, Twitter wants to show that it does not approve of this situation but it does not want to, again, confront the Turkish authorities that put a blanket ban on YouTube and Twitter in March 2014 (Akdeniz, 2015; Karakaş, 2015). Akdeniz says that Twitter does not want to lose Turkey, which is an important market with millions of users, and Facebook puts in force every ban it receives for the same reason (Karakaş, 2015). Therefore, the political power has the upper hand against social media platforms. The attitude of the platforms is not baseless. After the blanket ban of March 2014, Akdeniz and his colleagues filed a complaint in the Constitutional Court and succeeded in overturning the action (Karakaş, 2015). Thus, a blanket ban for Twitter constitutes a breach of the freedom of expression. However, similar bans were also applied after the murder of a prosecutor in March 2015 and the ISIS terror attack in Suruç in July 2015 (Karakaş, 2015).

According to the watchdog organization, Freedom House (2014, p. 3), Turkey is a critical "swing state" in Internet policy given that the battle on policy would possibly influence other countries, creating a democratic or a repressive model. However, the picture is not promising; according to the President of the organization, Mark P. Lagon, 90 percent of all demands that Twitter and Facebook received in 2015 for deleting comments were from Turkey (Çamlıbel, 2016). According to Lagon, especially the cases of insulting the President have become a central strategy of oppression with a new case being brought every four days in 2015 (Çamlıbel, 2016). The power holders are not very keen on accepting criticism and the judiciary does not resist political demands. Furthermore, regularly charging people with insulting the President is restricting the democratic usage of social media.

The Minister of Justice, Bekir Bozdağ, confirmed in March 2016 that there were 1,845 cases of insulting the President and said that nobody should have the right to denigrate another person ("Erdoğan'a hakaretten," 2016). Erdoğan's lawyer Hüseyin Aydın declared in August 2016 that there are still more than 3,000 cases to be heard ("Erdoğan withdraws," 2016). Contrary to Bozdağ's comments, not all the cases are concerned with insults; rather, people are deterred from freely criticizing the political power in social media and there are various examples displaying the determination of the political power. For example, a case of insulting the President was opened in August 2016 against a 14-year-old because of the comments in his Facebook account ("'Erdoğan'a hakaret'te bugün," 2016). It is indicated that the case was started after a tip-off to the Prime Minister Office's Communication Center (BİMER).

The current law pertaining to social media forbids people from disseminating criminal content. However, the interpretation of what is criminal sometimes turns into a Kafkaesque case. There is a case in which the authorities detained a dissident journalist for re-sharing a critical message while leaving untouched the original writer (Doğan, 2016). Similarly, sharing news reports of the legal media organizations can be enough for being charged with terror propaganda ("Serbest gazeteci," 2016).

Media blackouts worsen the situation. In addition to corruption cases, attacks of ISIS and PKK have been increasing since 2015. Turkey has lived with terror outbreaks, but the latest attacks were at an unprecedented scale and occurred in metropolitan areas. Between July 2015 and August 2016, more than 340 people died and 1,680 were wounded in 16 different attacks ("Son bir yılda," 2016). Ever-recurring attacks created questions concerning the policies and abilities of the government, but the discussion has been prevented by media blackouts (http://bianet.org/konu/yayin-yasagi).

The mainstream Turkish media respect the blackouts and then in the absence of information, people use social media intensively and criticize the government. This was the case after the murder of a State prosecutor in his office in March 2015. Just after the declaration of the media blackout, Aktrolls mobilized and *Esat Ç.* demanded the screenshots of social media accounts that did not abide by the blackout ("Yayın yasağı," 2016). In every crisis, Aktrolls scan social media and identify the critical comments and their authors in order to send them to the authorities that are not reluctant to open cases. Additionally, the authorities continuously warn people not to share "incorrect" information on social media in crisis moments. For instance, BTK announced that users have legal responsibility for their messages in social media after the ISIS attack in Istanbul Atatürk Airport ("BTK sosyal medyayı," 2016). After the failed coup, the National Police wanted to be informed about messages in social media "praising terror and the coup" (Yıldırım, 2016).

Turkish people have access to foreign news networks that do not abide by the blackouts. Nevertheless, it would not be logical to expect from foreign networks the clarification of serious events by comprehensive discussions. Given that it is among the most important sources of information in Turkey restricting social media aggravates the existing problems. According to *Digital News Report 2016* of the Reuters Institute of Oxford University (2016, pp. 72-73), because of the pressure on traditional media, Turkish people prefer the Internet and social media as major sources of information. In Turkey, 90 percent of the weekly news traffic happens on the Internet (social media included), with the specific share of social media is being 73 percent. The respective shares of television, newspapers and radio are 80 percent, 54 percent and 41 percent.

As terror attacks intensify, judicial cases of terror propaganda on social media also multiply. In particular, after the termination of the peace process with PKK, the number of cases increased and many people were arrested with terror propaganda and sentenced to prison. The same is valid for the period after the failed coup, in which some social media users were arrested for allegedly praising the coup attempt ("İnternette darbe," 2016). The problem is that the line between propaganda and criticism is very vague.

Technical measures for controlling the Internet and social media are among the tools of political power. According to the news from Reuters, the preferred technical method for Turkish government in critical periods is no longer blanket bans but to throttle bandwidth (Abutaleb & Sezer, 2016). Reuters claims that this method is increasingly used by countries wishing to control the Internet. News coverage reveals that Turkey Blocks, a watchdog group on Internet censorship, confirmed that Turkey blocked the Internet at least seven times with bandwidth throttling in 2015. Lastly, Facebook, Twitter and YouTube were inaccessible for more than 105 minutes after the deadly ISIS terror attack in Gaziantep in August 2016 and this is the sixth case of throttling in 2016 (Sozeri, 2016). According to Reuters, Turkey rejects claims by saying that the slowing down of social media platforms is due to intensive traffic. The agency also emphasized that throttling is more difficult to detect and more complicated to object to given that it is difficult to appeal in the absence of an actual ban.

As a counter-measure, Virtual Private Network (VPN) services have become increasingly popular (Demirel, 2016). After the ISIS attack in Istanbul Atatürk Airport, the downloading of the Android application of ZenMate, a private VPN company, increased by 1,300 percent and the rate of increase for the iPhone application was 2,400 percent.

VPN services are especially important for overcoming the ban on access to news sites. It is estimated that TİB banned more than 100,000 websites ("Turkey shuts down," 2016). Akdeniz claims that between April 2015 and July 2016, more than 3,000 news link were blocked mainly by requests from ministers ("1 yılda 3 bin haber," 2016). He adds that the bans are not being applied for a specific content but for the whole sites, which is a breach of the Constitution and "absolute censorship".

CONCLUSION

In Turkey, due to the strategies of the political power, there are important obstacles in using social media in advocacy campaigns. In this context, it is important to inquire about the adaptation of advocacy campaigners in the country for having a better understanding of the social reality. Though such an inquiry basically falls out of the scope of this chapter which principally focuses on the social media strategies of the political power in Turkey, a couple of interviews were conducted with the staff of the several non-governmental organizations (NGO) pursuing advocacy goals and expert scholars in order to verify the results in the chapter and to assist further elaborated researches. The identities of the interviewees are kept secret because of the security concerns.

An important point emphasized in the interviews is that the government has gained the upper hand in social media though the NGOs and activists were using it efficiently just after the Gezi Park Protest in 2013. This is in line with the findings of the chapter. According to an interviewee, NGOs were able to reach masses through their social media accounts with thousands of followers but the failed coup in 2016 and the subsequent declaration of the state of emergency has completely changed the situation. With the restriction of the freedom of expression in the country, she claims that it is not easy to use social media efficiently; the reports of the NGOs are being considered as criminal documents and social media postings can be a cause for prosecution. Thus, she observes a decline in the use of social media among advocacy campaigners. Moreover, both organizations and activists, in a form of self-censorship, check their social media histories and delete dangerous messages for not being prosecuted. These confirm the results of the chapter as well.

According to a scholar working on the subject, Turkish activists are keeping their hope for the future though they acknowledge the domination of the political power in social media. These activists view the Gezi Park Protest as an unfinished process and believe that they can create once again creative solutions for defying the authoritarian power. In this framework, the fact that the government opens criminal cases against dissident youngsters makes sense according to an interviewee given that these are the people who use social media in the most creative way as was witnessed in the Gezi Park Protest. This also verifies the findings mentioned in the chapter.

On the other hand, according to another interviewee, these problems are not for all advocacy initiatives. Those who pursue a cause approved by the government, such as fighting against Islamophobia, can work freely and use social media without having restrictions. He stresses that organizing advocacy campaigns against the political power is considered as an act of revolt to be suppressed. The fact that approximately 3 or 4 thousand associations have been forcibly closed after the coup attempt confirms his concerns. In this context, he says, it is better to keep a low profile than defying the political power in order to have a better chance of survival. Several incidents, in which the authorities arrested the most prominent advocacy campaigners by ignoring all sorts of objections, are in line with his concerns. In the fall of 2017, Osman Kavala, the most prominent supporter of the civil society in Turkey, was arrested on terror charges. Moreover, in the summer of 2017 the country director of the Amnesty International was arrested on the same charges along with several well-known activists while having a meeting on digital security in a hotel of Istanbul.

The findings in the chapter and the expressions of interviewees shows that social media is not a tool of emancipation *per se*. The trajectory of this new medium depends on the social struggle between the forces of emancipation and domination. The authoritarian power in Turkey, after experiencing the emancipatory potential of social media, has developed the efficient strategies which hamper advocacy activities in this digital environment. However, social media and the Internet are still the best options available for advocacy campaigners.

REFERENCES

1 yılda 3 bin haber linkine erişim engeli! (2016, July 4). Retrieved September 1, 2016, from http://t24.com.tr/haber/1-yilda-3-bin-haber-linkine-erisim-engeli,348456

10 maddede Aktrolleri tanıma rehberi. (2015, September 30). Retrieved August 16, 2016, from http://politikkedi.com/10-maddede-aktrolleri-tanima-rehberi.html

9 Soruda yeni internet yasası. (2014, February 6). Retrieved September 1, 2016, from http://www.diken.com.tr/gecmis-olsun-aknetli-donem-basliyor/

Abutaleb, Y., & Sezer, C. (2016, July 6). Turkey appears to be in vanguard of 'throttling' social media after attacks. *Reuters*. Retrieved September 1, 2016, from http://www.reuters.com/article/us-mideast-crisis-socialmedia-idUSKCN0ZM2O3

AK Parti'den 6 bin kişilik sosyal medya ordusu. (2013, November 14). Retrieved August 31, 2016, from http://www.hurriyet.com.tr/ak-partiden-6-bin-kisilik-sosyal-medya-ordusu-25115336

AK Parti'den sosyal medya atağı. (2013, June 14). Retrieved August 31, 2016, from http://www.milliyet.com.tr/ak-parti-den-sosyal-medya-atagi/gundem/detay/1722933/default.htm

'Ak Trol' Esat Ç.'nin kimliğini deşifre eden Taraf'a beraat. (2015, April 26). Retrieved August 31, 2016, from http://www.diken.com.tr/ak-trol-esat-c-nin-kimligini-desifre-eden-tarafa-beraat/

'Ak Trol'lerin haritası çıkarıldı: Merkezde Erdoğan'ın danışmanı Varank var. (2015, October 14). Retrieved August 31, 2016, from http://www.diken.com.tr/ak-trollerin-haritasi-cikarildi-merkezde-erdoganin-danismani-varank-var/

Akdeniz, Y. (2015, August 13). Twitter sansürlemede dünya lideriyiz. *Diken*. Retrieved August 31, 2016, from http://www.diken.com.tr/twitter-sansurlemede-dunya-lideriyiz/

Akgül, E. (2015, February 5). Yeni İnternet "Yasası"nı Anlama Kılavuzu. *Bianet*. Retrieved September 1, 2016, from http://bianet.org/bianet/medya/162080-yeni-internet-yasasi-ni-anlama-kilavuzu

Aktroller ne kadar maaş alıyor? (2015, September 29). Retrieved August 31, 2016, from http://www.sozcu.com.tr/2015/gunun-icinden/aktroller-ne-kadar-maas-aliyor-945937/

Altuntaş, Ö. (2015a, May 18). AKP Sosyal Medya Merkezi'nde bir gün. *BBC Türkçe*. Retrieved August 31, 2016, from http://www.bbc.com/turkce/haberler/2015/05/150515_akp_sosyal_medya

Altuntaş, Ö. (2015b, June 1). CHP Sosyal Medya Merkezi: 'Amaç, AKP Türkiyesi ile CHP Türkiyesi arasındaki farkı göstermek'. *BBC Türkçe*. Retrieved August 31, 2016, from http://www.bbc.com/turkce/haberler/2015/06/150601_chp_sosyal_medya_gs2015

Arınç'tan Ak Trol ve 'troliçe'lere sert cevap. (2016, February 1). Retrieved August 31, 2016, from http://www.abcgazetesi.com/arinctan-ak-trol-ve-trolicelere-sert-cevap-7298h.htm

Baerthlein, T. (2016, August 6). The rise of political bots on social media. *Deutsche Welle*. Retrieved August 31, 2016, from http://www.dw.com/en/the-rise-of-political-bots-on-social-media/a-19450562

BTK sosyal medyayı uyardı: Saldırıyla ilgili paylaşım yapanların yasal sorumluluğu var. (2016, June 29). Retrieved September 1, 2016, from http://www.diken.com.tr/btk-sosyal-medyayi-uyardi-saldiriyla-ilgili-paylasimda-bulunanlarin-yasal-sorumlulugu-var/

Çamlıbel, C. (2016, February 8). Freedom House Başkanı Lagon: Mülteci akını Batı'nın hatası. *Hürriyet*. Retrieved September 1, 2016, from http://www.hurriyet.com.tr/freedom-house-baskani-lagon-multeci-akini-batinin-hatasi-40050749

Castells, M. (2015). *Networks of Outrage and Hope: Social Movements in the Internet Age*. Cambridge, UK: Polity.

CHP 'AKtroller' için komisyon kurulmasını istedi. (2016, March 23). Retrieved August 31, 2016, from http://t24.com.tr/haber/chp-aktroller-icin-komisyon-kurulmasini-istedi,333304

Deibert, R., & Rohozinski, R. (2010). Beyond Denial: Introducing Next-Generation Information Access Controls. In R. Deibert, J. Palfrey, R. Rohozinski, & J. Zittrain (Eds.), *Access Controlled: The Shaping of Power, Rights, and Rule in Cyberspace* (pp. 3–13). Cambridge, MA: The MIT Press.

Deibert, R., & Rohozinski, R. (2012). Contesting Cyberspace and the Coming Crisis of Authority. In R. Deibert, J. Palfrey, R. Rohozinski, & J. Zittrain (Eds.), *Access Contested: Security, Identity, and Resistance in Asian Cyberspace* (pp. 21–41). Cambridge, MA: The MIT Press.

Demirel, F. (2016, July 1). Zenmate'in Türkiye'deki iOS ve Android indirme sayıları ortalama yüzde 1850 arttı. *Webrazzi*. Retrieved September 1, 2016, from http://webrazzi.com/2016/07/01/zenmatein-turkiyedeki-ios-ve-android-indirme-sayilari-ortalama-yuzde-1850-artti/

Demirhan, K. (2014). Social Media Effects on the Gezi Park Movement in Turkey: Politics Under Hashtags. In B. Pătruţ & M. Pătruţ (Eds.), *Social Media in Politics: Case Studies on the Political Power of Social Media* (pp. 281–314). New York: Springer.

Doğan, R. (2016, August 10). 'Erdoğan'a hakaret'te bugün: Facebook paylaşımı nedeniyle gözaltı. *Diken*. Retrieved September 1, 2016, from http://www.diken.com.tr/erdogana-hakarette-bugun-facebook-paylasimi-nedeniyle-gozalti/

Erdoğan withdraws defamation cases except for HDP. (2016, August 1). Retrieved September 1, 2016, from http://bianet.org/english/freedom-of-expression/177406-erdogan-withdraws-defamation-cases-except-for-hdp

Erdoğan Biliyorsunuz ben bu sosyal medyaya karşıyım. (2016, July 2). Retrieved August 31, 2016, from http://tr.sputniknews.com/turkiye/20160702/1023691179/erdogan-ataturk-havalimani-ziyaret.html

'Erdoğan'a hakaret'te bugün: 14 yaşındaki A.Ş'nin Facebook yorumuna iddianame. (2016, August 9). Retrieved September 1, 2016, from http://www.diken.com.tr/erdogana-hakarette-bugun-14-yasindaki-s-nin-facebook-yorumuna-iddianame/

Erdoğan'a hakaretten 1845 dosya. (2016, March 2). Retrieved September 1, 2016, from http://www.cumhuriyet.com.tr/haber/siyaset/490484/Erdogan_a_hakaretten_1845_dosya.html

Freedom House. (2014). *The Struggle for Turkey's Internet*: Retrieved September 1, 2016, from https://freedomhouse.org/sites/default/files/The%20Struggle%20for%20Turkey's%20Internet.pdf

Fuchs, C. (2011a). New media, web 2.0 and surveillance. *Sociology Compass*, *5*(2), 134–147. doi:10.1111/j.1751-9020.2010.00354.x

Fuchs, C. (2011b). Web 2.0, prosumption, and surveillance. *Surveillance & Society*, *8*(3), 288–309. Retrieved from http://ojs.library.queensu.ca/index.php/surveillance-and-society/article/view/4165/4167

Fuchs, C. (2012a). Some Reflections on Manuel Castells' Book Networks of Outrage and Hope. Social Movements in the Internet Age. *TripleC*, *10*(2), 775–797.

Fuchs, C. (2012b). Critique of the Political Economy of Web 2.0 Surveillance. In C. Fuchs, K. Boersma, A. Albrechtslund, & M. Sandoval (Eds.), *Internet and Surveillance: The Challenges of Web 2.0 and Social Media* (pp. 31–70). New York: Routledge.

Fuchs, C. (2014). *Social Media: A Critical Introduction*. London: Sage.

Fuchs, C. (2015). Social Media Surveillance. In S. Coleman & D. Freelon (Eds.), *Handbook of Digital Politics* (pp. 395–414). Cheltenham, UK: Edward Elgar.

Gerbaudo, P. (2012). *Tweets and the Streets: Social Media and Contemporary Activism*. London: Pluto.

Gladwell, M. (2010, October 4). Small Change: Why the Revolution Will Not Be Tweeted. *The New Yorker*, 42-49.

Gül'ün eski danışmanı Sever: Pelikan'a izin en yukarıdan, trollerin başında Varank var. (2016, May 9). Retrieved August 31, 2016, from http://www.diken.com.tr/gulun-danismani-sever-pelikana-izin-en-yukaridan-trollerin-basinda-varank-var/

Information and Communication Technologies Authority. (2016). *Electronic Communications in Turkey, 2016*, Q1. Ankara: BTK.

İnternet 'zincir'lendi: Artık erişim yasağı bir bakanın iki dudağı arasında. (2015, March 27). Retrieved September 1, 2016, from http://www.diken.com.tr/internete-zincir-geldi-tibe-genis-yetkiler-veren-internet-duzenlemesi-yasalasti/

İnternette darbe girişimini övdüğü iddiasıyla 4 kişi tutuklandı. (2016, July 20). Retrieved September 1, 2016, from http://t24.com.tr/haber/internette-darbe-girisimini-ovdugu-iddiasiyla-2-kisi-tutuklandi,350931

İşte 10 maddede internet sansürü. (2014, February 5). Retrieved September 1, 2016, from http://www.cumhuriyet.com.tr/haber/bilim-teknik/38013/iste_10_maddede_internet_sansuru.html

Karakaş, B. (2015, October 9). Prof. Yaman Akdeniz: İnternet yasası Bilal Erdoğan gibi büyük çocuklar için değişti. *Diken*. Retrieved September 1, 2016, from http://www.diken.com.tr/prof-yaman-akdeniz-internet-yasasi-bilal-erdogan-gibi-buyuk-cocuklar-icin-degistirildi/

Kasapoğlu, Ç. (2014, August 7). Cumhurbaşkanı adaylarının sosyal medya kampanyaları. *BBC Türkçe*. Retrieved August 31, 2016, from http://www.bbc.com/turkce/haberler/2014/08/140806_sosyalmedya_secim

King, G., Pan, J., & Roberts, M. (2013). How Censorship in China Allows Government Criticism but Silences Collective Expression. *The American Political Science Review*, *107*(2), 326–343. doi:10.1017/S0003055413000014

Kürtlere 'satır gösteren' 'Ak Trol'ün nikah şahidi Cumhurbaşkanı Erdoğan. (2015, June 13). Retrieved August 31, 2016, from http://www.diken.com.tr/kurtlere-satir-gosteren-ak-trolun-nikah-sahidi-cumhurbaskani-erdogan/

McNair, B. (2011). *An Introduction to Political Communication*. London: Routledge.

Morozov, E. (2009a, Fall). Iran: Downside to the "Twitter Revolution". *Dissent*, 10–14. Retrieved from http://www.evgenymorozov.com/morozov_twitter_dissent.pdf

Morozov, E. (2009b). *Brave New World Of Slacktivism*. Retrieved December 4, 2016, from http://www.npr.org/templates/story/story.php?storyId=104302141

Morozov, E. (2011). *The Net Delusion: The Dark Side of Internet Freedom*. New York: PublicAffairs.

Oremus, W. (2013, June 3). Turkish Prime Minister Blames Twitter for Unrest, Calls It "the Worst Menace to Society". *Slate*. Retrieved September 3, 2016, from http://www.slate.com/blogs/future_tense/2013/06/03/turkey_protests_prime_minister_erdogan_blames_twitter_calls_social_media.html

Poell, T. (2015). Social Media Activism and State Censorship. In D. Trottier & C. Fuchs (Eds.), *Social Media, Politics and the State: Protests, Revolutions, Riots, Crime and Policing in the Age of Facebook, Twitter and Youtube* (pp. 189–206). New York: Routledge.

Reuters Institute. (2016). *Reuters Institute Digital News Report 2016*: Retrieved September 1, 2016, from https://reutersinstitute.politics.ox.ac.uk/sites/default/files/Digital-News-Report-2016.pdf

Serbest gazeteci Emin Demir tutuklandı. (2016, May 31). Retrieved September 1, 2016, from https://www.evrensel.net/haber/281413/serbest-gazeteci-emin-demir-tutuklandi

Sezgin Tanrıkulu Profiline Atatürk resmi koymuş, AKP'li troller... (2016, March 13). Retrieved August 31, 2016, from http://www.abcgazetesi.com/sezgin-tanrikulu-profiline-ataturk-resmi-koymus-akpli-troller-10561h.htm

Shirk, S. L. (2011). *Changing Media, Changing China*. Oxford, UK: Oxford University Press.

Shirky, C. (2011). The Political Power of Social Media: Technology, the Public Sphere, and Political Change. *Foreign Affairs*, *90*(1), 28–41.

Sokullu, S., & Demir, B. (2013, September 19). AKP'den sosyal medya atağı. *Deutsche Welle Türkçe*. Retrieved August 31, 2016, from http://www.dw.com/tr/akpden-sosyal-medya-ata%C4%9F%C4%B1/a-17101383

Son bir yılda 6 bombalı saldırıda 344 kişi hayatını kaybetti, 1682'si yaralandı. (2016, August 21). Retrieved September 1, 2016, from http://www.diken.com.tr/son-bir-yilda-16-bombali-saldirida-344-kisi-hayatini-kaybetti-1682si-yaralandi/

'Sövme Timi' En Az Bin Lira Maaş Alıyormuş... (2015, September 29). Retrieved September 1, 2016, from https://onedio.com/haber/-sovme-timi-en-az-bin-lira-maas-aliyormus--595545

Sozeri, E. K. (2016, August 27). Social media throttling in Turkey points to wartime censorship efforts. *The Daily Dot*. Retrieved September 1, 2016, from http://www.dailydot.com/layer8/turkey-wartime-censorship-syria/

Sullivan, A. (2009, June 13). The Revolution Will Be Twittered. *The Atlantic*. Retrieved December 4, 2016, from http://www.theatlantic.com/daily-dish/archive/2009/06/the-revolution-will-be-twittered/200478/

Trollere ne kadar maaş ödeniyor? (2016, March 16). Retrieved August 31, 2016, from http://www.birgun.net/haber-detay/trollere-ne-kadar-maas-odeniyor-106445.html

Trottier, D., & Lyon, D. (2012). Key Features of Social Media Surveillance. In C. Fuchs, K. Boersma, A. Albrechtslund, & M. Sandoval (Eds.), *Internet and Surveillance: The Challenges of Web 2.0 and Social Media* (pp. 89–105). New York: Routledge.

Turkey PM Erdogan says 'tapped' phone call to son 'fabricated'. (2014, February 25). Retrieved September 2, 2016, from http://www.bbc.com/news/world-europe-26336354

Turkey shuts down TIB internet surveillance and censorship bureau. (2016, August 15). Retrieved September 1, 2016, from https://d8news.com/turkey-shuts-tib-internet-surveillance-censorship-bureau-1327

Turkish ministers accuse Twitter of plotting against Erdoğan. (2016, March 30). Retrieved August 31, 2016, from http://www.hurriyetdailynews.com/turkish-ministers-accuse-twitter-of-plotting-against-erdogan-.aspx?PageID=238&NID=97106&NewsCatID=338

Turkish Statistical Institute. (2016). *Hanehalkı Bilişim Teknolojileri Kullanım Araştırması, 2016*. Ankara: TUİK. Retrieved September 5, 2016, from http://www.tuik.gov.tr/PreTablo.do?alt_id=1028

Twitter is blocked in Turkey as Erdogan vows to 'wipe out' the social network. (2014, March 21). Retrieved September 3, 2016, from http://www.telegraph.co.uk/news/worldnews/europe/turkey/10713393/Twitter-is-blocked-in-Turkey-as-Erdogan-vows-to-wipe-out-the-social-network.html

Vergeer, M. (2012). Politics, Elections and Online Campaigning: Past, Present... and a Peek into the Future. *New Media & Society*, *15*(1), 9–17. doi:10.1177/1461444812457327

Vergeer, M., Hermans, L., & Sams, S. (2011). Is the Voter Only a Tweet Away? Micro-blogging During the 2009 European Parliament Election Campaign in the Netherlands. *First Monday*, *16*(8). Retrieved from http://firstmonday.org/article/view/3540/3026

Walker, S. (2015, April 2). Salutin' Putin: inside a Russian troll house. *The Guardian*. Retrieved September 3, 2016, from https://www.theguardian.com/world/2015/apr/02/putin-kremlin-inside-russian-troll-house

We Are Social. (2016). *Digital in 2016*. Retrieved September 5, 2016, from http://wearesocial.com/uk/special-reports/digital-in-2016

Williams, C. B., & Gulati, G. J. (2007). *Social Networks in Political Campaigns: Facebook and the 2006 Midterm Elections*. Paper presented at the 2007 Annual Meeting of the American Political Science Association, Chicago, IL. Retrieved December 28, 2016, from http://tranb300.ulb.ac.be/2012-2013/groupe141/archive/files/c65d6cf6f5d34b49f79d9e68a315bb41.pdf

Yang, G. (2009). *The Power of the Internet in China: Citizen Activism Online*. New York: Colombia University Press.

Yayın yasağı 'Ak Trol'e emanet: 'Tivit atanı not edin, bize gönderin'. (2015, March 31). Retrieved September 1, 2016, from http://www.diken.com.tr/yayin-yasagi-ak-trole-emanet-tivit-atani-not-edin-bize-gonderin/

Yıldırım, Ö. (2016, July 17). Sosyal medyadan terörü destekleyen profiller emniyete bildirilecek. *Anadolu Ajansı*. Retrieved September 1, 2016, from http://aa.com.tr/tr/15-temmuz-darbe-girisimi/sosyal-medyadan-teroru-destekleyen-profiller-emniyete-bildirilecek/609584

KEY TERMS AND DEFINITIONS

AKP: Abbreviation for the Justice and Development Party, which has been in power in Turkey since 2002.

Aktrolls: A group of social media users in Turkey who try to promote the ideas of the ruling party and oppress opponents by violent and unethical means.

Anonymity: The state of using the Internet and social media platforms by covering the users' real identity and thus making comments without being detected.

Bandwidth Throttling: An increasingly adopted way of censoring the Internet and social media by slowing down online traffic instead of applying a ban.

Bot Accounts: Automated social media accounts without an actual user. They are useful for inflating follower numbers or setting agenda on social media by creating trending topics.

Gülen Movement: A religious movement led by US-based Turkish cleric Fethullah Gülen, who is accused by Turkish government of masterminding the failed coup of July 15, 2016.

Internet Troll: An Internet or social media user deliberately hijacking online discussions by making provocative, irrelevant or harmful comments.

Chapter 9
Euphoria and Delusion of Digital Activism:
Case Study of #ZumaMustFall

Ufuoma Akpojivi
University of the Witwatersrand, South Africa

ABSTRACT

This chapter seeks to question and problematize the concept of cyber-utopianism that has characterized the phenomenal increase of digital activism in the African continent in the last decade. Using tweets collected between November 1, 2015 and May 1, 2016 on the #ZumaMustFall digital activism as a case study, the chapter argues that the ability of new media technologies in digital activism to create awareness has created a sense of euphoria that digital activism can bring about political, economic and socio-cultural changes. The study revealed that #ZumaMustFall digital activism has had limited impact as Zuma has not fallen and this can be attributed to the elite nature of the movement that has excluded vast majority of ordinary South Africans from the activities of the movement. In addition, the racial coloration of the movement (i.e. identity) hindered the movement from reaching out to the public who could have actively participated in translating the movement from the online space to the offline space and achieve their goals and objectives.

INTRODUCTION

The inspiration of digital media developments has altered activism and ushered in new and dynamic ways of generating awareness and participation (Diani 2000; Meyer & Bray 2013). The need for contestation of authority through constant interactions with power holders in order to stimulate change has been facilitated by

DOI: 10.4018/978-1-5225-2854-8.ch009

new media technology. Activism, described by Cammaerts (2007) as the practice of individuals challenging the status quo in order to bring about social, political, or economic change, has been transformed by the wizardry of digital technology to a large extent. While the intensity of involvement in activism ranges from determined participation to passive compliance, the advent of digital activism has increased people's intensity of involvement and power as they have become strong and far-reaching (Tilly 2005).

Groups and individuals have been allowed to negotiate their influence across time and space in ways that are more cost-effective and environmentally friendly while tackling essential political, economic, and social issues either at local, national and transnational levels (see Porta & Tarrow 2005). Consequently, there has been a rise of digital movements across the globe most especially from the global south. As the last decade has witnessed the growth and rapid spread of digital movements across the African continent. For instance, from Occupy Nigeria to Occupy Ghana, down to #ThisFlag of Zimbabwe to #BringBackOurGirls, to #RhodesMustFall, and #FeesMustFall amongst others. One common feature amongst these digital movements is the cyber utopian believe that these movements are instrumental in bringing about the needed political and economic changes that will help advance accountability and strengthen democratic institutions which have been a major bane in the continent. This perception is further echoed by cyber utopian studies of digital movements that believe that the adoption of new media technologies by social movement or digital movements will facilitate development and bring about the needed change due to the sense of empowerment and participation associated with such digital movements (see Castells 2012; Tilly 2004; Tarrow 2005).

However, recent studies have established that beyond the normative ideas of empowerment and participation that characterize digital movements, the success of any digital activism depends on other social relationships and structures in society (Fenton & Barassi 2011). In other words, the socio-cultural, political and economic context of any society does to a large extent determine the success of any digital movement campaign in relation to the attainment of their goals and objectives.

Therefore, this study seeks to examine #ZumaMustFall movement that was established in 2015 at the wake of political and economic crises in South Africa, where President Jacob Zuma had series of accusations against him, including the Nkandla Scandal[1], the Gupta family link[2], and his indecisive appointments of finance ministers, among others. Given the ability of digital activism to mobilize via digital media, and based on the cyber utopian arguments of Castells, Tilly and Tarrow amongst others, one may be compelled to enquire about the extent to which #ZumaMustFall movement can realize its set objectives, and if the movement is not just basking on the euphoria of cyber possibilities, hence lacking the active citizen participation and engagement that is salient in translating from the digital space to the physical space in order to realize goals and objectives (Postill 2013). These are pertinent issues which should be examined especially as South Africa is currently witnessing unprecedented increase in digital movements' activities[3] thus the need to ask who digital movements are established for, with what purpose and who are those involved in the activities of digital activism (Fenton & Barassi 2011). In this study I seek to challenge the normative idea that social media platforms offer unprecedented access for digital activism by encouraging citizens' participation. I will argue that although social media offer access, this access is mainly capitalized by the elites who use digital movements to advance their agenda/interests to the exclusion of the vast majority of the public, hence the limited impact of digital activism in society.

WHAT IS DIGITAL ACTIVISM?

Digital activism also known as online activism campaign is an organized public effort, making collective claim(s) on targeted authority(s), in which civic initiators or supporters use digital media (Edwards et al, 2013 p. 4). To Joyce (2010) digital activism must not be limited to the idea of regime change which is often the way people contextualize digital movement, but refers to the use of digital technology tools to facilitate campaigns for policy reform in the political, economic and social realms. These tools include the World Wide Web (WWW) based applications, the internet in its various applications, mobile phones, and other social media platforms found on digital platforms and websites such as Facebook groups, Twitter, YouTube amongst others. Consequently, McCaughey and Ayers (2003) conceptualize digital activism as activism that relies on the internet. And the use of hashtags is fundamental to digital activism. According to Olson (2016) digital activism revolves around hashtags, and it has been effective at drawing attention to issues confronting societies both at national and global levels. Because the discourse produced using these hashtags challenge dominant elites and the power dynamic of society (Ghobadi & Clegg 2015).

The ability of these digital technologies to offer safety of the cyberspace devoid of government control and monopoly has made people to embrace digital activism. According to Castells (2012) social media or new media has "become a place where history happens, a place people identify with" because of the potential to engage with each other devoid of preying eyes of governments. To Castells, this identity formation and construction is made possible by a network society which has bridged time and space and made it possible for people to connect together and take control over "the condition of their living" (Barney 2004 p. 31). Consequently, people embrace digital activism as a platform to establish and form a collective identity in pressing and demanding for change (political, economic or cultural) in societies.

Porta and Mosca (2005) argue that new media technologies are fundamental strategies or tools to digital movements as movements solely depend on new media technologies and platforms for communication, and creating awareness. In other words, without these platforms or technologies digital movements would not be in existence. Castells while expounding further held that in the contestation for power, communication is central, as communication helps in spreading the messages or ideologies of the digital movement and in the process construct the identity of the movement before society. To Tilly (2004), this contestation of power through the interactions between the citizens and the state via the institution of social movements leads to citizens' empowerment because of the participation of the public in the societal discourse which in most cases is not possible without this space of digital movement. Galusky (2003) while buttressing this point held that social movement or digital activism is a genuine tool for citizens' empowerment because, within this platform of interaction, everyone has the right to speak and to be heard, thus bringing about social change and development. Wilkins (2000) developed this further by stating that the alternative platform of engagement created by digital activism affords the state and social actors the opportunity to address the issue of distrust which prompted the formation and institutionalization of the digital movement in the first place, thus making civic engagement germane.

However, this idea of empowerment and participation that has embodied cyber utopian beliefs of digital movements have been widely criticized by Morozov (2009), Fenton and Barassi (2011) amongst others. According to Morozov (2009), the idea that new media and the internet offers safety and encourages participation should be dismissed as governments across the world have started using the internet to their advantage by regulating activities on new media technologies that might pose a threat to them. This is evident in other countries like China, Turkey, Brazil or Zimbabwe where telecommunication operators were asked to stop or suspend the services of social media platforms in order to regulate or filter the flow of information. In addition, Morozov questioned the activities of these digital movements by interrogating the decision-making process of these movements. This is in line with Fenton and Barassi (2011) where they problematized the individualization within digital movements as against the collective identity that surrounds the establishment of digital movements. According to Fenton and Barassi (2011) the power of the individual does to a large extent negate the collective dimension and idea of participatory communication, as most often the individual's decision or participation reflects his/her self-interest and might not be in accordance with the overall goal or interest of the movement. The examples of Fouad Mourtada, jailed for impersonating the Moroccan king's brother on Facebook, Cheng Jianping, who was sent to a labour camp for sending a tweet and Brit Chambers arrested for a joke about blowing up Robin Hood airport (Fairweather 2010; Sutherland 2010; Hughes & Walsh 2010) supports the assertions of Morozov (2009) and Fenton and Barassi (2011). Nevertheless, to some extent digital activism is not low risk related as there are potential dangers associated with it. Such danger(s) will depend on the willingness or openness of the state to criticism and the interplay and relationship between the movement and the state (see Akpojivi n/d), as governments could criminalize the activities of such digital activism as was the case in Nigeria with the #BringBackOurGirls movement under President Goodluck Johnathan and #ThisFlag of Zimbabwe.

RISE OF DIGITAL ACTIVISM IN AFRICA

The coming of digital revolution in Africa reformed the manner in which activism is done forcing activists to adapt to new ways and rethink digital activism strategies if they are to remain relevant in the global world of activism. In Africa, the Internet arrived first and then the mobile phone later. Although the internet arrived first, due to lack of supporting infrastructure it was not well received. When the mobile phone arrived in the mid-1990s, Africa adopted it and adapted the manner of doing activism (Otieno 2010). The integration of the mobile phones and new media proves terrific impact on freedom of expression, information gathering, packaging, and dissemination in Africa (Uchenna 2011; Huang et al, 2006; Erdal 2009).

In the 1990s the potential of digital media especially the Internet to widen participation in the public sphere were seen as signaling a new era for African democracy. However, Etzo and Collender quoted in Wasserman (2010) contend that digital activism in Africa was propelled by the use of mobile phones based on their affordability and quickness in information dissemination. As a result, Africans enthusiastically embraced mobile phones with more than 350 million mobile phone subscribers on the continent in the five years between 2003 and 2008 (Wasserman 2010). The ability of the mobile phone to multitask makes them ideal tools for digital activism than anything else. Berger (2008) advances that there are "1001 uses" of cell phones beyond voice communication. For instance, mobile phones are used to take photographs, make films, watch television (Berger 2010) search the Internet and to Facebook and to tweet or even read a newspaper (Berger 2008; Etzo & Collender 2010). This range of functionalities of mobile phones makes it a versatile technology for activists to plan campaigns long in advance or respond quickly to events.

This therefore, facilitates the rise of digital activism in the African continent, and Ghobadi and Clegg (2015) argue that digital activism has helped in changing the dynamic of relationship that exist between powers of the state and the citizens. According to Ghobadi and Clegg (2015) digital activism has recorded success in countries like Britain, South Africa and amongst others based on studies conducted by Steenkamp and Hyde-Clarke (2012), Castells (2012) and Wills and Reeves (2009). However, it can be argued that Tunisia and Egypt, 2010/2011 marked the climax of digital activism in Africa as the revolutions were largely organized, supported and driven through the use of digital media which consists of social media-based tools such as Facebook, Twitter and mobile phone technology among other devices for an extensive political expression against the government (Muller & van der Merwe 2011). The Arab springs in Algeria, Egypt, Libya, Morocco, Sudan, Tunisia, Libya and Western Sahara which began on the 18th of December 2010 was an unprecedented form of digital activism in Africa which forced leaders out of power in Tunisia, Egypt and Libya. In addition to the Arab springs, #Koni2012 campaign, #BringBackOurgirls movement, #ZumaMustFall, and the Zimbabwean #ThisFlag campaign indicates the rise of digital activism in Africa as people seek to disentangle themselves from the claws of poor governance, corrupt leadership, unemployment, and other economic and social ills. But the question remains: to what extent can digital activism inform real change in a politically charged and serious economic charged country like South Africa.

SLACKTIVISM, ARMCHAIR ACTIVISM, AND THE ULTIMATE GOAL ACHIEVEMENT

The effectiveness and value of digital activism is more often questioned and as a result, it has been problematic to understand whether or not it can work towards goal achievement. Edwards *et al* (2013) opine that because of the ability of digital activism to help draw people into the streets for public demonstrations, it is often misconstrued that such will bring about the needed change. Shirky (2008 p. 160) concurs but adds that activism success is defined along two dimensions: goal achievement and realization of benefit. Although the need for getting people into the street forms a crucial stage in the process, but being successful in bringing people to the streets does not always indicate success but it must be coupled with the achievement of either political, social or economic change. The ultimate goal of the #ZumaMustFall campaign is to pressure President Zuma to step down in the same manner Mr. Zine al-Abidine Ben Alihe of Tunisia (Bryant 2011) and President Hosni Mubarak of Egypt resigned (Aljazeera, Feb 11, 2011). In addition to stepping down, there must be some restoration of a better and safer country with work, enough food, clean water, electricity, houses for all, better education, better service delivery and better hospitals among others (Zumamustfall petition 2016). It therefore follows that in the absence of these demands, the #ZumaMustFall campaign would have not succeeded.

The above task entails that although it is nice to embrace technology, revolution does not happen when society adopts new technologies; it happens when society adopts new behaviours and demand reforms. While Howards' (2013) observation that people get physical and march in the streets to stay connected is not far from the truth, it is the achievement of the objectives of marching into the street which matters most. In 2011, thousands of Egyptians refused to leave Cairo's central Tahrir Square calling for an end to President Hosni Mubarak's three decades rule (The guardian 2011). The effectiveness and success of digital activism to bring about political, economic and social change have been put to test and succeeded well in this instance. In essence, online or digital activism also be complemented by offline activities to achieve the campaign's set goals.

Dismissing digital activism, Gladwell (2010) argues that digital activism is based on weak ties which can only demand low-risk participation. He argues that digital activism networks are not hierarchically organized, they are leaderless and cannot think strategically making it easier for activists to express themselves, but harder for that expression to have any impact in established political, economic and social realms. Although these sentiments have been defied to a greater extent in the Egypt and Tunisia springs, it has been established that over-reliance on digital activism degenerates into slacktivism, an online activism that has no tangible outcome (Kristofferson, White, & Peloza 2013). The belief that one could bring about change with a simple tweet, Facebook post or a click on mobile device is unfounded. For instance, the #Kony2012 campaign movement oversimplified their issues to a hashtag in order to draw attention to capture Ugandan war criminal, Joseph Kony. The campaign took a complicated issue and reduced it to a video. The complex political and socioeconomic issues of Uganda were overlooked as participants became convinced that demanding Kony's arrest via Facebook was enough to create change leading to doubts over the effectiveness of digitally mediated activism in bringing the needed change (LaRiviere et al, 2012). In the same manner the #ZumaMustFall's digitally mediated campaign needs further mutation into offline lest it will be prone to suffer a still birth like the fizzling out of Zimbabwe's #ThisFlag campaign.

Whereas some view virtual communities as revolutionary platforms of civic participation, others believe that they do not actually exist (Harasim 1993; Baudrillard 1995). Digital activism has become extensive and has the potential to alter the perceptions of the public on the media as the media and the 'real' merge into one (Baudrillard 1995). A closer analysis of digital activism in Africa, from the Nigeria's #BringBackOurGirls and the recent #ZumaMustFall in South Africa as well as #ThisFlag campaign in Zimbabwe indicate that a sense of real activism has been distorted. Online realities are not matched with offline realities, as people feel just tweeting or posting comments without offline support or strategies is actual activism, thus little achievements have been recorded when it comes to digital activism (Gladwell 2010). Indeed, the representation of activism through digital means has outperformed actual activism as we are now witnessing what Nyamnjoh

(2016) termed #whatwillfall to #whatwillrise due to the belief that digital activism is the key to addressing problems. For instance, in the #BringBackOurgirls campaign, the global world is intervening through both new and traditional media, liking the Facebook pages, signing online petitions, sending pictures on Instagram, forwarding consolation and prayer messages through SMS and Whatsapp messaging, a typical example of media referring to each other creating "a copy without origin" and no real offline action is taking place to rescue the girls from captivity (Baudrillard, 1995; Akpojivi n.d.). Likewise, the mega #ZumaMustFall support online is deceiving; it is just a representational image or simulacrum (Baudrillard 1995) with no corresponding offline action to pressure the President out of office. According to Baudrillard (1995) simulacrum means the creation of an impression of reality or "hyperreal" which isn't true but a false representation of society. And digital activism via clickactivisim or slacktivism helps create this feeling of hyperreal as people feel good about themselves as they equate tweeting or posting about a social cause as bringing about change without an active offline strategy. This false representation of reality leads to euphoria within digital activism.

Fenton and Barassi (2011) while elaborating on this euphoria argued that due to the potential of social media and new media technologies there is the belief that digital activism will bring about change without an understanding that the success of any digital activism is centered around other structural factors. And this has impacted significantly on most digital activism and the realization of their goals and objectives. To a larger extent, the success of the #BringBackOurGirls has remained lukewarm, not convincingly enough regardless of the awareness efforts put in place. The campaign has proved unhelpful in summoning Nigerian and global political will and resources to bring back the more than 250 girls abducted by Boko Haram in the northern Nigerian town of Chibok in April 2014 (Luckscheiter 2014). Although it is true that awareness can equate to power, the importance of balancing online and offline activism, ability to move from awareness to action plays a crucial role in the success of activism. While the campaign was media boosted by the support of international celebrities such as US First Lady Michelle Obama, World leaders like UK Prime Minister David Cameron and US President Barack Obama, the girls remained at large. The girls may have remained at large mainly because the support received was mostly digital consolation, a case of one media referring to another with no real physical effort to search for the girls (Akpojivi, n.d.).

To illuminate the mystery, Gladwell (2010, p. 9) explains that digital activism is made up of "Smart mobs" who are anonymous individuals who become linked by pervasive digital devices, such as phones and computers, which connect themselves via the Internet and locative technology. Although digital activism makes it easier for activists to express themselves, it is harder for that expression to have any impact, he adds. Furthermore, the relationships on which online activism is based are too weak to bring about substantial political, economic and social changes. Such types of activism which challenges the status quo in political realms and attacks deep rooted problems need very strong ties to achieve its objectives.

Morozov (2009) points that "click-based activism", undermine dedicated activism through discouragement from practical engagement. He further opines that shifting towards digital activism is a shift away from practical activism. In addition, he further argued that tweeting, liking a group or a post does not make one an activist as compared to those who are practically working in the streets, meeting with people. Furthermore, online activism often creates an echo-chamber effect, where communication only reaches the same narrow circle of activists limiting the rate of the project success (Melki & Mallat, 2014).

Whereas issues that triggered a successful revolution in Tunisia such as widespread discontent over unemployment, corruption levels, low living standards, failing economy and others are almost similar to issues being raised in #ZumaMustFall, the Tunisian campaign was unique because it was triggered by an offline event, the death of a 26-year-old Mohammad Bouazizi, a street vendor who set himself on fire in protest over a police officer who wouldn't allow him to sale his wares (Hassan, 2015). One may argue that this revolution was actioned offline with digital media helping to mobilize the masses only.

In as far as digital media is concerned; interrogation into the success and failure of #ZumaMustFall movement should not be based on its ability to create awareness only, but on goals and benefits achievement. This has remained the challenge of digitally mediated activism in the global world. In addition, the relationship between digital activism and the political, economic and social environment occupies a major place in the success or failure of digital activism.

SYNOPSIS OF PROTEST AND DIGITAL ACTIVISM IN SOUTH AFRICA

Protest is not new in South Africa as it has become a common phenomenon, and this is rooted in issues bothering on basic service delivery such as water, housing, power, toilet etc (Von Lieres 2014). According to a report from the police, in 2014 there were "just more than 3000 protests between January 2009 and August 2012" (News24, February 9, 2014). Although, protest has been rooted in South African history from colonialism to apartheid in which black South Africans where fighting against apartheid. These protests have continued even in post-apartheid era for two reasons. Firstly, Brunlof (2017) argues that on the institutionalization of democracy, South Africans were sold a "pipe dream" that democracy will bring about the needed political and economic transformation. The failure to achieve these economic benefits despite political transition after 23 years of independence has significantly contributed to the rise of protest. Secondly, protest is the weapon available to the ordinary South African to make the government or other actors respond to their pressing needs (Von Lieres, 2014).

Although these protests have been violent in nature i.e. destruction of properties, and confrontation with the police, therefore attracting the needed attention, however, the emergence of new media technologies and formation of social movements has transformed the nature of protest from being just an offline reality into online or mixture of both online and offline. According to Ballard et al. (2005) the year 1990 witnessed the emergence of social movement in South Africa which takes different forms like trade unions, civil societies, NGO's and political parties. These movements were struggling for better living conditions of the working class and citizens (von Holdt, 2002). It is only of recent that social movement has moved or integrated the use of online technologies thus the concept of digital or online activism.

The digital activism of #RhodesMustFall that started March 9, 2015 can be regarded as the pinnacle of social movements that changed the nature of protest in South Africa and moved into the digital space. As #RhodesMustFall saw the integration of digital technologies in protest to challenge deep rooted societal issues such as racial transformation, decolonization of education and transformation of university (see Nyamnjoh, 2016). Due to the ability of this movement to attract the needed responds and open debates to inherent educational practices, almost every digital movement have adopted the fallist campaign slogan e.g. #feesmustfall, #datamustfall etc, consequently, Nyamnjoh (2016, p. i) stated that "from #WhatMustFall to #WhatMustRise is a dynamic process of ongoing cultural creation and societal regeneration". In other words, digital activism is a process that will be affected by societal factors. This means that the embrace of digital activism will not lead to automatic change as portrayed by technological determinist (see Castells, 2010), but this change is a process and when completed will lead to regeneration of society which Nyamnjoh (2016) elucidated about.

#ZUMAMUSTFALL: THE ODYSSEY

The actual start date of #ZumaMustFall movement is uncertain as one cannot easily pin point the date the movement started. However, despite the uncertain start date, the movement gained momentum following the sack of the then Finance Minister Nhlanhla Nene on December 9, 2015. Following the sack of the Minister, the economy was badly affected as the South African Rands (South African Currency) dropped to a level low of 5.4 percent against the dollar within a day, and the market was severely affected. It should be noted that prior to the removal of the Finance

Minister, President Jacob Zuma according to the Business Day has made "11 cabinet reshuffles since coming to power in May 2009" (cited in Pauw, 2017, p. 79). Pauw (2017, p. 79) while expanding on the above held that President Jacob Zuma had made "126 changes to the national executives: 62 changes to ministerial positions, 63 changes to deputy ministerial positions, and one change to the deputy presidency", and these changes had impacted on the socioeconomic development of the country.

According to the #ZumaMustFall movement, the worsening economic situation i.e. "poor economic growth rate, investor confidence and subsequent plummeting of economic outputs in the face of policy uncertainty and lack of leadership during times of social unrest" facilitated the need for the movement (zumamustfall.org/why-zumamustfall/). In addition, the movement held that South Africa is in need of redemption and this cannot come from the leadership of President Jacob Zuma due to his questionable leadership issues as Zuma is perceived "as a leader who is serving himself first and his loyal comrades second", consequently, the call and challenge to the African National Congress (ANC) to recall President "Jacob Zuma and install a leader who will restore faith in the Presidency" (zumamustfall.org/why-zumamustfall/). Pauw (2017) sums this up by arguing that President Zuma puts his interest over that of the state and this is evident in the high cases i.e. corruption, fraud, money laundering and racketeering against him. And the Supreme Court of Appeal recently restated the 783 criminal charges against President Zuma in October 2017 (News24, October 16, 2017).

The call for the removal of President Jacob Zuma makes the movement to be political inclined, and likewise the economic interests surrounding the movement makes the movement a capitalism movement that seeks to protect the economic interests of the White minority whose business interests were mostly affected by the sack of the finance minister (Cloete 2015). While buttressing the above, Cloete (2015) held that on numerous salient issues that affect the black majority in South Africa, there has never been a movement from the whites to support the black however, because the removal of the Finance Minister has affected the business interest of the white, the "big business and pro-capitalist … are the main drivers of the #ZumaMustFall campaign." In addition, Erasmus (2005) while supporting the above claim posited that there is still economic inequality in South Africa despite the end of apartheid as the economy of South Africa is still in the hands of few white South Africans, and this has necessitated the radical economic transformation program of the state as a way of increasing and facilitating economic equality (Mkentane, 2017). Likewise, although the movement held that it has no link with "political parties" or "racial definition", however the complex polity of South Africa where race defines political and economic compositions, therefore, it is difficult to separate race from the vested economic and political interests of the movement.

METHODOLOGY

A study of this nature that seeks to examine the euphoria behind digital activism i.e. how people engage with hashtags and participate in a digital movement, there is the need to examine the hashtag in relation to the number of tweets, people that were involved in the movement and those excluded, and a brief examination of the twitter profiles of the people who were actively involved in the digital movement. This will enable me show that the success of any digital movements is centered on participation that can be translated from the digital space into the physical space (Postill, 2012). As failure to transcend from the digital space into the physical space of achieving goals and objectives behind the movement will lead to delusion that digital movements are able to bring about needed change due to euphoria of tweeting and retweeting and thinking (Akpojivi cited in Findhey, 2015), that just engaging in these actions make a digital movement successful (Fenton & Barassi, 2011).

As earlier stated this study examined tweets from the #ZumaMustFall movement. The tweets that were collected and examined for this study were between the timeframe of November 1, 2015 to 1 May 2016. The rationale for these dates is because the movement started gaining momentum following the sack of the then Finance Minister Nhlanhla Nene on December 9, 2015. Therefore, examining tweets between this timeframe I will be able to establish the euphoria and delusion behind the digital movement and also establish the transnational nature of the campaign. Furthermore, I will examine the actors (national and transnational) behind the digital movement and how these actors which are predominantly elites who are using the movement to promote their selfish interests that excludes the vast majority of South Africans that did not participate in the movement due to social and economic inequalities. What this chapter is focused on is in buttressing the technical mechanics of twitter as a platform for digital movement such as #ZumaMustFall, as there is the assumption that social media platforms such as twitter offers an open platform for everyone to be heard, which is largely untrue for a country like South Africa. As social media platform is largely a platform for the few elites to voice their views thus making it egalitarian utopian. And this to a large extent will impact on the success of the movement.

#ZUMAMUSTFALL PITFALLS: HAS ZUMA FALLEN?

A critical examination of the #ZumaMustFall digital movement shows that outside the political and economic issues confronting the country that gave birth to #ZumaMustFall, other movements such as #FeesMustFall influenced the formation of the movement. Before this movement, other movements such as #RhodesMustFall[4] and #FeesMustFall have successfully engaged with the state and the issues behind these movements were partially addressed like the #RhodesMustFall where the statue of Cecil Rhodes was removed, and the President freezing the higher education tuition fees for 2015 academic year, and there is currently a debate surrounding the feasibility of free and decolonized education in South Africa. Therefore, it can be argued that due to the success of these movements, which could be attributed to the ability of these digital movements to translate their activities within the digital space into the physical space i.e. the public actively participated and engaged with the relevant stakeholders (see Postill, 2012), the organisers of the #ZumaMustFall movement adopted a similar approach i.e. digital activism.

As earlier stated, the movement came into limelight when the former finance minister Nhlanhla Nene was removed by President Jacob Zuma from office on December 9, 2015. As before his removal from office (i.e. in the month of November) there were less than 200 tweets about #ZumaMustFall. For instance, between November 1, to December 9, 2015 the tweets ranged from 12 to 112 (see Table 1). Nevertheless, the days following the removal of the Minister, the tweets increased and moved to record high of 3977 tweets/retweets. For example, on December 10, 2015 a day after the sack there were 1026 tweets/retweets on #ZumaMustFall, as against 112 tweets/retweets of December 9, 2015. The economic slump that witnessed the fall of the Rands and other investments consequently led to the sack of the newly appointed finance minister Van Rooyen just three (3) days after his appointment due to the negative market reactions, and that period witnessed the rise in tweets/retweets of #ZumaMustFall. For instance, at the peak of the crisis there were 3977 tweets/retweets on December 16, 2015. See Figure 1 for details of numbers of tweets as against dates and Figure 2 for trend of the tweets.

Figure 1. Number of Tweets as against dates

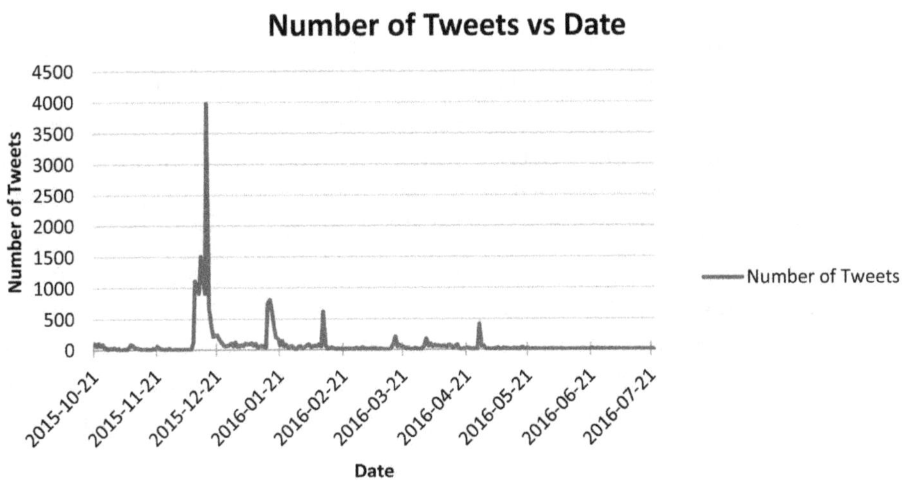

Figure 2. Trend of Tweets movement

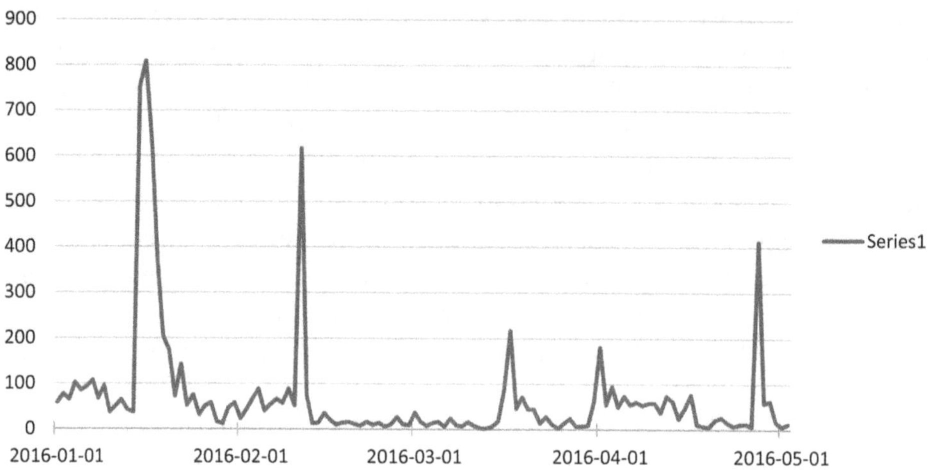

From the above tables, it can be established that significant events in the country witnessed the rise of tweets/retweets under the hashtag. This increase in tweets can be argued to be facilitated by the few elites[5] who tweeted under the hashtag. For example, the huge followers of these elites who tweeted/retweeted about #ZumaMustFall show that the #ZumaMustFall digital movement was capitalized by the elites to push an economic and political agenda. For example, key twitter personalities like Mmusi Maimane (leader of opposition party, Democratic Alliance (DA)) with followers of 366900 had a retweet of 777, Floyd Shivambu (activist and deputy president of the Economic Freedom Fighters (EFF)) with 191955 followers had 179 retweets, Robert Marawa (Sport journalist) with 446335 followers had a retweet of 412, Jacqui Mackway (blogger) with 38019 followers had a retweet of 748 and Shamrita Singh (lawyer and social justice advocate) with 1184 followers had a retweet of 871.

It should be noted that these retweets by followers of these elites/prominent personalities in South Africa cannot be ignored because of the significant role these retweets must have played in creating awareness about the digital movement. As earlier stated the highest number of tweets for the digital movement was 3977 which was recorded on December 16, 2015, and taking into consideration that Mmusi Maimane the leader of the opposition party (Democratic Alliance) had a retweet of 777 from his followers, this only shows that followers of these elites helped in magnifying the movement. This was the trend with all the twitter accounts examined under the given timeframe as most celebrities, politicians and bloggers that tweeted under the #ZumaMustFall had their followers retweet the hashtag, hence raising the momentum of the digital movement and giving a sense of euphoria that ordinary South

Africans are supporting and participating in the digital movement. This is evident in the number of people that participated in the actual march of #ZumaMustFall in Johannesburg, Pretoria and Cape Town in support of the movement. According to news reports there were less than 200 people that participated in the #ZumaMustFall march in the capital city of Pretoria, and the story is almost the same in cities like Johannesburg and Cape Town (News24, Enca). In addition, news stories reported that majority of the people that participated in the #ZumaMustFall march at Pretoria and Johannesburg were middle-class white South Africans (Daily Maverick, April 7, 2017). This shows that against the normative idea that social media platform affords digital movement the space for everyone to engage and participate (Castells 2012), this engagement and participation is egalitarian utopian.

The inability of the movement to attract South Africans to be actively involved in the march i.e. moving from the digital space to the physical space is predominately centered on the identity of the movement. The movement was seen largely as a white capitalist movement that seeks to promote the interest of the few whites in South Africa to the detriment of the poor black working-class South Africans. According to Cloete (2015) "…would Zuma's removal necessarily bring about the resolution of deepening levels of poverty, unemployment, inequality and corruption? In other words, what does the working class stand to gain from the #ZumaMustFall campaign?" This question raises two fundamental issues about the movement, firstly that the movement's interest is not in-line with the interest of the black majority of South Africans who have continued to endure the economic injustice of the past. This idea is buttressed further by Cloete (2015) that "the working class cannot perpetually subordinate its interest to hyenas who promise heaven and earth, but conceal their corrupt capitalist agenda". Therefore, this establishes the fact that the movement was largely seen as an instrument to push an agenda by the white capitalists, hence the need to boycott the movement or not participate in their activities.

This notion was echoed by Julius Malema[6] who tweeted on December 13, 2015 that "I refused to sign the #ZumaMustFall petition because it was initiated by the white capital which called #Marikana workers criminals...". Although Julius Malema and his Economic Freedom Fighters party (EFF) a predominately black political party that believes in nationalizing mines and banks, and promote economic equality refused to participate in the #ZumaMustFall protest, however the Democratic Alliance (DA) supported the campaign. It is noteworthy to state that the DA is perceived as a white political party. Secondly that the movement is an elite based movement that excludes others. From the above, it can be argued that the movement has an identity of "being white", with all the resources needed (access to digital space and technical knowledge to drive a digital movement both online and offline), thus buttressing the egalitarian utopianism of the movement. For instance, Munusamy (n/d) alleged that R500,000 was spent on making a banner that states #ZumaMustFall and renting a space for the erection of the banner which was destroyed a day after erection by some youths. The amount spent on making and erecting just one banner in a Cape Town Flat indicates that the campaign has financial resources at its disposal to promote the cause. Therefore, substantiating the idea that the movement was built around the elites and middle-class white South Africans who can afford the resources to push the cause.

This idea of egalitarian utopianism is further buttressed by the need to examine or ask who has access to new media and social media in a country like South Africa that is characterized by economic inequality, and where access to internet data is still relatively expensive, thus excluding people from participation in digital activism. According to Research ICT Africa, pricing is still a very big issue in South Africa as the country ranks 30th out of 46 countries examined in affordability and connectivity (Research ICT Research Brief 1, 2012). For instance, the cost of 1 GB of data between the various telecommunication operators ranges between R99 to R160. The high cost of data and internet accessibility gave birth to the #DataMustFall campaign which is currently in action. Therefore, from the above it can be argued that digital activism and participation is limited to those that could afford to get the devices and data in order to participate, thus creating a divide. Although, most digital movements claim to be open to all to engage and participate just like the #ZumaMustFall, however, social mechanism of society (digital divide) and the critical infrastructure of these social movement platforms exclude vast majority of the people. The initial euphoria of most digital movements in creating awareness both nationally and internationally tend to over shadow or ignore the fact that certain people are excluded. This exclusion is evident within the #ZumaMustFall digital movement as an examination of the devices used predominately for tweets/retweets showed that majority of the tweets/retweets were done using expensive devices such as Apple and Android devices. See Figure 3 below showing the list of devices used in tweeting and retweeting under the hashtag.

From the above figure, it can be argued that #ZumaMustFall social movement is elite driven based on the kind of devices used in tweeting and retweeting, as these devices are beyond the cost range of the poor and ordinary South Africans that should really be worried about the political and economic implications that gave birth to the movement. For example, the average cost of a mobile phone regarded as "entry level Android smartphone" with social media apps cost between R500 to R600 (mybroadband.co.za), and this is expensive in a country where the minimum wage is R3193.12 per month or R18.25 per hour (Department of Labour South Africa 2017). In addition, statistics South Africa argued that in 2015 about 55.5% of the population was at the poverty level. This further indicates that this group of people will be more worried about meeting their basic household needs than purchasing data in order to participate in this digital movement.

Figure 3. Devices used for top tweets/retweets

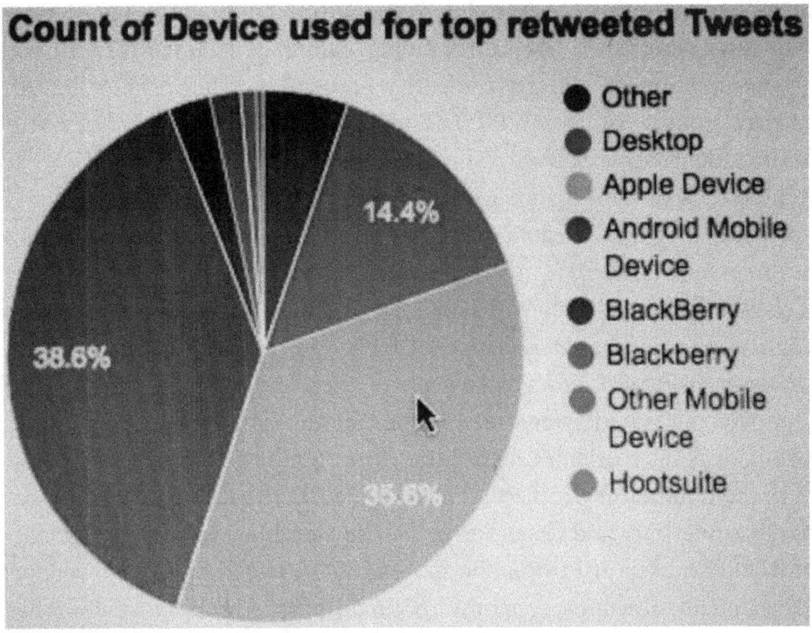

**For a more accurate representation see the electronic version.*

Since these elites have both the resources and technical manpower, they were able to create awareness that is necessary in projecting the activities of the digital movement both at national and at transnational levels. According to Porta and Mosca (2005) the embrace of new media and social media technologies are fundamental for social movements to have a transnational reach through creating of awareness. According to them, the purpose is to create awareness about their campaigns and this can only be achieved with the aid of communication via social media or new media technologies that are devoid of government control or censorship. In addition, since economic and political performances do not largely remain at the sphere of national level but at transnational level due to globalized nature of the societies; #ZumaMustFall became a transnational issue. South Africa is regarded as the second largest economy in Africa (Africaranking.com), and any political and economic factor(s) that will likely affect foreign direct investments of other countries within the space of South Africa will attract global attention. A lucid review of the tweets during the timeframe of study showed that key international media organizations such as CNN, BBC World, Economist, Wall Street Journal (WSJ), Times magazine and Reuter amongst others also tweeted/retweeted under the #ZumaMustFall. Furthermore, international celebrity Trevor Noah, of The Daily Show, also talked about the #ZumaMustFall movement.

The involvement of these international media organizations and celebrities did not only help in migrating the digital movement from national level to transnational level, but also established the transnational nature of #ZumaMustFall activism through the creation of collective identity across boarders despite the different cultural backgrounds (Tarrow 2005). This collective identity is centered on the need for President Jacob Zuma to be recalled or sacked due to economic crisis that followed the sack of the Finance Minister. Hence, the allegation from the African National Congress (ANC) general secretary Gwede Mantashe that the rise of digital activism in South Africa are instruments being used by the West in calling for regime change in South Africa which must be resisted (Munusamy 2016). However, it can be argued that the participation of these international media organizations in the hashtag in form of news and tweets further helped in creating the euphoria that the movement is widely embraced by all South Africans, ignoring the fact that the movement is elite oriented with little or no grassroots mobilization power as evident in the number of people that participated in the #ZumaMustFall march in Pretoria, Johannesburg and Cape Town. This further buttresses the argument made by Fenton and Barassi (2011) that the success of any social movement is dependent on wider social relationships, economic, political and cultural factors which has been difficult to achieve in this movement due to the complexity of the South African polity[7]. The difficulty in translating or moving the participation from the digital space into the physical space has impacted on the realization of the movement's goals and objectives, as President Jacob Zuma has not fallen but is still in power and has survived all the scandals and tantrums directed at him, and will probably complete his term in office as president.. Hence, the assertion that #ZumaMustFall has had limited impact on the South African polity. This can be zeroed down to the lack of active participation of the ordinary South Africans who are excluded from the movement, and the perception that the movement represents the economic interests of the white minority to the detriment of the black majority who are in favour of economic restructuring that will address the economic injustice of the past.

Nevertheless, this discussion will not undermine the fact that the #ZumaMustFall provided a platform for people to discuss political and economic issues confronting the country i.e. acting as a mediated space for people to deliberate on national issues. An examination of the different tweets under the hashtag shows that majority of the tweets touched on political, economic and racial issues. For instance, @justGlenT tweeted that "I love the ANC the history and everything but I love this country and my future more #ZumaMustFall". @GivenMahwayi tweeted that "this is how the currency behaved before Zuma was appointed on 2009 and amp; now, he made a wrong turn #ZumaMustFall". Similarly, @TomEatonSA tweeted that "I see #ZumaMustFall being blamed on racist whites. Because obviously black people can't spot a failing, corrupt government" and @UJrichjvV held that "zuma replacing

Finance Minister Nhlanhle Nene with Van Rooyen is spine chilling! #ZumaMustFall or South Africa will!!".

The above selected tweets touched on salient issues of race, corruption, economic and political developments of the country. These are issues that are constantly being debated on a daily basis and which to a large extent further establish the divide between the (white and black South Africans) that already exist in South Africa. For instance, the notion of loyalty to the ruling and liberation party ANC, and the need to protect the future of the country or the idea that black people are corrupt hence cannot identify with the #ZumaMustFall movement which is seen to be white oriented. These complexities outlined in the examined tweets can be attributed to why the #ZumaMustFall has had a limited effect hence the notion of delusion behind digital activism as earlier argued.

CONCLUSION

This study sets out to examine digital activism in relation to the attainment of their goals focusing on #ZumaMustFall movement that was established in 2015. The study established that behind the cyber utopian ideology that surrounds digital movements due to the notions of participation and empowerment that should invariable facilitate the attainment of goals and objectives, the #ZumaMustFall movement has had limited impact on society. This can be attributed to the elite nature of the movement that has excluded vast majority of ordinary South Africans from participating in digital activism due to social divide and social structure/mechanism of new media technology (Twitter) in the case of this study. Social divide such as class impacted greatly on the movement as according to Statistic South Africa 55.5% of the population are at the poverty level in 2015, this invariably means that these people have been excluded from participating in the movement as they would be more interested in getting basic household necessities than getting expensive data in order to participate in digital activism. The study also showed that the movement was affected by significant events happening in the country, and the ability of these elites and their followers in tweeting and retweeting led to the delusion that that movement has a wider or grassroots reach. This is reflected in the inability of the movement to translate the euphoria of tweeting/retweeting into reality in terms of actual participation and engagement with other stakeholders during their marches at Johannesburg, Pretoria and Cape Town.

In addition, the study argued that the complex nature of the South African state where race determines the economic, political and cultural composition to a large extent influenced the public perception of the movement and discouraged people from participating, hence giving the movement a racial coloration (white movement) that seeks to promote the white capitalist's interests. This buttresses the argument of Fenton and Barassi (2011) that the success of any digital movement is dependent on social relationships i.e. economic, political and cultural factors of society. Therefore, establishing that for any digital movement to go beyond awareness creation, they must actively recognize the place/role of inherent societal social relationships in digital movement activities i.e. both online (digital space) and offline (physical space).

REFERENCES

Akpojivi, U. (forthcoming). #BringBackOurGirls: Mediated space for citizens empowerment or disempowerment. *New Media & Society*.

Aljazeera. (2011, February 11). Hosni Mubarak resigns as president. Retrieved from: http://www.aljazeera.com/news/middleeast/2011/02/201121125158705862.htmlaaa

Ballard, R., Habib, A., Valodia, I., & Zuern, E. (2005). Globalization, marginalization and contemporary social movements in South Africa. *African Affairs*, *104*(417), 615–634. doi:10.1093/afraf/adi069

Baudrillard, J. (1995). *The gulf war did not take place. Translated by P. pattons*. Sydney: Sage Publications.

Beaumont, P., & Shenker, J. (2011). Egypt's protesters refuse to leave the streets until Mubarak steps down. *The Guardian*. Retrieved from https://www.theguardian.com/world/2011/feb/01/egypt-protest-mubarak-step-down

Barney, D. (2004). *The network society*. Cambridge: Polity Press.

Brunlof, H. (2017). Editorial: Protest show that nothing has changed. *MG*. Retrieved from http://mg.co.za/article/2017-05-12-00-editorial-protest-show-that-nothing-has-changed

Bryant, L. (2011). Tunisian Prime Minister resigns amid protests. *Voanews*. Retrieved from http://www.voanews.com/a/police-break-up-demonstrations-in-tunis-117009313/135706.html

Cammaerts, B. (2007). Introduction: Activism and media. In B. Cammaerts & N. Carpentier (Eds.), *Reclaiming the media: Communication rights and democratic media roles* (pp. 217–224). Chicago, IL: University of Chicago Press.

Castells, M. (2001). *The Internet galaxy: Reflections on the Internet, business and society*. Oxford: Oxford University Press. doi:10.1007/978-3-322-89613-1

Castells, M. (2009). *Communication power*. Oxford: Oxford University Press.

Castells, M. (2012). *Networks of outrage and hope social movements in the Internet age*. Cambridge: Polity Press.

Cerise, L. G. (2015). Activism or "Slacktivism?": Digital media and organizing for social change. *Communication Teacher*, *29*(2), 81–85. doi:10.1080/17404622.2014.1003310

Cleaver, H. (1998). The Zapatista effect: The Internet and the rise of an alternative public fabric. *Journal of International Affairs*, *51*, 621–632.

Cloete, K. (2015). What does the working class stand to gain from the #ZumaMustFall campaign? *Daily Maverick*. Retrieved from: http://www.dailymaverick.co.za/opinionista/2015-12-15-what-does-the-working-class-stand-to-gain-from-the-zumamustfall-campaign/#.V8_CQPl96Hs

Department of Labour (2017). Hospitality sector minimum wage for 2017/2018. Retrieved from: www.labour.gov.za/DOL/media-statements/2017/hospitality-sector-minimum-wage-for-2017-2018

Diani, M. (2000). Social movement networks virtual and real. *Information Communication and Society*, *3*(3), 386–401. doi:10.1080/13691180051033333

Downing, J. (2001). *Radical media*. Thousand Oaks: Sage Publications.

EWN. (2017). SCA Upholds High Court Decision on Zuma Charges.

Fenton, N., & Barassi, V. (2011). Alternative media and social networking sites: The politics of individuation and political participation. *Communication Review*, *14*(3), 179–196. doi:10.1080/10714421.2011.597245

Findlay, S. (2016). Hashtag Fail? #BringBackOurGirls has 'nothing to show.' Retrieved from: http://www.heraldlive.co.za/news/world/2016/04/14/hashtag-fail-bringbackourgirls-nothing-show/

Galusky, W. (2003). Identifying with information citizen empowerment, the Internet and the environment anti-toxins movement. In M. McCaughey & M. Ayers (Eds.), *Cyberactivism online activism in theory and practice* (pp. 185–199). London: Routledge.

Ghobadi, S., & Clegg, S. (2015). "These days will never be forgotten…": A critical mass approach to online activism. *Information and Organization*, *25*(1), 52–71. doi:10.1016/j.infoandorg.2014.12.002

Gladwell, M. (2010, October 4). Small change: Why the revolution will not be tweeted. *The New Yorker*.

Hassa, S. H. (2015). *Social media and the Arab Spring*. USA: The State University of New Jersey.

Melki, J., & Mallat, S. (2014). Digital activism: Efficacies and burdens of social media for civic activism. *Arab Media and Society*, *19*.

Meyer, M., & Workman, B. C. (2013). Emerging adult usage of social networks as sites of activism: A critical examination of the TOMS and TWLOHA movements. *Ohio Communication Journal*, *51*, 53–77. Retrieved from http://ohiocomm.org/main/

Mkentane, L. (2017) Radical economic transformation will save SA's economy: Dlamini-Zuma. *IOL*. Retrieved from http://www.iol.co.za/news/politics/development/radical-economic-transformation-save-sas-economy-dlamini-zuma-10757750

Morozov, E. (2009b). Texting toward utopia: Does the Internet spread democracy? *Boston Review*. Retrieved from http://bostonreview.net/BR34.2/morozov.php

Morozov, E. (2011). *The net delusion*. New York: Public Affairs.

Munusamy, R. (2016). Chasing Butterflies and Bogeymen: Mantashe beats 'regime change' drum. *Daily Maverick*. Retrieved from http://www.dailymaverick.co.za/article/2016-05-13-chasing-butterflies-and-bogeymen-mantashe-beats-regime-change-drum/

Munusamy, R. (2017). #ZumaMustFall: A misguided campaign, Zuma's helping hand. Daily Maverick. Retrieved from firstthings.dailymaverick.co.za/article?id=73576#WhGpgROCzsE

News24. (2017). Zuma sidesteps flames. Retrieved from:http://www.news24.com/Archives/City-Press/Zuma-sidesteps-flames-20150429

Norris, P. (2004). The bridging and bonding role of online communities. In P. N. Howard & S. Jones (Eds.), *Society online: The Internet in context* (pp. 31–41). Thousand Oaks: Sage. doi:10.4135/9781452229560.n2

Nyamnjoh, F. (2016). *#RhodesMustFall: Nibbling at resilient colonialism in South Africa*. Mankon Bamenda: Langaa Research & Publishing CIG.

Pauw, J. (2017). *The President's Keepers: Those keeping Zuma in power and out of prison*. Cape Town: Tafelberg.

Porta, D., & Mosca, L. (2005). Global-net for global movement? A network for networks for a movement of movement. *Journal of Public Policy*, *25*(1), 165–190. doi:10.1017/S0143814X05000255

Postill, J. (2012). Digital politics and political engagement. In H. Horst & D. Miller (Eds.), *Digital anthropology* (pp. 165–184). London: Berg Publishers.

Tarrow, S. (2005). *The new transnational activism*. Cambridge: Cambridge University Press. doi:10.1017/CBO9780511791055

Tilly, C. (1995). *From mobilization to revolution*. Reading, MA: Addison-Wesley.

Tilly, C. (2004). *Social movements 1768-2004*. London: Paradigm Publishers.

Van de Donk, W., Loader, B. D., Nixon, P. G., & Rucht, D. (Eds.). (2004). *Cyber protest: New media, citizens and social movements*. New York, NY: Routledge.

Von Holdt, K. (2002). Social movement unionism: The case of South Africa. *Work, Employment and Society*, *16*(2), 283–304. doi:10.1177/095001702400426848

Von Lieres, B. (2014). Citizenship from below: The Politics of citizen action and resistance in South Africa and Angola. In E. Obadare & W. Willems (Eds.), *Civic agency in Africa: Arts of resistance in the 21st Century* (pp. 49–62). Suffolk: James Currey.

Wassermann, H. (2010). *Mobile phones, popular media and everyday African democracy: transmissions and transgressions*. Unpublished paper, Rhodes University.

ENDNOTES

1 The public protector, an anti-corruption body, ruled in 2014 that $23m (£15m) of public money had been improperly spent on Mr Zuma's rural home in Nkandla in KwaZulu-Natal province, and ordered him to reimburse part of the expense.

2 President Zuma's alleged corrupt link with the wealth Gupta family has been exposed.

3 The last two years has witnessed phenomena increase in digital movements from #RhodesMustFall, #FeesMustFall, #ZumaMustFall, #OccupyLuthuliHouse and #BlackHair amongst others.

4 It should be noted that the #RhodesMustFall movement wasn't about the removal of the statue of Cecil Rhodes from University of Cape Town, South

Africa but includes deep issues such as transformation of the higher education sector in South Africa, and decolonization of the learning space.

5 The concept of elite is difficult to define due to the nuance from which it can be viewed. I have used elites from the social construct perspective. It's not a fixed category but based on the idea that not all are allowed to participate due to exclusion which might be caused by political, economic and cultural factors. Therefore, elite in this context is someone who is privileged economically, politically and culturally.

6 Julius Malema is the founder of the Economic Freedom Fighters (EFF) political party, and he is considered to be a revolutionary activist with strong views regarding hatred for white capitalism as he believes in nationalization and forceful taking over of the lands in South Africa. This has made him win the hearts of most black South Africa.

7 As earlier stated, the history of apartheid and race construction impact on political, economic and cultural discourses. Most people viewed the #ZumaMustFall as a white capitalist tool to project and protect their interests.

Chapter 10
Using Social Media to Advocate LGBT Rights in Black Africa:
A Study of Nigerian and Cameroonian Gay Bloggers and "Facebookers"

Floribert Patrick C. Endong
University of Calabar, Nigeria

ABSTRACT

The prevalence of draconian homophobic laws in Cameroon and Nigeria has systematically stultified sympathy for the LGBT communities and made pro-gay street activism a risky venture in these two countries. In view of this, a good number of gay rights activists have resorted to the social media as a suitable platform for a less risky advocacy. Using the social media has afforded them the opportunity to explore interactive, post-modern, and personified approaches to sensitizing and mobilizing their readership in favour of gay proselytism in Cameroon, Nigeria, and some other parts of Africa. Based on a content analysis of 200 blog posts and web/ facebook pages generated by Cameroonian and Nigerian gay activists, this chapter measures the extent to which gay activists adopt a national/local perspective versus the level to which they adopt an international perspective in their online advocacy. The chapter equally examines the degree to which these citizen journalist/activists construct their advocacy discourse from the prism of a cultural war between the West and Africa.

DOI: 10.4018/978-1-5225-2854-8.ch010

INTRODUCTION

Apart from South Africa, virtually all Black African countries have adopted draconian legislations which severely criminalise homosexuality and systematically discourage any form of sympathy for the LGBT people. Being mainly inspired by doctrinaire religions and other conservative/fundamentalist social arbiters, these legislations have not only instituted a homophobic atmosphere at all spheres of most African societies, but have equally attempted to literally stultify any form of advocacy for LGBT rights in these Black African nations. The homophobic legislations and atmosphere have engendered a situation where in pro-gay and human rights activists face constant death threats, intimidation, humiliation and physical elimination by anti-gay thugs and conservative arbiters. In countries like Nigeria, Mauritania, Senegal, Uganda and Cameroon (just to name a few), legal dispositions have even been taken to systematically neutralise media advocacy in favour of the LGBT rights movement (Egbert, 2013; Endong, 2015a; Karaim, 2011; Pen American Centre, 2015). Media regulatory organs have thus, in their codes, prescribed heavy penalties to be meted on "rebellious" media outlets that will dare celebrate and push a concept which, according to popular imaginations is just a symbol of Western cultural corruption, a vector of "*westoxification*", thus a socio-cultural pathology. In its chapter 3 devoted to program standards, the *Nigerian Broadcasting Code* (2010) for instance, provides a set of principles to clarify media professionals on morality and decency. It states that "sex-related acts such as adultery, prostitution, rape, bestiality, homosexuality, lesbianism, incest, etc, which are considered bad, shall not be presented, except as destructive practices to be avoided or denounced" (Article 3.7.5.). In many other African countries, such homophobic media codes guide all media operations, particularly in government owned media outlets (Endong & Vareba, 2015; Karaim, 2011).

It goes without saying that the (anti-gay) legislations and media codes adopted by most African countries actually violate a multitude of civil rights. They breed a climate of socio-political intimidation and fear which is immensely un-friendly to media advocacy and activism for LGBT rights. These legislations and media codes equally threaten self-expression by LGBT people and their allies; and systematically hinder the expression of support for LGBT human rights. Furthermore, the anti-LGBT legislations indirectly affect African peoples' literary, artistic, and cultural communities as they put LGBT and pro-gay writers and artists at risk of criminal prosecution and violent physical attacks, as well as limit their ability to publish and distribute their works in the homophobic African countries. Additionally, the anti-gay legislations directly threaten freedom of expression thereby eroding the strength of African democracies.

In view of all these indexes, the act by an African, of publicly supporting the LGBT right movement has, in most Black African countries, been a matter of being a courageous, off rooted and pertinacious advocate/activist. Meanwhile, putting up a stiff, rigid and uncompromising demonization of the LGBT people and wanton stigmatisation, blackmailing, seclusion and lynching of gays have been the rule, if not a range of patriotic prerogatives for all. As most political leaders and Africanist ideologues quasi unanimously echoed, homosexuality is purely "un-African", thus a bane to the authentic African social system.

Despite this asphyxiating homophobia and the strong stultification of media advocacy for the LGBT rights movement in African communities, (pro-)gay entities and other LGBT people have designed a variety of tactics to resist the "violation" of their freedom of expression, freedom of thought and freedom to protest. Some have used media productions, in the forms of documentaries, religious teachings and books to "clandestinely" and daringly raise awareness on the plight of homosexuals in Black African communities. With the help of both endogenous and exogenous civil society organisations, some have created programmes and schemes aimed at making journalists more sensitive to LGBT rights in their reporting of news events. The greatest media communication technique adopted by this strand of LGBT advocates has, perhaps, been guerrilla communication tactics centred on citizen journalism/online journalism. This citizen journalism has mostly been through blogging, tweeting and "facebooking" which offer them (the [pro-]gay activists) serious interactive options and alternative means to canvass support for pro-gay proselytism not only from their immediate geographical communities but from a transnational pool of online commenters and sympathisers.

The social media have thus provided a wide range of opportunities to (pro-) gay advocates from African countries to join the global momentum for the LGBT rights movement, with particular emphasis on their respective countries of origin. A herculean task or challenge faced by these pro-gay citizen journalists has been to properly deal with the conservative, but dominant theory which stipulates that homosexuality, same-sex marriage and the LGBT rights movement are *un-african* and thus a set of traditions that are to be "confined" to the West. This has motivated African bloggers, "facebookers" and users of other forms of social media networks to adopt varied advocacy tactics and axioms. While some have formulated their advocacy on a rhetoric which associates the above-mentioned neologisms (homosexuality, same-sex marriage and LGBT rights) with a number of cultural traditions within some traditionalist African social systems; others have totally neglected/overlooked the origin of these neologisms to principally underscore their nature as human rights and their being indispensible for a modern(izing) Africa. Using Nigerian and Cameroonian pro-gay bloggers and "facebookers" as a composite case study, this chapter examines the tone and scope of on-line advocacy for the LGBT rights movement by Black African gays (LGBT people) and pro-gay activists. Based on both quantitative and qualitative content analyses of 200 blogs, Facebook and web pages generated by gay activists, this chapter seeks to measure the extent to which gay activists adopt a national/local perspective *versus* the level to which they adopt an international perspective in their online advocacy. Additionally, the present discourse examines the degree to which these citizen journalist/activists construct their advocacy discourse from the prism of a cultural war between the West and Africa.

THEORETICAL FRAMEWORK

This study is anchored on two theories namely media advocacy and framing. These two theories are more or less broad. It will therefore be expedient in this section of the discourse, to highlight the particular keystones of these respective theories, that will be considered in our analyses.

Media Advocacy Theory

The media advocacy framework is principally defined with close respect to the meaning of the term "advocacy". Advocacy is popularly construed as the process by which an organisation, a group of individual or a person deploys well designed strategies to influence public policies, regulations or public opinions. Such a process is generally driven by motives which may be to protect the general interest or public assets. Advocacy may equally be driven by socio-cultural, religious or political motives among others. In line with this, the media advocacy theory stipulates that the media of mass communication are at the vanguards of advocacy in any given society. They enjoy an immeasurable potential to influence public opinion or public policies, in favour of particular social ideals. In effect, communication is one of the central components of any advocacy campaign. The mass media therefore provide a platform for the kind of communication that may secure a snowflake effect within the masses. A cardinal principle in the process of advocacy consists in getting well formulated messages across to various pockets of the masses and specific stakeholders in order to mobilize and push them to take (positive) action. The media of mass communication offer this opportunity for massive mobilisation through radio/TV advertisement, announcements, advertorial and human-interest programs on the issue being advocated.

The social media have, in recent time proven to be suitable tools for mass mobilisation and advocacy; hence the conception of the neologism "social media advocacy". The 2011 Arab Spring – which led to the overthrow of dictatorship and dramatic socio-political changes in various Middle East and Maghrebian countries

– is an egregious illustration of this thesis. The social media platforms such as Facebook, Twitter, YouTube, Google+, blogs and Pinterest among others are today considered suitable tools for media advocacy. They have been "appropriated" by activists and advocates of various causes – including the LGBT rights movement – for the purpose of socio-political advocacy. Even global opinion leaders as such as the UN have launched various forms of social media based movements for specific causes. The UN, in particular, initiated the Free and Equal Campaign to combat prejudice, discrimination and violence against Lesbian, gay, Bisexual and Transgender across the world.

Framing Theory

Framing – as a concept or a theoretical construction – has variously been envisaged. It is often described as a complex, elusive or scattered conceptualisation. Some critics juxtapose it with the three "similar" concepts of "priming", "script" and "schema" while others – for instance McComb, Shaw and Weaver (1996) – equate it (framing) to an extension of the Agenda Setting theory, which postulates that there is an automatic and cogent correlation between the emphasis placed on certain issues by the media and the way the audiences perceive these issues. McComb, Shaw and Weaver actually use the term "second-level agenda setting" in reference to the phenomenon, partially on account of its effect-related nature. Because of this terminological inconsistency, communication scholars have sometimes tended to use "Priming Effect", Agenda Setting and Framing as one and the same thing.

In the context of this work however, Framing is viewed as the way in which events and issues are organised and made sense of by both media message designers (in this case bloggers, citizen journalists and online activists) and the audiences. The theory is based on the assumption that the way an issue is presented in the media contents can have an influence on how the audience understands this issue. Most often, the media content designer (blogger for instance), actively sets the frames of reference that readers or viewers employ or consider to read, do an exegesis and discuss issues. (Scheufele, 1999). With this, the Framing theory is operationalized on the basis of a social constructivism which takes into account the impacts of media discourse on the audiences' construction of meaning and the public opinion's effects, on the process of meaning development and crystallization by media men in public discourse. The assumption here is that the bloggers' diction, ordering of ideas or use of other artefacts may twist or spin the information he or she is presenting. As Auerbash and Bloch-Elkon (2005) put it, when the media place stories in specific frames, "they lend a different meaning to the news". Through such a process the media systematically increase or decrease the salience of issues. This causes the public to remember and make judgments on such issues. Framing assumes that subtle changes in the wording used to describe a situation might affect how audience members think about this situation. It is also important to note that the bloggers' frame is not always harmonized with those of the audiences. It may happen that a bloggers' representation or framing of a certain experience diametrically conflicts with those of his/her readers.

LITERATURE REVIEW

A large body of literature has endeavoured to explore various aspects of the use of the social media for transnational or national advocacy in favour of LGBT rights. In this section of the chapter, the author will particularly be interested in studies which have critically examined the social media as working tools for human rights advocacy and those which have looked at the LGBT rights movement in Black Africa, particularly in Nigeria and Cameroon. This will help build a rich background for the present study.

Social Media as a Tool for (Human Rights) Advocacy

The uses and functions of social media have remarkably been dynamic over the last decades. In effects the social media have ceased to exclusively be typologies of platforms for entertainment, recreation and socializing. They have actually morphed or evolved into more versatile forums, and suitable tools/forums for activism. This could be evidenced by the fact that national, regional and global forces involved in advocacy have seen the enormous potential of the social networks. Most organisations ranging from political formations through non-profit foundations to business enterprises now consider the social media as valuable communication strategies for massive mobilisation and as strategic weapons to influence legislators or public opinion. As Aurora (2013) rightly observes, the line of thinking has these last decades, shifted from using social media merely as platforms for pictures sharing, chatting and socialising, to using say an image or a link to sensitize and mobilize social media users.

According to many human rights foundations and political activists, "sitting" on Facebook for the purpose of social media advocacy has become more like marching, shouting slogans, and waving signs over the heads of the crowds on a quotidian basis and in a creative way. This is not however, to insinuate that social media advocacy can replace the other foundational advocacy strategies. As Nisbet (2013) succinctly remarks, digital activism can only complement and strengthen essential movement strategies such as coalition building, legal actions, media outreach, street protests or canvassing. Although very instrumental, digital advocacy is unlikely to ever be able to replace these movement strategies. Social media advocacy therefore constitutes only one of the communication strategies envisaged in a movement context and for it to be efficacious, it must be diligently strengthened with other tools notably street protest. Street activism has always played a central role in educating and provoking evidential social change. Corroborating this position, Hackl (2013) cites examples such as the Stonewall Riots of 1969 which witnessed a success grace to well coordinated street mobilizations, organized to fight societal marginalization.

Also important to mention here is the 1980s HIV/AIDS epidemic movements which, to be fruitful, necessitated radical street protests against the ACT UP that challenged societal misinformation and lack of governmental response. In the same line of argument, Hestre (2013) remarks that global advocacy groups such as the 1Sky and 350 org combined offline protests to their online activism to effectively mobilize efforts in favor of climate change in the world. All these are apt evidences of the fact that, in most cases, the social media platforms are basically used as organizational tool for offline protest and other essential movement strategies. They help – or are supposed to help – inform and mobilize constituents around grassroots efforts (DeNardis, 2012; Hackl 2013).

Though not "self-sufficient", digital activism remains a robust approach at engaging and reaching audiences. It may involve the creation of "crowd-speaking" platforms (which can enable campaign organizers to rally facebook or twitter users to mass-tweet in unison). It may equally involve the creation of specific sites through which campaigns may spread messages through unified profile badges as well as platforms enabling users to tweet at a person or entity in an organized tweeted protest (Nonprofit Technology Network, 2013). To this list of social media advocacy strategies, it is expedient to add the creation of blogs and other social media outlets through which various interactions on the idea(l) been advocated may be done. Blogs are generally adapted for discussing human rights topics which most often have been sensitive, controversial and which are circumstantially unfavorable to the economics of traditional media. Given the fact that they must not always follow the cannons of mainstream journalism, they can be partisan, in questionable taste and totally individualistic. All these characteristics make for lively, interactive and exciting contents (Dominick 2011; Endong 2015, a, b).

Digital activism or social media advocacy has been instrumental to the success of various forms of socio-political mobilisation across the world. Aurora (2013) counts it among the principal factors responsible for the repeal of the death penalty in the Maryland State of the USA in 2013. According to her, early campaigns by both state and national advocacy groups aimed at pushing for the repeal of the death penalty in this State paid little attention to digital activism and suffered for such serious "omission" or insufficient attention. These human right activists saw the imperative to re-strategize. As she concedes,

We needed an innovative and strategic digital campaign that would not only promote our messages, but mobilize constituents and influence policymakers. Marylanders — and the state's politicians — had been hearing about the inefficacy and inequality of the death penalty from the same people for years. It became our job to find new ways to turn up the pressure, publicly. Our digital media campaign launched just before the 2013 Maryland General Assembly. Every detail of each social media action was considered, down to the timing, and it paid off — we won. In May 2013, Governor Martin O'Malley signed a bill making Maryland the eighteenth state to repeal the death penalty. (para 3)

Another egregious illustration of the power of the social media in human rights and political activism is the 2011 fruitful Arab Spring that brought about sweeping socio-political mutations in parts of the Maghreb and the Middle East. As a serious socio-political force, the Arab spring enabled the overthrow of dictatorial regimes and the introduction of democracy in a number of Arab monarchies. The movement actually witnessed the flexible and creative implementation of the social media for activism in a context of authoritarian media system. The different social media enabled human right activists to surmount or beat regular censorship of the media by the authoritarian governments in these Arab countries. Digital activism was thus critical during riots in these countries as the government could not easily control social media platforms. This "advantage" was however to an extent as the governments later responded to the uprisings by shutting down the Internet.

Another major realm in which digitally enabled activism has been tested and proven technically efficacious is the LGBT rights advocacy. Some of the LGBT rights include – but are not limited to – the following:

- Recognition of same-sex relationships (through same-sex marriage or similar unions)
- The right to adopt children
- Recognition to LGBT parenting
- Immigration equality right
- The right to donate blood
- The right for protection against discrimination in employment and housing procedures
- Protection against any form of bullying
- Equal access to reproductive technology and
- Access to sex re-assignment surgery and hormones, among others

The relative success registered by activists involved in online LGBT rights activism is an evidence that digital advocacy does not work exclusively in context of political protests. In most western countries, online advocacy for the LGBT rights has been effective, except in countries like Russia where the government has adopted a number of federal legislations that criminalise the promotion of homosexual propaganda and has provided jail sentences and stiff fines to be meted out on refractors of these laws (Gevisser, 2015; Salzburg Academy, 2015). Such homophobic legislations are partially responsible for the multiple challenges faced by Russian pro-gay activists, in the latter's use of the social media. The law actually handicaps pro-LGBT activism in the country. On June 2013, a prominent Russian human rights activist Nikolai Alexeyev initiated an online petition aimed at blacklisting the visas of some principal artisans of the federal laws which criminalizes pro-gay propaganda in the country. The move did not yield positive fruits as the targeted anti-gay legislators counter-threatened the activist with a criminal case (Salzburg Academy, 2015).

America represents an egregious example of a country where online LGBT activism has somehow been very productive. As earlier as 2010, there has been a surge in LGBT social media campaigns following a number of major incidents. One of such incidents is the suicide act committed by Justin Aaberg and Billy Lucas (two American adolescents) on account of their being constantly bullied by peers for their gayness. This incident in particular motivated movements such as the "It Gets Better" Campaign to advocate governmental measures designed to check the bullying of teenagers for their sexualities. Apart from the "It Gets Better" Campaigns, American LGBT rights activists have been using social media such as Twitter, Facebook and YouTube among others to canvas support in favour of LGBT equality, receiving the support of a broad base of online communities including celebrities and philanthropists. Even heavy weights from the realm of politics (notably President Obama and former Secretary of State Hilary Clinton) joined in this online razzmatazz for LGBT proselytism. President Obama for instance tweeted his support for same-sex-marriage shortly after the US Supreme Court overruled the famous Defence of Marriage Act (DOMA) which rejected same-sex marriage and denied gays financial benefits emanating from such marriages. Obama's tweet was received by more than 150 million social media users.

Online activism has in general been acclaimed for a number of successful mobilization of efforts in favour of socio-political and human rights causes. However, the phenomenon has shown a number of weaknesses, particularly in this last decade. It has for instance been highlighted that social media advocacy perpetrates or is based on the mobilization of weak-tie networks of constituents. This brings to the fore the phenomenon of mere "clicktivism" or "like-tivism" which of course has serious limitations in the sense that, constituents presumed subscription to the idea advocated may not be sincere or enthusiastic. As Egbert (2013) argues, one of the dangers of digitally enabled awareness campaigns is that "they risk being [mere] online popularity contests". A number of observers have presented social media as tools not properly used by activists. Hackl (2013) notes for instance that some critics are of the opinion that future socio-political revolutions may not be masterfully "tweeted". Such beliefs feed on the observation that in major uprisings (notably the 2011 Arab Spring), the social media were cardinally deployed as mere sources of information instead of being employed as an arsenal for protest organization. During the Arab Spring specifically, attention to Twitter came primarily from outside the protest region.

Another area of concern has been the lack of tact (by online activists) and the poor enunciation of the themes or strophes of some online advocacy campaigns. Egbert (2013) makes such an observation with reference to *Hivo* and Human Right Watch's 2013 international campaign titled "Wanted For Love", a campaign aimed at sensitizing the world about homophobia and draconian anti-gay legislations in Africa. She notes particularly that, though well intentioned, the "Wanted For Love" campaign functioned as a tool aimed to further a "pink-washed" or "homo-nationalist" agenda. This has been so as it was solidly grounded on the faulty/misleading rhetoric which presents Africa as the most homophobic continent (a hell), and a place contrastable to Europe, a heaven for the LGBT people. As Egbert (2013) explains:

The campaign discursively constructs a specific image of "Africa," rights, and culture which it, then, exploits for rhetorical purposes. Contrastingly, it constructs the fantasy of "Europe" as a bastion of freedom for LGBT people. In its bid to support activists in Africa Wanted For Love ends up juxtaposing a "homophobic Africa" with a "liberal Europe." Thus, "Africa" is made to serve as "homophobic Other" for Dutch homonationalism. (Egbert, 2013, para 8)

A similar project by the European Refugee Fund and the Dutch Ministry of Justice and Security exploited the same rhetoric by anchoring their activism on the idea (the theme) of "*Fleeing Homophobia. Seeking Safety in Europe*". In view of such evidences and other factors, it may be argued that it has progressively become a maxim for Euro-centric LGBT activists to tap into myths that present Africa as a dangerous clime and a place diametrically different from the "dreamed land", Europe or the West in general (Endong, 2015; Okanlawon, 2011). While such myths and imaginations may have a relative degree of pertinence, they contribute in furthering the stereotyping of Africa and African poeples. They equally project a somehow false, illusory or artificial image of the West. As can be argued with reference to the state of the LGBT rights in Europe, the image of Europe as a heaven for the LGBT people is somehow mythical and misleading as recent reports by organizations such as the European Union Agency for Fundamental Human Right (2015) indicate that homophobia continues to exist in varied facets, in European socio-cultural context. Even European countries with pro-gay laws have not been totally exempted from this phenomenon.

The LGBT Rights Movement in Black Africa

The LGTB rights movement has, over the years, spread to Black African countries, inspiring to a hot debate which has basically opposed conservative or fundamentalist socio-political forces to modernist/westernised forces. In effect, "gayness" and the tolerance of homosexuality (the LGBT rights movement) have mainly been read as markers of the western culture. This has caused the LGBT rights concept to be popularly labelled as an *un-African* ploy aimed at advocating or perpetrating an "infamous" western cultural intoxication on African soil. A vitriolic political narrative has thus been developed and homophobic legislations have been adopted in most Black African countries. The political discourse prevailing in these African states derogatorily brand LGBT communities and makes LGBT activism (particularly street protests) not just a risky mission but a derisory act. Zimbabwe's President Robert Mugabe's critique of gayness and the LGBT movement is perhaps the most virulent of African opponents to the LGBT rights movement. Mugabe equated (African) gays in particular with beings whose sexual orientations are not just inordinate but of lower status to those of animals. To him, gays have subhuman inclinations; they are less than dogs and pigs. On the same note, he described the LGBT movement as an abomination and intolerable enterprise. As he put it:

Homosexuality degrades human dignity. It's unnatural, and there is no question ever of allowing these people to behave worse than dogs and pigs. If dogs and pigs do not do it, why must human beings? We have our own culture, and we must rededicate ourselves to our traditional values that make us human beings. What we are being persuaded to accept is a sub-animal behaviour and we will never allow it here [in Zimbabwe]. (cited in Endong 2015b, p.56)

With the same measure of intolerance, Gambian President, Jammeh, used the metaphoric expression of "mosquitoes" to refer to the queer community. Even in acclaimed African democracies such as Ghana, the political discourse has been antithetical to the LGBT movement. President John Mills (of Ghana) has equated homosexuality to a cultural oddity. The Head of State has lambasted the LGBT movement "vowing" "never [to] initiate or support any attempt to legalize [homosexuality]" (BBC News, 2011; Endong, 2016). The vitriolic political discourse adopted by African leaders has either systematically inspired or been re-enforced by the passing of homophobic bills in various Black African countries. These bills severely repress homosexuality and encourage the wanton humiliation, lynching and ostracism of the LGBT communities – including pro-gay activists – in Black African countries. All these negative indexes indicate how difficult it has been for both endogenous and exogenous anti-homophobia forces to mount vocal LGBT activism strategies in Black African countries.

Despite these challenges, a number of transnational advocacy campaigns have been initiated by such global forces as Human Rights Watch (HRW), the UNO, the European Refugee Fund and European Union Agency for Human Rights among others. In collaboration with H*i*vo, the HRW initiated a broad online campaign captioned "Wanted for Love". This campaign took place in 2013 and was aimed at drawing global attention to the plight of LGBT communities in Africa. A similar campaign – captioned "Fleeing Homophobia. Seeking Safety in Europe" – was initiated by the European Refugee Fund. Other LGBT advocacy initiatives have been designed by Africans with or without the support of exogenous forces. One of such has been the efforts of the anti-Apartheid icon, Desmond Tutu. In most of his advocacy efforts, Arch Bishop Tutu has been seeking to debunk the religious arguments advanced by doctrinaire Christian forces in Africa, to fuel anti-gay proselytism. In the occasion of the launch of UN's 2014 "Free and Equal" Campaign (an event aimed at promoting homosexual rights in South Africa), Archbishop Desmond Tutu alluded to the fact that he will prefer going to hell than going to a homophobic heaven. This allusion is captured in his saying that "I would refuse to go to a homophobic heaven. No, I would say sorry. I mean, I would much rather go to the other place" (cited in Endong 2015b, p. 52). Tutu equally uses platforms such as the *Gay Humanist Quarterly* – a journal devoted to LGBT advocacy – to lambast Black African countries' socio-political hysteria about the LGBT right movement. He notes that:

I am deeply disturbed that in the face of some of the most horrendous problems facing Africa, we concentrate on 'what do I do in bed with whom'. For one to penalize someone for their sexual orientation is the same as penalizing someone for something they can do nothing about, like ethnicity or race. I cannot imagine persecuting a minority group which is already being persecuted. (cited in Gay Humanist Quarterly 2007, p.10)

Tutu's line of thought and advocacy style is emulated by Nigerian born Rev, Olajide Macaulay who, since 2006 has been using his gay-only church (House of Rainbow) as a transnational project aimed at advocating LGBT rights. House of Rainbow has been functioning more like a local support organization primarily devoted to the legitimization of homosexuality. The project is visibly less concerned with the holistic exploration of Christian spirituality. Through its concept of guerrilla spirituality, the church has been providing "spiritual" orientation to LGBT community Nigeria and numerous other African countries as well as survival strategies to withstand and challenge the prevailing homophobic atmosphere in African countries. As Obadare (2014) succinctly notes,

House of Rainbow's guerrilla spirituality is illustrative of the grit and feistiness of a small number of social agents determined not to leave the physical, if not social, ground uncontested to opponents of homosexuality; a reminder that though the debate is not always construed as such, the campaign against sexual bigotry in Nigeria and other African countries boils down in the end to these four things: what it means to be human, what it means to live in a democratic society, what it means for a society to have an autonomous public sphere, and what it means to be a free citizen, untrammeled in the pursuit of one's individual realization and upliftment. It is, at its core therefore, about the social projects of civil society. (p. 5)

LGBT activism on African soil has equally included the muscled efforts of western chancelleries such as Anglo-American and EU's resort to financial threats against homophobic countries within the continent. In effect, America, Britain and the EU have threatened to withdraw their financial aids to African countries which have adopted anti-gay laws. These threats have actually not yielded considerable fruits, given the fact that, anti-gay legislations continued to prevail in the continent. In the exception of South Africa virtually all the other African states have homophobic legislations. The threats have even instead worsened the already precarious conditions of LGBT communities as they (the threats) have largely been interpreted by the public opinion as an evidence of western "cultural aggression", violation of African countries' sovereignty and Western countries' superiority complex (Chika 2014; Endong, 2016). The threats seem not to have successfully reformed the minds of the African populace whose homophobic instincts have, since then, been manifested by persistent death threats, wanton lynching, intimidation, humiliation or assassination of local LGBT activists.

The Cameroonian Perspective

In Cameroon for instance, icons of the LGBT rights movement such as Alice Nkom and Michel Togue (all two lawyers) have faced countless moves and ploys by both the government and social institutions aimed at cowing and neutralizing their activism. In an interview she granted the French international Broadcaster *France 24*, Alice Nkom reveals the personal sacrifices she found herself obliged to make, in view of ensuring her own security: "I made arrangements. I have a security contract with a company, because the state doesn't ensure my safety. [...] Diplomacy has a very important role to play because, if I did not have outside help, they would have already killed me" (cited in *France 24*, 2014, para 6-8).

Alice Nkom's pro-gay activism has attracted acerb criticisms and pre-meditated assassinations of her character from various segments of the Cameroonian public opinion. She became a popularly perceived by some social and political arbiters as "notorious deviant" from the moment she embarked on censuring Article 347 of the Cameroonian Penal Code – which severely criminalizes "sexual relations with a person of the same sex"- as well as other social strictures and structures (the religious and conservative rhetoric) instituted to fuel homophobia in the country. Such public criticisms and hate against the activist got to their climax in January 2011 when she received a significant financial support (300 000 Euros) from the European Union, aimed at pushing a number of pro LGBT activities in the country. The financial support was actually destined to facilitate the execution by Nkom's outfit (Association for the Defense of the Rights of Homosexuals) of a project titled "Support and Training for Sexual Minority". EU's support was popularly read as Western countries' interference in the internal affairs of Cameroon; while Alice Nkom's act was interpreted as a serious violation of the country's law. Her "traitorous alliance" with the EU earned her several arrest charges.

At first sight, Nkom's predicament seems not as sepulchral as that of some of her colleagues. In 2013, a prominent figure of the LGBT rights movement in Cameroon, Eric Ohena Lebembe was gruesomely assassinated (presumably) by anti-gay thugs in Yaounde. The incident occurred shortly after the activist announced a series of frontal moves aimed at propelling his LGBT rights activism to a higher dimension. Up till today, the activist's assassins have not been brought to justice; and according to many critics, no diligent investigation has been initiated by the Cameroonian forces of law, to find and collar the thugs. The (presumed) lukewarm attitude of both the forces of law and the government towards the proper investigation of the matter has been viewed as a regrettable consequence of the country's homophobic nature. The widespread condemnations of the murder by the international community, have not been sufficient to trigger a pro-human right reaction from the Cameroonian government. One of the relatively "lukewarm" reactions of the government has been a press conference organized by the Cameroon Minister of Information during which neither condemnations nor comments on the murder were formulated. The gruesome murder of Lebembe in 2013, has seriously diluted and obliterated – if not totally quenched – the zeal of a good number of LGBT rights activists in the country. The murder has made activists more conscious of the level of insecurity in which they are compelled to manifest their activism. The general fear among them is that their activism may expose them to be next targets of anti-gay thugs.

The Nigerian Perspective

A similar situation prevails in Nigeria with the *Same Sex Marriage (Prohibition) Act* which severely criminalizes homosexuality and technically discourages street protests or any other form of public activism in favor of LGBT rights. Prominent gay or bisexual activist such as Bisi Alimi, Jide Macaulay and Yemisi Illesanmi among others have been subject to multifaceted threats, attempts at intimidation and violent aggressions for their ("inordinate") sexual orientation and activism (Illesanmi, 2016; Macaulay, 2013). Most of these gay activists are on self-imposed exile in Western countries. The Nigerian government has consistently frustrated most of the major internal and external moves (by activists) aimed at reversing the homophobic atmosphere reigning in the country. LGBT rights activist Dammian Ugwu (cited by Duke, 2014) makes allusion to such governmental opposition to gay activism when he remarks that Nigerian law makers' instinctive alliance with other social forces (religious conservative and fundamentalists) to frustrate pro gay agitations against the draconian anti-gay bill adopted by the country. He buttresses his position by highlighting the undemocratic tactics deployed by the Nigerian government to sideline pro-gay activists in the promulgation process of *Same Sex Marriage (Prohibition) Act.* As he notes,

Supporters of the bill were given ample time to organize and mobilize their supporters, while LGBT activists and civil society organizations opposed to the bill were refused permission to attend the public hearing. Those who managed to scale the security barriers to attend the hearing were constantly jeered at and booed by religious fundamentalists while being intimidated by legislators. (cited in Duke, 2014, para 11)

In view of the asphyxiating conditions reigning in their countries of origin, many African LGBT right activists – particularly in Nigeria and Cameroon – have had no other options than fleeing to seek asylum in western countries or/and to heavily resort to online protest in guise of mobilization strategies. The social media have thus become platforms *par excellence* for sensitizing/mobilizing and pushing Africans to "positive" actions. They have become suitable weapons to push for a pro-gay agenda.

METHODOLOGY

Sample and Measurement

This study is based on the content analysis of a corpus of 200 posts generated by Nigerian and Cameroonian gay bloggers or "facebookers" from June 2012 to June 2016. The posts were randomly selected from blogs, tweets and Facebook or web pages designed by Nigerian and Cameroonian gay or pro-gay activists. The author considered paragraphs as units of analysis and therefore content analyzed a total of 2814 paragraphs. The choice of the paragraph as unit of analysis is justifiable by the fact that it constitutes a suitable unit or sequence of text construction with potential to carry dominant ideas developed by the blogger or citizen journalists. The author equally considered five (5) variable labels for the study, namely:

1. **(Geographical) Perspective:** Local/national or international,
2. **Tone:** Simple sensitization or provocative mobilization,
3. **Angle:** Cultural war; human rights, religion, or others,
4. **Level of Politicization:** Political or neutral, and
5. **Level of Sensationalism:** Sensational or non-sensational.

Definition of the Various Categories Considered

The local or international perspective of blog and web pages' contents were determined by the level of attention the bloggers gave to LGBT rights related issues happening in their countries vis-à-vis the attention they gave to issues happening in foreign countries. The "simple sensitization" category (featuring under the tone) was defined by the bloggers or Facebookers' efforts to simply inform and sensitize their readership on the plight of LGBT people and homophobia related issues; meanwhile the "provocative mobilization" (tone) was determine by the bloggers' visible attempt to extrinsically push their readership to action (notably street protest).

It is the belief of this author that categories related to the three variable labels of "angle", "level of politicization" and "level of sensationalism" are self-explanatory. Nevertheless, it should be noted that this author associated politicization of issues with bloggers' manifest tendency to relate the LGBT rights movement to poor governance and "obnoxious" government policies in their countries. The author equally viewed sensationalism from the angle of bloggers' clear attempt at getting their readership interested or moved through the use of shocking materials (for instance graphic pictures, obscene language, and links to websites with shocking material among others).

Data Analysis and Presentation

The data collected with the aid of a data sheet was statistically analyzed using the SPSS (Statistical Package for Social Sciences) program, and presented in tabular form (see tables 1, 2, 3, 4 and 5). Simple statistical manipulations were used including simple frequencies distributions. These data was discussed, and buttressed with the aid of suitable anecdotal evidences drawn from the sample (the posts considered for the study).

FINDINGS AND DISCUSSION

Findings indicate that Cameroonian and Nigerian LGBT right activists dominantly adopted a national or local perspective in their advocacy discourse. Over 77.93% of the blog and web pages' contents attest to this observation (see Table 1). This is consistent with the maxim which states that "charity begins at home". In line with this, Cameroonian and Nigerian bloggers sought principally to influence public opinion in their respective countries, by addressing factors at domestic level which directly or indirectly affect the social debate and government policies on homosexuality. The paragraphs devoted to the international perspective on the issue (LGBT right movement) are few as they amount to 22.07% of the overall content of the blogs and web pages. Cameroonian bloggers and gay-activists happened to be the principal breed to have explored this international perspective. This is indicated by the fact that 26.19% of their advocacy messages focused on attacking homophobia and preaching for positive (pro-gay) social changes not only in their countries but in other African and Arab countries.

Findings equally reveal that most of the activists limited themselves to sensitizing and raising awareness to the plight of the LGBT communities in African countries (particularly in Cameroon and Nigeria). Over 97.40% of the blog and web/facebook pages' content attests to this fact (see Table 2). A relatively insignificant portion of these

Table 1. Local versus international perspective

Geographic Perspective	Cam. Activists		Nig. Activists		Total	
	n	%	n	%	n	%
Local	851	73.81	1342	80.79	2193	77.93
International	302	26.19	319	19.21	621	22.07
Total	1153	100	1661	100	2814	100

Key: Cam: Cameroonian; Nig: Nigerian

Table 2. Activists' tone

Tone	Cam. Activists		Nig. Activists		Total	
	n	%	n	%	n	%
Sensitizing	1103	95.66	1638	98.61	2741	97.40
Mobilizing	50	4.34	23	1.39	73	2.6
Total	1153	100	1661	100	2814	100

online contents (2.6%) was devoted to "creating a spark" or pushing local readers to mobilize against the prevailing laws or status quo. Here again, Cameroonian activists sounded more "aggressive", more "ambitious" than their Nigerian counterparts as 4.34% of their advocacy messages contained highly motivational cues, susceptible to galvanize and directly push their Cameroonian readership to resisting anti-gay legislations. In one of her published post – particularly addressed to her colleagues and composed in the face of imminent arrest charges, Alice Nkom (one of the Cameroonian activist considered for this study) galvanized her Cameroonian and international allies saying "If we unite our efforts and our resources, we will get the Supreme court to join the other supreme courts in the world to firmly condemn the use of Article 347 as a basis for legal action or verdicts". It is expedient here to reiterates the fact that Article 347 of the Cameroonian Penal Code is the central anti-gay aspect of the Cameroonian legislation.

Furthermore, findings reveal that most of the activists considered in this study composed their advocacy discourse from the angle of the so-called cultural war between the West and Black African countries (see Table 3). In line with this, 40.86% of the their posts' contents was devoted to constructing an advocacy message aimed at debunking popular – but questionable – views/myths that homosexuality and the LGBT rights concept are essentially "un-African" – and that they represent typical markers of Western cultural "intoxication". Such portions of the posts fervidly

Table 3. Angles mostly exploited by the activists

Angle	Cam. Activists		Nig. Activists		Total	
	n	%	n	%	n	%
Cultural War	451	39.11	699	42.08	1150	40.86
Human Rights	625	54.20	461	27.75	1086	38.59
Religion	26	2.27	221	13.32	247	8.76
Others	51	4.42	280	16.85	331	11.76
Total	1153	100	1661	100	2814	100

challenged maxims which associated the LGBT rights movement with facets of neocolonialism and expression of Western cultural supremacy. It should however be noted that activists' tendency to censure the above mentioned myths of Western cultural supremacy and neocolonialism is more accentuated among Nigerian activists. Over 42.08% of their messages were composed from this angle, compared to 39.11% of the ones composed by Cameroonian activists.

The other dominant angles from which both Cameroonian and Nigerian developed their advocacy discourses include human rights (38.59%) and other issues (11.76%). In line with this, most of the activists pushed for the acceptance of LGBT rights as fundamental human rights. An interesting finding of the study is that, the religious argument was less explored by the activists. Although fundamental religious arbiters and doctrines have constituted central obstacles to gay-proselytism and the LGBT rights movement in the two countries, the activists have devoted less of their energy to challenging them or pushing LGBT rights on religious basis. This may partially be justified by the fact that it has always been a herculean task for most activists to unarguably make a case for LGBT rights on purely religious bases (be it in relation to Christian aphorisms or Islamic doctrines). The "best solution" most activists seem to have so far, found to deal with this religious equation has been to simply attack religious doctrines and theologies – in an atheistic manner – by relegating them to anti-progressive forces. Nigerian born LGBT right activist Yemisi Illasanmi exemplifies this breed of gay activist with her statement that "We must rid ourselves of mental slavery, self-righteousness and religious stupidity before we can truly empathize with another human being or other earthlings. We must break the need to justify our actions with quotes from some imported 'holy books'".

It was also observed that a small portion (28.15%) of the blogs and Facebook/web pages' contents was devoted to attempts at politicizing anti-gayness and the LGBT rights movement (see Table 4). In the process of advocating gay rights, a number of Cameroonian and Nigeria activists associated the homophobic atmosphere reigning in their countries with bad governance and African leaders' penchant for

Table 4. Level of politicization

Level of politicization	Cam. Bloggers		Nig. Bloggers		Total	
	n	%	n	%	n	%
Political	351	30.45	441	26.56	792	28.15
Neutral	802	69.55	1220	73.44	2022	71.85
Total	1153	100	1661	100	2814	100

populism. In tandem with this, the activists enjoined their readership to view Black African state men's homophobic stances and reluctance to embrace the LGBT rights movement as a political ploy meant to attract votes or increase their chances of success in upcoming elections. Such activists, equally interpreted Cameroon and Nigerian governments' adoption of populist anti-gay agendas and legislations as an avenue to opportunistically escape pressing and vital imperatives at the political level. For some Nigerian activists for instance, it is incomprehensive that the government insists on cracking down on an already marginalized community of gays, meanwhile it seems not to give sufficient attention to the deadly Boko Haram insurgency which is ravaging the North of the country. The anti-gay campaigns systematically sustained in the two countries are therefore framed by some of the activists as a way for the governments to cover-up for numerous failures at the socio-political realm.

Activists' tendency to politicize the LGBT right debate was however not accentuated, given the fact that a greater portion (71.85%) of their posts' contents was neutral. Cameroonian bloggers appear to be the most noted for this politicization tradition as their posts and web pages' contents was 30.45% constructed with paragraphs that politicize the anti-gay campaigns and other homophobic attitudes demonstrated by the Cameroonian government and populace.

In the course of criticizing the lukewarm attitude of local authorities and populace towards gay-proselytism – particularly the repeated violence against LGBT communities in their countries – activists from both countries sometimes resorted to various methods of sensationalism. In line with this, a small proportion (12.12%) of their messages contained sensational materials, mostly chocking expressions (see Table 5).

The sensational cues were mostly deployed in contexts where the activists attempted to describe the methods of torture, lynching, humiliation and other typologies of violence suffered by the LGBT communities in the two countries. These efforts were visibly geared at associating homophobia with barbarism and incivility.

Table 5. Level sensationalism in the posts

Level of Sensationalism	Cam. Bloggers		Nig. Bloggers		Total	
	n	%	n	%	n	%
Sensational	102	8.85	239	14.39	341	12.12
Non-Sensational	1051	91.15	1422	85.61	2473	87.88
Total	1153	100	1661	100	2814	100

CONCLUSION

A highly homophobic atmosphere persists in most black countries, particularly in Cameroon and Nigeria; and from multiple indexes this uneasy situation may last for some decades given the "slow" rate of social acceptance/toleration of gayness in the two countries. The existence of draconian legislations which severely criminalize homosexuality and gay-proselytism has complicated street advocacy (for instance street protests), making them very risky ventures for human right activists. No doubt, a number of Cameroonian and Nigerian gay activists have gruesomely perished in their attempt to defy social strictures and fundamentalist religious arbiters to advocate LGBT equality. Some have been obliged to either live in silent darkness or to seek asylum in Western countries as an in-extremis approach to protect their lives. In the face of such a rigid and inhuman resistance to LGBT right activism many human rights "preachers" and apostles have resorted to the social media as a platform par excellence for advocacy. Online advocacy has thus been viewed as a less risky form of activism, even though engaging in it has not totally inhumed gay activists from death threats, bulling, and other forms of soft or hard aggressions.

The social media have afforded African gay activists – notably Cameroonian and Nigerian human right activists – the opportunity to explore new and personalized styles of advocacy. This study has argued that online activists from both countries have mainly be driven by the maxim which states that "charity begins at home"; that is, they have dominantly explore a national perspective in their online advocacy messages. This national orientation is symbolic of their zeal to primordially affect public opinion in their respective countries, while not losing sight of the need to support the LGBT right movement in other parts of Africa and the Arad/Asian world. This study equally established the fact that online activists from both countries dominantly limit themselves to sensitizing their readership and drawing attention to the plight of LGBT communities in homophobic African settings. Only little energy is devoted to concretely mobilize the readership and push it to street advocacy – notably street protests in favor of gay proselytism.

This study equally illustrated that Nigerian and Cameroonian online activists dominantly construct their advocacy discourses from the angles of the cultural wars between the West and Africa and human rights. Most of them have found it difficult to anchor their activism on religious arguments. Another interesting discussion has been that a number of activists resort to politicization of the LGBT right related issues which they raise in their posts and also deploy sensational cues, visibly, in other to emphasize the crude and animalistic nature of homophobia.

REFERENCES

Auerbach, Y., & Bloch-Elkon, Y. (2005). Media framing and foreign policy: The elite press vis-a-vis US policy in Bosnia. *Journal of Peace Research*, *42*(1), 83–99. doi:10.1177/0022343305049668

Aurora, M. (2015). Social media for social change. *Connect: TEN*. Retrieved September 7, 2016, from https://www.nten.org/article/social-media-for-social-change/

BBC News. (2011). *Ghana refuses to grant gays' rights despite aid threat*. Retrieved from http://www.bbc.co.uk/news/world-africa-15558769 Accessed on the 27/04/2016

Bucholz, L., & Wuggenig, U. (2015). Cultural globalization between myth and reality: A case of contemporary visual art. *ART-e-FACT*, *4*, 12–34.

DeNardis, L. (2012). Hidden levers of Internet control: An infrastructure-based theory of Internet governance. *Journal of Information Communicatio Socialis*, *15*(3), 720–738.

Duke, B. (2014). Religious fanatics blamed for Nigeria's draconian anti-gay bill, approved this week. *The Free Thinker*. Retrieved from http://www.religious-fanatics-blamed-for-nigerias-draconian-antigay-bill-approved-this-week/thefreethinker.com.

Egbert, A. M. (2013). Wanted for Love but not here: The travelling right of LGBT Activists. *Critical Legal Thinker*. Retrieved September 7, 2016, from http://criticallegalthinking.com/2013/08/12/wanted-for-love-but-not-here-the-travelling-rights-of-african-lgbt-activists/

Endong, F. P. C. (2015a). Christian resistance to gay-proselytism in a secular Nigeria: Anathema or social heroism? *ERAS: European Review of Applied Sociology*, *8*(11), 5–13.

Endong, F. P. C. (2015b). Framing the queers and the LGBT right movement in Africa: A study of Nigerian bloggers and web journalists. *Journal of Global Research in Education and Social Sciences*, *6*(4), 50–60.

Endong, F. P. C. (2016). The LGBT right movement in Africa and the myth of the Whiteman's superiority. *Journal of Globalization Studies*, *7*(1), 3–15.

Endong, F. P. C., & Vareba, A. L. (2015). Resisting anti-gay laws through media advocacy and online communities of meaning: A study of Nigerian homosexuals. *Journal for Studies in Management and Planning*, *10*(2), 94–106.

Federal Republic of Nigeria. (2012). *Same sex marriage prohibition act.* Abuja: Government Printer.

Gay and Lesbian Humanist Association. (2007b). Nigeria: Humanist jeered for supporting gay rights. *Gay Humanist Quarterly*, *7*, 23–24.

Gevisser, M. (2015). Homosexuality and the global culture wars. *International Journal of Mass Communication*, *16*(3), 10–25.

Hackl, A. (2013). *Digital activism and the future of the LGBT movement: Insight from recent research and case study*. Retrieved September 7, 2016, from http://climateshiftproject.org/2013/12/08/digital-activism-and-the-future-of-the-glbt-movement-insights-from-recent-research-and-case-studies/

Hardwick, N. A. (2012). Theoretically justifying human right: A critical analysis. *The International Relation Student*. Retrieved September, 13, 2016; from http://www.e-ir.info/2012/08/05/theoretically-justifying-human-rights-a-critical-analysis/

Hestres, L. (n.d.). Preaching to the choir: Internet-mediated advocacy, issue public mobilization and climate change. *New Media & Society*, *56*, 87–99.

Ilesanmi, Y. (2016). Would the percentage of Nigerians condemning jungle justice decrease if the ALUU 4 victims were gays caught in the act? YEMMYnisting. *Free Thought Blogs*. Retrieved from http://www.yemmynisting/freethought-blogs.com

Initiative for Equal Rights. (2014). *Survey on homosexuality perception in Nigeria*. Lagos: TIERs – The Initiative for Equal Rights.

Karaim, R. (2011). Gay rights. Has the movement's success sparked a backlash? *CQ Global Researcher*, *5*(5), 107–132.

Macaulay, J. R. (2013). Africa and homosexuality. *AGW: A Globe of Witness – The Witness Magazine*. Retrieved from http://www.thewitness.org-marriage-in-church-in-africa_queering-the-church.htm

McComb, M., Shaw, D. L., & Weaver, D. (1997). *Communication and democracy: Exploring the intellectual frontiers of agenda-setting theory*. Erlbaum.

McGuinness, E. (2014) Insight into social media usage by advocacy groups in the area of same-sex marriage. *EMCG Public Relations*. Retrieved September 7, 2016, from http://emcgpr.com/blog/insights-social-media-usage-advocacy-groups-area-sex-marriage/

National Broadcasting Commission. (2012). *N.B.C. Code*. Abuja: NBC.

National Economic and Social Right Initiative. (2015). *What are the Basis Principles of the Human Rights Framework*? New York: NESRI. Retrieved September 13, 2016, from https://www.nesri.org/programs/what-are-the-basic-principles-of-the-human-rights-framework

Nisbet, M. (2013). *Digital activism and the future of the LGBT movement: Insight from recent research and case study*. Retrieved September 7, 2016, from http://climateshiftproject.org/2013/12/08/digital-activism-and-the-future-of-the-glbt-movement-insights-from-recent-research-and-case-studies/

Obadare, E. (2014). Dangerous associations: Legal homophobia and the changing politics of civil society. *ISTR Africa: Civil Society Research Network*, *8*(1), 4–6.

Okanlawon, K. (2011). *Same gender marriage prohibition bill: Public hearing at the senate hearing room, National Assembly complex*. Abuja: MCD.

Olivier, M. (2013). Transnational sex politics, conservative Christianity and antigay activism in Uganda. *Studies in Social Justice*, *7*(1), 83–105. doi:10.26522sj.v7i1.1056

Pen American Centre. (2015). *Silenced voices, threatened lives: The impact of Nigeria's anti-LGBTI laws on freedom of expression*. Abuja: Pen Nigeria.

Salzburg Academy. (2015). *The social media and the LGBT community. Finding a voice through the social media: The LGBT community*. Retrieved September 7, 2016, from http://www.salzburg.umd.edu/unesco/social-media-and-lgbt-community

Scheufele, D. (1999, Winter). Framing as a theory of media effects. *Journal of Communication*, 103-122.

Sen, A. (2005). Elements of a theory of human rights. *Philosophy & Public Affairs*, *32*(4), 315–356. doi:10.1111/j.1088-4963.2004.00017.x

Social Pathologist. (2010). *Traditionalism and conservatism: The old versus the right*. Retrieved from http://traditionalism-and-conservatism/theoldvstheright/the-social-pathologist.com

Stewart, C. (2014). *21 varieties of traditional African homosexuality*, Retrieved from http://www.21_varities_of_traditional_african_homosexuality.htm

Suny Levin Institute. (2014). *Globalization*. London: Suny Levin Institute.

KEY TERMS AND DEFINITIONS

Advocacy: This term is used in reference to strategies or well-designed actions deployed by an organization, a group of individuals, or a person seeking to systematically influence public policy or public opinion in a geographical space. It is often driven by moral, ethical, socio-political, or religious motives and ultimately aims to protect an interest, an asset, or an idea.

Civil Society: A community of citizens linked by a common interest and having the same activity. This community comprises organizations that are non-governmental and non-profit in nature and that work for the interest of citizens. Examples of civil society organizations include churches, labor unions, NGOs, and other non-profit organizations that work for the common good, providing very important services in a society; this for very little or nothing in return.

Homophobia: A term used to refer to any irrational fear or hatred of homosexual feelings, behaviors, thoughts, or people. It equally means a bias evaluation of homosexual identities which may—or always—lead to discrimination against homosexual individuals.

Homosexuality: A term invented by nineteenth century German sexologists to describe an attraction between two individuals of the same sex at the physical, sexual, emotional, intellectual, and spiritual levels.

Human Rights: The concept of human rights framework actually protects civil, political, socio-cultural, and economic rights. It is guided by the principles of universality, people's participation, indivisibility, transparency, accountability, and non-discrimination.

LGBT Right Movement: The abbreviation LGBT stands for lesbian, gay, bisexual, and transgender. Some authors prefer to employ a longer abbreviation which includes intersexual and queers, thus LGBTIQ. The LGBT right movement is a complex form of program aimed at advocating the rights of non-heterosexuals. LGBT rights include but are not limited to (1) recognition of same-sex relationships (through same-sex marriage or similar unions), (2) right to adopt children, (3) right to donate blood, (4) recognition of LGBT parenting, (5) immigration equality rights, (6) right for protection against discrimination in employment and housing procedures, (7) protection against bullying of any sort, (8) equal access to assisted reproductive technology, and (9) access to sex reassignment surgery and hormones, among others.

Related References

To continue our tradition of advancing academic research, we have compiled a list of recommended IGI Global readings. These references will provide additional information and guidance to further enrich your knowledge and assist you with your own research and future publications.

Adeyemo, O. (2013). The nationwide health information network: A biometric approach to prevent medical identity theft. In *User-driven healthcare: Concepts, methodologies, tools, and applications* (pp. 1636–1649). Hershey, PA: IGI Global. doi:10.4018/978-1-4666-2770-3.ch081

Adler, M., & Henman, P. (2009). Justice beyond the courts: The implications of computerisation for procedural justice in social security. In A. Martínez & P. Abat (Eds.), *E-justice: Using information communication technologies in the court system* (pp. 65–86). Hershey, PA: IGI Global. doi:10.4018/978-1-59904-998-4.ch005

Aflalo, E., & Gabay, E. (2013). An information system for coping with student dropout. In L. Tomei (Ed.), *Learning tools and teaching approaches through ICT advancements* (pp. 176–187). Hershey, PA: IGI Global. doi:10.4018/978-1-4666-2017-9.ch016

Ahmed, M. A., Janssen, M., & van den Hoven, J. (2012). Value sensitive transfer (VST) of systems among countries: Towards a framework. *International Journal of Electronic Government Research, 8*(1), 26–42. doi:10.4018/jegr.2012010102

Aikins, S. K. (2008). Issues and trends in internet-based citizen participation. In G. Garson & M. Khosrow-Pour (Eds.), *Handbook of research on public information technology* (pp. 31–40). Hershey, PA: IGI Global. doi:10.4018/978-1-59904-857-4.ch004

Aikins, S. K. (2009). A comparative study of municipal adoption of internet-based citizen participation. In C. Reddick (Ed.), *Handbook of research on strategies for local e-government adoption and implementation: Comparative studies* (pp. 206–230). Hershey, PA: IGI Global. doi:10.4018/978-1-60566-282-4.ch011

Aikins, S. K. (2012). Improving e-government project management: Best practices and critical success factors. In *Digital democracy: Concepts, methodologies, tools, and applications* (pp. 1314–1332). Hershey, PA: IGI Global. doi:10.4018/978-1-4666-1740-7.ch065

Akabawi, M. S. (2011). Ghabbour group ERP deployment: Learning from past technology failures. In E. Business Research and Case Center (Ed.), Cases on business and management in the MENA region: New trends and opportunities (pp. 177-203). Hershey, PA: IGI Global. doi:10.4018/978-1-60960-583-4.ch012

Akabawi, M. S. (2013). Ghabbour group ERP deployment: Learning from past technology failures. In *Industrial engineering: Concepts, methodologies, tools, and applications* (pp. 933–958). Hershey, PA: IGI Global. doi:10.4018/978-1-4666-1945-6.ch051

Akbulut, A. Y., & Motwani, J. (2008). Integration and information sharing in e-government. In G. Putnik & M. Cruz-Cunha (Eds.), *Encyclopedia of networked and virtual organizations* (pp. 729–734). Hershey, PA: IGI Global. doi:10.4018/978-1-59904-885-7.ch096

Akers, E. J. (2008). Technology diffusion in public administration. In G. Garson & M. Khosrow-Pour (Eds.), *Handbook of research on public information technology* (pp. 339–348). Hershey, PA: IGI Global. doi:10.4018/978-1-59904-857-4.ch033

Al-Shafi, S. (2008). Free wireless internet park services: An investigation of technology adoption in Qatar from a citizens' perspective. *Journal of Cases on Information Technology*, *10*(3), 21–34. doi:10.4018/jcit.2008070103

Al-Shafi, S., & Weerakkody, V. (2009). Implementing free wi-fi in public parks: An empirical study in Qatar. *International Journal of Electronic Government Research*, *5*(3), 21–35. doi:10.4018/jegr.2009070102

Aladwani, A. M. (2002). Organizational actions, computer attitudes and end-user satisfaction in public organizations: An empirical study. In C. Snodgrass & E. Szewczak (Eds.), *Human factors in information systems* (pp. 153–168). Hershey, PA: IGI Global. doi:10.4018/978-1-931777-10-0.ch012

Aladwani, A. M. (2002). Organizational actions, computer attitudes, and end-user satisfaction in public organizations: An empirical study. *Journal of Organizational and End User Computing*, *14*(1), 42–49. doi:10.4018/joeuc.2002010104

Allen, B., Juillet, L., Paquet, G., & Roy, J. (2005). E-government and private-public partnerships: Relational challenges and strategic directions. In M. Khosrow-Pour (Ed.), *Practicing e-government: A global perspective* (pp. 364–382). Hershey, PA: IGI Global. doi:10.4018/978-1-59140-637-2.ch016

Alshawaf, A., & Knalil, O. E. (2008). IS success factors and IS organizational impact: Does ownership type matter in Kuwait? *International Journal of Enterprise Information Systems*, *4*(2), 13–33. doi:10.4018/jeis.2008040102

Ambali, A. R. (2009). Digital divide and its implication on Malaysian e-government: Policy initiatives. In H. Rahman (Ed.), *Social and political implications of data mining: Knowledge management in e-government* (pp. 267–287). Hershey, PA: IGI Global. doi:10.4018/978-1-60566-230-5.ch016

Amoretti, F. (2007). Digital international governance. In A. Anttiroiko & M. Malkia (Eds.), *Encyclopedia of digital government* (pp. 365–370). Hershey, PA: IGI Global. doi:10.4018/978-1-59140-789-8.ch056

Amoretti, F. (2008). Digital international governance. In A. Anttiroiko (Ed.), *Electronic government: Concepts, methodologies, tools, and applications* (pp. 688–696). Hershey, PA: IGI Global. doi:10.4018/978-1-59904-947-2.ch058

Amoretti, F. (2008). E-government at supranational level in the European Union. In A. Anttiroiko (Ed.), *Electronic government: Concepts, methodologies, tools, and applications* (pp. 1047–1055). Hershey, PA: IGI Global. doi:10.4018/978-1-59904-947-2.ch079

Amoretti, F. (2008). E-government regimes. In A. Anttiroiko (Ed.), *Electronic government: Concepts, methodologies, tools, and applications* (pp. 3846–3856). Hershey, PA: IGI Global. doi:10.4018/978-1-59904-947-2.ch280

Amoretti, F. (2009). Electronic constitution: A Braudelian perspective. In F. Amoretti (Ed.), *Electronic constitution: Social, cultural, and political implications* (pp. 1–19). Hershey, PA: IGI Global. doi:10.4018/978-1-60566-254-1.ch001

Amoretti, F., & Musella, F. (2009). Institutional isomorphism and new technologies. In M. Khosrow-Pour (Ed.), *Encyclopedia of information science and technology* (2nd ed.; pp. 2066–2071). Hershey, PA: IGI Global. doi:10.4018/978-1-60566-026-4.ch325

Andersen, K. V., & Henriksen, H. Z. (2007). E-government research: Capabilities, interaction, orientation, and values. In D. Norris (Ed.), *Current issues and trends in e-government research* (pp. 269–288). Hershey, PA: IGI Global. doi:10.4018/978-1-59904-283-1.ch013

Anderson, K. V., & Henriksen, H. Z. (2005). The first leg of e-government research: Domains and application areas 1998-2003. *International Journal of Electronic Government Research, 1*(4), 26–44. doi:10.4018/jegr.2005100102

Anttiroiko, A. (2009). Democratic e-governance. In M. Khosrow-Pour (Ed.), *Encyclopedia of information science and technology* (2nd ed.; pp. 990–995). Hershey, PA: IGI Global. doi:10.4018/978-1-60566-026-4.ch158

Association, I. R. (2010). *Networking and telecommunications: Concepts, methodologies, tools and applications* (Vols. 1–3). Hershey, PA: IGI Global. doi:10.4018/978-1-60566-986-1

Association, I. R. (2010). *Web-based education: Concepts, methodologies, tools and applications* (Vols. 1–3). Hershey, PA: IGI Global. doi:10.4018/978-1-61520-963-7

Baker, P. M., Bell, A., & Moon, N. W. (2009). Accessibility issues in municipal wireless networks. In C. Reddick (Ed.), *Handbook of research on strategies for local e-government adoption and implementation: Comparative studies* (pp. 569–588). Hershey, PA: IGI Global. doi:10.4018/978-1-60566-282-4.ch030

Becker, S. A., Keimer, R., & Muth, T. (2010). A case on university and community collaboration: The sci-tech entrepreneurial training services (ETS) program. In S. Becker & R. Niebuhr (Eds.), *Cases on technology innovation: Entrepreneurial successes and pitfalls* (pp. 68–90). Hershey, PA: IGI Global. doi:10.4018/978-1-61520-609-4.ch003

Becker, S. A., Keimer, R., & Muth, T. (2012). A case on university and community collaboration: The sci-tech entrepreneurial training services (ETS) program. In Regional development: Concepts, methodologies, tools, and applications (pp. 947-969). Hershey, PA: IGI Global. doi:10.4018/978-1-4666-0882-5.ch507

Bernardi, R. (2012). Information technology and resistance to public sector reforms: A case study in Kenya. In T. Papadopoulos & P. Kanellis (Eds.), *Public sector reform using information technologies: Transforming policy into practice* (pp. 59–78). Hershey, PA: IGI Global. doi:10.4018/978-1-60960-839-2.ch004

Bernardi, R. (2013). Information technology and resistance to public sector reforms: A case study in Kenya. In *User-driven healthcare: Concepts, methodologies, tools, and applications* (pp. 14–33). Hershey, PA: IGI Global. doi:10.4018/978-1-4666-2770-3.ch002

Bolívar, M. P., Pérez, M. D., & Hernández, A. M. (2012). Municipal e-government services in emerging economies: The Latin-American and Caribbean experiences. In Y. Chen & P. Chu (Eds.), *Electronic governance and cross-boundary collaboration: Innovations and advancing tools* (pp. 198–226). Hershey, PA: IGI Global. doi:10.4018/978-1-60960-753-1.ch011

Borycki, E. M., & Kushniruk, A. W. (2010). Use of clinical simulations to evaluate the impact of health information systems and ubiquitous computing devices upon health professional work. In S. Mohammed & J. Fiaidhi (Eds.), *Ubiquitous health and medical informatics: The ubiquity 2.0 trend and beyond* (pp. 552–573). Hershey, PA: IGI Global. doi:10.4018/978-1-61520-777-0.ch026

Borycki, E. M., & Kushniruk, A. W. (2011). Use of clinical simulations to evaluate the impact of health information systems and ubiquitous computing devices upon health professional work. In *Clinical technologies: Concepts, methodologies, tools and applications* (pp. 532–553). Hershey, PA: IGI Global. doi:10.4018/978-1-60960-561-2.ch220

Buchan, J. (2011). Developing a dynamic and responsive online learning environment: A case study of a large Australian university. In B. Czerkawski (Ed.), *Free and open source software for e-learning: Issues, successes and challenges* (pp. 92–109). Hershey, PA: IGI Global. doi:10.4018/978-1-61520-917-0.ch006

Buenger, A. W. (2008). Digital convergence and cybersecurity policy. In G. Garson & M. Khosrow-Pour (Eds.), *Handbook of research on public information technology* (pp. 395–405). Hershey, PA: IGI Global. doi:10.4018/978-1-59904-857-4.ch038

Burn, J. M., & Loch, K. D. (2002). The societal impact of world wide web - Key challenges for the 21st century. In A. Salehnia (Ed.), *Ethical issues of information systems* (pp. 88–106). Hershey, PA: IGI Global. doi:10.4018/978-1-931777-15-5.ch007

Burn, J. M., & Loch, K. D. (2003). The societal impact of the world wide web-Key challenges for the 21st century. In M. Khosrow-Pour (Ed.), *Advanced topics in information resources management* (Vol. 2, pp. 32–51). Hershey, PA: IGI Global. doi:10.4018/978-1-59140-062-2.ch002

Bwalya, K. J., Du Plessis, T., & Rensleigh, C. (2012). The "quicksilver initiatives" as a framework for e-government strategy design in developing economies. In K. Bwalya & S. Zulu (Eds.), *Handbook of research on e-government in emerging economies: Adoption, e-participation, and legal frameworks* (pp. 605–623). Hershey, PA: IGI Global. doi:10.4018/978-1-4666-0324-0.ch031

Cabotaje, C. E., & Alampay, E. A. (2013). Social media and citizen engagement: Two cases from the Philippines. In S. Saeed & C. Reddick (Eds.), *Human-centered system design for electronic governance* (pp. 225–238). Hershey, PA: IGI Global. doi:10.4018/978-1-4666-3640-8.ch013

Camillo, A., Di Pietro, L., Di Virgilio, F., & Franco, M. (2013). Work-groups conflict at PetroTech-Italy, S.R.L.: The influence of culture on conflict dynamics. In B. Christiansen, E. Turkina, & N. Williams (Eds.), *Cultural and technological influences on global business* (pp. 272–289). Hershey, PA: IGI Global. doi:10.4018/978-1-4666-3966-9.ch015

Capra, E., Francalanci, C., & Marinoni, C. (2008). Soft success factors for m-government. In A. Anttiroiko (Ed.), *Electronic government: Concepts, methodologies, tools, and applications* (pp. 1213–1233). Hershey, PA: IGI Global. doi:10.4018/978-1-59904-947-2.ch089

Cartelli, A. (2009). The implementation of practices with ICT as a new teaching-learning paradigm. In A. Cartelli & M. Palma (Eds.), *Encyclopedia of information communication technology* (pp. 413–417). Hershey, PA: IGI Global. doi:10.4018/978-1-59904-845-1.ch055

Charalabidis, Y., Lampathaki, F., & Askounis, D. (2010). Investigating the landscape in national interoperability frameworks. *International Journal of E-Services and Mobile Applications, 2*(4), 28–41. doi:10.4018/jesma.2010100103

Charalabidis, Y., Lampathaki, F., & Askounis, D. (2012). Investigating the landscape in national interoperability frameworks. In A. Scupola (Ed.), *Innovative mobile platform developments for electronic services design and delivery* (pp. 218–231). Hershey, PA: IGI Global. doi:10.4018/978-1-4666-1568-7.ch013

Chen, I. (2005). Distance education associations. In C. Howard, J. Boettcher, L. Justice, K. Schenk, P. Rogers, & G. Berg (Eds.), *Encyclopedia of distance learning* (pp. 599–612). Hershey, PA: IGI Global. doi:10.4018/978-1-59140-555-9.ch087

Chen, I. (2008). Distance education associations. In L. Tomei (Ed.), *Online and distance learning: Concepts, methodologies, tools, and applications* (pp. 562–579). Hershey, PA: IGI Global. doi:10.4018/978-1-59904-935-9.ch048

Chen, Y. (2008). Managing IT outsourcing for digital government. In A. Anttiroiko (Ed.), *Electronic government: Concepts, methodologies, tools, and applications* (pp. 3107–3114). Hershey, PA: IGI Global. doi:10.4018/978-1-59904-947-2.ch229

Chen, Y., & Dimitrova, D. V. (2006). Electronic government and online engagement: Citizen interaction with government via web portals. *International Journal of Electronic Government Research, 2*(1), 54–76. doi:10.4018/jegr.2006010104

Chen, Y., & Knepper, R. (2005). Digital government development strategies: Lessons for policy makers from a comparative perspective. In W. Huang, K. Siau, & K. Wei (Eds.), *Electronic government strategies and implementation* (pp. 394–420). Hershey, PA: IGI Global. doi:10.4018/978-1-59140-348-7.ch017

Chen, Y., & Knepper, R. (2008). Digital government development strategies: Lessons for policy makers from a comparative perspective. In H. Rahman (Ed.), *Developing successful ICT strategies: Competitive advantages in a global knowledge-driven society* (pp. 334–356). Hershey, PA: IGI Global. doi:10.4018/978-1-59904-654-9.ch017

Cherian, E. J., & Ryan, T. W. (2014). Incongruent needs: Why differences in the iron-triangle of priorities make health information technology adoption and use difficult. In C. El Morr (Ed.), *Research perspectives on the role of informatics in health policy and management* (pp. 209–221). Hershey, PA: IGI Global. doi:10.4018/978-1-4666-4321-5.ch012

Cho, H. J., & Hwang, S. (2010). Government 2.0 in Korea: Focusing on e-participation services. In C. Reddick (Ed.), *Politics, democracy and e-government: Participation and service delivery* (pp. 94–114). Hershey, PA: IGI Global. doi:10.4018/978-1-61520-933-0.ch006

Chorus, C., & Timmermans, H. (2010). Ubiquitous travel environments and travel control strategies: Prospects and challenges. In M. Wachowicz (Ed.), *Movement-aware applications for sustainable mobility: Technologies and approaches* (pp. 30–51). Hershey, PA: IGI Global. doi:10.4018/978-1-61520-769-5.ch003

Chuanshen, R. (2007). E-government construction and China's administrative litigation act. In A. Anttiroiko & M. Malkia (Eds.), *Encyclopedia of digital government* (pp. 507–510). Hershey, PA: IGI Global. doi:10.4018/978-1-59140-789-8.ch077

Ciaghi, A., & Villafiorita, A. (2012). Law modeling and BPR for public administration improvement. In K. Bwalya & S. Zulu (Eds.), *Handbook of research on e-government in emerging economies: Adoption, e-participation, and legal frameworks* (pp. 391–410). Hershey, PA: IGI Global. doi:10.4018/978-1-4666-0324-0.ch019

Ciaramitaro, B. L., & Skrocki, M. (2012). mHealth: Mobile healthcare. In B. Ciaramitaro (Ed.), Mobile technology consumption: Opportunities and challenges (pp. 99-109). Hershey, PA: IGI Global. doi:10.4018/978-1-61350-150-4.ch007

Comite, U. (2012). Innovative processes and managerial effectiveness of e-procurement in healthcare. In A. Manoharan & M. Holzer (Eds.), *Active citizen participation in e-government: A global perspective* (pp. 206–229). Hershey, PA: IGI Global. doi:10.4018/978-1-4666-0116-1.ch011

Cordella, A. (2013). E-government success: How to account for ICT, administrative rationalization, and institutional change. In J. Gil-Garcia (Ed.), *E-government success factors and measures: Theories, concepts, and methodologies* (pp. 40–51). Hershey, PA: IGI Global. doi:10.4018/978-1-4666-4058-0.ch003

Cropf, R. A. (2009). ICT and e-democracy. In M. Khosrow-Pour (Ed.), *Encyclopedia of information science and technology* (2nd ed.; pp. 1789–1793). Hershey, PA: IGI Global. doi:10.4018/978-1-60566-026-4.ch281

Cropf, R. A. (2009). The virtual public sphere. In M. Pagani (Ed.), *Encyclopedia of multimedia technology and networking* (2nd ed.; pp. 1525–1530). Hershey, PA: IGI Global. doi:10.4018/978-1-60566-014-1.ch206

D'Abundo, M. L. (2013). Electronic health record implementation in the United States healthcare industry: Making the process of change manageable. In V. Wang (Ed.), *Handbook of research on technologies for improving the 21st century workforce: Tools for lifelong learning* (pp. 272–286). Hershey, PA: IGI Global. doi:10.4018/978-1-4666-2181-7.ch018

Damurski, L. (2012). E-participation in urban planning: Online tools for citizen engagement in Poland and in Germany. *International Journal of E-Planning Research*, *1*(3), 40–67. doi:10.4018/ijepr.2012070103

de Almeida, M. O. (2007). E-government strategy in Brazil: Increasing transparency and efficiency through e-government procurement. In M. Gascó-Hernandez (Ed.), *Latin America online: Cases, successes and pitfalls* (pp. 34–82). Hershey, PA: IGI Global. doi:10.4018/978-1-59140-974-8.ch002

de Juana Espinosa, S. (2008). Empirical study of the municipalitites' motivations for adopting online presence. In A. Anttiroiko (Ed.), *Electronic government: Concepts, methodologies, tools, and applications* (pp. 3593–3608). Hershey, PA: IGI Global. doi:10.4018/978-1-59904-947-2.ch262 de Souza Dias, D. (2002). Motivation for using information technology. In C. Snodgrass & E. Szewczak (Eds.), *Human factors in information systems* (pp. 55–60). Hershey, PA: IGI Global. doi:10.4018/978-1-931777-10-0.ch005

Demediuk, P. (2006). Government procurement ICT's impact on the sustainability of SMEs and regional communities. In S. Marshall, W. Taylor, & X. Yu (Eds.), *Encyclopedia of developing regional communities with information and communication technology* (pp. 321–324). Hershey, PA: IGI Global. doi:10.4018/978-1-59140-575-7.ch056

Devonshire, E., Forsyth, H., Reid, S., & Simpson, J. M. (2013). The challenges and opportunities of online postgraduate coursework programs in a traditional university context. In B. Tynan, J. Willems, & R. James (Eds.), *Outlooks and opportunities in blended and distance learning* (pp. 353–368). Hershey, PA: IGI Global. doi:10.4018/978-1-4666-4205-8.ch026

Di Cerbo, F., Scotto, M., Sillitti, A., Succi, G., & Vernazza, T. (2007). Toward a GNU/Linux distribution for corporate environments. In S. Sowe, I. Stamelos, & I. Samoladas (Eds.), *Emerging free and open source software practices* (pp. 215–236). Hershey, PA: IGI Global. doi:10.4018/978-1-59904-210-7.ch010

Diesner, J., & Carley, K. M. (2005). Revealing social structure from texts: Meta-matrix text analysis as a novel method for network text analysis. In V. Narayanan & D. Armstrong (Eds.), *Causal mapping for research in information technology* (pp. 81–108). Hershey, PA: IGI Global. doi:10.4018/978-1-59140-396-8.ch004

Dologite, D. G., Mockler, R. J., Bai, Q., & Viszhanyo, P. F. (2006). IS change agents in practice in a US-Chinese joint venture. In M. Hunter & F. Tan (Eds.), *Advanced topics in global information management* (Vol. 5, pp. 331–352). Hershey, PA: IGI Global. doi:10.4018/978-1-59140-923-6.ch015

Drnevich, P., Brush, T. H., & Luckock, G. T. (2011). Process and structural implications for IT-enabled outsourcing. *International Journal of Strategic Information Technology and Applications*, *2*(4), 30–43. doi:10.4018/jsita.2011100103

Dwivedi, A. N. (2009). *Handbook of research on information technology management and clinical data administration in healthcare* (Vols. 1–2). Hershey, PA: IGI Global. doi:10.4018/978-1-60566-356-2

Elbeltagi, I., McBride, N., & Hardaker, G. (2006). Evaluating the factors affecting DSS usage by senior managers in local authorities in Egypt. In M. Hunter & F. Tan (Eds.), *Advanced topics in global information management* (Vol. 5, pp. 283–307). Hershey, PA: IGI Global. doi:10.4018/978-1-59140-923-6.ch013

Eom, S., & Fountain, J. E. (2013). Enhancing information services through public-private partnerships: Information technology knowledge transfer underlying structures to develop shared services in the U.S. and Korea. In J. Gil-Garcia (Ed.), *E-government success around the world: Cases, empirical studies, and practical recommendations* (pp. 15–40). Hershey, PA: IGI Global. doi:10.4018/978-1-4666-4173-0.ch002

Esteves, T., Leuenberger, D., & Van Leuven, N. (2012). Reaching citizen 2.0: How government uses social media to send public messages during times of calm and times of crisis. In K. Kloby & M. D'Agostino (Eds.), *Citizen 2.0: Public and governmental interaction through web 2.0 technologies* (pp. 250–268). Hershey, PA: IGI Global. doi:10.4018/978-1-4666-0318-9.ch013

Estevez, E., Fillottrani, P., Janowski, T., & Ojo, A. (2012). Government information sharing: A framework for policy formulation. In Y. Chen & P. Chu (Eds.), *Electronic governance and cross-boundary collaboration: Innovations and advancing tools* (pp. 23–55). Hershey, PA: IGI Global. doi:10.4018/978-1-60960-753-1.ch002

Ezz, I. E. (2008). E-governement emerging trends: Organizational challenges. In A. Anttiroiko (Ed.), *Electronic government: Concepts, methodologies, tools, and applications* (pp. 3721–3737). Hershey, PA: IGI Global. doi:10.4018/978-1-59904-947-2.ch269

Fabri, M. (2009). The Italian style of e-justice in a comparative perspective. In A. Martínez & P. Abat (Eds.), *E-justice: Using information communication technologies in the court system* (pp. 1–19). Hershey, PA: IGI Global. doi:10.4018/978-1-59904-998-4.ch001

Fagbe, T., & Adekola, O. D. (2010). Workplace safety and personnel well-being: The impact of information technology. *International Journal of Green Computing*, *1*(1), 28–33. doi:10.4018/jgc.2010010103

Fagbe, T., & Adekola, O. D. (2011). Workplace safety and personnel well-being: The impact of information technology. In *Global business: Concepts, methodologies, tools and applications* (pp. 1438–1444). Hershey, PA: IGI Global. doi:10.4018/978-1-60960-587-2.ch509

Farmer, L. (2008). Affective collaborative instruction with librarians. In S. Kelsey & K. St.Amant (Eds.), *Handbook of research on computer mediated communication* (pp. 15–24). Hershey, PA: IGI Global. doi:10.4018/978-1-59904-863-5.ch002

Favier, L., & Mekhantar, J. (2007). Use of OSS by local e-administration: The French situation. In K. St.Amant & B. Still (Eds.), *Handbook of research on open source software: Technological, economic, and social perspectives* (pp. 428–444). Hershey, PA: IGI Global. doi:10.4018/978-1-59140-999-1.ch033

Fernando, S. (2009). Issues of e-learning in third world countries. In M. Khosrow-Pour (Ed.), *Encyclopedia of information science and technology* (2nd ed.; pp. 2273–2277). Hershey, PA: IGI Global. doi:10.4018/978-1-60566-026-4.ch360

Filho, J. R., & dos Santos, J. R. Jr. (2009). Local e-government in Brazil: Poor interaction and local politics as usual. In C. Reddick (Ed.), *Handbook of research on strategies for local e-government adoption and implementation: Comparative studies* (pp. 863–878). Hershey, PA: IGI Global. doi:10.4018/978-1-60566-282-4.ch045

Fletcher, P. D. (2004). Portals and policy: Implications of electronic access to U.S. federal government information services. In A. Pavlichev & G. Garson (Eds.), *Digital government: Principles and best practices* (pp. 52–62). Hershey, PA: IGI Global. doi:10.4018/978-1-59140-122-3.ch004

Fletcher, P. D. (2008). Portals and policy: Implications of electronic access to U.S. federal government information services. In A. Anttiroiko (Ed.), *Electronic government: Concepts, methodologies, tools, and applications* (pp. 3970–3979). Hershey, PA: IGI Global. doi:10.4018/978-1-59904-947-2.ch289

Forlano, L. (2004). The emergence of digital government: International perspectives. In A. Pavlichev & G. Garson (Eds.), *Digital government: Principles and best practices* (pp. 34–51). Hershey, PA: IGI Global. doi:10.4018/978-1-59140-122-3.ch003

Franzel, J. M., & Coursey, D. H. (2004). Government web portals: Management issues and the approaches of five states. In A. Pavlichev & G. Garson (Eds.), *Digital government: Principles and best practices* (pp. 63–77). Hershey, PA: IGI Global. doi:10.4018/978-1-59140-122-3.ch005

Gaivéo, J. M. (2013). Security of ICTs supporting healthcare activities. In M. Cruz-Cunha, I. Miranda, & P. Gonçalves (Eds.), *Handbook of research on ICTs for human-centered healthcare and social care services* (pp. 208–228). Hershey, PA: IGI Global. doi:10.4018/978-1-4666-3986-7.ch011

Garson, G. D. (1999). *Information technology and computer applications in public administration: Issues and trends*. Hershey, PA: IGI Global. doi:10.4018/978-1-87828-952-0

Garson, G. D. (2003). Toward an information technology research agenda for public administration. In G. Garson (Ed.), *Public information technology: Policy and management issues* (pp. 331–357). Hershey, PA: IGI Global. doi:10.4018/978-1-59140-060-8.ch014

Garson, G. D. (2004). The promise of digital government. In A. Pavlichev & G. Garson (Eds.), *Digital government: Principles and best practices* (pp. 2–15). Hershey, PA: IGI Global. doi:10.4018/978-1-59140-122-3.ch001

Garson, G. D. (2007). An information technology research agenda for public administration. In G. Garson (Ed.), *Modern public information technology systems: Issues and challenges* (pp. 365–392). Hershey, PA: IGI Global. doi:10.4018/978-1-59904-051-6.ch018

Gasco, M. (2007). Civil servants' resistance towards e-government development. In A. Anttiroiko & M. Malkia (Eds.), *Encyclopedia of digital government* (pp. 190–195). Hershey, PA: IGI Global. doi:10.4018/978-1-59140-789-8.ch028

Gasco, M. (2008). Civil servants' resistance towards e-government development. In A. Anttiroiko (Ed.), *Electronic government: Concepts, methodologies, tools, and applications* (pp. 2580–2588). Hershey, PA: IGI Global. doi:10.4018/978-1-59904-947-2.ch190

Ghere, R. K. (2010). Accountability and information technology enactment: Implications for social empowerment. In E. Ferro, Y. Dwivedi, J. Gil-Garcia, & M. Williams (Eds.), *Handbook of research on overcoming digital divides: Constructing an equitable and competitive information society* (pp. 515–532). Hershey, PA: IGI Global. doi:10.4018/978-1-60566-699-0.ch028

Gibson, I. W. (2012). Simulation modeling of healthcare delivery. In A. Kolker & P. Story (Eds.), *Management engineering for effective healthcare delivery: Principles and applications* (pp. 69–89). Hershey, PA: IGI Global. doi:10.4018/978-1-60960-872-9.ch003

Gil-Garcia, J. R. (2007). Exploring e-government benefits and success factors. In A. Anttiroiko & M. Malkia (Eds.), *Encyclopedia of digital government* (pp. 803–811). Hershey, PA: IGI Global. doi:10.4018/978-1-59140-789-8.ch122

Gil-Garcia, J. R., & González Miranda, F. (2010). E-government and opportunities for participation: The case of the Mexican state web portals. In C. Reddick (Ed.), *Politics, democracy and e-government: Participation and service delivery* (pp. 56–74). Hershey, PA: IGI Global. doi:10.4018/978-1-61520-933-0.ch004

Goldfinch, S. (2012). Public trust in government, trust in e-government, and use of e-government. In Z. Yan (Ed.), *Encyclopedia of cyber behavior* (pp. 987–995). Hershey, PA: IGI Global. doi:10.4018/978-1-4666-0315-8.ch081

Goodyear, M. (2012). Organizational change contributions to e-government project transitions. In S. Aikins (Ed.), *Managing e-government projects: Concepts, issues, and best practices* (pp. 1–21). Hershey, PA: IGI Global. doi:10.4018/978-1-4666-0086-7.ch001

Gordon, S., & Mulligan, P. (2003). Strategic models for the delivery of personal financial services: The role of infocracy. In S. Gordon (Ed.), *Computing information technology: The human side* (pp. 220–232). Hershey, PA: IGI Global. doi:10.4018/978-1-93177-752-0.ch014

Gordon, T. F. (2007). Legal knowledge systems. In A. Anttiroiko & M. Malkia (Eds.), *Encyclopedia of digital government* (pp. 1161–1166). Hershey, PA: IGI Global. doi:10.4018/978-1-59140-789-8.ch175

Graham, J. E., & Semich, G. W. (2008). Integrating technology to transform pedagogy: Revisiting the progress of the three phase TUI model for faculty development. In L. Tomei (Ed.), *Adapting information and communication technologies for effective education* (pp. 1–12). Hershey, PA: IGI Global. doi:10.4018/978-1-59904-922-9.ch001

Grandinetti, L., & Pisacane, O. (2012). Web services for healthcare management. In D. Prakash Vidyarthi (Ed.), *Technologies and protocols for the future of internet design: Reinventing the web* (pp. 60–94). Hershey, PA: IGI Global. doi:10.4018/978-1-4666-0203-8.ch004

Groenewegen, P., & Wagenaar, F. P. (2008). VO as an alternative to hierarchy in the Dutch police sector. In G. Putnik & M. Cruz-Cunha (Eds.), *Encyclopedia of networked and virtual organizations* (pp. 1851–1857). Hershey, PA: IGI Global. doi:10.4018/978-1-59904-885-7.ch245

Gronlund, A. (2001). Building an infrastructure to manage electronic services. In S. Dasgupta (Ed.), *Managing internet and intranet technologies in organizations: Challenges and opportunities* (pp. 71–103). Hershey, PA: IGI Global. doi:10.4018/978-1-878289-95-7.ch006

Gronlund, A. (2002). Introduction to electronic government: Design, applications and management. In Å. Grönlund (Ed.), *Electronic government: Design, applications and management* (pp. 1–21). Hershey, PA: IGI Global. doi:10.4018/978-1-930708-19-8.ch001

Gupta, A., Woosley, R., Crk, I., & Sarnikar, S. (2009). An information technology architecture for drug effectiveness reporting and post-marketing surveillance. In J. Tan (Ed.), *Medical informatics: Concepts, methodologies, tools, and applications* (pp. 631–646). Hershey, PA: IGI Global. doi:10.4018/978-1-60566-050-9.ch047

Hallin, A., & Lundevall, K. (2007). mCity: User focused development of mobile services within the city of Stockholm. In I. Kushchu (Ed.), Mobile government: An emerging direction in e-government (pp. 12-29). Hershey, PA: IGI Global. doi:10.4018/978-1-59140-884-0.ch002

Hallin, A., & Lundevall, K. (2009). mCity: User focused development of mobile services within the city of Stockholm. In S. Clarke (Ed.), Evolutionary concepts in end user productivity and performance: Applications for organizational progress (pp. 268-280). Hershey, PA: IGI Global. doi:10.4018/978-1-60566-136-0.ch017

Hallin, A., & Lundevall, K. (2009). mCity: User focused development of mobile services within the city of Stockholm. In D. Taniar (Ed.), Mobile computing: Concepts, methodologies, tools, and applications (pp. 3455-3467). Hershey, PA: IGI Global. doi:10.4018/978-1-60566-054-7.ch253

Hanson, A. (2005). Overcoming barriers in the planning of a virtual library. In M. Khosrow-Pour (Ed.), *Encyclopedia of information science and technology* (pp. 2255–2259). Hershey, PA: IGI Global. doi:10.4018/978-1-59140-553-5.ch397

Haque, A. (2008). Information technology and surveillance: Implications for public administration in a new word order. In T. Loendorf & G. Garson (Eds.), *Patriotic information systems* (pp. 177–185). Hershey, PA: IGI Global. doi:10.4018/978-1-59904-594-8.ch008

Hauck, R. V., Thatcher, S. M., & Weisband, S. P. (2012). Temporal aspects of information technology use: Increasing shift work effectiveness. In J. Wang (Ed.), *Advancing the service sector with evolving technologies: Techniques and principles* (pp. 87–104). Hershey, PA: IGI Global. doi:10.4018/978-1-4666-0044-7.ch006

Hawk, S., & Witt, T. (2006). Telecommunications courses in information systems programs. *International Journal of Information and Communication Technology Education*, *2*(1), 79–92. doi:10.4018/jicte.2006010107

Helms, M. M., Moore, R., & Ahmadi, M. (2009). Information technology (IT) and the healthcare industry: A SWOT analysis. In J. Tan (Ed.), *Medical informatics: Concepts, methodologies, tools, and applications* (pp. 134–152). Hershey, PA: IGI Global. doi:10.4018/978-1-60566-050-9.ch012

Hendrickson, S. M., & Young, M. E. (2014). Electronic records management at a federally funded research and development center. In J. Krueger (Ed.), *Cases on electronic records and resource management implementation in diverse environments* (pp. 334–350). Hershey, PA: IGI Global. doi:10.4018/978-1-4666-4466-3.ch020

Henman, P. (2010). Social policy and information communication technologies. In J. Martin & L. Hawkins (Eds.), *Information communication technologies for human services education and delivery: Concepts and cases* (pp. 215–229). Hershey, PA: IGI Global. doi:10.4018/978-1-60566-735-5.ch014

Hismanoglu, M. (2011). Important issues in online education: E-pedagogy and marketing. In U. Demiray & S. Sever (Eds.), *Marketing online education programs: Frameworks for promotion and communication* (pp. 184–209). Hershey, PA: IGI Global. doi:10.4018/978-1-60960-074-7.ch012

Ho, K. K. (2008). The e-government development, IT strategies, and portals of the Hong Kong SAR government. In A. Anttiroiko (Ed.), *Electronic government: Concepts, methodologies, tools, and applications* (pp. 715–733). Hershey, PA: IGI Global. doi:10.4018/978-1-59904-947-2.ch060

Holden, S. H. (2003). The evolution of information technology management at the federal level: Implications for public administration. In G. Garson (Ed.), *Public information technology: Policy and management issues* (pp. 53–73). Hershey, PA: IGI Global. doi:10.4018/978-1-59140-060-8.ch003

Holden, S. H. (2007). The evolution of federal information technology management literature: Does IT finally matter? In G. Garson (Ed.), *Modern public information technology systems: Issues and challenges* (pp. 17–34). Hershey, PA: IGI Global. doi:10.4018/978-1-59904-051-6.ch002

Holland, J. W. (2009). Automation of American criminal justice. In M. Khosrow-Pour (Ed.), *Encyclopedia of information science and technology* (2nd ed.; pp. 300–302). Hershey, PA: IGI Global. doi:10.4018/978-1-60566-026-4.ch051

Holloway, K. (2013). Fair use, copyright, and academic integrity in an online academic environment. In *Digital rights management: Concepts, methodologies, tools, and applications* (pp. 917–928). Hershey, PA: IGI Global. doi:10.4018/978-1-4666-2136-7.ch044

Horiuchi, C. (2005). E-government databases. In L. Rivero, J. Doorn, & V. Ferraggine (Eds.), *Encyclopedia of database technologies and applications* (pp. 206–210). Hershey, PA: IGI Global. doi:10.4018/978-1-59140-560-3.ch035

Horiuchi, C. (2006). Creating IS quality in government settings. In E. Duggan & J. Reichgelt (Eds.), *Measuring information systems delivery quality* (pp. 311–327). Hershey, PA: IGI Global. doi:10.4018/978-1-59140-857-4.ch014

Hsiao, N., Chu, P., & Lee, C. (2012). Impact of e-governance on businesses: Model development and case study. In *Digital democracy: Concepts, methodologies, tools, and applications* (pp. 1407–1425). Hershey, PA: IGI Global. doi:10.4018/978-1-4666-1740-7.ch070

Huang, T., & Lee, C. (2010). Evaluating the impact of e-government on citizens: Cost-benefit analysis. In C. Reddick (Ed.), *Citizens and e-government: Evaluating policy and management* (pp. 37–52). Hershey, PA: IGI Global. doi:10.4018/978-1-61520-931-6.ch003

Hunter, M. G., Diochon, M., Pugsley, D., & Wright, B. (2002). Unique challenges for small business adoption of information technology: The case of the Nova Scotia ten. In S. Burgess (Ed.), *Managing information technology in small business: Challenges and solutions* (pp. 98–117). Hershey, PA: IGI Global. doi:10.4018/978-1-930708-35-8.ch006

Hurskainen, J. (2003). Integration of business systems and applications in merger and alliance: Case metso automation. In T. Reponen (Ed.), *Information technology enabled global customer service* (pp. 207–225). Hershey, PA: IGI Global. doi:10.4018/978-1-59140-048-6.ch012

Iazzolino, G., & Pietrantonio, R. (2011). The soveria.it project: A best practice of e-government in southern Italy. In D. Piaggesi, K. Sund, & W. Castelnovo (Eds.), *Global strategy and practice of e-governance: Examples from around the world* (pp. 34–56). Hershey, PA: IGI Global. doi:10.4018/978-1-60960-489-9.ch003

Imran, A., & Gregor, S. (2012). A process model for successful e-government adoption in the least developed countries: A case of Bangladesh. In F. Tan (Ed.), *International comparisons of information communication technologies: Advancing applications* (pp. 321–350). Hershey, PA: IGI Global. doi:10.4018/978-1-61350-480-2.ch014

Inoue, Y., & Bell, S. T. (2005). Electronic/digital government innovation, and publishing trends with IT. In M. Khosrow-Pour (Ed.), *Encyclopedia of information science and technology* (pp. 1018–1023). Hershey, PA: IGI Global. doi:10.4018/978-1-59140-553-5.ch180

Islam, M. M., & Ehsan, M. (2013). Understanding e-governance: A theoretical approach. In M. Islam & M. Ehsan (Eds.), *From government to e-governance: Public administration in the digital age* (pp. 38–49). Hershey, PA: IGI Global. doi:10.4018/978-1-4666-1909-8.ch003

Jaeger, B. (2009). E-government and e-democracy in the making. In M. Khosrow-Pour (Ed.), *Encyclopedia of information science and technology* (2nd ed.; pp. 1318–1322). Hershey, PA: IGI Global. doi:10.4018/978-1-60566-026-4.ch208

Jain, R. B. (2007). Revamping the administrative structure and processes in India for online diplomacy. In A. Anttiroiko & M. Malkia (Eds.), *Encyclopedia of digital government* (pp. 1418–1423). Hershey, PA: IGI Global. doi:10.4018/978-1-59140-789-8.ch217

Jain, R. B. (2008). Revamping the administrative structure and processes in India for online diplomacy. In A. Anttiroiko (Ed.), *Electronic government: Concepts, methodologies, tools, and applications* (pp. 3142–3149). Hershey, PA: IGI Global. doi:10.4018/978-1-59904-947-2.ch233

Jauhiainen, J. S., & Inkinen, T. (2009). E-governance and the information society in periphery. In C. Reddick (Ed.), *Handbook of research on strategies for local e-government adoption and implementation: Comparative studies* (pp. 497–514). Hershey, PA: IGI Global. doi:10.4018/978-1-60566-282-4.ch026

Jensen, M. J. (2009). Electronic democracy and citizen influence in government. In C. Reddick (Ed.), *Handbook of research on strategies for local e-government adoption and implementation: Comparative studies* (pp. 288–305). Hershey, PA: IGI Global. doi:10.4018/978-1-60566-282-4.ch015

Jiao, Y., Hurson, A. R., Potok, T. E., & Beckerman, B. G. (2009). Integrating mobile-based systems with healthcare databases. In J. Erickson (Ed.), *Database technologies: Concepts, methodologies, tools, and applications* (pp. 484–504). Hershey, PA: IGI Global. doi:10.4018/978-1-60566-058-5.ch031

Joia, L. A. (2002). A systematic model to integrate information technology into metabusinesses: A case study in the engineering realms. In F. Tan (Ed.), *Advanced topics in global information management* (Vol. 1, pp. 250–267). Hershey, PA: IGI Global. doi:10.4018/978-1-930708-43-3.ch016

Jones, T. H., & Song, I. (2000). Binary equivalents of ternary relationships in entity-relationship modeling: A logical decomposition approach. *Journal of Database Management, 11*(2), 12–19. doi:10.4018/jdm.2000040102

Juana-Espinosa, S. D. (2007). Empirical study of the municipalitites' motivations for adopting online presence. In L. Al-Hakim (Ed.), *Global e-government: Theory, applications and benchmarking* (pp. 261–279). Hershey, PA: IGI Global. doi:10.4018/978-1-59904-027-1.ch015

Jun, K., & Weare, C. (2012). Bridging from e-government practice to e-government research: Past trends and future directions. In K. Bwalya & S. Zulu (Eds.), *Handbook of research on e-government in emerging economies: Adoption, e-participation, and legal frameworks* (pp. 263–289). Hershey, PA: IGI Global. doi:10.4018/978-1-4666-0324-0.ch013

Junqueira, A., Diniz, E. H., & Fernandez, M. (2010). Electronic government implementation projects with multiple agencies: Analysis of the electronic invoice project under PMBOK framework. In J. Cordoba-Pachon & A. Ochoa-Arias (Eds.), *Systems thinking and e-participation: ICT in the governance of society* (pp. 135–153). Hershey, PA: IGI Global. doi:10.4018/978-1-60566-860-4.ch009

Juntunen, A. (2009). Joint service development with the local authorities. In C. Reddick (Ed.), *Handbook of research on strategies for local e-government adoption and implementation: Comparative studies* (pp. 902–920). Hershey, PA: IGI Global. doi:10.4018/978-1-60566-282-4.ch047

Kamel, S. (2001). *Using DSS for crisis management.* Hershey, PA: IGI Global. doi:10.4018/978-1-87828-961-2.ch020

Kamel, S. (2006). DSS for strategic decision making. In M. Khosrow-Pour (Ed.), *Cases on information technology and organizational politics & culture* (pp. 230–246). Hershey, PA: IGI Global. doi:10.4018/978-1-59904-411-8.ch015

Kamel, S. (2009). The software industry in Egypt as a potential contributor to economic growth. In M. Khosrow-Pour (Ed.), *Encyclopedia of information science and technology* (2nd ed.; pp. 3531–3537). Hershey, PA: IGI Global. doi:10.4018/978-1-60566-026-4.ch562

Kamel, S., & Hussein, M. (2008). Xceed: Pioneering the contact center industry in Egypt. *Journal of Cases on Information Technology, 10*(1), 67–91. doi:10.4018/jcit.2008010105

Kamel, S., & Wahba, K. (2003). The use of a hybrid model in web-based education: "The Global campus project. In A. Aggarwal (Ed.), *Web-based education: Learning from experience* (pp. 331–346). Hershey, PA: IGI Global. doi:10.4018/978-1-59140-102-5.ch020

Kardaras, D. K., & Papathanassiou, E. A. (2008). An exploratory study of the e-government services in Greece. In G. Garson & M. Khosrow-Pour (Eds.), *Handbook of research on public information technology* (pp. 162–174). Hershey, PA: IGI Global. doi:10.4018/978-1-59904-857-4.ch016

Kassahun, A. E., Molla, A., & Sarkar, P. (2012). Government process reengineering: What we know and what we need to know. In *Digital democracy: Concepts, methodologies, tools, and applications* (pp. 1730–1752). Hershey, PA: IGI Global. doi:10.4018/978-1-4666-1740-7.ch086

Khan, B. (2005). Technological issues. In B. Khan (Ed.), *Managing e-learning strategies: Design, delivery, implementation and evaluation* (pp. 154–180). Hershey, PA: IGI Global. doi:10.4018/978-1-59140-634-1.ch004

Khasawneh, A., Bsoul, M., Obeidat, I., & Al Azzam, I. (2012). Technology fears: A study of e-commerce loyalty perception by Jordanian customers. In J. Wang (Ed.), *Advancing the service sector with evolving technologies: Techniques and principles* (pp. 158–165). Hershey, PA: IGI Global. doi:10.4018/978-1-4666-0044-7.ch010

Khatibi, V., & Montazer, G. A. (2012). E-research methodology. In A. Juan, T. Daradoumis, M. Roca, S. Grasman, & J. Faulin (Eds.), *Collaborative and distributed e-research: Innovations in technologies, strategies and applications* (pp. 62–81). Hershey, PA: IGI Global. doi:10.4018/978-1-4666-0125-3.ch003

Kidd, T. (2011). The dragon in the school's backyard: A review of literature on the uses of technology in urban schools. In L. Tomei (Ed.), *Online courses and ICT in education: Emerging practices and applications* (pp. 242–257). Hershey, PA: IGI Global. doi:10.4018/978-1-60960-150-8.ch019

Kidd, T. T. (2010). My experience tells the story: Exploring technology adoption from a qualitative perspective - A pilot study. In H. Song & T. Kidd (Eds.), *Handbook of research on human performance and instructional technology* (pp. 247–262). Hershey, PA: IGI Global. doi:10.4018/978-1-60566-782-9.ch015

Kieley, B., Lane, G., Paquet, G., & Roy, J. (2002). e-Government in Canada: Services online or public service renewal? In Å. Grönlund (Ed.), Electronic government: Design, applications and management (pp. 340-355). Hershey, PA: IGI Global. doi:10.4018/978-1-930708-19-8.ch016

Kim, P. (2012). "Stay out of the way! My kid is video blogging through a phone!": A lesson learned from math tutoring social media for children in underserved communities. In *Wireless technologies: Concepts, methodologies, tools and applications* (pp. 1415–1428). Hershey, PA: IGI Global. doi:10.4018/978-1-61350-101-6.ch517

Kirlidog, M. (2010). Financial aspects of national ICT strategies. In S. Kamel (Ed.), *E-strategies for technological diffusion and adoption: National ICT approaches for socioeconomic development* (pp. 277–292). Hershey, PA: IGI Global. doi:10.4018/978-1-60566-388-3.ch016

Kisielnicki, J. (2006). Transfer of information and knowledge in the project management. In E. Coakes & S. Clarke (Eds.), *Encyclopedia of communities of practice in information and knowledge management* (pp. 544–551). Hershey, PA: IGI Global. doi:10.4018/978-1-59140-556-6.ch091

Kittner, M., & Van Slyke, C. (2006). Reorganizing information technology services in an academic environment. In M. Khosrow-Pour (Ed.), *Cases on the human side of information technology* (pp. 49–66). Hershey, PA: IGI Global. doi:10.4018/978-1-59904-405-7.ch004

Knoell, H. D. (2008). Semi virtual workplaces in German financial service enterprises. In P. Zemliansky & K. St.Amant (Eds.), *Handbook of research on virtual workplaces and the new nature of business practices* (pp. 570–581). Hershey, PA: IGI Global. doi:10.4018/978-1-59904-893-2.ch041

Koh, S. L., & Maguire, S. (2009). Competing in the age of information technology in a developing economy: Experiences of an Indian bank. In S. Koh & S. Maguire (Eds.), *Information and communication technologies management in turbulent business environments* (pp. 326–350). Hershey, PA: IGI Global. doi:10.4018/978-1-60566-424-8.ch018

Kollmann, T., & Häsel, M. (2009). Competence of information technology professionals in internet-based ventures. In I. Lee (Ed.), *Electronic business: Concepts, methodologies, tools, and applications* (pp. 1905–1919). Hershey, PA: IGI Global. doi:10.4018/978-1-60566-056-1.ch118

Kollmann, T., & Häsel, M. (2009). Competence of information technology professionals in internet-based ventures. In A. Cater-Steel (Ed.), *Information technology governance and service management: Frameworks and adaptations* (pp. 239–253). Hershey, PA: IGI Global. doi:10.4018/978-1-60566-008-0.ch013

Kollmann, T., & Häsel, M. (2010). Competence of information technology professionals in internet-based ventures. In *Electronic services: Concepts, methodologies, tools and applications* (pp. 1551–1565). Hershey, PA: IGI Global. doi:10.4018/978-1-61520-967-5.ch094

Kraemer, K., & King, J. L. (2006). Information technology and administrative reform: Will e-government be different? *International Journal of Electronic Government Research*, *2*(1), 1–20. doi:10.4018/jegr.2006010101

Kraemer, K., & King, J. L. (2008). Information technology and administrative reform: Will e-government be different? In D. Norris (Ed.), *E-government research: Policy and management* (pp. 1–20). Hershey, PA: IGI Global. doi:10.4018/978-1-59904-913-7.ch001

Lampathaki, F., Tsiakaliaris, C., Stasis, A., & Charalabidis, Y. (2011). National interoperability frameworks: The way forward. In Y. Charalabidis (Ed.), *Interoperability in digital public services and administration: Bridging e-government and e-business* (pp. 1–24). Hershey, PA: IGI Global. doi:10.4018/978-1-61520-887-6.ch001

Lan, Z., & Scott, C. R. (1996). The relative importance of computer-mediated information versus conventional non-computer-mediated information in public managerial decision making. *Information Resources Management Journal*, *9*(1), 27–0. doi:10.4018/irmj.1996010103

Law, W. (2004). *Public sector data management in a developing economy*. Hershey, PA: IGI Global. doi:10.4018/978-1-59140-259-6.ch034

Law, W. K. (2005). Information resources development challenges in a cross-cultural environment. In M. Khosrow-Pour (Ed.), *Encyclopedia of information science and technology* (pp. 1476–1481). Hershey, PA: IGI Global. doi:10.4018/978-1-59140-553-5.ch259

Law, W. K. (2009). Cross-cultural challenges for information resources management. In M. Khosrow-Pour (Ed.), *Encyclopedia of information science and technology* (2nd ed.; pp. 840–846). Hershey, PA: IGI Global. doi:10.4018/978-1-60566-026-4.ch136

Law, W. K. (2011). Cross-cultural challenges for information resources management. In *Global business: Concepts, methodologies, tools and applications* (pp. 1924–1932). Hershey, PA: IGI Global. doi:10.4018/978-1-60960-587-2.ch704

Malkia, M., & Savolainen, R. (2004). eTransformation in government, politics and society: Conceptual framework and introduction. In M. Malkia, A. Anttiroiko, & R. Savolainen (Eds.), eTransformation in governance: New directions in government and politics (pp. 1-21). Hershey, PA: IGI Global. doi:10.4018/978-1-59140-130-8.ch001

Mandujano, S. (2011). Network manageability security. In D. Kar & M. Syed (Eds.), *Network security, administration and management: Advancing technology and practice* (pp. 158–181). Hershey, PA: IGI Global. doi:10.4018/978-1-60960-777-7.ch009

Marich, M. J., Schooley, B. L., & Horan, T. A. (2012). A normative enterprise architecture for guiding end-to-end emergency response decision support. In M. Jennex (Ed.), *Managing crises and disasters with emerging technologies: Advancements* (pp. 71–87). Hershey, PA: IGI Global. doi:10.4018/978-1-4666-0167-3.ch006

Markov, R., & Okujava, S. (2008). Costs, benefits, and risks of e-government portals. In G. Putnik & M. Cruz-Cunha (Eds.), *Encyclopedia of networked and virtual organizations* (pp. 354–363). Hershey, PA: IGI Global. doi:10.4018/978-1-59904-885-7.ch047

Martin, N., & Rice, J. (2013). Evaluating and designing electronic government for the future: Observations and insights from Australia. In V. Weerakkody (Ed.), *E-government services design, adoption, and evaluation* (pp. 238–258). Hershey, PA: IGI Global. doi:10.4018/978-1-4666-2458-0.ch014

i. Martinez, A. C. (2008). Accessing administration's information via internet in Spain. In F. Tan (Ed.), *Global information technologies: Concepts, methodologies, tools, and applications* (pp. 2558–2573). Hershey, PA: IGI Global. doi:10.4018/978-1-59904-939-7.ch186

Mbarika, V. W., Meso, P. N., & Musa, P. F. (2006). A disconnect in stakeholders' perceptions from emerging realities of teledensity growth in Africa's least developed countries. In M. Hunter & F. Tan (Eds.), *Advanced topics in global information management* (Vol. 5, pp. 263–282). Hershey, PA: IGI Global. doi:10.4018/978-1-59140-923-6.ch012

Mbarika, V. W., Meso, P. N., & Musa, P. F. (2008). A disconnect in stakeholders' perceptions from emerging realities of teledensity growth in Africa's least developed countries. In F. Tan (Ed.), *Global information technologies: Concepts, methodologies, tools, and applications* (pp. 2948–2962). Hershey, PA: IGI Global. doi:10.4018/978-1-59904-939-7.ch209

Means, T., Olson, E., & Spooner, J. (2013). Discovering ways that don't work on the road to success: Strengths and weaknesses revealed by an active learning studio classroom project. In A. Benson, J. Moore, & S. Williams van Rooij (Eds.), *Cases on educational technology planning, design, and implementation: A project management perspective* (pp. 94–113). Hershey, PA: IGI Global. doi:10.4018/978-1-4666-4237-9.ch006

Melitski, J., Holzer, M., Kim, S., Kim, C., & Rho, S. (2008). Digital government worldwide: An e-government assessment of municipal web sites. In G. Garson & M. Khosrow-Pour (Eds.), *Handbook of research on public information technology* (pp. 790–804). Hershey, PA: IGI Global. doi:10.4018/978-1-59904-857-4.ch069

Memmola, M., Palumbo, G., & Rossini, M. (2009). Web & RFID technology: New frontiers in costing and process management for rehabilitation medicine. In L. Al-Hakim & M. Memmola (Eds.), *Business web strategy: Design, alignment, and application* (pp. 145–169). Hershey, PA: IGI Global. doi:10.4018/978-1-60566-024-0.ch008

Meng, Z., Fahong, Z., & Lei, L. (2008). Information technology and environment. In Y. Kurihara, S. Takaya, H. Harui, & H. Kamae (Eds.), *Information technology and economic development* (pp. 201–212). Hershey, PA: IGI Global. doi:10.4018/978-1-59904-579-5.ch014

Mentzingen de Moraes, A. J., Ferneda, E., Costa, I., & Spinola, M. D. (2011). Practical approach for implementation of governance process in IT: Information technology areas. In N. Shi & G. Silvius (Eds.), *Enterprise IT governance, business value and performance measurement* (pp. 19–40). Hershey, PA: IGI Global. doi:10.4018/978-1-60566-346-3.ch002

Merwin, G. A. Jr, McDonald, J. S., & Odera, L. C. (2008). Economic development: Government's cutting edge in IT. In M. Raisinghani (Ed.), *Handbook of research on global information technology management in the digital economy* (pp. 1–37). Hershey, PA: IGI Global. doi:10.4018/978-1-59904-875-8.ch001

Meso, P., & Duncan, N. (2002). Can national information infrastructures enhance social development in the least developed countries? An empirical investigation. In M. Dadashzadeh (Ed.), *Information technology management in developing countries* (pp. 23–51). Hershey, PA: IGI Global. doi:10.4018/978-1-931777-03-2.ch002

Meso, P. N., & Duncan, N. B. (2002). Can national information infrastructures enhance social development in the least developed countries? In F. Tan (Ed.), *Advanced topics in global information management* (Vol. 1, pp. 207–226). Hershey, PA: IGI Global. doi:10.4018/978-1-930708-43-3.ch014

Middleton, M. (2008). Evaluation of e-government web sites. In G. Garson & M. Khosrow-Pour (Eds.), *Handbook of research on public information technology* (pp. 699–710). Hershey, PA: IGI Global. doi:10.4018/978-1-59904-857-4.ch063

Mingers, J. (2010). Pluralism, realism, and truth: The keys to knowledge in information systems research. In D. Paradice (Ed.), *Emerging systems approaches in information technologies: Concepts, theories, and applications* (pp. 86–98). Hershey, PA: IGI Global. doi:10.4018/978-1-60566-976-2.ch006

Mital, K. M. (2012). ICT, unique identity and inclusive growth: An Indian perspective. In A. Manoharan & M. Holzer (Eds.), *E-governance and civic engagement: Factors and determinants of e-democracy* (pp. 584–612). Hershey, PA: IGI Global. doi:10.4018/978-1-61350-083-5.ch029

Mizell, A. P. (2008). Helping close the digital divide for financially disadvantaged seniors. In F. Tan (Ed.), *Global information technologies: Concepts, methodologies, tools, and applications* (pp. 2396–2402). Hershey, PA: IGI Global. doi:10.4018/978-1-59904-939-7.ch173

Molinari, F., Wills, C., Koumpis, A., & Moumtzi, V. (2011). A citizen-centric platform to support networking in the area of e-democracy. In H. Rahman (Ed.), *Cases on adoption, diffusion and evaluation of global e-governance systems: Impact at the grass roots* (pp. 282–302). Hershey, PA: IGI Global. doi:10.4018/978-1-61692-814-8.ch014

Molinari, F., Wills, C., Koumpis, A., & Moumtzi, V. (2013). A citizen-centric platform to support networking in the area of e-democracy. In H. Rahman (Ed.), *Cases on progressions and challenges in ICT utilization for citizen-centric governance* (pp. 265–297). Hershey, PA: IGI Global. doi:10.4018/978-1-4666-2071-1.ch013

Monteverde, F. (2010). The process of e-government public policy inclusion in the governmental agenda: A framework for assessment and case study. In J. Cordoba-Pachon & A. Ochoa-Arias (Eds.), *Systems thinking and e-participation: ICT in the governance of society* (pp. 233–245). Hershey, PA: IGI Global. doi:10.4018/978-1-60566-860-4.ch015

Moodley, S. (2008). Deconstructing the South African government's ICT for development discourse. In A. Anttiroiko (Ed.), *Electronic government: Concepts, methodologies, tools, and applications* (pp. 622–631). Hershey, PA: IGI Global. doi:10.4018/978-1-59904-947-2.ch053

Moodley, S. (2008). Deconstructing the South African government's ICT for development discourse. In C. Van Slyke (Ed.), *Information communication technologies: Concepts, methodologies, tools, and applications* (pp. 816–825). Hershey, PA: IGI Global. doi:10.4018/978-1-59904-949-6.ch052

Mora, M., Cervantes-Perez, F., Gelman-Muravchik, O., Forgionne, G. A., & Mejia-Olvera, M. (2003). DMSS implementation research: A conceptual analysis of the contributions and limitations of the factor-based and stage-based streams. In G. Forgionne, J. Gupta, & M. Mora (Eds.), *Decision-making support systems: Achievements and challenges for the new decade* (pp. 331–356). Hershey, PA: IGI Global. doi:10.4018/978-1-59140-045-5.ch020

Mörtberg, C., & Elovaara, P. (2010). Attaching people and technology: Between e and government. In S. Booth, S. Goodman, & G. Kirkup (Eds.), *Gender issues in learning and working with information technology: Social constructs and cultural contexts* (pp. 83–98). Hershey, PA: IGI Global. doi:10.4018/978-1-61520-813-5.ch005

Murphy, J., Harper, E., Devine, E. C., Burke, L. J., & Hook, M. L. (2011). Case study: Lessons learned when embedding evidence-based knowledge in a nurse care planning and documentation system. In A. Cashin & R. Cook (Eds.), *Evidence-based practice in nursing informatics: Concepts and applications* (pp. 174–190). Hershey, PA: IGI Global. doi:10.4018/978-1-60960-034-1.ch014

Mutula, S. M. (2013). E-government's role in poverty alleviation: Case study of South Africa. In H. Rahman (Ed.), *Cases on progressions and challenges in ICT utilization for citizen-centric governance* (pp. 44–68). Hershey, PA: IGI Global. doi:10.4018/978-1-4666-2071-1.ch003

Nath, R., & Angeles, R. (2005). Relationships between supply characteristics and buyer-supplier coupling in e-procurement: An empirical analysis. *International Journal of E-Business Research, 1*(2), 40–55. doi:10.4018/jebr.2005040103

Nissen, M. E. (2006). Application cases in government. In M. Nissen (Ed.), *Harnessing knowledge dynamics: Principled organizational knowing & learning* (pp. 152–181). Hershey, PA: IGI Global. doi:10.4018/978-1-59140-773-7.ch008

Norris, D. F. (2003). Leading-edge information technologies and American local governments. In G. Garson (Ed.), *Public information technology: Policy and management issues* (pp. 139–169). Hershey, PA: IGI Global. doi:10.4018/978-1-59140-060-8.ch007

Norris, D. F. (2008). Information technology among U.S. local governments. In G. Garson & M. Khosrow-Pour (Eds.), *Handbook of research on public information technology* (pp. 132–144). Hershey, PA: IGI Global. doi:10.4018/978-1-59904-857-4.ch013

Northrop, A. (1999). The challenge of teaching information technology in public administration graduate programs. In G. Garson (Ed.), *Information technology and computer applications in public administration: Issues and trends* (pp. 1–22). Hershey, PA: IGI Global. doi:10.4018/978-1-87828-952-0.ch001

Northrop, A. (2003). Information technology and public administration: The view from the profession. In G. Garson (Ed.), *Public information technology: Policy and management issues* (pp. 1–19). Hershey, PA: IGI Global. doi:10.4018/978-1-59140-060-8.ch001

Northrop, A. (2007). Lip service? How PA journals and textbooks view information technology. In G. Garson (Ed.), *Modern public information technology systems: Issues and challenges* (pp. 1–16). Hershey, PA: IGI Global. doi:10.4018/978-1-59904-051-6.ch001

Null, E. (2013). Legal and political barriers to municipal networks in the United States. In A. Abdelaal (Ed.), *Social and economic effects of community wireless networks and infrastructures* (pp. 27–56). Hershey, PA: IGI Global. doi:10.4018/978-1-4666-2997-4.ch003

Okunoye, A., Frolick, M., & Crable, E. (2006). ERP implementation in higher education: An account of pre-implementation and implementation phases. *Journal of Cases on Information Technology*, *8*(2), 110–132. doi:10.4018/jcit.2006040106

Olasina, G. (2012). A review of egovernment services in Nigeria. In A. Tella & A. Issa (Eds.), *Library and information science in developing countries: Contemporary issues* (pp. 205–221). Hershey, PA: IGI Global. doi:10.4018/978-1-61350-335-5.ch015

Orgeron, C. P. (2008). A model for reengineering IT job classes in state government. In G. Garson & M. Khosrow-Pour (Eds.), *Handbook of research on public information technology* (pp. 735–746). Hershey, PA: IGI Global. doi:10.4018/978-1-59904-857-4.ch066

Owsinski, J. W., & Pielak, A. M. (2011). Local authority websites in rural areas: Measuring quality and functionality, and assessing the role. In Z. Andreopoulou, B. Manos, N. Polman, & D. Viaggi (Eds.), *Agricultural and environmental informatics, governance and management: Emerging research applications* (pp. 39–60). Hershey, PA: IGI Global. doi:10.4018/978-1-60960-621-3.ch003

Owsiński, J. W., Pielak, A. M., Sęp, K., & Stańczak, J. (2014). Local web-based networks in rural municipalities: Extension, density, and meaning. In Z. Andreopoulou, V. Samathrakis, S. Louca, & M. Vlachopoulou (Eds.), *E-innovation for sustainable development of rural resources during global economic crisis* (pp. 126–151). Hershey, PA: IGI Global. doi:10.4018/978-1-4666-4550-9.ch011

Pagani, M., & Pasinetti, C. (2008). Technical and functional quality in the development of t-government services. In A. Anttiroiko (Ed.), *Electronic government: Concepts, methodologies, tools, and applications* (pp. 2943–2965). Hershey, PA: IGI Global. doi:10.4018/978-1-59904-947-2.ch220

Pani, A. K., & Agrahari, A. (2005). On e-markets in emerging economy: An Indian experience. In M. Khosrow-Pour (Ed.), *Advanced topics in electronic commerce* (Vol. 1, pp. 287–299). Hershey, PA: IGI Global. doi:10.4018/978-1-59140-819-2.ch015

Papadopoulos, T., Angelopoulos, S., & Kitsios, F. (2011). A strategic approach to e-health interoperability using e-government frameworks. In A. Lazakidou, K. Siassiakos, & K. Ioannou (Eds.), *Wireless technologies for ambient assisted living and healthcare: Systems and applications* (pp. 213–229). Hershey, PA: IGI Global. doi:10.4018/978-1-61520-805-0.ch012

Papadopoulos, T., Angelopoulos, S., & Kitsios, F. (2013). A strategic approach to e-health interoperability using e-government frameworks. In *User-driven healthcare: Concepts, methodologies, tools, and applications* (pp. 791–807). Hershey, PA: IGI Global. doi:10.4018/978-1-4666-2770-3.ch039

Papaleo, G., Chiarella, D., Aiello, M., & Caviglione, L. (2012). Analysis, development and deployment of statistical anomaly detection techniques for real e-mail traffic. In T. Chou (Ed.), *Information assurance and security technologies for risk assessment and threat management: Advances* (pp. 47–71). Hershey, PA: IGI Global. doi:10.4018/978-1-61350-507-6.ch003

Papp, R. (2003). Information technology & FDA compliance in the pharmaceutical industry. In M. Khosrow-Pour (Ed.), *Annals of cases on information technology* (Vol. 5, pp. 262–273). Hershey, PA: IGI Global. doi:10.4018/978-1-59140-061-5.ch017

Parsons, T. W. (2007). Developing a knowledge management portal. In A. Tatnall (Ed.), *Encyclopedia of portal technologies and applications* (pp. 223–227). Hershey, PA: IGI Global. doi:10.4018/978-1-59140-989-2.ch039

Passaris, C. E. (2007). Immigration and digital government. In A. Anttiroiko & M. Malkia (Eds.), *Encyclopedia of digital government* (pp. 988–994). Hershey, PA: IGI Global. doi:10.4018/978-1-59140-789-8.ch148

Pavlichev, A. (2004). The e-government challenge for public administration. In A. Pavlichev & G. Garson (Eds.), *Digital government: Principles and best practices* (pp. 276–290). Hershey, PA: IGI Global. doi:10.4018/978-1-59140-122-3.ch018

Penrod, J. I., & Harbor, A. F. (2000). Designing and implementing a learning organization-oriented information technology planning and management process. In L. Petrides (Ed.), *Case studies on information technology in higher education: Implications for policy and practice* (pp. 7–19). Hershey, PA: IGI Global. doi:10.4018/978-1-878289-74-2.ch001

Planas-Silva, M. D., & Joseph, R. C. (2011). Perspectives on the adoption of electronic resources for use in clinical trials. In M. Guah (Ed.), *Healthcare delivery reform and new technologies: Organizational initiatives* (pp. 19–28). Hershey, PA: IGI Global. doi:10.4018/978-1-60960-183-6.ch002

Pomazalová, N., & Rejman, S. (2013). The rationale behind implementation of new electronic tools for electronic public procurement. In N. Pomazalová (Ed.), *Public sector transformation processes and internet public procurement: Decision support systems* (pp. 85–117). Hershey, PA: IGI Global. doi:10.4018/978-1-4666-2665-2.ch006

Postorino, M. N. (2012). City competitiveness and airport: Information science perspective. In M. Bulu (Ed.), *City competitiveness and improving urban subsystems: Technologies and applications* (pp. 61–83). Hershey, PA: IGI Global. doi:10.4018/978-1-61350-174-0.ch004

Poupa, C. (2002). Electronic government in Switzerland: Priorities for 2001-2005 - Electronic voting and federal portal. In Å. Grönlund (Ed.), *Electronic government: Design, applications and management* (pp. 356–369). Hershey, PA: IGI Global. doi:10.4018/978-1-930708-19-8.ch017

Powell, S. R. (2010). Interdisciplinarity in telecommunications and networking. In *Networking and telecommunications: Concepts, methodologies, tools and applications* (pp. 33–40). Hershey, PA: IGI Global. doi:10.4018/978-1-60566-986-1.ch004

Priya, P. S., & Mathiyalagan, N. (2011). A study of the implementation status of two e-governance projects in land revenue administration in India. In M. Shareef, V. Kumar, U. Kumar, & Y. Dwivedi (Eds.), *Stakeholder adoption of e-government services: Driving and resisting factors* (pp. 214–230). Hershey, PA: IGI Global. doi:10.4018/978-1-60960-601-5.ch011

Prysby, C., & Prysby, N. (2000). Electronic mail, employee privacy and the workplace. In L. Janczewski (Ed.), *Internet and intranet security management: Risks and solutions* (pp. 251–270). Hershey, PA: IGI Global. doi:10.4018/978-1-878289-71-1.ch009

Prysby, C. L., & Prysby, N. D. (2003). Electronic mail in the public workplace: Issues of privacy and public disclosure. In G. Garson (Ed.), *Public information technology: Policy and management issues* (pp. 271–298). Hershey, PA: IGI Global. doi:10.4018/978-1-59140-060-8.ch012

Prysby, C. L., & Prysby, N. D. (2007). You have mail, but who is reading it? Issues of e-mail in the public workplace. In G. Garson (Ed.), *Modern public information technology systems: Issues and challenges* (pp. 312–336). Hershey, PA: IGI Global. doi:10.4018/978-1-59904-051-6.ch016

Radl, A., & Chen, Y. (2005). Computer security in electronic government: A state-local education information system. *International Journal of Electronic Government Research, 1*(1), 79–99. doi:10.4018/jegr.2005010105

Rahman, H. (2008). Information dynamics in developing countries. In C. Van Slyke (Ed.), *Information communication technologies: Concepts, methodologies, tools, and applications* (pp. 104–114). Hershey, PA: IGI Global. doi:10.4018/978-1-59904-949-6.ch008

Ramanathan, J. (2009). Adaptive IT architecture as a catalyst for network capability in government. In P. Saha (Ed.), *Advances in government enterprise architecture* (pp. 149–172). Hershey, PA: IGI Global. doi:10.4018/978-1-60566-068-4.ch007

Ramos, I., & Berry, D. M. (2006). Social construction of information technology supporting work. In M. Khosrow-Pour (Ed.), *Cases on information technology: Lessons learned* (Vol. 7, pp. 36–52). Hershey, PA: IGI Global. doi:10.4018/978-1-59140-673-0.ch003

Ray, D., Gulla, U., Gupta, M. P., & Dash, S. S. (2009). Interoperability and constituents of interoperable systems in public sector. In V. Weerakkody, M. Janssen, & Y. Dwivedi (Eds.), *Handbook of research on ICT-enabled transformational government: A global perspective* (pp. 175–195). Hershey, PA: IGI Global. doi:10.4018/978-1-60566-390-6.ch010

Reddick, C. G. (2007). E-government and creating a citizen-centric government: A study of federal government CIOs. In G. Garson (Ed.), *Modern public information technology systems: Issues and challenges* (pp. 143–165). Hershey, PA: IGI Global. doi:10.4018/978-1-59904-051-6.ch008

Reddick, C. G. (2010). Citizen-centric e-government. In C. Reddick (Ed.), *Homeland security preparedness and information systems: Strategies for managing public policy* (pp. 45–75). Hershey, PA: IGI Global. doi:10.4018/978-1-60566-834-5.ch002

Reddick, C. G. (2010). E-government and creating a citizen-centric government: A study of federal government CIOs. In C. Reddick (Ed.), *Homeland security preparedness and information systems: Strategies for managing public policy* (pp. 230–250). Hershey, PA: IGI Global. doi:10.4018/978-1-60566-834-5.ch012

Reddick, C. G. (2010). Perceived effectiveness of e-government and its usage in city governments: Survey evidence from information technology directors. In C. Reddick (Ed.), *Homeland security preparedness and information systems: Strategies for managing public policy* (pp. 213–229). Hershey, PA: IGI Global. doi:10.4018/978-1-60566-834-5.ch011

Reddick, C. G. (2012). Customer relationship management adoption in local governments in the United States. In S. Chhabra & M. Kumar (Eds.), *Strategic enterprise resource planning models for e-government: Applications and methodologies* (pp. 111–124). Hershey, PA: IGI Global. doi:10.4018/978-1-60960-863-7.ch008

Reeder, F. S., & Pandy, S. M. (2008). Identifying effective funding models for e-government. In A. Anttiroiko (Ed.), *Electronic government: Concepts, methodologies, tools, and applications* (pp. 1108–1138). Hershey, PA: IGI Global. doi:10.4018/978-1-59904-947-2.ch083

Riesco, D., Acosta, E., & Montejano, G. (2003). An extension to a UML activity graph from workflow. In L. Favre (Ed.), *UML and the unified process* (pp. 294–314). Hershey, PA: IGI Global. doi:10.4018/978-1-93177-744-5.ch015

Ritzhaupt, A. D., & Gill, T. G. (2008). A hybrid and novel approach to teaching computer programming in MIS curriculum. In S. Negash, M. Whitman, A. Woszczynski, K. Hoganson, & H. Mattord (Eds.), *Handbook of distance learning for real-time and asynchronous information technology education* (pp. 259–281). Hershey, PA: IGI Global. doi:10.4018/978-1-59904-964-9.ch014

Roche, E. M. (1993). International computing and the international regime. *Journal of Global Information Management, 1*(2), 33–44. doi:10.4018/jgim.1993040103

Rocheleau, B. (2007). Politics, accountability, and information management. In G. Garson (Ed.), *Modern public information technology systems: Issues and challenges* (pp. 35–71). Hershey, PA: IGI Global. doi:10.4018/978-1-59904-051-6.ch003

Rodrigues Filho, J. (2010). E-government in Brazil: Reinforcing dominant institutions or reducing citizenship? In C. Reddick (Ed.), *Politics, democracy and e-government: Participation and service delivery* (pp. 347–362). Hershey, PA: IGI Global. doi:10.4018/978-1-61520-933-0.ch021

Rodriguez, S. R., & Thorp, D. A. (2013). eLearning for industry: A case study of the project management process. In A. Benson, J. Moore, & S. Williams van Rooij (Eds.), Cases on educational technology planning, design, and implementation: A project management perspective (pp. 319-342). Hershey, PA: IGI Global. doi:10.4018/978-1-4666-4237-9.ch017

Roman, A. V. (2013). Delineating three dimensions of e-government success: Security, functionality, and transformation. In J. Gil-Garcia (Ed.), *E-government success factors and measures: Theories, concepts, and methodologies* (pp. 171–192). Hershey, PA: IGI Global. doi:10.4018/978-1-4666-4058-0.ch010

Ross, S. C., Tyran, C. K., & Auer, D. J. (2008). Up in smoke: Rebuilding after an IT disaster. In H. Nemati (Ed.), *Information security and ethics: Concepts, methodologies, tools, and applications* (pp. 3659–3675). Hershey, PA: IGI Global. doi:10.4018/978-1-59904-937-3.ch248

Ross, S. C., Tyran, C. K., Auer, D. J., Junell, J. M., & Williams, T. G. (2005). Up in smoke: Rebuilding after an IT disaster. *Journal of Cases on Information Technology*, *7*(2), 31–49. doi:10.4018/jcit.2005040103

Roy, J. (2008). Security, sovereignty, and continental interoperability: Canada's elusive balance. In T. Loendorf & G. Garson (Eds.), *Patriotic information systems* (pp. 153–176). Hershey, PA: IGI Global. doi:10.4018/978-1-59904-594-8.ch007

Rubeck, R. F., & Miller, G. A. (2009). vGOV: Remote video access to government services. In A. Scupola (Ed.), Cases on managing e-services (pp. 253-268). Hershey, PA: IGI Global. doi:10.4018/978-1-60566-064-6.ch017

Saekow, A., & Boonmee, C. (2011). The challenges of implementing e-government interoperability in Thailand: Case of official electronic correspondence letters exchange across government departments. In Y. Charalabidis (Ed.), *Interoperability in digital public services and administration: Bridging e-government and e-business* (pp. 40–61). Hershey, PA: IGI Global. doi:10.4018/978-1-61520-887-6.ch003

Saekow, A., & Boonmee, C. (2012). The challenges of implementing e-government interoperability in Thailand: Case of official electronic correspondence letters exchange across government departments. In *Digital democracy: Concepts, methodologies, tools, and applications* (pp. 1883–1905). Hershey, PA: IGI Global. doi:10.4018/978-1-4666-1740-7.ch094

Sagsan, M., & Medeni, T. (2012). Understanding "knowledge management (KM) paradigms" from social media perspective: An empirical study on discussion group for KM at professional networking site. In M. Cruz-Cunha, P. Gonçalves, N. Lopes, E. Miranda, & G. Putnik (Eds.), *Handbook of research on business social networking: Organizational, managerial, and technological dimensions* (pp. 738–755). Hershey, PA: IGI Global. doi:10.4018/978-1-61350-168-9.ch039

Sahi, G., & Madan, S. (2013). Information security threats in ERP enabled e-governance: Challenges and solutions. In *Enterprise resource planning: Concepts, methodologies, tools, and applications* (pp. 825–837). Hershey, PA: IGI Global. doi:10.4018/978-1-4666-4153-2.ch048

Sanford, C., & Bhattacherjee, A. (2008). IT implementation in a developing country municipality: A sociocognitive analysis. *International Journal of Technology and Human Interaction*, *4*(3), 68–93. doi:10.4018/jthi.2008070104

Schelin, S. H. (2003). E-government: An overview. In G. Garson (Ed.), *Public information technology: Policy and management issues* (pp. 120–138). Hershey, PA: IGI Global. doi:10.4018/978-1-59140-060-8.ch006

Schelin, S. H. (2004). Training for digital government. In A. Pavlichev & G. Garson (Eds.), *Digital government: Principles and best practices* (pp. 263–275). Hershey, PA: IGI Global. doi:10.4018/978-1-59140-122-3.ch017

Schelin, S. H. (2007). E-government: An overview. In G. Garson (Ed.), *Modern public information technology systems: Issues and challenges* (pp. 110–126). Hershey, PA: IGI Global. doi:10.4018/978-1-59904-051-6.ch006

Schelin, S. H., & Garson, G. (2004). Theoretical justification of critical success factors. In G. Garson & S. Schelin (Eds.), *IT solutions series: Humanizing information technology: Advice from experts* (pp. 4–15). Hershey, PA: IGI Global. doi:10.4018/978-1-59140-245-9.ch002

Scime, A. (2002). Information systems and computer science model curricula: A comparative look. In M. Dadashzadeh, A. Saber, & S. Saber (Eds.), *Information technology education in the new millennium* (pp. 146–158). Hershey, PA: IGI Global. doi:10.4018/978-1-931777-05-6.ch018

Scime, A. (2009). Computing curriculum analysis and development. In M. Khosrow-Pour (Ed.), *Encyclopedia of information science and technology* (2nd ed.; pp. 667–671). Hershey, PA: IGI Global. doi:10.4018/978-1-60566-026-4.ch108

Scime, A., & Wania, C. (2008). Computing curricula: A comparison of models. In C. Van Slyke (Ed.), *Information communication technologies: Concepts, methodologies, tools, and applications* (pp. 1270–1283). Hershey, PA: IGI Global. doi:10.4018/978-1-59904-949-6.ch088

Seidman, S. B. (2009). An international perspective on professional software engineering credentials. In H. Ellis, S. Demurjian, & J. Naveda (Eds.), *Software engineering: Effective teaching and learning approaches and practices* (pp. 351–361). Hershey, PA: IGI Global. doi:10.4018/978-1-60566-102-5.ch018

Seifert, J. W. (2007). E-government act of 2002 in the United States. In A. Anttiroiko & M. Malkia (Eds.), *Encyclopedia of digital government* (pp. 476–481). Hershey, PA: IGI Global. doi:10.4018/978-1-59140-789-8.ch072

Seifert, J. W., & Relyea, H. C. (2008). E-government act of 2002 in the United States. In A. Anttiroiko (Ed.), *Electronic government: Concepts, methodologies, tools, and applications* (pp. 154–161). Hershey, PA: IGI Global. doi:10.4018/978-1-59904-947-2.ch013

Seufert, S. (2002). E-learning business models: Framework and best practice examples. In M. Raisinghani (Ed.), *Cases on worldwide e-commerce: Theory in action* (pp. 70–94). Hershey, PA: IGI Global. doi:10.4018/978-1-930708-27-3.ch004

Shareef, M. A., & Archer, N. (2012). E-government service development. In M. Shareef, N. Archer, & S. Dutta (Eds.), *E-government service maturity and development: Cultural, organizational and technological perspectives* (pp. 1–14). Hershey, PA: IGI Global. doi:10.4018/978-1-60960-848-4.ch001

Shareef, M. A., & Archer, N. (2012). E-government initiatives: Review studies on different countries. In M. Shareef, N. Archer, & S. Dutta (Eds.), *E-government service maturity and development: Cultural, organizational and technological perspectives* (pp. 40–76). Hershey, PA: IGI Global. doi:10.4018/978-1-60960-848-4.ch003

Shareef, M. A., Kumar, U., & Kumar, V. (2011). E-government development: Performance evaluation parameters. In M. Shareef, V. Kumar, U. Kumar, & Y. Dwivedi (Eds.), *Stakeholder adoption of e-government services: Driving and resisting factors* (pp. 197–213). Hershey, PA: IGI Global. doi:10.4018/978-1-60960-601-5.ch010

Shareef, M. A., Kumar, U., Kumar, V., & Niktash, M. (2012). Electronic-government vision: Case studies for objectives, strategies, and initiatives. In M. Shareef, N. Archer, & S. Dutta (Eds.), *E-government service maturity and development: Cultural, organizational and technological perspectives* (pp. 15–39). Hershey, PA: IGI Global. doi:10.4018/978-1-60960-848-4.ch002

Shukla, P., Kumar, A., & Anu Kumar, P. B. (2013). Impact of national culture on business continuity management system implementation. *International Journal of Risk and Contingency Management*, *2*(3), 23–36. doi:10.4018/ijrcm.2013070102

Shulman, S. W. (2007). The federal docket management system and the prospect for digital democracy in U S rulemaking. In G. Garson (Ed.), *Modern public information technology systems: Issues and challenges* (pp. 166–184). Hershey, PA: IGI Global. doi:10.4018/978-1-59904-051-6.ch009

Simonovic, S. (2007). Problems of offline government in e-Serbia. In A. Anttiroiko & M. Malkia (Eds.), *Encyclopedia of digital government* (pp. 1342–1351). Hershey, PA: IGI Global. doi:10.4018/978-1-59140-789-8.ch205

Simonovic, S. (2008). Problems of offline government in e-Serbia. In A. Anttiroiko (Ed.), *Electronic government: Concepts, methodologies, tools, and applications* (pp. 2929–2942). Hershey, PA: IGI Global. doi:10.4018/978-1-59904-947-2.ch219

Singh, A. M. (2005). Information systems and technology in South Africa. In M. Khosrow-Pour (Ed.), *Encyclopedia of information science and technology* (pp. 1497–1502). Hershey, PA: IGI Global. doi:10.4018/978-1-59140-553-5.ch263

Singh, S., & Naidoo, G. (2005). Towards an e-government solution: A South African perspective. In W. Huang, K. Siau, & K. Wei (Eds.), *Electronic government strategies and implementation* (pp. 325–353). Hershey, PA: IGI Global. doi:10.4018/978-1-59140-348-7.ch014

Snoke, R., & Underwood, A. (2002). Generic attributes of IS graduates: An analysis of Australian views. In F. Tan (Ed.), *Advanced topics in global information management* (Vol. 1, pp. 370–384). Hershey, PA: IGI Global. doi:10.4018/978-1-930708-43-3.ch023

Sommer, L. (2006). Revealing unseen organizations in higher education: A study framework and application example. In A. Metcalfe (Ed.), *Knowledge management and higher education: A critical analysis* (pp. 115–146). Hershey, PA: IGI Global. doi:10.4018/978-1-59140-509-2.ch007

Song, H., Kidd, T., & Owens, E. (2011). Examining technological disparities and instructional practices in English language arts classroom: Implications for school leadership and teacher training. In L. Tomei (Ed.), *Online courses and ICT in education: Emerging practices and applications* (pp. 258–274). Hershey, PA: IGI Global. doi:10.4018/978-1-60960-150-8.ch020

Speaker, P. J., & Kleist, V. F. (2003). Using information technology to meet electronic commerce and MIS education demands. In A. Aggarwal (Ed.), *Web-based education: Learning from experience* (pp. 280–291). Hershey, PA: IGI Global. doi:10.4018/978-1-59140-102-5.ch017

Spitler, V. K. (2007). Learning to use IT in the workplace: Mechanisms and masters. In M. Mahmood (Ed.), *Contemporary issues in end user computing* (pp. 292–323). Hershey, PA: IGI Global. doi:10.4018/978-1-59140-926-7.ch013

Stellefson, M. (2011). Considerations for marketing distance education courses in health education: Five important questions to examine before development. In U. Demiray & S. Sever (Eds.), *Marketing online education programs: Frameworks for promotion and communication* (pp. 222–234). Hershey, PA: IGI Global. doi:10.4018/978-1-60960-074-7.ch014

Straub, D. W., & Loch, K. D. (2006). Creating and developing a program of global research. *Journal of Global Information Management, 14*(2), 1–28. doi:10.4018/jgim.2006040101

Straub, D. W., Loch, K. D., & Hill, C. E. (2002). Transfer of information technology to the Arab world: A test of cultural influence modeling. In M. Dadashzadeh (Ed.), *Information technology management in developing countries* (pp. 92–134). Hershey, PA: IGI Global. doi:10.4018/978-1-931777-03-2.ch005

Straub, D. W., Loch, K. D., & Hill, C. E. (2003). Transfer of information technology to the Arab world: A test of cultural influence modeling. In F. Tan (Ed.), *Advanced topics in global information management* (Vol. 2, pp. 141–172). Hershey, PA: IGI Global. doi:10.4018/978-1-59140-064-6.ch009

Suki, N. M., Ramayah, T., Ming, M. K., & Suki, N. M. (2013). Factors enhancing employed job seekers intentions to use social networking sites as a job search tool. In A. Mesquita (Ed.), *User perception and influencing factors of technology in everyday life* (pp. 265–281). Hershey, PA: IGI Global. doi:10.4018/978-1-4666-1954-8.ch018

Suomi, R. (2006). Introducing electronic patient records to hospitals: Innovation adoption paths. In T. Spil & R. Schuring (Eds.), *E-health systems diffusion and use: The innovation, the user and the use IT model* (pp. 128–146). Hershey, PA: IGI Global. doi:10.4018/978-1-59140-423-1.ch008

Swim, J., & Barker, L. (2012). Pathways into a gendered occupation: Brazilian women in IT. *International Journal of Social and Organizational Dynamics in IT, 2*(4), 34–51. doi:10.4018/ijsodit.2012100103

Tarafdar, M., & Vaidya, S. D. (2006). Adoption and implementation of IT in developing nations: Experiences from two public sector enterprises in India. In M. Khosrow-Pour (Ed.), *Cases on information technology planning, design and implementation* (pp. 208–233). Hershey, PA: IGI Global. doi:10.4018/978-1-59904-408-8.ch013

Tarafdar, M., & Vaidya, S. D. (2008). Adoption and implementation of IT in developing nations: Experiences from two public sector enterprises in India. In G. Garson & M. Khosrow-Pour (Eds.), *Handbook of research on public information technology* (pp. 905–924). Hershey, PA: IGI Global. doi:10.4018/978-1-59904-857-4.ch076

Thesing, Z. (2007). Zarina thesing, pumpkin patch. In M. Hunter (Ed.), *Contemporary chief information officers: Management experiences* (pp. 83–94). Hershey, PA: IGI Global. doi:10.4018/978-1-59904-078-3.ch007

Thomas, J. C. (2004). Public involvement in public administration in the information age: Speculations on the effects of technology. In M. Malkia, A. Anttiroiko, & R. Savolainen (Eds.), *eTransformation in governance: New directions in government and politics* (pp. 67–84). Hershey, PA: IGI Global. doi:10.4018/978-1-59140-130-8.ch004

Treiblmaier, H., & Chong, S. (2013). Trust and perceived risk of personal information as antecedents of online information disclosure: Results from three countries. In F. Tan (Ed.), *Global diffusion and adoption of technologies for knowledge and information sharing* (pp. 341–361). Hershey, PA: IGI Global. doi:10.4018/978-1-4666-2142-8.ch015

van Grembergen, W., & de Haes, S. (2008). IT governance in practice: Six case studies. In W. van Grembergen & S. De Haes (Eds.), *Implementing information technology governance: Models, practices and cases* (pp. 125–237). Hershey, PA: IGI Global. doi:10.4018/978-1-59904-924-3.ch004

van Os, G., Homburg, V., & Bekkers, V. (2013). Contingencies and convergence in European social security: ICT coordination in the back office of the welfare state. In M. Cruz-Cunha, I. Miranda, & P. Gonçalves (Eds.), *Handbook of research on ICTs and management systems for improving efficiency in healthcare and social care* (pp. 268–287). Hershey, PA: IGI Global. doi:10.4018/978-1-4666-3990-4.ch013

Velloso, A. B., Gassenferth, W., & Machado, M. A. (2012). Evaluating IBMEC-RJ's intranet usability using fuzzy logic. In M. Cruz-Cunha, P. Gonçalves, N. Lopes, E. Miranda, & G. Putnik (Eds.), *Handbook of research on business social networking: Organizational, managerial, and technological dimensions* (pp. 185–205). Hershey, PA: IGI Global. doi:10.4018/978-1-61350-168-9.ch010

Villablanca, A. C., Baxi, H., & Anderson, K. (2009). Novel data interface for evaluating cardiovascular outcomes in women. In A. Dwivedi (Ed.), *Handbook of research on information technology management and clinical data administration in healthcare* (pp. 34–53). Hershey, PA: IGI Global. doi:10.4018/978-1-60566-356-2.ch003

Villablanca, A. C., Baxi, H., & Anderson, K. (2011). Novel data interface for evaluating cardiovascular outcomes in women. In *Clinical technologies: Concepts, methodologies, tools and applications* (pp. 2094–2113). Hershey, PA: IGI Global. doi:10.4018/978-1-60960-561-2.ch806

Virkar, S. (2011). Information and communication technologies in administrative reform for development: Exploring the case of property tax systems in Karnataka, India. In J. Steyn, J. Van Belle, & E. Mansilla (Eds.), *ICTs for global development and sustainability: Practice and applications* (pp. 127–149). Hershey, PA: IGI Global. doi:10.4018/978-1-61520-997-2.ch006

Virkar, S. (2013). Designing and implementing e-government projects: Actors, influences, and fields of play. In S. Saeed & C. Reddick (Eds.), *Human-centered system design for electronic governance* (pp. 88–110). Hershey, PA: IGI Global. doi:10.4018/978-1-4666-3640-8.ch007

Wallace, A. (2009). E-justice: An Australian perspective. In A. Martínez & P. Abat (Eds.), *E-justice: Using information communication technologies in the court system* (pp. 204–228). Hershey, PA: IGI Global. doi:10.4018/978-1-59904-998-4.ch014

Wang, G. (2012). E-democratic administration and bureaucratic responsiveness: A primary study of bureaucrats' perceptions of the civil service e-mail box in Taiwan. In K. Kloby & M. D'Agostino (Eds.), *Citizen 2.0: Public and governmental interaction through web 2.0 technologies* (pp. 146–173). Hershey, PA: IGI Global. doi:10.4018/978-1-4666-0318-9.ch009

Wangpipatwong, S., Chutimaskul, W., & Papasratorn, B. (2011). Quality enhancing the continued use of e-government web sites: Evidence from e-citizens of Thailand. In V. Weerakkody (Ed.), *Applied technology integration in governmental organizations: New e-government research* (pp. 20–36). Hershey, PA: IGI Global. doi:10.4018/978-1-60960-162-1.ch002

Wedemeijer, L. (2006). Long-term evolution of a conceptual schema at a life insurance company. In M. Khosrow-Pour (Ed.), *Cases on database technologies and applications* (pp. 202–226). Hershey, PA: IGI Global. doi:10.4018/978-1-59904-399-9.ch012

Whybrow, E. (2008). Digital access, ICT fluency, and the economically disadvantages: Approaches to minimize the digital divide. In F. Tan (Ed.), *Global information technologies: Concepts, methodologies, tools, and applications* (pp. 1409–1422). Hershey, PA: IGI Global. doi:10.4018/978-1-59904-939-7.ch102

Whybrow, E. (2008). Digital access, ICT fluency, and the economically disadvantages: Approaches to minimize the digital divide. In C. Van Slyke (Ed.), *Information communication technologies: Concepts, methodologies, tools, and applications* (pp. 764–777). Hershey, PA: IGI Global. doi:10.4018/978-1-59904-949-6.ch049

Wickramasinghe, N., & Geisler, E. (2010). Key considerations for the adoption and implementation of knowledge management in healthcare operations. In M. Saito, N. Wickramasinghe, M. Fuji, & E. Geisler (Eds.), *Redesigning innovative healthcare operation and the role of knowledge management* (pp. 125–142). Hershey, PA: IGI Global. doi:10.4018/978-1-60566-284-8.ch009

Wickramasinghe, N., & Geisler, E. (2012). Key considerations for the adoption and implementation of knowledge management in healthcare operations. In *Organizational learning and knowledge: Concepts, methodologies, tools and applications* (pp. 1316–1328). Hershey, PA: IGI Global. doi:10.4018/978-1-60960-783-8.ch405

Wickramasinghe, N., & Goldberg, S. (2007). A framework for delivering m-health excellence. In L. Al-Hakim (Ed.), *Web mobile-based applications for healthcare management* (pp. 36–61). Hershey, PA: IGI Global. doi:10.4018/978-1-59140-658-7.ch002

Wickramasinghe, N., & Goldberg, S. (2008). Critical success factors for delivering m-health excellence. In N. Wickramasinghe & E. Geisler (Eds.), *Encyclopedia of healthcare information systems* (pp. 339–351). Hershey, PA: IGI Global. doi:10.4018/978-1-59904-889-5.ch045

Wyld, D. (2009). Radio frequency identification (RFID) technology. In J. Symonds, J. Ayoade, & D. Parry (Eds.), *Auto-identification and ubiquitous computing applications* (pp. 279–293). Hershey, PA: IGI Global. doi:10.4018/978-1-60566-298-5.ch017

Yaghmaei, F. (2010). Understanding computerised information systems usage in community health. In J. Rodrigues (Ed.), *Health information systems: Concepts, methodologies, tools, and applications* (pp. 1388–1399). Hershey, PA: IGI Global. doi:10.4018/978-1-60566-988-5.ch088

Yee, G., El-Khatib, K., Korba, L., Patrick, A. S., Song, R., & Xu, Y. (2005). Privacy and trust in e-government. In W. Huang, K. Siau, & K. Wei (Eds.), *Electronic government strategies and implementation* (pp. 145–190). Hershey, PA: IGI Global. doi:10.4018/978-1-59140-348-7.ch007

Yeh, S., & Chu, P. (2010). Evaluation of e-government services: A citizen-centric approach to citizen e-complaint services. In C. Reddick (Ed.), *Citizens and e-government: Evaluating policy and management* (pp. 400–417). Hershey, PA: IGI Global. doi:10.4018/978-1-61520-931-6.ch022

Young-Jin, S., & Seang-tae, K. (2008). E-government concepts, measures, and best practices. In A. Anttiroiko (Ed.), *Electronic government: Concepts, methodologies, tools, and applications* (pp. 32–57). Hershey, PA: IGI Global. doi:10.4018/978-1-59904-947-2.ch004

Yun, H. J., & Opheim, C. (2012). New technology communication in American state governments: The impact on citizen participation. In K. Bwalya & S. Zulu (Eds.), *Handbook of research on e-government in emerging economies: Adoption, e-participation, and legal frameworks* (pp. 573–590). Hershey, PA: IGI Global. doi:10.4018/978-1-4666-0324-0.ch029

Zhang, N., Guo, X., Chen, G., & Chau, P. Y. (2011). User evaluation of e-government systems: A Chinese cultural perspective. In F. Tan (Ed.), *International enterprises and global information technologies: Advancing management practices* (pp. 63–84). Hershey, PA: IGI Global. doi:10.4018/978-1-60960-605-3.ch004

Zuo, Y., & Hu, W. (2011). Trust-based information risk management in a supply chain network. In J. Wang (Ed.), *Supply chain optimization, management and integration: Emerging applications* (pp. 181–196). Hershey, PA: IGI Global. doi:10.4018/978-1-60960-135-5.ch013

Compilation of References

@UKBLM (n.d.). Official Twitter Page Black Lives Matter UK. Twitter. Retrieved from https://twitter.com/ukblm

1 yılda 3 bin haber linkine erişim engeli! (2016, July 4). Retrieved September 1, 2016, from http://t24.com.tr/haber/1-yilda-3-bin-haber-linkine-erisim-engeli,348456

10 maddede Aktrolleri tanıma rehberi. (2015, September 30). Retrieved August 16, 2016, from http://politikkedi.com/10-maddede-aktrolleri-tanima-rehberi.html

9 Soruda yeni internet yasası. (2014, February 6). Retrieved September 1, 2016, from http://www.diken.com.tr/gecmis-olsun-aknetli-donem-basliyor/

Aboud, F. E. (2003). The formation of in-group favoritism and out-group prejudice in young children: Are they distinct attitudes? *Developmental Psychology*, *39*(1), 48–60. doi:10.1037/0012-1649.39.1.48 PMID:12518808

Abunimah, A. (2009). An ideal medium for a stateless people. *Electronic Intifada*. Retrieved September 1, 2016 from https://electronicintifada.net/content/ideal-medium-stateless-people/9745

Abunimah, A. (2016). Facebook disables accounts of Palestinian editors. *Electronic Intifada*. Retrieved September 29, 2016 from https://electronicintifada.net/blogs/ali-abunimah/facebook-disables-accounts-palestinian-editors

Abutaleb, Y., & Sezer, C. (2016, July 6). Turkey appears to be in vanguard of 'throttling' social media after attacks. *Reuters*. Retrieved September 1, 2016, from http://www.reuters.com/article/us-mideast-crisis-socialmedia-idUSKCN0ZM2O3

Ackerman, S. (2001, January). Uprising without explanation. *EXTRA!* Retrieved September 5, 2016 from http://fair.org/extra/uprising-without-explanation/

Acosta, A. M. (2013). The Impact and Effectiveness of Accountability and Transparency Initiatives: The Governance of Natural Resources. *Development Policy Review*, *31*(1), 89–105. doi:10.1111/dpr.12021

Action.org. (2007). Best practices for advocacy; A dozen tactics, tools and strategies. Retrieved November 2007, from http://www.action.org/documents/ACTION_Best_Practices_Guide_small.pdf

Agnihotri, M. (2015, July 2). XKEYSCORE: NSA's Google for the World's Private Communications. *LinkedIn*. Retrieved from https://www.linkedin.com/pulse/xkeyscore-nsas-google-worlds-private-communications-mayur-agnihotri?published=t

AK Parti'den 6 bin kişilik sosyal medya ordusu. (2013, November 14). Retrieved August 31, 2016, from http://www.hurriyet.com.tr/ak-partiden-6-bin-kisilik-sosyal-medya-ordusu-25115336

AK Parti'den sosyal medya atağı. (2013, June 14). Retrieved August 31, 2016, from http://www.milliyet.com.tr/ak-parti-den-sosyal-medya-atagi/gundem/detay/1722933/default.htm

'Ak Trol' Esat Ç.'nin kimliğini deşifre eden Taraf'a beraat. (2015, April 26). Retrieved August 31, 2016, from http://www.diken.com.tr/ak-trol-esat-c-nin-kimligini-desifre-eden-tarafa-beraat/

'Ak Trol'lerin haritası çıkarıldı: Merkezde Erdoğan'ın danışmanı Varank var. (2015, October 14). Retrieved August 31, 2016, from http://www.diken.com.tr/ak-trollerin-haritasi-cikarildi-merkezde-erdoganin-danismani-varank-var/

Akdeniz, Y. (2015, August 13). Twitter sansürlemede dünya lideriyiz. *Diken*. Retrieved August 31, 2016, from http://www.diken.com.tr/twitter-sansurlemede-dunya-lideriyiz/

Akgül, E. (2015, February 5). Yeni İnternet "Yasası"nı Anlama Kılavuzu. *Bianet*. Retrieved September 1, 2016, from http://bianet.org/bianet/medya/162080-yeni-internet-yasasi-ni-anlama-kilavuzu

Akpojivi, U. (forthcoming). #BringBackOurGirls: Mediated space for citizens empowerment or disempowerment. *New Media & Society*.

Aktroller ne kadar maaş alıyor? (2015, September 29). Retrieved August 31, 2016, from http://www.sozcu.com.tr/2015/gunun-icinden/aktroller-ne-kadar-maas-aliyor-945937/

Aljazeera. (2011, February 11). Hosni Mubarak resigns as president. Retrieved from: http://www.aljazeera.com/news/middleeast/2011/02/201121125158705862.htmlaaa

Al-Jazeera. (2016, April 26). Waiting for 3G: Palestinians call for connections. *Al-Jazeera*. Retrieved November 20, 2017 from http://www.aljazeera.com/news/2016/04/waiting-3g-palestinians-call-connections-160426133858205.html

Allan, S. (2009). Histories of citizen journalism. In S. Allan & E. Thorsen (Eds.), *Citizen journalism: global perspectives* (pp. 17–32). New York: Peter Lang Publishing.

Allan, S., & Thorsen, E. (Eds.). (2009). *Citizen journalism: global perspectives*. New York: Peter Lang Publishing.

Allport, G. W. (1954). *The nature of prejudice*. Cambridge, MA: Addison-Wesley.

Alsaafin, L. (2013). Israel restricts entry of foreigners into Palestinian territories. *Al-Monitor*. Retrieved September 30, 2016 from http://www.al-monitor.com/pulse/originals/2013/03/israel-restricts-foreign-nationals-entry.html

Altuntaş, Ö. (2015a, May 18). AKP Sosyal Medya Merkezi'nde bir gün. *BBC Türkçe*. Retrieved August 31, 2016, from http://www.bbc.com/turkce/haberler/2015/05/150515_akp_sosyal_medya

Altuntaş, Ö. (2015b, June 1). CHP Sosyal Medya Merkezi: 'Amaç, AKP Türkiyesi ile CHP Türkiyesi arasındaki farkı göstermek'. *BBC Türkçe*. Retrieved August 31, 2016, from http://www.bbc.com/turkce/haberler/2015/06/150601_chp_sosyal_medya_gs2015

Amnesty International. (2015). *"Our job is shoot, slaughter and kill". Boko Haram's reign of terror in North-East Nigeria*. London: Amnesty International Ltd.

Amnesty International. (2017). Israel and the Occupied Palestinian Territories. Retrieved November 19, 2017 from https://www.amnesty.org/en/countries/middle-east-and-north-africa/israel-and-occupied-palestinian-territories/report-israel-and-occupied-palestinian-territories/

Anderson, M., & Hitlin, P. (2016). *Social Media Conversations About Race*. New York: Pew Research Center.

Aouragh, M. (2012). *Palestine online: Transnationalism, the internet and the construction of identity*. London: I.B Tauris.

Arınç'tan Ak Trol ve 'troliçe'lere sert cevap. (2016, February 1). Retrieved August 31, 2016, from http://www.abcgazetesi.com/arinctan-ak-trol-ve-trolicelere-sert-cevap-7298h.htm

Armistead, A. L., & Starman, S. (2015). Perception Shaping and Cyber Macht: Russia and Ukraine. In J. Zaaiman and L. Leenen (Eds.), *Proceedings of the 10th International Conference on Cyber Warfare and Security*, Reading, UK (pp. 14-19). Academic Conferences.

Armistead, A. L., & Starman, S. (2014). Global Influence and Cyber Macht. *Journal of Information Warfare*, *13*(1), 47–57.

Associated Press. (2011, March 4). Libya Shuts Down Internet Service Ahead of Planned Anti-Government Protests. Retrieved from http://www.foxnews.com/world/2011/03/04/libya-shuts-internet-service-ahead-planned-anti-government-protests.html

Athwal, H., & Burnett, J. (2014). Investigated or ignored? An analysis of race-related deaths since the Macpherson Report. *Race & Class*, *56*(1), 22–42. doi:10.1177/0306396814531694

Auerbach, Y., & Bloch-Elkon, Y. (2005). Media framing and foreign policy: The elite press vis-a-vis US policy in Bosnia. *Journal of Peace Research*, *42*(1), 83–99. doi:10.1177/0022343305049668

Aurora, M. (2015). Social media for social change. *Connect: TEN*. Retrieved September 7, 2016, from https://www.nten.org/article/social-media-for-social-change/

Baerthlein, T. (2016, August 6). The rise of political bots on social media. *Deutsche Welle*. Retrieved August 31, 2016, from http://www.dw.com/en/the-rise-of-political-bots-on-social-media/a-19450562

Bakr, R. (2012). How we made the world hear Gaza, as citizen journalists. *Electronic Intifada.* Retrieved August 29, 2016 from http://electronicintifada.net/blogs/rana-baker/how-we-made-world-hear-gaza-citizen-journalists

Balkaran, S. (2015, May 27). Post Racial America in the Age of Obama. The Huffington Post. Retrieved September 27, 2016, from http://www.huffingtonpost.com

Ballard, R., Habib, A., Valodia, I., & Zuern, E. (2005). Globalization, marginalization and contemporary social movements in South Africa. *African Affairs*, *104*(417), 615–634. doi:10.1093/afraf/adi069

Banday, M. T., & Mattoo, M. M. (2013). Social Media in e-Governance: A Study with Special Reference to India. *Social Networking*, 2(2), 47–56. doi:10.4236n.2013.22006

Bannister, F., & Connolly, R. (2011). The Trouble with Transparency: A Critical View of Openness in e-governance. *Policy and Internet*, *3*(1), 1–30. doi:10.2202/1944-2866.1076

Barberá, P., Wang, N., Bonneau, R., Jost, J. T., Nagler, J., Tucker, J., & González-Bailón, S. (2015). The critical periphery in the growth of social protests. *PLoS One*, *10*(11), 1–15. doi:10.1371/journal.pone.0143611 PMID:26618352

Barghouti, O. (2011). *Boycott, divestment, sanctions: The global struggle for Palestinian human rights*. Chicago: Haymarket.

Barney, D. (2004). *The network society*. Cambridge: Polity Press.

Baudrillard, J. (1995). *The gulf war did not take place. Translated by P. pattons*. Sydney: Sage Publications.

BBC News. (2011). *Ghana refuses to grant gays' rights despite aid threat*. Retrieved from http://www.bbc.co.uk/news/world-africa-15558769 Accessed on the 27/04/2016

BBC. (2011). England riots: Maps and timeline. Retrieved from http://www.bbc.co.uk

BBC. (2015, September 19). China censors Hong Kong protest posts on social media. Retrieved from http://www.bbc.com/news/world-asia-china-29411270

Beauchemin, C., Borrel, C., & Régnard, C. (2010b). Migrations : Les immigrés et les autres. In P. Simon, C. Beauchemin, & C. Hamel, (Eds.), Trajectoires et Origines. Enquête sur la diversité des populations en France. Premiers résultats (Ch. 2). Paris: Institut national d'études démographiques, pp 19-24.

Beauchemin, C., Hamel, C., Simon, P., & Equipe Te, O. (2010a). *Trajectoires et origines : enquête sur la diversité des populations en France. Premiers résultats*. Paris: Institut National d'Études Démographiques.

Beauchemin, C., Lagrange, H., & Safi, M. (2011). *Transnationalism and immigrant assimilation in France: Between here and there?* Paris: HAL et INED.

Beaumont, P., & Shenker, J. (2011). Egypt's protesters refuse to leave the streets until Mubarak steps down. *The Guardian*. Retrieved from https://www.theguardian.com/world/2011/feb/01/egypt-protest-mubarak-step-down

Begag, A. (2016). La France en panne d'intégration. *Contemporary French Civilization*, *41*(2), 273–277. doi:10.3828/cfc.2016.14

Berggren, E., & Bernshteyn, R. (2007). Organizational transparency drives company performance. *Journal of Management Development*, *26*(5), 411–417. doi:10.1108/02621710710748248

Bertaux, S. (2016). Towards the unmaking of the French mainstream: The empirical turn in immigrant assimilation and the making of Frenchness. *Journal of Ethnic and Migration Studies*, *42*(9), 1496–1512. doi:10.1080/1369183X.2015.1119651

Bidabad, B., Amirostovar, A., & Sherafati, M. (2017). Financial transparency, corporate governance and information disclosure of the entrepreneur's corporation in Rastin banking. *International Journal of Law and Management*, *59*(5), 636–651. doi:10.1108/IJLMA-01-2016-0003

Black, I., & Chulov, M. (2011, February 18). Bahrain, Libya and Yemen try to crush protests with violence. Retrieved from http://www.guardian.co.uk/world/2011/feb/18/bahrain-libya-yemen-protestsviolence

Blumenthal, M., & Carmel, J. (2015). Exposed: Pro-Israel modern day McCarthyites going to extremes to slime human rights activists. *AlterNet*. Retrieved September 30, 2016 from http://www.alternet.org/tea-party-and-right/modern-day-mccarthyists-are-going-extremes-slime-activists-fighting-israels

Bogart, N. (2014, May 9). Can social media really help #BringBackOurGirls and end terrorism in Nigeria? *Global News*, 32-36.

Bolarinwa, O. A. (2015). Principles and methods of validity and reliability testing of questionnaires used in social and health science researches. *The Nigerian Postgraduate Medical Journal*, *22*(4), 195–201. doi:10.4103/1117-1936.173959 PMID:26776330

Bonilla-Silva, E. (2004). From bi-racial to tri-racial: Towards a new system of racial stratification in the USA. *Ethnic and Racial Studies*, *27*(6), 931–950. doi:10.1080/0141987042000268530

Bonilla, Y., & Rosa, J. (2015). # Ferguson: Digital protest, hashtag ethnography, and the racial politics of social media in the United States. *American Ethnologist*, *42*(1), 4–17. doi:10.1111/amet.12112

Boulle, P. H. (2002). La construction du concept de race dans la France d'Ancien Régime. *Outre-mers*, *89*(336/337), 155–175. doi:10.3406/outre.2002.3987

Boyoung, I., & Jinwoo, J. (2001). *Using ICT for Strengthening Government Transparency*. Retrieved September 20, 2016, from http://www.oecd.org/dataoecd/53/55/2537402.pdf

Brahm Levey, G., & Modood, T. (2009). *Secularism, Religion and Multicultural Citizenship*. Cambridge: Cambridge University Press.

Brand, E. S., Ruiz, R. A., & Padilla, A. M. (1974). Ethnic identification and preference: A review. *Psychological Bulletin, 81*(11), 860–890. doi:10.1037/h0037266

Breindl, Y. (2010). Internet-based protest in European policymaking: The case of digital activism. *International Journal of E-Politics, 1*(1), 57–72. doi:10.4018/jep.2010102204

Brown v. Board of Education of Topeka, 347 U.S. 483, 74 S. Ct. 686; 98 L. Ed. 873. (1954).

Brunlof, H. (2017). Editorial: Protest show that nothing has changed. *MG*. Retrieved from http://mg.co.za/article/2017-05-12-00-editorial-protest-show-that-nothing-has-changed

Bryant, L. (2011). Tunisian Prime Minister resigns amid protests. *Voanews*. Retrieved from http://www.voanews.com/a/police-break-up-demonstrations-in-tunis-117009313/135706.html

BTK sosyal medyayı uyardı: Saldırıyla ilgili paylaşım yapanların yasal sorumluluğu var. (2016, June 29). Retrieved September 1, 2016, from http://www.diken.com.tr/btk-sosyal-medyayi-uyardi-saldiriyla-ilgili-paylasimda-bulunanlarin-yasal-sorumlulugu-var/

Bucholz, L., & Wuggenig, U. (2015). Cultural globalization between myth and reality: A case of contemporary visual art. *ART-e-FACT, 4*, 12–34.

Bulman, M. (2016). Death of black teenager detained by police sparks Black Lives Matter protests in UK cities. *The Independent*. Retrieved from http://www.independent.co.uk

Burnett, J. (2013). *Racial Violence: Facing Reality*. London: Institute of Race Relations.

Butler, M. (1996). Clicktivism, slacktivism or real activism. Cultural codes of American activism in the internet era. A M.A. Thesis submitted to the faculty of graduate School, University of Colorado.

Caleffi, P. M. (2015). The 'hashtag': A new word or a new rule? *Skase Journal of Theoretical Linguistics, 13*(2).

Camay, P., & Gordon, A.J. (1998). *Advocacy in Southern Africa: Lessons for the future*. Johannesburg: Cooperative for Research and Education (CORE).

Çamlıbel, C. (2016, February 8). Freedom House Başkanı Lagon: Mülteci akını Batı'nın hatası. *Hürriyet*. Retrieved September 1, 2016, from http://www.hurriyet.com.tr/freedom-house-baskani-lagon-multeci-akini-batinin-hatasi-40050749

Cammaerts, B. (2007). Introduction: Activism and media. In B. Cammaerts & N. Carpentier (Eds.), *Reclaiming the media: Communication rights and democratic media roles* (pp. 217–224). Chicago, IL: University of Chicago Press.

Cammaerts, B. (2015). Social media and activism. In R. Hwa (Ed.), *The international encyclopedia of digital communication and society* (pp. 1027–1034). Oxford: Willey-Blackwell.

Cammearts, B. (2015). 'Technologies of self – medication: Affordances and constraints of social media for protest movements. In J. Udam & A. Vestergaard (Eds.), *Civic Engagement and Social Media: Political Participation Beyond Protest* (pp. 87–110). New York: Palgrave Macmillan. doi:10.1057/9781137434166_5

Campbell, K. K. (2005). Agency: Promiscuous and prote-an. *Communication and Critical/ Cultural Studies*, *2*(1). doi:10.1080/1479142042000332134

Cashmore, E., & McLaughlin, E. (Eds.). (1991). *Out of Order: Policing Black People*. Routledge.

Castelliti, C. (2016, July 24). Reportage au cœur de la première manifestation "Black Lives Matter France. *Les Inrocks*. Retrieved from http://www.lesinrocks.com/2016/07/24/actualite/reportage-coeur-de-manifestation-black-live-matter-france-11855472/

Castells, M. (1996). *The rise of the network society*. Blackwell.

Castells, M. (1996). *The rise of the network society. Malden MA: Blackwell.*

Castells, M. (2001). *The Internet galaxy: Reflections on the Internet, business and society*. Oxford: Oxford University Press. doi:10.1007/978-3-322-89613-1

Castells, M. (2009). *Communication power*. Oxford: Oxford University Press.

Castells, M. (2012). *Networks of outrage and hope social movements in the Internet age*. Cambridge: Polity Press.

Castells, M. (2015). *Networks of Outrage and Hope: Social Movements in the Internet Age*. Cambridge, UK: Polity.

Castles, S. (2000). *Ethnicity and globalization: From migrant worker to transnational citizen*. London: Sage.

Catron, J. (2012). Gaza thwarts Israeli propaganda with Twitter. *Electronic Intifada*. Retrieved August 26, 2016 from http://electronicintifada.net/content/gaza-thwarts-israeli-propaganda-twitter/11964

Cerise, L. G. (2015). Activism or "Slacktivism?": Digital media and organizing for social change. *Communication Teacher*, *29*(2), 81–85. doi:10.1080/17404622.2014.1003310

Chabrow, E. (2012, March 6). LulzSec Leader Strikes Deal with Feds, Government Information Security. Retrieved from http://www.govinfosecurity.com/articles.php?art_id=4558&opg=1

Chehata, H. (2010). Israeli censorship. *Middle East Monitor*. Retrieved September 8, 2016 from http://www.middleeastmonitor.com/reports/by-dr-hanan-chehata/1449-israeli-censorship

CHP 'AKtroller' için komisyon kurulmasını istedi. (2016, March 23). Retrieved August 31, 2016, from http://t24.com.tr/haber/chp-aktroller-icin-komisyon-kurulmasini-istedi,333304

Christoph, S., Enrico, C., & Alison, G. (2013). Internet going mobile: internet access and use in 11 African countries. *info, 15*(5), 34-51.

Cleaver, H. (1998). The Zapatista effect: The Internet and the rise of an alternative public fabric. *Journal of International Affairs*, *51*, 621–632.

Cloete, K. (2015). What does the working class stand to gain from the #ZumaMustFall campaign? *Daily Maverick*. Retrieved from: http://www.dailymaverick.co.za/opinionista/2015-12-15-what-does-the-working-class-stand-to-gain-from-the-zumamustfall-campaign/#.V8_CQPl96Hs

Cockerham, C. (2011). The defining moment: Children's conceptualization of race and experiences with racial discrimination. *Ethnic and Racial Studies*, *34*(4), 662–682. doi:10.1080/01419870.2011.535906 PMID:21532908

Cole, N. (2015).h What is Globalization, A Sociological Definition: About Education. Retrieved from: http://sociology.about.com/od/Ask-a-Sociologist/fl/Globalization.htm

Collaboration on International ICT Policy in East and Southern Africa. (2015). *ICT in Governance in Tanzania*. Kampala: CIPESA. Retrieved September 29, 2016, from http://www.cipesa.org/?wpfb_dl=205

Communication Security Group. (2017). Seecrypt. Retrieved from http://www.seecrypt.com/

Comninos, A. (2011, June). Twitter revolutions and cyber crackdowns, Association for Progressive Communications. Retrieved from http://www.apc.org/en/system/files/AlexComninos_MobileInternet.pdf

Cook, J. (2009). Internet users paid to spread Israeli propaganda. *Electronic Intifada*. Retrieved September 19, 2016 from http://electronicintifada.net/content/internet-users-paid-spread-israeli-propaganda/8355

Cook, J. (2008). *Disappearing Palestine: Israel's experiments in human despair*. London: Zed Books.

Cooper, F. (1996). *Decolonization and African society: The labor question in French and British Africa*. Cambridge University Press. doi:10.1017/CBO9780511584091

CRAN. (2007). Les discriminations à l'encontre des populations noires de France (short report). Retrieved from le-cran.fr/document-cran-associations-noires-de-france/63-tns-sofres-premiere-enquete-statistique-sur-les-noirs-de-france.pdf

Crush, J., & Ramachandran, S. (2014). *Xenophobic violence in South Africa: Denialism, minimalism & realism*. Cape Town: International Migration Research Centre.

Dadoo, S. (2013). Using Twitter to spread the word about #AhavaCrimes. *Mondoweiss*. Retrieved September 27, 2016, from http://mondoweiss.net/2013/04/twitter-spread-ahavacrimes/#sthash.Vqh2gyZ9.dpuf

Dadoo, S. (2014, August 4). Israel is losing the war in Gaza one tweet at a time. *The Star*. Retrieved September 27, 2016 from http://mediareviewnet.com/2014/08/israel-is-losing-the-war-in-gaza-one-tweet-at-a-time/

Dahlgren, P. (2000). Media citizens and civic culture. In M. Gurevitch & J. Curran (Eds.), *Mass Media and society* (3rd ed.). London: Edward Arnold.

Dahlgren, P. (2000). The Internet and the democratisation of civic culture. *Political Communication, 17*(4), 335–340. doi:10.1080/10584600050178933

Dahlgren, P. (2005). *Internet, public spheres and political communication.* London: Routledge.

Daniel, P. (1973). *The Shadow of Slavery: Peonage in the South, 1901-1969.* London, Oxford: Oxford University Press.

Daniel, P. (1979). The Metamorphosis of Slavery, 1865-1900. *The Journal of American History, 66*(1), 88–99. doi:10.2307/1894675

Darwish, A., & Lakhtaria, K. I. (2011). The Impact of the New Web 2.0 Technologies in Communication, Development, and Revolutions of Societies. *Journal of Advanced Information Technologies, 2*(4), 204–216.

De Choudhury, M., Jhaver, S., Sugar, B., & Weber, I. (2016). Social Media Participation in an Activist Movement for Racial Equality. AAAI In (Ed.), *Proceedings of the Tenth International AAAI Conference on Web and Social Media* (pp. 92-101).

de Wet, P. (2015, February 27). What the 'spy cables' taught us, Mail and Guardian. Retrieved from http://mg.co.za/article/2015-02-27-what-the-spy-cables-taught-us

Deibert, R., & Rohozinski, R. (2010). Beyond Denial: Introducing Next-Generation Information Access Controls. In R. Deibert, J. Palfrey, R. Rohozinski, & J. Zittrain (Eds.), *Access Controlled: The Shaping of Power, Rights, and Rule in Cyberspace* (pp. 3–13). Cambridge, MA: The MIT Press.

Deibert, R., & Rohozinski, R. (2012). Contesting Cyberspace and the Coming Crisis of Authority. In R. Deibert, J. Palfrey, R. Rohozinski, & J. Zittrain (Eds.), *Access Contested: Security, Identity, and Resistance in Asian Cyberspace* (pp. 21–41). Cambridge, MA: The MIT Press.

Demirel, F. (2016, July 1). Zenmate'in Türkiye'deki iOS ve Android indirme sayıları ortalama yüzde 1850 arttı. *Webrazzi.* Retrieved September 1, 2016, from http://webrazzi.com/2016/07/01/zenmatein-turkiyedeki-ios-ve-android-indirme-sayilari-ortalama-yuzde-1850-artti/

Demirhan, K. (2014). Social Media Effects on the Gezi Park Movement in Turkey: Politics Under Hashtags. In B. Pătruţ & M. Pătruţ (Eds.), *Social Media in Politics: Case Studies on the Political Power of Social Media* (pp. 281–314). New York: Springer.

DeNardis, L. (2012). Hidden levers of Internet control: An infrastructure-based theory of Internet governance. *Journal of Information Communicatio Socialis, 15*(3), 720–738.

Dencik, L., & Cable, J. (2017). The Advent of Surveillance Realism: Public Opinion and Activist Responses to the Snowden Leaks. *International Journal of Communication, 11*, 763–781.

Department of Arts and Culture, South Africa. (2016). *Social cohesion programme.* Retrieved from http://www.dac.gov.za/social-cohesion

Department of Justice and Constitutional Development, Republic of South Africa. (1996). Constitution of the Republic of South Africa.

Department of Labour (2017). Hospitality sector minimum wage for 2017/2018. Retrieved from: www.labour.gov.za/DOL/media-statements/2017/hospitality-sector-minimum-wage-for-2017-2018

Diani, M. (2000). Social movement networks virtual and real. *Information Communication and Society*, *3*(3), 386–401. doi:10.1080/13691180051033333

Digital Governance Initiative. (2016). *Interactive Service Model.* Retrieved September 30, 2016, from http://www.digitalgovernance.org/index.php/models/interactive-service

Dodd, V. (2016). Police blame worst rise in recorded hate crime on EU referendum: The Guardian. Retrieved September 20, 2016 from https://www.theguardian.com

Doğan, R. (2016, August 10). 'Erdoğan'a hakaret'te bugün: Facebook paylaşımı nedeniyle gözaltı. *Diken*. Retrieved September 1, 2016, from http://www.diken.com.tr/erdogana-hakarette-bugun-facebook-paylasimi-nedeniyle-gozalti/

Dombeu, J., & Rannyai, N. (2013). African E-government Research Land Scape. *African Journal of Information Systems*, *6*(3), 85–119.

Downing, J. (2001). *Radical media*. Thousand Oaks: Sage Publications.

Dugard, J. (2007). Report of the Special Rapporteur on the situation of human rights in the Palestinian territories occupied since 1967. Retrieved November 19, 2017 from http://www.diakonia.se/Documents/public/IHL/Publications/Dugard_January2008.pdf

Duggan, P. (2016, January 8). Why Special Operations Forces in US Cyber-Warfare? *The Cyber Defense Review*. Retrieved from http://www.cyberdefensereview.org/2016/01/08/why-special-operations-forces-in-us-cyber-warfare/

Duke, B. (2014). Religious fanatics blamed for Nigeria's draconian anti-gay bill, approved this week. *The Free Thinker*. Retrieved from http://www.religious-fanatics-blamed-for-nigerias-draconian-antigay-bill-approved-this-week/thefreethinker.com.

Durham, C. W. (Ed.). (2015). *Religion and the Secular State*. Madrid: International Center for Law and Religion Studies, Universidad Complutense.

East African Community. (2013). *Protocol on Regional Information and Communication Technology*. Retrieved September 5, 2016, from www.eac.int

Edwards, F., Howard, P., & Joyce, M. (2013). *Digital activism and non-violent conflicts. Digital Activism Project*. Seattle: University of Washington.

Egbert, A. M. (2013). Wanted for Love but not here: The travelling right of LGBT Activists. *Critical Legal Thinker*. Retrieved September 7, 2016, from http://criticallegalthinking.com/2013/08/12/wanted-for-love-but-not-here-the-travelling-rights-of-african-lgbt-activists/

End the Occupation. (2010). 'Stolen Beauty' victory: Costco feels the love. *End The Occupation*. Retrieved September 29, 2016 from http://blog.endtheoccupation.org/2010/01/stolen-beauty-victory-costco-feels-love.html

Endong, F. P. C. (2015a). Christian resistance to gay-proselytism in a secular Nigeria: Anathema or social heroism? *ERAS: European Review of Applied Sociology*, *8*(11), 5–13.

Endong, F. P. C. (2015b). Framing the queers and the LGBT right movement in Africa: A study of Nigerian bloggers and web journalists. *Journal of Global Research in Education and Social Sciences*, *6*(4), 50–60.

Endong, F. P. C. (2016). The LGBT right movement in Africa and the myth of the Whiteman's superiority. *Journal of Globalization Studies*, *7*(1), 3–15.

Endong, F. P. C., & Vareba, A. L. (2015). Resisting anti-gay laws through media advocacy and online communities of meaning: A study of Nigerian homosexuals. *Journal for Studies in Management and Planning*, *10*(2), 94–106.

England, S. (2010). Mixed and multiracial in Trinidad and Honduras: Rethinking mixed-race identities in Latin America and the Caribbean. *Ethnic and Racial Studies*, *33*(2), 195–213. doi:10.1080/01419870903040169

Entous, A., Nakashima, E., & Miller, G. (2016, December 9). Secret CIA assessment says Russia was trying to help Trump win White House. *The Washington Post*. Retrieved from https://www.washingtonpost.com/world/national-security/obama-orders-review-of-russian-hacking-during-presidential-campaign/2016/12/09/31d6b300-be2a-11e6-94ac-3d324840106c_story.html

Erdoğan Biliyorsunuz ben bu sosyal medyaya karşıyım. (2016, July 2). Retrieved August 31, 2016, from http://tr.sputniknews.com/turkiye/20160702/1023691179/erdogan-ataturk-havalimani-ziyaret.html

Erdoğan withdraws defamation cases except for HDP. (2016, August 1). Retrieved September 1, 2016, from http://bianet.org/english/freedom-of-expression/177406-erdogan-withdraws-defamation-cases-except-for-hdp

'Erdoğan'a hakaret'te bugün: 14 yaşındaki A.Ş'nin Facebook yorumuna iddianame. (2016, August 9). Retrieved September 1, 2016, from http://www.diken.com.tr/erdogana-hakarette-bugun-14-yasindaki-s-nin-facebook-yorumuna-iddianame/

Erdoğan'a hakaretten 1845 dosya. (2016, March 2). Retrieved September 1, 2016, from http://www.cumhuriyet.com.tr/haber/siyaset/490484/Erdogan_a_hakaretten_1845_dosya.html

EWN. (2017). SCA Upholds High Court Decision on Zuma Charges.

Falk, R. (2010). Report of the Special Rapporteur on the situation of human rights in the Palestinian territories occupied since 1967. Retrieved November 19, 2017 from http://www.un.org/ga/search/view_doc.asp?symbol=A/65/331

Favell, A. (2001). Philosophies of Integration. Immigration and the Idea of Citizenship in France and Britain (2nd ed.), New York: Palgrave in association with Centre for Research in Ethnic Relations, University of Warwick. doi:10.1057/9780333992678

FBI. (2016). Hate Crime Statistics: Criminal Justice Information Services Division: Government website. Retrieved November 22, 2017 from https://www.fbi.gov/news/stories/2016-hate-crime-statistics

FBI. (2017, August 3) Black Identity Extremists Likely Motivated to Target Law Enforcement Officer. Counterterrorism Division, Government report: Retrieved November 22, 2017 fromhttps://assets.documentcloud.org/documents/4067711/BIE-Redacted.pdf

Federal Republic of Nigeria. (2012). *Same sex marriage prohibition act.* Abuja: Government Printer.

Fenton, N., & Barassi, V. (2011). Alternative media and social networking sites: The politics of individuation and political participation. *Communication Review*, *14*(3), 179–196. doi:10.1080/10714421.2011.597245

Ferraro, T. (2012). Determining the beginning and end of an occupation under international humanitarian law. *International Review of the Red Cross*, *94*(885), 133–163. Retrieved November 19, 2017 from https://www.icrc.org/eng/assets/files/review/2012/irrc-885-ferraro.pdf doi:10.1017/S181638311200063X

Findlay, S. (2016). Hashtag Fail? #BringBackOurGirls has 'nothing to show.' Retrieved from: http://www.heraldlive.co.za/news/world/2016/04/14/hashtag-fail-bringbackourgirls-nothing-show/

Fisk, R. (2001, September 3). CNN caves in to Israel over its references to illegal settlements. *The Independent*. Retrieved September 3, 2016 from http://www.commondreams.org/headlines.shtml?/headlines01/0903-01.htm

Fjeldstad, O.-H., & Moore, M. (2009). Revenue Authorities and Public Authoriesin Africa. *The Journal of Modern African Studies*, *47*(1). doi:10.1017/S0022278X08003637

Flock, E. (2011, June 3). Syria internet services shut down as protesters fill streets. *The Washington Post*. Retrieved from https://www.washingtonpost.com/blogs/blogpost/post/syria-internet-services-shut-down-as-protesters-fill-streets/2011/06/03/AGtLwxHH_blog.html?utm_term=.ee1d83e83848

Franklin, J. (2013, November 17). Camila Vallejo, student leader, gets ready for a seat in Chilean congress. *The Guardian*. Retrieved from https://www.theguardian.com/world/2013/nov/17/chilean-student-activists-congress

Franklin, S. M. (2014). *After the rebellion: Black youth, social movement activism, and the post-civil rights generation*. NYU Press. doi:10.18574/nyu/9780814789384.001.0001

Freedom House. (2014). *The Struggle for Turkey's Internet*: Retrieved September 1, 2016, from https://freedomhouse.org/sites/default/files/The%20Struggle%20for%20Turkey's%20Internet.pdf

Freelon, D., McIlwain, C. D., & Clarke, M. D. (2016). *Beyond The Hashtags: #Ferguson, #Blacklivesmatter and the online struggle for offline justice*. Washington, DC: Centre for Media & Social Impact. American University.

Freeman, G. P. (2015). *Immigrant labor and racial conflict in industrial societies: The French and British experience, 1945-1975*. Princeton University Press.

Friel, H., & Falk, R. (2007). *Israel-Palestine on record: How the New York Times misreports conflict in the Middle East*. London and New York: Verso.

Fuchs, C. (2011a). New media, web 2.0 and surveillance. *Sociology Compass*, *5*(2), 134–147. doi:10.1111/j.1751-9020.2010.00354.x

Fuchs, C. (2011b). Web 2.0, prosumption, and surveillance. *Surveillance & Society*, *8*(3), 288–309. Retrieved from http://ojs.library.queensu.ca/index.php/surveillance-and-society/article/view/4165/4167

Fuchs, C. (2012a). Some Reflections on Manuel Castells' Book Networks of Outrage and Hope. Social Movements in the Internet Age. *TripleC*, *10*(2), 775–797.

Fuchs, C. (2012b). Critique of the Political Economy of Web 2.0 Surveillance. In C. Fuchs, K. Boersma, A. Albrechtslund, & M. Sandoval (Eds.), *Internet and Surveillance: The Challenges of Web 2.0 and Social Media* (pp. 31–70). New York: Routledge.

Fuchs, C. (2014). *Social Media: A Critical Introduction*. London: Sage.

Fuchs, C. (2015). Social Media Surveillance. In S. Coleman & D. Freelon (Eds.), *Handbook of Digital Politics* (pp. 395–414). Cheltenham, UK: Edward Elgar.

Galusky, W. (2003). Identifying with information citizen empowerment, the Internet and the environment anti-toxins movement. In M. McCaughey & M. Ayers (Eds.), *Cyberactivism online activism in theory and practice* (pp. 185–199). London: Routledge.

García, C., Chauveau, P., Ledezma, J., & Pinto, M. (2013, August 11-13). What can social media teach us about protests? In *Proceedings of the 4th International Conference on Collaborative Innovation Networks (COINs13),* Santiago de Chile.

Gauthier-Faure, M. (2016, July 31). Mort d'Adama Traoré: le New York Times dénonce l'impunité de la police française. Retrieved from http://www.marianne.net/mort-adama-traore-new-york-times-denonce-impunite-police-francaise-100244747.html

Gay and Lesbian Humanist Association. (2007b). Nigeria: Humanist jeered for supporting gay rights. *Gay Humanist Quarterly*, *7*, 23–24.

Geneva International Organisation for Migration (2013). Advocacy role. Retrieved September 28, 2016 from, http://www.unhcr.org/advocacy.html

Gentzkow, M., & Allcott, H. (2017, January). Social Media and Fake News in the 2016 Election. *Sanford University*. Retrieved from https://people.stanford.edu/gentzkow/papers

Gerbaudo, P. (2012). *Tweets and the Streets: Social Media and Contemporary Activism*. London: Pluto.

Gerbaudo, P. (2017). From cyber-autonomism to cyber-populism: An ideological history of digital activism. *Journal for a Global Sustainable Information Society*, *15*(2), 15–34.

Gevisser, M. (2015). Homosexuality and the global culture wars. *International Journal of Mass Communication*, *16*(3), 10–25.

Ghobadi, S., & Clegg, S. (2015). "These days will never be forgotten...": A critical mass approach to online activism. *Information and Organization*, *25*(1), 52–71. doi:10.1016/j.infoandorg.2014.12.002

Gibson, M. (2014, May 7). Can a social media campaign really #BringBackOurGirls? *TIME Magazine*.

Gideon, Z., & Alouis, M. (2013). Systems, Processes and Challenges of Public Revenue Collection in Zimbabwe. *American International Journal of Contemporary Research*, *3*(2), 49–59.

Giglietto, F. A., Rossi, L., & Bennato, D. (2014). The Open Laboratory: Limits and Possibilities of Using Facebook, Twitter, and Youtube as a Research Data Source. In K. Bredl, J. Hunniger, & J. L. Jensen (Eds.), *Methods for Analyzing Social Media* (pp. 5–19). London, New York: Routledge.

Gladwell, M. (2010, October 4). Small Change: Why the Revolution Will Not Be Tweeted. *The New Yorker*, 42-49.

Gladwell, M. (2010, October 4). Small change: Why the revolution will not be tweeted. *The New Yorker*.

Goffman, E. (1963). *Stigma: Notes on the management of spoiled identity*. London: Pelican Books.

Goode, L. (2009). Social news, citizen journalism and democracy. *New Media & Society*, *11*(11), 1287–1305. doi:10.1177/1461444809341393

Greenwald, G. (2016, September 12). Facebook is collaborating with the Israeli government to determine what should be censored. *The Intercept*. Retrieved September 30, 2016 from https://theintercept.com/2016/09/12/facebook-is-collaborating-with-the-israeli-government-to-determine-what-should-be-censored/

Grierson, J. (2016). Black Lives Matter activists admit trespass after City airport protest. Retrieved from, https://www.theguardian.com

Gross, G. (2017, March 7). WikiLeaks' CIA document dump shows agency can compromise Android, TVs. *Computer World*. Retrieved from http://www.computerworld.com/article/3177797/security/wikileaks-cia-document-dump-shows-agency-can-compromise-android-tvs.html

Groves, H. E. (1951). Separate but Equal--The Doctrine of Plessy v. Ferguson. *Phylon*, *12*(1), 66–72. doi:10.2307/272323

Grzywinska, I., & Batorsski, D. (2016). How the influence of social networking sites challenges agenda-setting theory. *Nontekst y Spoleczne*, *4*(1), 19–32.

Guardian. (2016, September 12). Facebook and Israel to work to monitor posts that incite violence. *Guardian*. Retrieved September 30, 2016 from https://www.theguardian.com/technology/2016/sep/12/facebook-israel-monitor-posts-incite-violence-social-media?CMP=twt_gu

Gül'ün eski danışmanı Sever: Pelikan'a izin en yukarıdan, trollerin başında Varank var. (2016, May 9). Retrieved August 31, 2016, from http://www.diken.com.tr/gulun-danismani-sever-pelikana-izin-en-yukaridan-trollerin-basinda-varank-var/

Gumede, P. (2015, September 3). Till jam protest at Woolworths. *South Coast Fever*. Retrieved September 30, 2016 from http://www.news24.com/SouthAfrica/Local/South-Coast-Fever/Till-jam-protest-at-Woolworths-20150902

Gumede, W. (2015, March 1). Spy leaks have revealed the rot, Independent Online. Retrieved from http://www.iol.co.za/sundayindependent/spy-leaks-have-revealed-the-rot-1.1825190

Guo, C., & Saxton, G. (2013, January). 8). Tweeting social change: How social media are changing non-profit advocacy. *Nonprofit and Voluntary Sector Quarterly*, 43–57.

Gur, H., & Winer, S. (2016, July 20). Bill cracking down on social media incitement passes initial reading. *Times of Israel*. Retrieved September 29, 2016 from http://www.timesofisrael.com/bill-cracking-down-on-social-media-incitement-passes-initial-reading/

Habermas, J. (1989). *The structural transformation of the public sphere: an inquiry into a category of bourgeois society*. Cambridge, MA: MIT Press.

Hackl, A. (2013). *Digital activism and the future of the LGBT movement: Insight from recent research and case study*. Retrieved September 7, 2016, from http://climateshiftproject.org/2013/12/08/digital-activism-and-the-future-of-the-glbt-movement-insights-from-recent-research-and-case-studies/

Hardwick, N. A. (2012). Theoretically justifying human right: A critical analysis. *The International Relation Student*. Retrieved September, 13, 2016; from http://www.e-ir.info/2012/08/05/theoretically-justifying-human-rights-a-critical-analysis/

Hassa, S. H. (2015). *Social media and the Arab Spring*. USA: The State University of New Jersey.

Hestres, L. (n.d.). Preaching to the choir: Internet-mediated advocacy, issue public mobilization and climate change. *New Media & Society*, *56*, 87–99.

Hitchcock, J. (2016, January-March). Social media rhetoric of the transnational Palestinian-led boycott, divestment, and sanctions movement. *Social Media + Society*, *2*(1). doi:10.1177/2056305116634367

Hjarvard, S. (2001). New media and the globalization of the public sphere. In S. Hjarvard (Ed.), *News in a globalized society*. Goteborg: Nordicom.

Hoberman, J. M. (1997). *Darwin's Athletes: How Sport has Damaged Black America and Preserved the Myth of Race*. Boston: Houghton Mifflin Co.

Howard, N. P., & Hussain, M. M. (2013). *Democracy's fourth wave?* Oxford: Oxford University Press. doi:10.1093/acprof:oso/9780199936953.001.0001

Human Rights Watch. (2006). Written statement: Human Rights Council special session on the Occupied Palestinian Territories. Retrieved November 19, 2017 from https://www.hrw.org/news/2006/07/05/human-rights-council-special-session-occupied-palestinian-territories-july-6-2006

Human Rights Watch. (2010). Separate and unequal: Israel's discriminatory treatment of Palestinians in the Occupied Palestinian Territories. Retrieved November 19, 2017 from http://www.hrw.org/en/reports/2010/12/19/separate-and-unequal

Iazzolino, G. (2010). Digital shahid: From broadcast media to citizen journalism in Palestine. *Arab Media and Society*. Retrieved September 25, 2016 from http://www.arabmediasociety.com/?article=763

Ibahrine, M. (2017). Women Hashtactivism: Civic Engagement in Saudi Arabia. *World Academy of Science, Engineering and Technology. International Journal of Information and Communication Engineering*, *11*(3), 79.

Ibeh, N. (2014, June 14). Interview: Meet the man who generated #BringBackOurGirls hashtag. *Premium Times*, 32-36.

Ilesanmi, Y. (2016). Would the percentage of Nigerians condemning jungle justice decrease if the ALUU 4 victims were gays caught in the act? YEMMYnisting. *Free Thought Blogs*. Retrieved from http://www.yemmynisting/freethought-blogs.com

Information and Communication Technologies Authority. (2016). *Electronic Communications in Turkey*, *2016*, Q1. Ankara: BTK.

Initiative for Equal Rights. (2014). *Survey on homosexuality perception in Nigeria*. Lagos: TIERs – The Initiative for Equal Rights.

INQUEST. (2017). BAME deaths in police custody. Retrieved from http://inquest.org.uk/statistics/bame-deaths-in-police-custody

Institute of Middle East Understanding (IMEU). (2015). In their own words: Senior Israeli officials on the Palestinian question. Retrieved September 30, 2016 from http://imeu.org/article/in-their-own-words-senior-israeli-officials-on-the-palestinian-question

International Communications Union. (2017). Measuring the Information Society Report (Vol. 1).

International Court of Justice. (2004). Legal consequences of the construction of a wall in the Occupied Palestinian Territory (Request for advisory opinion). Retrieved November 19, 2017 from http://www.unrod.org/docs/ICJ-Advisory2004.pdf

International Federation for Accountants. (2013). *Good Governance in the Public Sector*. New York: IFAC.

International Organisation for Migration. (2015). 'Global migration trends fact sheet, Retrieved September 26, 2016 from, https://www.iom.int/news/iom-releases-global-migration-trends-2015-factsheet

İnternet 'zincir'lendi: Artık erişim yasağı bir bakanın iki dudağı arasında. (2015, March 27). Retrieved September 1, 2016, from http://www.diken.com.tr/internete-zincir-geldi-tibe-genis-yetkiler-veren-internet-duzenlemesi-yasalasti/

İnternette darbe girişimini övdüğü iddiasıyla 4 kişi tutuklandı. (2016, July 20). Retrieved September 1, 2016, from http://t24.com.tr/haber/internette-darbe-girisimini-ovdugu-iddiasiyla-2-kisi-tutuklandi,350931

IRR. (2013). Facing up to racial violence. Retrieved September from http://www.irr.org.uk/news/facing-up-to-racial-violence/

IRR. (2014). Investigated or ignored? Press Release. Retrieved from http://www.irr.org.uk/news/investigated-or-ignored/

IRR. (n.d.). Criminal justice system statistics. Retrieved from http://www.irr.org.uk/research/statistics/criminal-justice/

Isin, E., & Ruppert, E. (2017). Citizen Snowden. *International Journal of Communication*, *11*, 843–857.

İşte 10 maddede internet sansürü. (2014, February 5). Retrieved September 1, 2016, from http://www.cumhuriyet.com.tr/haber/bilim-teknik/38013/iste_10_maddede_internet_sansuru.html

Jacobs, B., & Murray, W. (2017, August 13) Donald Trump under fire after failing to denounce Virginia white supremacists. *The Guardian*. Retrieved November 22, 2017 from www.theguardian.com

Jansen, F. (2010). Digital activism in the Middle East: Mapping issue networks in Egypt, Iran, Syria and Tunisia. *Knowledge Management for Development Journal*, *6*(1), 37–52. doi:10.1080/19474199.2010.493854

Jausset, J. S. (2016, Aug 8). France: abattu par la police, Babacar Guèye a été accusé de tentative de meurtre par deux des policiers. Jeune Afrique http://www.jeuneafrique.com/346546/societe/abattu-par-police-babacar-gueye-accuse-de-tentative-de-meurtre/

Jhally, S., & Ratzkoff, B. (2003). Peace, propaganda and the promised land. *Media Education Foundation*. Retrieved August 5, 2016 from https://www.youtube.com/watch?v=GSXFNSvInIE

Jones, A., & Lobianco, T. (2016, September 5). Obama: Colin Kaepernick 'exercising constitutional right'. *CNN*. Retrieved from http://edition.cnn.com

Jordan, T., & Taylor, P. A. (2004). *Hacktivism and cyberwars. Rebels with a cause?* London: Routledge.

Kamzi, A. (2011, September 27). How anonymous emerged to occupy Wall Street, The Guardian. Retrieved from http://www.guardian.co.uk/commentisfree/cifamerica/2011/sep/27/occupy-wall-street-anonymous

Karaim, R. (2011). Gay rights. Has the movement's success sparked a backlash? *CQ Global Researcher*, *5*(5), 107–132.

Karakaş, B. (2015, October 9). Prof. Yaman Akdeniz: İnternet yasası Bilal Erdoğan gibi büyük çocuklar için değişti. *Diken*. Retrieved September 1, 2016, from http://www.diken.com.tr/prof-yaman-akdeniz-internet-yasasi-bilal-erdogan-gibi-buyuk-cocuklar-icin-degistirildi/

Karatzogiani, A. (2017). Beyond hashtag: How a new wave of digital activists is changing society. *The Conversation*. Retrieved November 3, 2017, from https://theconversation.com/beyond-hashtags-how-a-new-wave-of-digital-activists-is-changing-society-57502

Kasapoğlu, Ç. (2014, August 7). Cumhurbaşkanı adaylarının sosyal medya kampanyaları. *BBC Türkçe*. Retrieved August 31, 2016, from http://www.bbc.com/turkce/haberler/2014/08/140806_sosyalmedya_secim

Keck, M., & Sikkink, K. (1998). *Activists beyond borders*. Ithaca: Cornell University Press.

Kelbert, A. W. (2016). Climate change is a racist crisis: that's why Black Lives Matter closed an airport. *The Guardian*. Retrieved from https://www.theguardian.com

Kestler-D'Amours, J. (2011). Israel investing $1.6 million in 'new media warriors'. *Electronic Intifada*. Retrieved September 8, 2016 from http://electronicintifada.net/content/israel-investing-16-million-new-media-warriors/9245

Khagram, S., Riker, J. V., & Sikkink, K. (2002). *Restructuring world politics: Transnational social movements, networks, and norms: Project MUSE*. Minneapolis: University of Minnesota Press.

Khalid, I. (2015, September 1). From Chibok to global reckoning: The impact of social media on the #BringBackOurGirls campaign. *Native Edge*. Retrieved November 2, 2017, from http://nativedge.com/blog/from-chibok-to-global-reckoning-the-impact-of-social-media-on-the-bringbackourgirls-campaign/

Khalidi, R. (2006). *The iron cage: The story of the Palestinian struggle for statehood*. Boston: Beacon Press.

Khan, J. (2015). Black Lives Matter has become a global movement. The root. Retrieved from: https://www.theroot.com

Kiel, C. (2011). How transnational advocacy networks mobilize: Applying the literature on interest groups to international action. *Josef Korbel Journal of Advanced International Studies*, *3*, 77–101.

Kim, S., & Lee, J. (2011). E-Participation, Transparency, and Trust in Local Government. In *Proceedings of the 1st Global Conference on Transparency Research*. Newark: Rutger University.

King, G., Pan, J., & Roberts, M. (2013). How Censorship in China Allows Government Criticism but Silences Collective Expression. *The American Political Science Review*, *107*(2), 326–343. doi:10.1017/S0003055413000014

Klein, N. (2014) Why #BlackLivesMatter Should Transform the Climate Debate. *The Nation*. Retrieved September 5, 2016 from: https://www.thenation.com

Kravets, D. (2011, January 27). Internet down, tens of thousands protest in Friday of wrath. *Wired*. Retrieved from http://www.wired.com/threatlevel/2011/01/egypt-internet-down/#

Kuntsman, A., & Stein, R. (2015). *Digital militarism: Israel's occupation in the social media age*. Stanford: Stanford University Press.

Kürtlere 'satır gösteren' 'Ak Trol'ün nikah şahidi Cumhurbaşkanı Erdoğan. (2015, June 13). Retrieved August 31, 2016, from http://www.diken.com.tr/kurtlere-satir-gosteren-ak-trolun-nikah-sahidi-cumhurbaskani-erdogan/

Lee, D. (2014, October 30). The role of social media in Occupy protests, on the ground and around the world, The South China Morning Post. Retrieved from http://www.scmp.com/news/hong-kong/article/1628305/role-social-media-occupy-protests-ground-and-around-world

Lee, M. (2011, February 1). Obama urges Mubarak to step down. *Columbia Missourian*. Retrieved from http://www.columbiamissourian.com/stories/2011/02/01/obama-urges-mubarak-step-down-now

Legal Centre for Freedom of Movement (Gisha). (2008). Gaza closure defined: Collective punishment position paper on the international law definition of Israeli restrictions on movement in and out of the Gaza Strip. Retrieved November 19, 2017 from http://www.gisha.org/userfiles/file/publications/GazaClosureDefinedEng.pdf

Lekic, S. (2011, February 11). Denmark prime minister Lars Loekke Rasmussen calls on Egypt's Mubarak to resign. *Huffingtonpost.com*. Retrieved from http://www.huffingtonpost.com/2011/02/11/denmark-lars-loekkerasmussen-mubarak-egypt_n_821804.html

Lentin, A. (2016) Luqman Onikosi's deportation shows we are all being asked to become border guards. *The Guardian*. Retrieved from, https://www.theguardian.com

Lewis, K., Gray, K., & Meierhenrich, J. (2014). The structure of online activism. *Sociological Science*, *1*, 1–9. doi:10.15195/v1.a1

Li, D. K. (2014, July 31). Soldier's selfies might prove Russia's direct role in Ukraine. *The New York Post*. Retrieved from http://nypost.com/2014/07/31/soldiers-selfies-might-prove-russias-role-in-ukraine/

Lindon, G., & Roe, S. (2017). *Deaths in police custody: A review of the international evidence. Research Report 95*. London: Home Office, Crown Copyright.

Loken, M. (2014). # BringBackOurGirls and the Invisibility of Imperialism. *Feminist Media Studies*, *14*(6), 1100–1101. doi:10.1080/14680777.2014.975442

Lokot, T. (2014, March 2). Ukrainian journalists take regime's corruption public with YanukovychLeaks. *Global Voices Online*. Retrieved from http://globalvoicesonline.org/2014/03/02/ukrainian-journalists-take-regimes-corruption-public-with-yanukovychleaks

Lowensohn, J. (2014, July 18). Russia Spotted editing Wikipedia page about downed Malaysia Airlines jet. *The Verge*. Retrieved from http://www.theverge.com/2014/7/18/5917099/russia-spotted-editing-wikipedia-page-of-downed-malaysia-air-jet

Lubua, E. W., & Maharaj, M. (2014). State Information Protection Laws and e-Transparency. In *ST-Africa 2014 Conference Proceedings*. Younde: IIMC International Information.

Lubua, E. (2014). E-Transparency and Information Sharing in the Public Sector. *International Journal of Computer Science and Business Informatics*, *14*(1), 1694–2108.

Macaulay, J. R. (2013). Africa and homosexuality. *AGW: A Globe of Witness – The Witness Magazine*. Retrieved from http://www.thewitness.org-marriage-in-church-in-africa_queering-the-church.htm

Machado, M. B. (2015). Between control and hacker activism: The political actions of Anonymous Brazil. *Historica, Ciencias. Saude*, *22*, 1–18.

Machery, E., & Faucher, L. (2005). Social construction and the concept of race. *Philosophy of Science*, *72*(5), 1208–1219. doi:10.1086/508966

Madrigal, A. (2011, January 24). The inside story of how Facebook responded to Tunisian hacks. *The Atlantic*. Retrieved from http://www.theatlantic.com/technology/archive/2011/01/the-inside-story-of-how-facebookresponded-to-tunisian-hacks/70044/#

Manley, D., & Lassourd, T. (2014). *Tanzania and Statoil: What Does the Leaked Agreement mean to Citizens.* Retrieved November 20, 2017, from https://resourcegovernance.org/sites/default/files/Tanzania_Statoil_20140808.pdf

Manning , K. (2014, November 28). In Chile, Protesting Students Tweak Tweets to Win Global Support. *Wired*. Retrieved from http://www.wired.com/2011/11/chile-students/

Mano W. & Mukhongo, L. L. (2016). Towards alternative media as critical media in Africa. *Journal of Alternative and Community,* (1).

Maskovsky, J. (2017). Toward the anthropology of white nationalist postracialism: Comments inspired by hall, goldstein, and Ingram's "The hands of donald trump". *HAU*, *7*(1), 433–440. doi:10.14318/hau7.1.030

Maslow, W., & Robison, J. B. (1953). Civil Rights Legislation and the Fight for Equality, 1862-1952. *The University of Chicago Law Review. University of Chicago. Law School*, *20*(3), 3. doi:10.2307/1597662

Mbarawa, M. (2014). (Interview). Retrieved August 28, 2016, from http://www.the-report.net/tanzania/nov2014/1166-interview-professor-makame-mbarawa-minister-of-communications-science-and-technology

McAuley, J. (2016). Black Lives Matter movement comes to France. But will it translate? Washington Post.

McComb, M., Shaw, D. L., & Weaver, D. (1997). *Communication and democracy: Exploring the intellectual frontiers of agenda-setting theory*. Erlbaum.

McGuinness, E. (2014) Insight into social media usage by advocacy groups in the area of same-sex marriage. *EMCG Public Relations*. Retrieved September 7, 2016, from http://emcgpr.com/blog/insights-social-media-usage-advocacy-groups-area-sex-marriage/

McLaughlin, M. (2016). The Dynamic History of #BlackLivesMatter Explained, This is how a transformed into a movement. *The Huffington Post*. Retrieved June 30, 2016, from http://www.huffingtonpost.co.uk

McNair, B. (2011). *An Introduction to Political Communication*. London: Routledge.

McQuail, D. (2009). *Mass communication theory* (5th ed.). London: Routledge.

Melki, J., & Mallat, S. (2014). Digital activism: Efficacies and burdens of social media for civic activism. *Arab Media and Society, 19*.

Meyer, M., & Workman, B. C. (2013). Emerging adult usage of social networks as sites of activism: A critical examination of the TOMS and TWLOHA movements. *Ohio Communication Journal, 51*, 53–77. Retrieved from http://ohiocomm.org/main/

Mhiripiri, N. A., & Mutsvairo, B. (2013). Social Media, New ICTs and the Challenges Facing the Zimbabwe Democratic Process. In A.A. Olorunnisola & A. Douai, (Eds.), New Media Influence on Social and Political Change in Africa (pp. 402 -421). Hershey, PA: IGI Global.

Miller, G. (2010, December 21). CIA launches task force to assess impact of U.S. cables' exposure by WikiLeaks. *Washington Post*. Retrieved from http://www.washingtonpost.com/wp-dyn/content/article/2010/12/21/AR2010122104599.html

Mitra, A. (2001). Marginal Voices in Cyberspace. *New Media & Society, 3*(1), 29–48. doi:10.1177/14614448010030010003

Mkentane, L. (2017) Radical economic transformation will save SA's economy: Dlamini-Zuma. *IOL*. Retrieved from http://www.iol.co.za/news/politics/development/radical-economic-transformation-save-sas-economy-dlamini-zuma-10757750

Monaghan, F. (2003). Seeing red: Social media and football fan activism. *The Information Society, 6*(20), 143–168.

Mondoweiss. (2011). Stolen Beauty boycott culture jam turns Ahava's online marketing contest into a social media #FAIL. *Mondoweiss*. Retrieved September 29, 2016 from http://mondoweiss.net/2011/05/stolen-beauty-boycott-culture-jam-turns-ahava%E2%80%99s-online-marketing-contest-into-a-social-media-fail/#sthash.DeAZ27TO.dpuf

Moore, H. L., & Selchow, S. (2012). 'Global Civil Society' and the Internet 2012: Time to Update Our Perspective. In M. Kaldor et al... (Eds.), *Global Civil Society 2012* (pp. 28–40). Palgrave Macmillan, UK. doi:10.1057/9780230369436_2

Mora, F. A. (2014). Emergent digital activism: The generational/technological connection. *Journal of Community Informatics*, *10*(1).

Morozov, E. (2009b). *Brave New World Of Slacktivism*. Retrieved December 4, 2016, from http://www.npr.org/templates/story/story.php?storyId=104302141

Morozov, E. (2009b). Texting toward utopia: Does the Internet spread democracy? *Boston Review*. Retrieved from http://bostonreview.net/BR34.2/morozov.php

Morozov, E. (2009a, Fall). Iran: Downside to the "Twitter Revolution". *Dissent*, 10–14. Retrieved from http://www.evgenymorozov.com/morozov_twitter_dissent.pdf

Morozov, E. (2011). *The net delusion*. New York: Public Affairs.

Morozov, E. (2011). *The Net Delusion: The Dark Side of Internet Freedom*. New York: PublicAffairs.

Morozow, E. (2011). *The net delusion: The dark side of Internet freedom*. New York: Perseus Book Group.

Morrison, K. (2015, July 30). Social Media Activism: Sandra Bland, Police Brutality and #BlackLivesMatter. *Adweek.com*. Retrieved from http://www.adweek.com

Morrow, M., & al-Omrani, K. (2011). Activists preparing for 'third intifada.' *Electronic Intifada*. Retrieved November 22, 2017 from https://electronicintifada.net/content/activists-preparing-third-intifada/9937

Morse, F. (2014, May 13). The bring back our girl campaign is working: Boko Haram should be scared of a hashtag. *The Independent*, 51-56.

Mortimer, C. (2017, January 3). M62 Shooting: Charts show difference between police shootings in the US and the UK. *The Independent*. Retrieved November 19, 2017 from http://www.independent.co.uk

Mothobi, L. (2016, September). (telephone interview) (e-mail communication).

Motion, J., Heath, R. L., & Leitch, S. (2016). *Social media and public relation: Fake friends and powerful publics*. New York: Taylor & Francis Group.

Moyer, J. (2017). Political activism on social media has grown some teeth. *Pacific Standards*. Retrieved November 3, 2017, from https://psmag.com/social-justice/social-media-activism

Moyo, D. (2010). 'The new media as monitors of democracy. Mobile phones and Zimbabwe's 2008 election'. Paper presented at the conference on election processes, liberation movements and democratic change in Africa, Maputo, April 8-11.

Moyo, D. (2010). The new media as monitors of democracy. Mobile phones and Zimbabwe's 2008 election. *Paper presented at the conference on election processes, liberation movements and democratic change in Africa*, Maputo, April 8-11.

Mpofu, S. (n.d.). The power of citizen journalism in Zimbabwe. Unpublished manuscript.

Mujere, J., & Mwatwara, W. (2015). Citizen Journalism and National Politics in Zimbabwe: The Case of the 2008 and 2013 Elections. In B. Mutsvairo (Ed.), Participatory Politics and Citizen Journalism in a Networked Africa: A Connected Continent (pp. 215 – 228). London: Palgrave, MacMillan.

Mullings, L. (2005). Interrogating Racism: Toward an Antiracist Anthropology. *Annual Review of Anthropology*, *34*(1), 667–693. doi:10.1146/annurev.anthro.32.061002.093435

Munusamy, R. (2016). Chasing Butterflies and Bogeymen: Mantashe beats 'regime change' drum. *Daily Maverick*. Retrieved from http://www.dailymaverick.co.za/article/2016-05-13-chasing-butterflies-and-bogeymen-mantashe-beats-regime-change-drum/

Munusamy, R. (2017). #ZumaMustFall: A misguided campaign, Zuma's helping hand. Daily Maverick. Retrieved from firstthings.dailymaverick.co.za/article?id=73576#WhGpgROCzsE

Murdoch, D. (2016). *Black power: America's armed resistance*. Documentary, UK: BBC; Retrieved from http://www.bbc.co.uk/programmes/p03t9g3j

Mutsvairo, B. (2015). Recapturing Citizen Journalism: Processes and Patterns Citizen Journalism and National Politics in Zimbabwe: The Case of the 2008 and 2013 Elections. In B. Mutsvairo (Ed.), Participatory Politics and Citizen Journalism in a Networked Africa: A Connected Continent. London: Palgrave, Macmillan.

Nabulsi, M. (2014). "Hungry for freedom": Palestine youth activism in the era of social media. In L. Herrera (Ed.), *Wired citizenship: Youth learning and activism in the Middle East* (pp. 105–119). New York: Routledge.

Nagarajan, C. (2013). How politicians and the media made us hate immigrants (Blog post). *Open Democracy Online*. Retrieved from https://www.opendemocracy.net/transformation/chitra-nagarajan/how-politicians-and-media-made-us-hate-immigrants

Naicker, C. (2016). From Marikana to #feesmustfall: The praxis of popular politics in South Africa. *Urbanisation*, *1*(1), 53–61. doi:10.1177/2455747116640434

National Broadcasting Commission. (2012). *N.B.C. Code*. Abuja: NBC.

National Economic and Social Right Initiative. (2015). *What are the Basis Principles of the Human Rights Framework*? New York: NESRI. Retrieved September 13, 2016, from https://www.nesri.org/programs/what-are-the-basic-principles-of-the-human-rights-framework

National Planning Commission, South Africa. (2009). *National development plan of South Africa 2030: Our future, make it work. The Department in the Presidency of South Africa.* Pretoria: Government Printers.

NCCHR. (2016). *Report on the prevention of racism, anti-semitism and xenophobia.* Paris: CNCDH.

Ndiaye, P. (2008). *La condition noire. Essai sur une minoritéfrançaise.* Paris: Calmann-Lévy.

News, N. B. C. (2015). Hashtag wars: Who is behind the Nigeria #BringBackOurGirls movement? *NBC News.* Retrieved from https://www.nbcnews.com/tech/social-media/hashtag-wars-whos-behind-nigeria-bringbackourgirls-movement-n100771

News24. (2017). Zuma sidesteps flames. Retrieved from:http://www.news24.com/Archives/City-Press/Zuma-sidesteps-flames-20150429

Nieman, D. G. (1994). *From Slavery to Sharecropping: White Land and Black Labor in the Rural South, 1865-1900.* London: Garland.

Nisbet, M. (2013). *Digital activism and the future of the LGBT movement: Insight from recent research and case study.* Retrieved September 7, 2016, from http://climateshiftproject.org/2013/12/08/digital-activism-and-the-future-of-the-glbt-movement-insights-from-recent-research-and-case-studies/

Norris, P. (2004). The bridging and bonding role of online communities. In P. N. Howard & S. Jones (Eds.), *Society online: The Internet in context* (pp. 31–41). Thousand Oaks: Sage. doi:10.4135/9781452229560.n2

Nyamnjoh, F. (2016). *#RhodesMustFall: Nibbling at resilient colonialism in South Africa.* Mankon Bamenda: Langaa Research & Publishing CIG.

Obadare, E. (2014). Dangerous associations: Legal homophobia and the changing politics of civil society. *ISTR Africa: Civil Society Research Network*, *8*(1), 4–6.

Oborne, P., & Jones, J. (2009). The pro-Israel lobby in Britain. *Open Democracy.* Retrieved September 18, 2016 from http://www.opendemocracy.net/ourkingdom/peter-oborne-james-jones/pro-israel-lobby-in-britain-full-text

Office for National Statistics. (2012a). *Ethnicity and National Identity in England and Wales: 2011. National Identity.* London Crown Copyright.

Office for National Statistics. (2012b). *Ethnicity and National Identity in England and Wales: 2011. Migration.* London: Crown Copyright.

Ogundimu, N.K. (2013). Facebook and digital activism: Conversation about peace building in Nigeria between a President and his "friends" on Facebook. *International Journal of social Sciences and Humanities Reviews*, *4*(1), 218-206.

Ojo, J. (2013). E-governance: An imperative for sustainable grass root development in Nigeria. *Journal of Public Administration and Policy Research*, *6*(4), 77–89. doi:10.5897/JPAPR2013.0264

Okanlawon, K. (2011). *Same gender marriage prohibition bill: Public hearing at the senate hearing room, National Assembly complex*. Abuja: MCD.

Oladepo, T. (2016). Digital activism and Nigeria's emerging public sphere. *Journal of Law. Social Justice and Global Development, 13*(4).

Olivier, M. (2013). Transnational sex politics, conservative Christianity and antigay activism in Uganda. *Studies in Social Justice, 7*(1), 83–105. doi:10.26522sj.v7i1.1056

Oluwatobi, S.O., & Ogunrinola, O.I. (2011). Government Expenditure on Human Capital Development: Implications for Economic Growth in Nigeria. *Journal of Sustainable Development, 4*(3), 72–80.

Omotoso A (2016, September). (Interview)..

Open Whisper Systems. (2016). Privacy that fits in your pocket. Retrieved from https://whispersystems.org/

Oremus, W. (2013, June 3). Turkish Prime Minister Blames Twitter for Unrest, Calls It "the Worst Menace to Society". *Slate*. Retrieved September 3, 2016, from http://www.slate.com/blogs/future_tense/2013/06/03/turkey_protests_prime_minister_erdogan_blames_twitter_calls_social_media.html

Osai, O. (2014). Hashtag activism makes the invisible visible. *The Mantle*. Retrieved November 3, 2017, from http://www.mantlethought.org/other/hashtag-activism-makes-invisible-visible

Pager, D. (2003). The Mark of a Criminal Record. *American Journal of Sociology, 108*(5), 937–975. doi:10.1086/374403

Painter, N. I. (2006). *Creating black Americans: African-American history and its meanings, 1619 to the present*. USA: Oxford University Press.

Palestinian Central Bureau of Statistics (PCBS). (2015). Statistics on internet usage in the OPT. Retrieved September 6, 2016 from http://pcbs.gov.ps/portals/_pcbs/PressRelease/Press_En_IntDyInfoSoc2015E.pdf

Papacharissi, Z. (2009). Introduction. In Z. Papacharissi (Ed.), Journalism and Citizenship: New Agendas in Communication. London: Routledge.

Pappé, I. (2006). *The ethnic cleansing of Palestine*. London: Oneworld.

Pauw, J. (2017). *The President's Keepers: Those keeping Zuma in power and out of prison*. Cape Town: Tafelberg.

Peace Now. (2017). Settlements data – population. Retrieved November 18, 2017 from http://peacenow.org.il/en/settlements-watch/settlements-data/jerusalem

Pen American Centre. (2015). *Silenced voices, threatened lives: The impact of Nigeria's anti-LGBTI laws on freedom of expression*. Abuja: Pen Nigeria.

Pew Research Center. (2013). King's Dream Remains an Elusive Goal; Many Americans See Racial Disparities. Retrieved from http://www.pewsocialtrends.org/2013/08/22/kings-dream-remains-an-elusive-goal-many-americans-see-racial-disparities/4/

Philo, G., & Berry, M. (2004). *Bad news from Israel*. London: Pluto Press.

Piccinini, E., Gregory, R., & Kolbe, L. M. (2015). Changes in the producer-consumer relationship – Towards digital Transformation. In *Proceedings of the 12th international Conference on Wirtschaftsinformatik*, Osnabruck, Germany, March 4-6.

Pidd, H. (2016). Thousands attend Black Lives Matter solidarity march in Manchester. The Guardian. Retrieved from https://www.theguardian.com/uk

Plessy v. Ferguson, 63 U.S. 537, 16 S. Ct. 1138; 41 L. Ed. 256. (1896).

Plumer, B. (2013, Aug 28). Ten charts show how the U.S. has changed for the better since MLK's speech. *The Washington Post*. Retrieved August 28, 2016 from www.washingtonpost.com

Poell, T. (2015). Social Media Activism and State Censorship. In D. Trottier & C. Fuchs (Eds.), *Social Media, Politics and the State: Protests, Revolutions, Riots, Crime and Policing in the Age of Facebook, Twitter and Youtube* (pp. 189–206). New York: Routledge.

Porta, D., & Mosca, L. (2005). Global-net for global movement? A network for networks for a movement of movement. *Journal of Public Policy*, *25*(1), 165–190. doi:10.1017/S0143814X05000255

Postill, J. (2012). Digital politics and political engagement. In H. Horst & D. Miller (Eds.), *Digital anthropology* (pp. 165–184). London: Berg Publishers.

Poulsen, K., & Zetter, K. (2010, June 6). U.S. Intelligence Analyst Arrested in Wikileaks Video Probe. *Wired*. Retrieved from http://www.wired.com/threatlevel/2010/06/leak/

Prison Reform Trust. (2016.). Projects & Research. Retrieved from http://www.prisonreformtrust.org.uk/ProjectsResearch/Race

Qawasmi, H., & Othman, D. (2016). *Hashtag Palestine: Palestinian social media activity during 2015*. Haifa: Arab Centre for Social Media Advancement (7amleh). Retrieved September 4, 2016 from http://www.7amleh.org/en/article/62

Quartz. (2015, November 19). Israel is finally allowing Palestine to have 3G. Retrieved September 28, 2016 from http://qz.com/554746/israel-is-finally-allowing-palestine-to-have-3g/

Racisme, S. O. S. (2016, July 12). Les discriminations dans l'accès à l'emploi public: un rapport bienvenu. Retrieved from http://sos-racisme.org/communique-de-presse/les-discriminations-dans-lacces-a-lemploi-public-un-rapport-de-bienvenue/

Ramluckan, T. (2016). Social Media as a Crisis Communications and Disaster Management Tool: A South African Governance Perspective [DAdmin Dissertation]. University of KwaZulu-Natal, Durban, South Africa.

Ramluckan, T., Sayeed Ally, S. E., & van Niekerk, B. (2017). Twitter Use in Student Protests: The Case of South Africa's #FeesMustFall Campaign. In M. E. Korstanje (Ed.), *Threat Mitigation and Detection of Cyber Warfare and Terrorism Activities* (pp. 221–254). Hershey, PA: IGI. doi:10.4018/978-1-5225-1938-6.ch010

Rashid, S. (2003). An overview of the role of the international media regarding the Palestinian-Israeli conflict. *Paper presented at the Alternative Information Centre seminar*, Boston. Retrieved September 27, 2016 from https://electronicintifada.net/content/role-international-media-palestinian-israeli-conflict/4853

Reitan, R. (2007). *Global activism*. New York: Routledge.

Reuters Institute. (2016). *Reuters Institute Digital News Report 2016*: Retrieved September 1, 2016, from https://reutersinstitute.politics.ox.ac.uk/sites/default/files/Digital-News-Report-2016.pdf

Robbins, A. (2016). BDS victory: Ahava moving factory out of occupied West Bank. *Mondoweiss*. Retrieved September 29, 2016 from http://mondoweiss.net/2016/03/bds-victory-ahava-moving-factory-out-of-occupied-west-bank/

Robinson, J. J. (2011, February 2). Maldavian president joins calls for Mubarak to step down. Retrieved from http://minivannews.com/politics/maldivian-president-joins-calls-for-mubarak-to-step-down-15715

Roche, J. P. (1951). The Future of "Separate but Equal". *Phylon*, *12*(3), 219–226. doi:10.2307/271632

Rushe, D., & Walker, S. (2014, July 20). MH17 crash: Kerry lays out evidence of pro-Russia separatists' responsibility. *The Guardian*. Retrieved from http://www.theguardian.com/world/2014/jul/20/mh17-crash-kerry-evidence-pro-russia-separatists-responsibility

Russel, A., & Waisbard, S. (2017). The Snowden Revelations and the Networked Fourth Estate. *International Journal of Communication*, *11*, 858–878.

Rutland, A., Hitti, A., Mulvey, K. L., Abrams, D., & Killen, M. (2015). When does the ingroup like the out-group? Bias among children as a function of group norms. *Psychological Science*, *26*(6), 834–842. doi:10.1177/0956797615572758 PMID:25888686

Sabanadze, N. (2010). Globalization and Nationalism: The Relationship Revisited. In *Globalization and Nationalism: The Cases of Georgia and the Basque Country* (pp. 169–186). Central European University Press.

Sabao, C. (2016). Shades of the GNU in Zimbabwe (2009 – 13). Linguistic discourse analysis of representations of transitional politics in Zimbabwean newspapers. In D. O. Orwenjo, O. Oketch, & A. H. Tunde (Eds.), *Political Discourse in Emergent, Fragile, and Failed Democracies* (pp. 306–327). Hershey, PA: IGI Global. doi:10.4018/978-1-5225-0081-0.ch017

Sabao, C., & Chingwaramusee, V. R. (2017). Citizen journalism on Facebook and the challenges of media regulation in Zimbabwe. In N. A. Mhiripiri & T. Chari (Eds.), *Media Law, Ethics, and Policy in the Digital Age* (pp. 193–206). Hershey, PA: IGI Global. doi:10.4018/978-1-5225-2095-5.ch011

Sadighi, D. (2017). How hashtag activism helped raise awareness about Boko Haram. *Teen Vogue*. Retrieved November 3, 2017 from https://www.teenvogue.com/story/hashtag-activism-raise-awareness-boko-haram/

Salzburg Academy. (2015). *The social media and the LGBT community. Finding a voice through the social media: The LGBT community*. Retrieved September 7, 2016, from http://www.salzburg.umd.edu/unesco/social-media-and-lgbt-community

Satell, G. (2014, January 18). If you doubt that social media has changed the World, take a look at Ukraine. *Forbes*. Retrieved from http://www.forbes.com/sites/gregsatell/2014/01/18/if-you-doubt-that-social-media-has-changed-the-world-take-a-look-at-ukraine/

Sawant, N. (2017, February 17). The Fake News problem in India can get out of hand if not controlled in due time; experts tell us why. *FirstPost*. Retrieved from http://tech.firstpost.com/news-analysis/the-fake-news-problem-in-india-can-get-out-of-hand-if-not-controlled-in-due-time-experts-tell-us-why-362791.html

Scheper-Hughes, N. (2017). Another country? racial hatred in the time of trump: A time for historical reckoning. *HAU*, *7*(1), 449–460. doi:10.14318/hau7.1.032

Scheufele, D. (1999, Winter). Framing as a theory of media effects. *Journal of Communication*, 103-122.

Schroeder, R. (2017). Towards a theory of digital media. *Information Communication and Society*, *33*(1), 1–18.

Schunemann, W. J., Stier, S., & Steiger, S. (2015). Is there a transnationalisation of public sphere? A comparism of two global political issues. Presented at ECPR General conference, Montreal, August 26-29.

Scott, J. T. & Maryman, J. (2016). Using social media as a tool to complement advocacy efforts. *Global Journal of Community Psychology Practice*, 7(5).

Segar, M. (2016, November 30). Shame as a political weapon: Donald Trump and the US presidential election. *The Conversation Africa*. Retrieved from http://theconversation.com/shame-as-a-political-weapon-donald-trump-and-the-us-presidential-election-69029

Sen, A. (2005). Elements of a theory of human rights. *Philosophy & Public Affairs*, *32*(4), 315–356. doi:10.1111/j.1088-4963.2004.00017.x

Serbest gazeteci Emin Demir tutuklandı. (2016, May 31). Retrieved September 1, 2016, from https://www.evrensel.net/haber/281413/serbest-gazeteci-emin-demir-tutuklandi

Sergeant, P., & Taggs, C. (2014). *The language of social media: Identity and community on the Internet*. New York: Palgrave MacMillan. doi:10.1057/9781137029317

Sezgin Tanrıkulu Profiline Atatürk resmi koymuş, AKP'li troller... (2016, March 13). Retrieved August 31, 2016, from http://www.abcgazetesi.com/sezgin-tanrikulu-profiline-ataturk-resmi-koymus-akpli-troller-10561h.htm

Shapiro, R. (2017, November 6). Trump says deadly Texas shooting isn't a guns issue, it's a mental health problem. *The Huffington Post*. Retrieved November 22, 2017 fromhttp://www.huffingtonpost.co.uk

Shearlaw, M. (2015, April 14). Did the #BringBackOurGirl campaign make a difference in Nigeria? *The Guardian*.

Sheen, D. (2014). Incitement to hate: Testimony to the Russell Tribunal on Palestine. Retrieved September 30, 2016 from https://www.youtube.com/watch?v=SDNFdjwolaI&list=PLBDtcbghfMdsKkGO9MFG5MPxC3s8gyGES&index=5

Shirk, S. L. (2011). *Changing Media, Changing China*. Oxford, UK: Oxford University Press.

Shirky, C. (2011). The Political Power of Social Media: Technology, the Public Sphere, and Political Change. *Foreign Affairs*, *90*(1), 28–41.

Silver, C. (2016). Mossad-linked group sues Facebook for $1 billion. *Electronic Intifada*. Retrieved September 30, 2016 from https://electronicintifada.net/blogs/charlotte-silver/mossad-linked-group-sues-facebook-1-billion

Sivitanides, M. & Shah, V. (2011). The era of digital activism. *Conference for Information Systems Applied Research (CONISAR) Proceedings*, *4*(1842), 1-8.

Sivitanides, M. & Shah, V. (2011). The era of digital activism. *Conference for Information Systems Applied Research (CONISAR) Proceedings*, *4*(1842).

Sky News. (2011). Middle East: See facts about all the countries in the region. Retrieved from http://news.sky.com/skynews/Interactive-Graphics/middleeast

Smedley, A., & Smedley, B. D. (2005). Race as biology is fiction, racism as a social problem is real: Anthropological and historical perspectives on the social construction of race. *The American Psychologist*, *60*(1), 16–26. doi:10.1037/0003-066X.60.1.16 PMID:15641918

Smith, C. (2015). The technology of hope: Twitter and the #BringBackOurGirls campaign [M.A. Thesis]. Royal Roads University.

Social Pathologist. (2010). *Traditionalism and conservatism: The old versus the right*. Retrieved from http://traditionalism-and-conservatism/theoldvstheright/the-social-pathologist.com

Sokullu, S., & Demir, B. (2013, September 19). AKP'den sosyal medya atağı. *Deutsche Welle Türkçe*. Retrieved August 31, 2016, from http://www.dw.com/tr/akpden-sosyal-medya-ata%C4%9F%C4%B1/a-17101383

Son bir yılda 6 bombalı saldırıda 344 kişi hayatını kaybetti, 1682'si yaralandı. (2016, August 21). Retrieved September 1, 2016, from http://www.diken.com.tr/son-bir-yilda-16-bombali-saldirida-344-kisi-hayatini-kaybetti-1682si-yaralandi/

South Africa, B. D. S. (2014). Successful #BoycottWoolworths "Seng Khatele" flashmob. *YouTube*. Retrieved September 30, 2016 from https://www.youtube.com/watch?v=_6Y-oHEw61U&list=PL_FuAw3qkivow_Li9JWKSI-OhlmU21A68&index=4

South African Human Rights Commission. (2010). *Report on the SAHRC investigation into issues of rule of law: Justice and impunity arising out of the 2008public violence against non-nationals*. Johannesburg: Human Rights Commission.

Southern African Development Community. (2012). *ICT Sector Plan*. Retrieved August 30, 2016, from http://www.sadc.int/files/9413/5293/3532/Regional_Infrastructure_Development_Master_Plan_ICT_Sector_Plan.pdf

'Sövme Timi' En Az Bin Lira Maaş Alıyormuş... (2015, September 29). Retrieved September 1, 2016, from https://onedio.com/haber/-sovme-timi-en-az-bin-lira-maas-aliyormus--595545

Sozeri, E. K. (2016, August 27). Social media throttling in Turkey points to wartime censorship efforts. *The Daily Dot*. Retrieved September 1, 2016, from http://www.dailydot.com/layer8/turkey-wartime-censorship-syria/

Spire, A., & Merllié, D. (1999). La question des origines dans les statistiques en France. Les enjeux d'une controverse. *Le Mouvement Social*, *188*(188), 119–130. doi:10.2307/3779961 PMID:22029101

Stache, L. C. (2015). Advocacy and political potential at the convergence of hashtag activism and commerce. *Feminist Media Studies*, *15*(1), 162–164. doi:10.1080/14680777.2015.987429

Statista. (2016). UK Social Media Statistics for 2016. Leading social networks worldwide as of September 2016, ranked by number of active users (in millions). Worldwide; We Are Social; WhatsApp; Tumblr; LinkedIn; Google. Retrieved from https://www.statista.com

Statista. (n.d.). Number of social media users worldwide 2010-2020. Retrieved from https://www.statista.com/statistics/278414/number-of-worldwide-social-network-users/

Statistics South Africa. (2015). Documented immigrants in South Africa. Statistics South Africa 10, Retrieved September 27, 2016, from http://www.statssa.gov.za/publications/P03514/P035142013.pdf

Steinberg, S. (1989). *The ethnic myth: Race, ethnicity, and class in America*. Boston: Beacon Press.

Steinmetz, K. (2014) #blacklivesmatter Is the American Dialect Society's 2014 Word of the Year: TIME online. Retrieved June 19, 2016 from http://time.com

Stewart, C. (2014). *21 varieties of traditional African homosexuality*, Retrieved from http://www.21_varities_of_traditional_african_homosexuality.htm

Stopwatch. (2015). Stop and Search Statistics 2014/2015. Retrieved from http://www.stop-watch.org/news-comment/story/new-stop-and-search-statistics-2014-2015

Sullivan, A. (2009, June 13). The Revolution Will Be Twittered. *The Atlantic*. Retrieved December 4, 2016, from http://www.theatlantic.com/daily-dish/archive/2009/06/the-revolution-will-be-twittered/200478/

Suny Levin Institute. (2014). *Globalization*. London: Suny Levin Institute.

Sussman, R. W. (2014). *The myth of race: The troubling persistence of an unscientific idea*. Cambridge: Harvard university press. doi:10.4159/harvard.9780674736160

Tanzania Communication Regulatory Authority. (2016). *Quarterly Communication Statistics Report*. Retrieved September 28, 2016, from http://tcra.go.tz/images/documents/telecommunication/CommStatMarch16.pdf

Tarrow, S. (2005). *The new transnational activism*. Cambridge: Cambridge University Press. doi:10.1017/CBO9780511791055

Taylor, K.-Y. (2016). *From #Blacklivesmatter To Black Liberation*. Haymarket Books Chicago.

Tharoor, I. (2016). Black Lives Matter is a global cause. *The Washington Post*. Retrieved September 5, 2016 from https://www.washingtonpost.com

Thrasher, S. W. (2015). Black Lives Matter has showed us: the oppression of black people is borderless. *The Guardian*. Retrieved March 7, 2015 from https://www.theguardian.com/uk

Tilley, V. (2009). Occupation, colonialism, apartheid? A re-assessment of Israel's practices in the Occupied Palestinian Territories under international law. Human Sciences Research Council, Pretoria. Retrieved November 19, 2017 from http://www.hsrc.ac.za/en/research-outputs/view/4634

Tilly, C. (1995). *From mobilization to revolution*. Reading, MA: Addison-Wesley.

Tilly, C. (2004). *Social movements 1768-2004*. London: Paradigm Publishers.

Tran, M. (2015). Malala Yousafzai criticizes weak effort to free girls kidnapped by Boko Haram. *The Guardian*. Retrieved November 15, 2017, from https://www.theguardian.com/world/2015/feb/08/malala-yousafzai-criticises-efforts-free-nigerian-girls-boko-haram

Transparency International. (2015). *Corruption Perception Index 2016*. Retrieved August 29, 2016, from https://www.transparency.org/news/feature/corruption_perceptions_index_2016

Traynor, L. (2016, July 16). Pleas for "justice" for 18-year-old Mzee Mohammed at Black Lives Matter march in Liverpool. Liverpool Echo. Retrieved from http://www.liverpoolecho.co.uk

Trollere ne kadar maaş ödeniyor? (2016, March 16). Retrieved August 31, 2016, from http://www.birgun.net/haber-detay/trollere-ne-kadar-maas-odeniyor-106445.html

Trottier, D., & Lyon, D. (2012). Key Features of Social Media Surveillance. In C. Fuchs, K. Boersma, A. Albrechtslund, & M. Sandoval (Eds.), *Internet and Surveillance: The Challenges of Web 2.0 and Social Media* (pp. 89–105). New York: Routledge.

Turkey PM Erdogan says 'tapped' phone call to son 'fabricated'. (2014, February 25). Retrieved September 2, 2016, from http://www.bbc.com/news/world-europe-26336354

Turkey shuts down TIB internet surveillance and censorship bureau. (2016, August 15). Retrieved September 1, 2016, from https://d8news.com/turkey-shuts-tib-internet-surveillance-censorship-bureau-1327

Turkish ministers accuse Twitter of plotting against Erdoğan. (2016, March 30). Retrieved August 31, 2016, from http://www.hurriyetdailynews.com/turkish-ministers-accuse-twitter-of-plotting-against-erdogan-.aspx?PageID=238&NID=97106&NewsCatID=338

Turkish Statistical Institute. (2016). *Hanehalkı Bilişim Teknolojileri Kullanım Araştırması, 2016*. Ankara: TUİK. Retrieved September 5, 2016, from http://www.tuik.gov.tr/PreTablo.do?alt_id=1028

Tuten, L., & Solomon, M. (2015). *Social Media Marketing Strategy*. New York: Sage Publications.

Twitter is blocked in Turkey as Erdogan vows to 'wipe out' the social network. (2014, March 21). Retrieved September 3, 2016, from http://www.telegraph.co.uk/news/worldnews/europe/turkey/10713393/Twitter-is-blocked-in-Turkey-as-Erdogan-vows-to-wipe-out-the-social-network.html

Udam, J., & Vestergaard, A. (2015). *Civic engagement and social media political participation beyond protest*. New York: Palgrave MacMillan.

Ukah, O. C. (2009). General Expenditure Management and Control Within the Framework of Ethiopia Economy. *African Research Review*, *3*(1), 206–213. doi:10.4314/afrrev.v3i1.43566

UNESCO Institute for Statistics (UIS). (2013). *Adult and youth literacy: National, regional and global trends, 1985 – 2015*. Retrieved September 30, 2016 from http://www.uis.unesco.org/Education/Documents/literacy-statistics-trends-1985-2015.pdf

United Nations ACICIT-ESCAP. (2014). Academy of ICT essentials for government leaders Version 2.0 Module 11: Social Media for Development. Republic of Korea. Retrieved June 11, 2014 from, http://www.unapcict.org/academy

United Nations Educational, Scientific and Cultural Organization (UNESCO). (2014). *Assessment of media development in Palestine*. Retrieved September 21, 2016 from http://unesdoc.unesco.org/images/0022/002277/227784e.pdf

United Nations General Assembly Human Rights Council. (2009). Report of the United Nations fact-finding mission on the Gaza Conflict. Retrieved November 19, 2017 from http://www2.ohchr.org/english/bodies/hrcouncil/docs/12session/A-HRC-12-48.pdf

United Nations General Assembly Human Rights Council. (2010). Report of the international fact-finding mission to investigate violations of international law, including international humanitarian and human rights law, resulting from the Israeli attacks on the flotilla of ships carrying humanitarian assistance. Retrieved November 19, 2017 from http://www2.ohchr.org/english/bodies/hrcouncil/docs/15session/A.HRC.15.21_en.pdf

United Nations Security Council Resolution 2334. (2016). Retrieved November 19, 2017 from http://www.un.org/webcast/pdfs/SRES2334-2016.pdf

United Nations. (2016). *Security Council Report of the Secretary General S/2016/796*. Geneva: UNO.

United States Department of State. (2011). 2010 country reports on human rights practices: Israel and the Occupied Territories. Retrieved November 19, 2017 from https://www.state.gov/j/drl/rls/hrrpt/2010/nea/154463.htm

Uwazi. (2010). *Tanzania's Tax Exemptions: Are they too high and making us too dependent on foreign aid?* Retrieved November 23, 2017, from http://twaweza.org/uploads/files/Tax%20 Exemptions.PDF

Vaidyanathan, R. (2016). The compass: America in black and white: Criminal Justice. *BBC*. Retrieved September 17, 2016, from http://www.bbc.co.uk/programmes/p03db7zh

Vaidyanathan, R. (2016). The compass: America in black and white: Economic Opportunity. *BBC*. Retrieved September 17, 2016, from http://www.bbc.co.uk/programmes/p03drnpt

Van de Donk, W., Loader, B. D., Nixon, P. G., & Rucht, D. (Eds.). (2004). *Cyber protest: New media, citizens and social movements*. New York, NY: Routledge.

van Niekerk, B., & Maharaj, M. S. (2011) The Information Warfare Life Cycle Model, SA Journal of Information Management 13(1). Retrieved from http://www.sajim.co.za/index.php/SAJIM/article/view/476

van Niekerk, B. (2015). Information Warfare in the 2013-2014 Ukraine Crisis. In J. Richet (Ed.), *Cybersecurity Policies and Strategies for Cyberwarfare Prevention* (pp. 307–339). Hershey, PA: IGI. doi:10.4018/978-1-4666-8456-0.ch012

van Niekerk, B., Pillay, K., & Maharaj, M. (2011). Analysing the Role of ICTs in the Tunisian and Egyptian Unrest from an Information Warfare Perspective. *International Journal of Communication, 5*, 1406–1416.

van Zyl, G. (2016a, June 15). Hack attack threat for Gupta sites, Oakbay and Sahara down. *Fin24*. Retrieved from http://www.fin24.com/Tech/Cyber-Security/anonymous-threatens-hack-attacks-on-gupta-websites-20160615

van Zyl, G. (2016b, July 12). Anonymous 'hacks' Armscor website. *Fin24*. Retrieved from http://www.fin24.com/Tech/News/anonymous-hacks-armscor-website-20160712

Vergeer, M. (2012). Politics, Elections and Online Campaigning: Past, Present… and a Peek into the Future. *New Media & Society, 15*(1), 9–17. doi:10.1177/ 1461444812457327

Vergeer, M., Hermans, L., & Sams, S. (2011). Is the Voter Only a Tweet Away? Micro-blogging During the 2009 European Parliament Election Campaign in the Netherlands. *First Monday, 16*(8). Retrieved from http://firstmonday.org/article/view/3540/3026

Vermeulen, J. (2016, June 13). This is how I took down the SABC: Anonymous hacker. *MyBroadband*. Retrieved from http://mybroadband.co.za/news/security/168303-this-is-how-i-took-down-the-sabc-anonymous-hacker.html

Voice of the Cape FM. (2014, November 14). Taking BDS to court 'risky': analyst. Retrieved September 29, 2016 from http://www.vocfm.co.za/taking-bds-to-court-risky-analyst/

von Clausewitz, C. (1832). *On War* (M. Howard & P. Paret, Trans.). Oxford, UK: Oxford University Press.

Von Holdt, K. (2002). Social movement unionism: The case of South Africa. *Work, Employment and Society*, *16*(2), 283–304. doi:10.1177/095001702400426848

Von Lieres, B. (2014). Citizenship from below: The Politics of citizen action and resistance in South Africa and Angola. In E. Obadare & W. Willems (Eds.), *Civic agency in Africa: Arts of resistance in the 21st Century* (pp. 49–62). Suffolk: James Currey.

Wahlquist, C. (2017, May 22). Black Lives Matter awarded 2017 Sydney peace prize. *The Guardian*. Retrieved November 18, 2017 from https://www.theguardian.com/uk

Walker, S. (2015, April 2). Salutin' Putin: inside a Russian troll house. *The Guardian*. Retrieved September 3, 2016, from https://www.theguardian.com/world/2015/apr/02/putin-kremlin-inside-russian-troll-house

Wassermann, H. (2010). *Mobile phones, popular media and everyday African democracy: transmissions and transgressions*. Unpublished paper, Rhodes University.

We Are Social. (2016). Digital In 2016. Retrieved from http://wearesocial.com/uk/special-reports/digital-in-2016

We Are Social. (2016). *Digital in 2016*. Retrieved September 5, 2016, from http://wearesocial.com/uk/special-reports/digital-in-2016

Weedston, L. (2014). 12 Hashtags That changed the world in 2014. *YES Magazine*. Retrieved from http://www.yesmagazine.org

Weiss, F., & Steiner, S. (2006). Transparency as an Element of Good Governance. *Fordham International Law Journal*, *30*(5), 1545–1580.

Wheatley, M. (2013, September 12). Botnets and Porn: It's What Tor's All About. *Silicon Angle*. Retrieved from http://siliconangle.com/blog/2013/09/12/botnets-and-porn-its-what-tors-all-about/

Williams, C. B., & Gulati, G. J. (2007). *Social Networks in Political Campaigns: Facebook and the 2006 Midterm Elections*. Paper presented at the 2007 Annual Meeting of the American Political Science Association, Chicago, IL. Retrieved December 28, 2016, from http://tranb300.ulb.ac.be/2012-2013/groupe141/archive/files/c65d6cf6f5d34b49f79d9e68a315bb41.pdf

Williams, S. (2015). Digital defense: Black feminists resist violence with hashtag activism. *Feminist Media Studies*, *15*(2), 341–344. doi:10.1080/14680777.2015.1008744

Witte, G. (2015, June 11). Do Britain's gunless bobbies provide answers for America's police? *The Washington Post*. Retrieved September 5, 2016, from https://www.washingtonpost.com

Wong, C. W. (2017, February 3). Uber CEO steps down from Trump advisory council after users boycott. *The Guardian*. Retrieved from https://www.theguardian.com/technology/2017/feb/02/travis-kalanick-delete-uber-leaves-trump-council

World Wide Web & Omico South Africa. (2017). South African social media landscape. Retrieved September 11, 2017 from http://www.worldwideworx.com/wp-content/uploads/2016/09/Social-Media-2017-Executive-Summary.pdf

Yang, G. (2009). *The Power of the Internet in China: Citizen Activism Online*. New York: Colombia University Press.

Yang, G. (2016). Narrative agency in hashtag activism: The case of# BlackLivesMatter. *Media and Communication*, *4*(4), 13–17. doi:10.17645/mac.v4i4.692

Yayın yasağı 'Ak Trol'e emanet: 'Tivit atanı not edin, bize gönderin'. (2015, March 31). Retrieved September 1, 2016, from http://www.diken.com.tr/yayin-yasagi-ak-trole-emanet-tivit-atani-not-edin-bize-gonderin/

Yıldırım, Ö. (2016, July 17). Sosyal medyadan terörü destekleyen profiller emniyete bildirilecek. *Anadolu Ajansı*. Retrieved September 1, 2016, from http://aa.com.tr/tr/15-temmuz-darbe-girisimi/sosyal-medyadan-teroru-destekleyen-profiller-emniyete-bildirilecek/609584

Zappavigna, M. (2014). CoffeTweets: Bonding Around the Bean on Twitter. In P. Sergeant & C. Taggs (Eds.), *The language of social media: Identity and community on the Internet* (pp. 139–160). New York: Palgrave MacMillan. doi:10.1057/9781137029317_7

Zappi, S. (2016). Rassemblement à Paris de "Black Lives Matter France" après la mort d'Adama Traoré. Le Monde. Retrieved from http://www.lemonde.fr/police-justice/article/2016/07/23/rassemblement-a-paris-de-black-lives-matter-france-apres-la-mort-d-adama-traore_4973930_1653578.html#7zT5dvQqPYTMwEgm.99

Zayyan, H., & Carter, C. (2009). Human rights and wrongs: Blogging news of everyday life in Palestine. In S. Allan & E. Thorsen (Eds.), *Citizen journalism: global perspectives* (pp. 85–96). New York: Peter Lang Publishing.

About the Contributors

Floribert Patrick C. Endong (PhD) is a research consultant in the humanities and social sciences. He is a reviewer and editor with many scientific journals in the social sciences. His current research interest focuses on international communication, gender studies, digital media, media laws, international relations, culture and religious communication He is author of numerous peer-reviewed articles and book chapters in the above-mentioned areas of interest.

* * *

Ufuoma Akpojivi is a lecturer at the Media Studies Department, University of Witwatersrand, South Africa. He holds a Ph.D and M.A. in Communications Studies from the University of Leeds, United Kingdom and a B.A. in Mass Communication from the Delta State University, Nigeria. He also holds a Certificate in Comparative Media Law from University of Oxford, United Kingdom and a Certificate in Strengthening Postgraduate Supervision from Rhode University, South Africa. He has over 4 years teaching experience, and he and his colleagues were recently awarded the Faculty of Humanities Team Teaching and Learning Award. He is an NRF rated researcher and he has published extensively.

Danella Campbell is a doctoral researcher in Journalism, Race and Political Movements.

Tendai Owen Chikara is a young academic with a keen interest in Systemic Functional Linguistics theory and Discourse Analysis. Currently, he lectures as a full timer at Bindura University of Science Education and part time at Solusi University and is working on his doctoral studies in Applied Linguistics.

Marie Chollier is a clinical Psychologist, Psychotherapist, Sexologist. Doctoral researcher in social sciences and health sciences.

Suraya Dadoo received her Master of Social Science degree in Sociology from Rhodes University in 2001. In 2002 she joined Media Review Network in Johannesburg as a researcher. She writes and presents widely on the impact of the Israeli occupation of Palestine and Israeli apartheid practices, and is the co-author of Why Israel? The Anatomy of Zionist Apartheid: A South African Perspective (2013, Porcupine Press). She is also the social media co-ordinator for the National Coalition for Palestine - an umbrella body representing over 40 South African civil society structures, ranging from trade unions to religious organisations, students groups, political structures and NGO's dedicated to ending the occupation and achieving a just peace in Palestine-Israel.

Edison Wazoel Lubua is a Senior Lecturer at the Institute of Accountancy Arusha. He is a postdoctoral fellow of the North-West University, with a PhD (IS&T) of the University of KwaZulu Natal, MCom (IS) of the University of Cape Town, MSc(HRM) of Mzumbe University and an Advanced Diploma from the Institute of Accountancy Arusha. Moreover, Dr. Lubua is a Certified Information Systems Auditor (CISA). In addition, he has published works which carry international reputation in journals and conferences in the area of ICT for Development. Equally, Dr. Lubua is a reviewer at the African Journal of Information Systems and the Journal of Information Technology Education.

Aifheli Makhwanya heads the Policy and Research Department at the National Film and Video Foundation (South Africa). She started her professional career as a Researcher: Broadcasting Policy Development at the Independent Communications Authority of South Africa in 2004. Aifheli holds LLB and LLM (Communications Law) degrees from the University of the Witwatersrand, Johannesburg. She is a final MA (Cultural Policy and Management) student at the same university. She writes in her personal capacity. Aifheli has conducted and contributed to researches, policies and strategies in the cultural industries (film and broadcasting) and serves on a number of government committees.

Collen Sabao (PhD) is a Senior Lecturer of Pure and Applied Linguistics in the Language and Literature Department at the University of Namibia and also in the English and Communication Department at the Midlands State University in Zimbabwe. His research interests lie in Phonetics and Phonological Theory, Journalism Studies, Applied Linguistics specifically Media Discourse and Political Discourse. He also has interests in Iconography, Symbology and Semiotics. His research has appeared in a variety of high impact journals across the world. He is also an African Humanities Program (AHP) Fellow as well as an American Council of Learned Societies (ACLS) Fellow.

Brett van Niekerk graduated with his PhD in 2012 from the University of KwaZulu-Natal, and has completed two years of postdoctoral research into information operations, information warfare, and critical infrastructure protection. He is currently works as a Senior Security Analyst, and continues his research as an Honorary Research Fellow at the University of KwaZulu-Natal. He also holds a BSc and a MSc in electronic engineering. He has over 10 journal articles and 15 conference presentations in the field. He is a member of the IFIP WG 9.10 on ICT in Peace and War. He has contributed to ISO/IEC standards on information security.

Hakan Yüksel received his MA in Information and Communication Sciences from University of Paris 13 in 2003. In 2007 he got his second MA in Journalism from Ankara University in Turkey. He was hired as Research Assistant by Ankara University in 2009. He received his PhD in Journalism from Ankara University in 2013. He worked as Junior Lecturer between 2013 and 2017 for the Faculty of Communication of Ankara University. He has various scientific publications on information society policies, new communication technologies, political economy of communication, and communication history.

Index

#thisflag 17-18, 20-22, 28-31, 33, 180, 183-185

A

activism 1, 5-6, 9, 36-42, 47-48, 51, 55-58, 73-74, 79, 82-83, 87, 89, 91-93, 104-105, 109, 134-135, 156, 179-188, 190-191, 194, 196-197, 203-204, 208-217, 223
advocacy 1-4, 8-11, 19-21, 41-42, 47, 55-60, 62-63, 66, 68-70, 73, 78-79, 88, 90-93, 101-102, 104, 120, 134, 148, 153-154, 158, 160, 169-170, 203-212, 214, 219-221, 223, 227
AKP 159-166, 178
Aktrolls 162-164, 168, 178
anonymity 10, 159-160, 163, 178
Assimilationism 134
availability 2, 5, 16, 143-144

B

Bandwidth Throttling 169, 178
BDS Movement 100
Blacks 102, 106-108, 110, 113, 120-121, 125
blog 48, 83, 100, 164-165, 203, 218-219
Boko Haram 36, 38, 42, 45-51, 186, 222
Bot Accounts 165, 178
bots 165

C

campaign 5, 9, 23, 29, 33, 36-38, 41-51, 55-58, 60-70, 74, 81-88, 90-91, 105-106, 108, 114, 117, 122, 155, 161, 163, 165, 180-181, 184-190, 193-194, 206-207, 209-212, 214-215
censorship 79, 88, 90, 93, 100, 155, 157, 159, 166, 169, 195, 210
citizen journalism 21, 24-27, 41, 78, 81, 93, 100, 205
clicktivism 36, 38, 47, 51, 211
Colour-Blindness 124, 135
communicative potential 17-23
confidentiality 2-5, 7, 9, 16
Cyber-Security 2, 16
cyber-warfare 2-3

D

deception 2-3, 9
denial of service 5-6, 16
digital activism 36, 38-42, 82, 91, 104, 179-188, 190-191, 194, 196-197, 208-210
digital propaganda 160-161

E

e-governance 136, 148, 152
Electronic Fiscal Device 152
Enterprise Resource Planning System 152

equality 101-104, 108, 113, 117, 120, 189, 193, 211, 223, 227
Erdoğan 159-162, 164-165, 167
e-transparency 136, 139, 143-145, 147-149, 152

G

Gezi Park Protest 153, 159, 161-164, 166, 169-170
global 3-4, 6, 18, 21, 27, 37-40, 42, 44, 50, 56, 58, 61-62, 65, 69, 73-74, 91-92, 102, 106-107, 109, 111, 119, 121, 125, 154, 180-181, 183, 186-187, 195, 205, 207-209, 214
governance 51, 62, 136-139, 141-144, 146-149, 152, 184, 218, 221
Gülen Movement 159-160, 178

H

hacktivism 5-6
hacktivist 3, 9, 16
Hashtactivism 104, 135
hashtag 28, 36-37, 41-43, 45-48, 51, 69, 80-81, 83-86, 88, 90, 100-102, 104-105, 107, 110, 122-123, 125, 165, 185, 190, 192, 194, 196
hashtag activism 36-37, 41-42, 48, 51, 104-105

I

immigrants 55-56, 61-66, 70
Infographics 81, 100
information security 1-3, 5, 9-11, 16
information warfare 1-3, 8, 16
integrity 2-5, 7, 9, 16, 136
Internationalization 36, 38, 42, 51, 102, 110-111
Internet censorship 169
Internet Troll 178

M

model 111, 139-141, 152, 154, 167
Multiculturalism 135

N

National Coalition for Palestine (NC4P) 74, 81, 87, 100
national politics 17-18, 23, 27, 32
Nationalism 124
non-governmental organisations 55, 61-62, 117

P

partnership 65-66, 70, 138
politics 17-19, 21, 23, 25, 27, 32, 52, 55-56, 60, 64, 88, 108-109, 120, 123, 125, 155, 211
Portal 142, 152
propaganda 6, 9, 20, 24, 81, 88, 90, 93, 100, 155, 160-162, 167-168, 211
protests 4-8, 17-18, 20, 22-23, 27-32, 37, 41, 46, 73, 81-84, 87-88, 92, 106-107, 115-117, 119, 123, 154-157, 159, 187-188, 208-209, 211, 213, 217, 223
psychological operations 2, 16

R

race 76, 104, 107, 109, 113, 117, 123-124, 155, 189, 197, 214
racism 23, 91, 106-107, 109-110, 112, 118, 120, 125

S

social media 1-3, 5-11, 17-24, 26-34, 37-42, 44, 47, 55-60, 63, 67-70, 73-74, 77, 79-93, 100, 102, 104, 106-108, 110, 117, 120-123, 135-139, 141-145, 148-149, 152-163, 165-170, 178, 181-182, 186, 190, 193-195, 203, 205-212, 217, 223

T

transparency 3-4, 136-144, 149, 152, 165, 227
trending 81-82, 86, 100, 165, 178
Turkey 117, 153-154, 157-162, 165-170, 178, 182
Twitter 17-19, 21-23, 26, 28, 31, 37-39, 41-44, 50-51, 58, 67, 69, 80-87, 89, 91, 93, 100, 105, 115-116, 120-122, 141, 154-156, 159-161, 163-167, 169, 181, 184, 190, 192, 197, 207, 209, 211-212
Twitterstorm 100

V

VPN 157, 169

X

xenophobia 56, 60-61, 63-69

Z

ZANU-PF 18-19, 24-26, 30, 32
Zimbabwe 17-22, 24-32, 62, 65, 180, 182-183, 185, 213

www.ingramcontent.com/pod-product-compliance
Lightning Source LLC
LaVergne TN
LVHW081335300926
849161LV00008B/1980